SALTERS ADVANCED CHEMISTRY

9

Chemic
Storylines

Central Team

George Burton

John Holman

Gwen Pilling

David Waddington

Heinemann

CONTENTS

Page

Introduction for students   **1**

The Elements of Life   2

EL1   What are we made of?   3
EL2   Take two elements …   4
EL3   Looking for patterns in elements   6
EL4   Where do the chemical elements come from?   9
EL5   The molecules of life   14
EL6   Summary   15

Developing Fuels   16

DF1   Petrol is popular …   17
DF2   Getting energy from fuels   18
DF3   Focus on petrol   20
DF4   Making petrol – getting the right octane rating   25
DF5   Trouble with emissions   31
DF6   Methanol – the key to future fuels?   35
DF7   What other solutions are there?   36
DF8   Summary   37

From Minerals to Elements   38

M1   Chemicals from the sea   39
M2   Copper from deep in the ground   44
M3   Mining Cornish tin   50
M4   Summary   53

The Atmosphere   54

A1   What's in the air?   55
A2   Screening the Sun   56
A3   Ozone: A vital sunscreen   58
A4   The CFC story   63
A5   How bad is the ozone crisis?   69
A6   Trouble in the troposphere   71
A7   Keeping the window open   75
A8   Focus on carbon dioxide   77
A9   Coping with carbon   80
A10   Summary   81

Page

The Polymer Revolution   82

PR1   Designer polymers   83
PR2   The polythene story   85
PR3   Towards high density polymers   87
PR4   Conducting polymers – breaking the rules   89
PR5   The invention of nylon   91
PR6   Kelvar   94
PR7   Taking temperature into account   95
PR8   Throwing it away… or not?   97
PR9   Summary   99

What's in a Medicine?   100

WM1   The development of modern ideas about medicines   101
WM2   Medicines from nature   102
WM3   Identifying the active chemical in willow bark   103
WM4   Instrumental analysis   103
WM5   The synthesis of salicylic acid and aspirin   106
WM6   Delivering the product   107
WM7   Development and safety testing of medicines   109
WM8   Summary   111

Using Sunlight   112

US1   The Sun: sustainer of life   113
US2   Exciting light   115
US3   Photosynthesis   117
US4   Fuel for the future   122
US5   Solar cells   126
US6   The hydrogen economy   131
US7   Summary   133

Engineering Proteins   134

EP1   Christopher's story   135
EP2   Protein building   138
EP3   Genetic engineering   147
EP4   Proteins in 3-D   148
EP5   Giving evolution a push   151
EP6   Enzymes   154
EP7   Summary   156

The Steel Story   158

		Page
SS1	What is steel?	159
SS2	How is steel made?	160
SS3	A closer look at the elements in steel	165
SS4	Rusting	167
SS5	What happens inside a 'tin' can?	171
SS6	Recycled steel	173
SS7	Summary	175

Aspects of Agriculture   176

AA1	What do we want from agriculture?	177
AA2	The world at your feet	178
AA3	How does the soil remain fertile?	186
AA4	Competition for food	193
AA5	Summary	199

Colour by Design   200

CD1	Ways of making colour	201
CD2	The Monastral Blue story	203
CD3	Chrome Yellow	204
CD4	Chemistry in the art gallery	208
CD5	At the start of the rainbow	213
CD6	Chemists design colours	219
CD7	Colour for cotton	220
CD8	High-tech colour	224
CD9	Summary	227

The Oceans   228

O1	The edge of the land	229
O2	Wider still and deeper	234
O3	Oceans of energy	237
O4	A safe place to grow	243
O5	Summary	251

Medicines by Design   252

		Page
MD1	Alcohol in the body	253
MD2	The drug action of ethanol	258
MD3	Medicines that send messages to nerves	261
MD4	Enzyme inhibitors as medicines	264
MD5	Targetting bacteria	267
MD6	Summary	271

Visiting the Chemical Industry   272

VCI1	Introduction	273
VCI2	The operation of a chemical manufacturing process	274
VCI3	People	276
VCI4	Raw materials and feedstock preparation	277
VCI5	The best conditions for the process	278
VCI6	Safety matters	281
VCI7	Environmental issues	282
VCI8	Costs	282
VCI9	Location	284

Index   287

ACKNOWLEDGEMENTS

The authors and publishers are grateful to the following for permission to reproduce text extracts:
Paul Brown© *The Guardian* (Fig. 7, p.59); Reprinted with permission from *Nature*, Vol. 315, No. 6016, pp. 207–210, Copyright 1985 Macmillan Magazines Ltd. (Fig. 14, p.65); WMO publication 'World Meteorological Organisation Global Ozone Research and Monitoring Project – Report No. 25, Scientific Assessment of Ozone depletion 1991' (Fig. 18, p.67); *The Independent* (Fig. 22 (top and bottom), p.70); Newman/*The Observer* (Fig. 23, p.70); Geoff Thompson/*The Independent Magazine* (Fig. 36, p.81); Murray J McEwan and Leon F Phillips, *Chemistry of the Atmosphere*, Edward Arnold Publishers (Fig. 18, p.122); BP Educational (Fig. 19, p.123); Hoechst *High Chem Magazine* (Fig. 21, p.124); *Which?*, February 1989, published by Consumers' Association, London (Fig. 22, p.169); Zeneca Pharmaceuticals (interview, pp.109–111); ICI (Fig. 30, p.187); Norsk Hydro (Fig. 35, p.190); Zeneca Agrochemicals © Zeneca Ltd (Figs 39 and 40, p.192); British Agrochemicals Association Ltd (Fig. 47, p.197); ICI (Fig. 24, p.216); *New Scientist – Inside Science No.44, Climate Now* by John Gribbin (Fig. 28, p.242); Reprinted with permission from *Nature*, Vol. 270, pp.567–572, Copyright 1977 Macmillan Magazines Ltd (Table 1, p.254); Adapted from Wilson P, *Drinking in England and Wales*, HMSO 1980 (Assignment 2 tables, p.255); Chemical Industries Association (Fig. 1, p.273); ICI (Assignment 5, p.278).

The authors and publishers are grateful to the following for permission to reproduce photographs:

Cover photo J. Paul Getty Museum, Malibu, California/Bridgeman Art Library

L = left, **R** = right, **T** = top, **B** = bottom

Page 3 Science Photo Library/Philippe Plailly; **page 5L** SPL/Jerry Mason, **R** Ann Marie McDonald; **page 6** ZEFA; **page 8L** Science Museum Library, **R** GT Woods; **page 10L** Royal Observatory, Edinburgh/AATB/SPL, **R** NOAO/SPL; **page 15** SPL/Roger Resmeyer/Starlight; **page 17** Daimler Benz; **page 19** Philip Parkhouse; **page 20T** Philip Parkhouse, **B** Quadrant Picture Library; **page 21** Eta Process Plant; **page 22** Shell Canada; **page 23** Brian and Cherry Alexander; **page 24** Philip Parkhouse; **page 30** South American Pictures; **page 31** SPL/David Parker; **page 34** Johnson-Matthay; **page 35** ICI; **page 36** Shell International Petroleum Co Ltd; **page 39** ZEFA; **page 40** Compix; **page 42** Michelin; **page 43** Research Division Kodak; **page 44** CM Dixon; **page 45L** SPL/ Martin Land, **R** GSF; **page 46** Eileen Barrett; **page 48** SPL/ Simon Fraser; **page 49** IMI Refiners; **page 51L** Mary Aitken, **R** GSF; **page 55** SPL; **page 56** Popperfoto; **page 58** Philip Parkhouse; **page 59** SPL/ Hattie Young; **page 62** Lord Porter/ Imperial College; **page 63T** Philip Parkhouse, **B** Sherry Rowland; **page 65L** SPL/ Simon Fraser, **R** SPL/Doug Allan; **page 66** SPL/Philippe Plailly; **page 69L** Hutchinson Libary, **R** SPL/Dr Jeremy Burgess; **page 74** SPL/NASA/Goddard Institute for Space Studies; **page 76T** SPL/Graham Ewens, B Rex Features/Sipa; **page 80** SPL/Andrew Syred; **page 83** The Bridgeman Art Library; **page 86L** Colin J Williamson, **R** Popperfoto; **page 87** Archiv fur Kunst und Geschichte Berlin; **page 88 both** BP Chemicals; **page 89** Fisher-Price; **page 90** SPL/BlairSeitz; **page 91** Zipperling Kessler and Co; **page 92** Topham Picture Source; **page 93** Fell/Hurworth Photography/ICI Chemicals and Polymers; **page 94** Sylvia Katz/ICI Fibres; **page 95 both** Dupont; **page 96** Fell/Hurworth Photography/ICI Chemicals and Polymers; **page 97L** Caradon Everest Ltd, **R** Zeneca Bioproducts; **page 98** Enak Ltd; **page 101** A-Z Botanical Collection; **page 102L** A-Z Botanical Collection, **R** Mary Evans Picture Library; **page 103T** Mary Evans Picture Library, **B** Perkin-Elmer Ltd; **page 105** ICI Chemicals and Polymers; **page 106** Bayer plc; **page 107** The Garden Picture Library; **page 108L** Bayer plc, **R** Steve Bicknell; **pages 109 and 111** Zeneca Pharmaceuticals; **page 113** SPL/ Susan McCartney; **page 114** J Allen Cash; **page 116** Robert Harding Picture Library; **page 117** SPL/Hank Morgan; **page 118** Professor Rachel M Leech; **page 121L** Barnaby's Picture Library, **R** Oxford Scientific Films; **page 122** Planet Earth Pictures; **page 125** Topham Picture Library; **page 126** SPL/Davio Ducros/Jerrican; **page 127 both** BP

Solar; **page 130L** SPL/Dr Jeremy Burgess, **R** Robert Harding Picture Library; **page 131L** BP Solar, **R** Mercedes-Benz; **page 135L** Mary Aitken, **R** Department of Chemistry/University of York; **page 136** J Allen Cash; **page 138** British Diabetic Association; **page 140** Philip Parkhouse; **page 145** SPL/Omikron; **page 146** European Molecular Biology Laboratory; **page 147** Novo Nordisk; **page 148L** SPL/Jerry Mason, **R** SPL/Peter Menzel; **page 149 ,150L and TR** Dr RE Hubbard/ Department of Chemistry/ University of York; **page 150BR** Dr G Dodson; **page 151** Department of Chemistry/University of York; **page 152TL** Dr RE Hubbard/ Department of Chemistry/ University of York, **BL** Xiao Bing Department of Chemistry/ University of York, **R** Novo Nordisk; **page 154L** SPL/ Chris Priest and Mark Clarke, **R** Dr RE Hubbard/Department of Chemistry/ University of York; **page 156** Barnaby's Picture Library; **page 157T** Novo Nordisk, **B** Barnaby's Picture Library; **page 159T** J Allan Cash, **B** Leslie Garland Picture Library; **page 160 to page 164T** British Steel Sections, Plates and Commercial Steels/Scunthorpe Works, **R** J Allan Cash; **page 165** British Steel Sections, Plates and Commercial Steels/ Scunthorpe Works; **page 166** Department of Chemistry/ University of York; **page 167** Jim Kershaw/ Reproduced by kind permission of the Dean and Chapter of York; **page 168** Haymarket Copyright Archives; **page 169T** Philip Parkhouse, **B** Advertising Archives; **page 170** Avesta/Sheffield; **page 171** Dr Stuart Thorne/courtesy of The Science Museum; **page 173L** Advertising Archives, **R** J Allan Cash; **page 175T** National Radiological Protection Board, **B** The Hulton Deutsch Collection; **page 177L** Holt Studios International, **R** J Allan Cash; **page 180T** SPL/Robert de Gugliemo, **B** Ace Photo Agency; **page 181L** The Natural History Museum, **R** GSF; **page 182** The Natural History Museum; **page 183 and 184** Ace Photo Agency; **page 185** Bruce Coleman Ltd; **page 187T both** Holt Studios International, **B** SPL/Nelson Medina; **page 189L** Rothamsted Experimental Station, **R** J Allan Cash; **page 190 and 191** BASF; **page 192** Hydro Media; **page 193L** J Allan Cash; **R a,c,d**, Holt Studios International, **b**, SPL/Vaughan Flemming; **page 194** British Agrochemicals Association Ltd; **page 195** Heather Angel; **page 197** Zeneca Agrochemicals; **page 199T** Holt Studios International, **B** SPL/Rodney Henson; **page 201** courtesy of Hoechst UK; **page 202** both Mary Evans Picture Library; **page 203** Milepost 92Y2; **page 204** Mary Evans Picture Library; **page 205** Philip Parkhouse; **page 206** The National Gallery; **page 207L** The Bridgeman Art Library, **R and to page 212** The National Gallery; **page 213** Dr Tony Travis; **page 214T** courtesy of Zeneca Specialties Research Department Archive, **B** adapted from The Rainbow Makers by Tony Travis/Lehigh University Press/ Associated University Presses; **page 215TL** Royal Society of Chemistry, **TR** courtesy of Hoechst UK, **B** Dr Tony Travis; **page 218** The Colour Museum/Bradford; **page 119** Dr Tony Travis; **page 220** The Science Museum Picture Library; **page 223** courtesy of Zeneca Specialties Research Department Archive; **page 224** Robert Harding Picture Library; **page 229B** J Allan Cash, **R** Robert Harding Picture Library **R inset** The British Museum; **page 230** Bruce Coleman Ltd; **page 232** The Salters Company; **page 233L** Maldon Crystal Salt Company Ltd, **R** J Allan Cash; **page 234L** Institute of Oceanographic Sciences, **R** Mary Evans Picture Library; **page 235** SPL/ Tom van Sant/Geosphere Project Santa Monica; **page 237** SPL/Jan Hinsdi; **page 240 and 245** both J Allan Cash; **page 247** GSF; **page 248** Planet Earth Pictures; **page 250** J Allan Cash; **page 251** Bruce Coleman Ltd; **page 253** SPL/JC Revy; **page 254** The British School of Motoring; **page 256** Lion Laboratories plc; **page 261** SPL/Simon Fraser; **page 262** SPL/ Chris Priest and Mark Clarke; **page 263** Zeneca Pharmaceuticals; **page 265T** SPL/Hattie Young, **B** Chris Mattison; **page 267** SPL/ Will and Deni McIntyre; **page 268** SPL/Andrew McClenaghan; **page 269 to 271** by kind permission of Smithkline Beecham; **page 273** Chemical Industries Association; **page 275T** Brian Ratcliffe, **B** Buxton Lime Industries; **page 276** Miranda Mapletoft; **page 277** Glaxo Group Research; **page 279** Chemical Industries Association; **page 280** Chemineer; **page 281T** SPL/Will and Deni McIntyre, **B** Chemical Industries Association; **page 282L** Bayer AG/Leverkusen, **R** Popperfoto; **page 284** courtesy of ICI Chemicals and Polymers .

CONTRIBUTORS

Many people have contributed to the Salters Advanced Chemistry course, and a full list of contributors is given in the Teacher's Guide. They include the following:

Central Team

George Burton	Cranleigh School and University of York
John Holman (Project Director)	Watford Grammar School and University of York
Margaret Ferguson (1990-1991)	King Edward VI School, Louth
Gwen Pilling	University of York
David Waddington (Chairman of Steering Committee)	University of York

Advisory Committee

Dr Peter Doyle	Zeneca Group
Dr Tony Kirby, FRS	University of Cambridge
Professor The Lord Lewis, FRS (Chairman)	University of Cambridge
Sir Richard Norman, FRS	University of Oxford
Mr John Raffan	University of Cambridge

Sponsors

Many industrial companies have contributed time and expertise to the development of the Salters Advanced Chemistry Course. The work has been made possible by generous donations from the following:

The Salters Institute for Industrial Chemistry
The Association of the British Pharmaceutical Industry
BP Chemicals
British Steel
Esso UK
Zeneca Agrochemicals
The Royal Society of Chemistry
Shell UK

Dedication

To Dick Norman

Heinemann Educational Publishers,
a division of Heinemann Publishers (Oxford) Ltd,
Halley Court, Jordan Hill, Oxford, OX2 8EJ

OXFORD LONDON EDINBURGH
MADRID ATHENS BOLOGNA PARIS
MELBOURNE SYDNEY AUCKLAND SINGAPORE TOKYO
IBADAN NAIROBI HARARE GABORONE
PORTSMOUTH NH (USA)

First published 1994

98 97 96 95
10 9 8 7 6 5 4 3

ISBN 0 435 63106 3

Designed, illustrated and typeset by Gecko Limited, Bicester, Oxon.

Printed in Spain by Mateu Cromo

INTRODUCTION FOR STUDENTS

The Salters Advanced Chemistry course is made up of 13 units, together with a structured industrial visit and an Individual Investigation. This book contains the **Chemical Storylines** which form the backbone of each unit. There is a separate book of **Chemical Ideas**, and **Activities**.

Each unit is driven by the Storyline. You work through the Storyline, making 'excursions' to Activities and Chemical Ideas at appropriate points.

The Storylines are broken down into sections and sub-sections. You will find that there are numbered Assignments at intervals. These are designed to help you through the Storyline and to probe understanding, and they are best done as you go along.

Excursions to Activities

As you work through each Storyline, you will find that there are references to Activities. Each Activity is referred to at that point in the Storyline to which it most closely relates. Of course, you may not be able to do the Activity straight away, but it should be done not too long after that part of the Storyline.

Activities are numbered to correspond to the relevant part of the Storyline.

Excursions to Chemical Ideas

As you work through the Storylines, you will also find that there are references to sections in the book of Chemical Ideas. These cover the chemical principles that are needed to understand that particular part of the Storyline, and you will probably need to study that section of the Chemical Ideas book before you can go much further.

As you study the Chemical Ideas you will find Problems to tackle. These are designed to check and consolidate your understanding of the chemical principles involved.

Building up the Chemical Ideas

Salters Advanced Chemistry has been planned so that you build up your understanding of chemical ideas gradually. For example, the idea of chemical equilibrium is introduced in a simple, qualitative way in *The Atmosphere* unit. A more detailed, quantitative treatment is given in *Engineering Proteins* and *Aspects of Agriculture*, and applied to acids and precipitation in *The Oceans*.

It is important to bear in mind that the Chemical Ideas book is not the only place where chemistry is covered! The Chemical Ideas cover chemical principles that are needed in more than one unit of the course. Chemistry that is specific to a particular unit is dealt with in the Storyline itself and in related Activities.

How much do you need to remember?

The syllabus for Salters Advanced Chemistry defines what you have to remember. Each unit concludes with a 'Check your Notes' activity, which you can use to check that you have mastered all the required knowledge, understanding and skills for that unit. 'Check your Notes' tells you whether a topic is to be found in the Chemical Ideas, Chemical Storylines or Activities.

We hope that you will learn as much about the fascinating world of chemistry from the Salters Advanced Chemistry books as we have learned writing them.

George Burton   John Holman   Gwen Pilling   David Waddington

THE ELEMENTS OF LIFE

Why a unit on THE ELEMENTS OF LIFE?

This unit tells the story of the elements of life: what they are, how they originated and how they can be detected and measured. It shows how studying the composition of stars can throw light on the formation of elements which make up our own bodies.

This storyline begins with the elements from which our bodies are formed. You learn how to measure amounts of these elements (in terms of atoms) and, thus, how to calculate chemical formulae. The story then looks in more depth at two elements – iron and calcium – and this leads into learning about patterns in the properties of elements and the Periodic Table.

The second part of the unit looks at the origins of the elements, and introduces you to ideas about the structure of atoms. It concludes with a brief look at how elements combine to form compounds such as the 'molecules of life' which form the body.

Overview of chemical principles

In this unit you will learn more about …

ideas you will probably have come across in your earlier studies

- the Periodic Table
- protons, neutrons and electrons
- radioactivity and ionising radiation
- the wave model of light
- the electromagnetic spectrum.

… as well as learning new ideas about

- relative atomic masses and relative molecular masses
- amount of substance (moles and the Avogadro constant)
- chemical formulae
- nuclear fusion and nuclear equations
- the photon model of light
- atomic spectra
- the electronic structure of atoms
- ionic and covalent bonding.

The chemical ideas about amount of substance, atomic structure and chemical bonding are only *introduced* in this unit. They will be consolidated and developed in later units.

This technique of taking ideas only as far as you need to know them in order to follow the storyline you are studying, and then building on them by repeating the process in later units, is central to the Salters' approach to chemistry at Advanced Level.

EL1 *What are we made of?*

Elements and the body

If you asked a number of people the question, 'What are you made of?' you would get a variety of different answers. Some people would use biological terms and talk about organs, bones and so on. Others might answer in more detail and mention proteins, fats and DNA. A chemist would be most likely to talk about atoms and molecules, or elements and compounds.

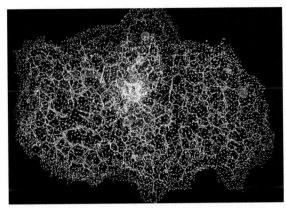

Figure 1 Termolysine – a biological molecule essential to human life

As a chemist, you know that you are not really made up of a mixture of elements but rather a mixture of compounds, many of which appear quite complicated. You will be finding out more about some of these compounds later in the unit. To begin with, however, you will look at the elements which are most likely to be in the compounds in your body.

Elements in the body are classified as one of three types:

- **major constituent elements**, which make up 2%–60% of all the atoms present, eg carbon and hydrogen
- **trace elements**, which make up 0.01%–1%, eg calcium and phosphorus
- **ultra-trace elements**, which make up less than 0.01%, eg iron and iodine.

Counting atoms of elements

Table 1 gives you the masses and proportions of the major constituent elements in a person of average mass (about 60 kg).

Element	Mass in 60 kg person/g	Percentage of atoms
oxygen	36 800	25.9
carbon	11 688	11.0
hydrogen	5326	59.4
nitrogen	2962	2.39

Table 1 The major constituent elements in the human body

Notice that in the two columns of numbers in Table 1 different elements appear to be more important in the body. For example, there are more atoms of hydrogen in your body than atoms of any other element, but hydrogen contributes far less than carbon or oxygen to the mass of your body. So a list of masses alone does not allow us to decide which of the three categories of 'elements of life' an element belongs to. To do this, we need to determine how many **atoms** of each element there are.

Chemists can convert masses of elements into a measure of the number of atoms they contain by making use of **moles**. When we are dealing with elements, one mole is the amount of an element which contains the same number of atoms as 12 g of carbon.

Because atoms have exceedingly small masses, the number of atoms in one mole of an element is large. In fact it is very, very large – approximately 6×10^{23} atoms per mole. There are almost 1000 moles of carbon in a 60 kg person, so there are an awful lot of carbon atoms in the human body.

Once the number of moles of atoms of each element in the body has been calculated from its mass, these can be added to give the total number of atoms in the body. The percentage of atoms in the body of each element can then be worked out using the total.

Chemical Ideas 1.1 tells you more about moles and how to use them in calculations.

Table 1 shows you that the ratio of hydrogen atoms to oxygen atoms in your body is almost 2:1. That's because 65% of the mass of your body is water and the chemical formula of water is H_2O. You have probably known that formula for a long time. But how did you know it? Did you ever work it out? It's not difficult – provided that you know about moles.

Activity EL1 gives you a chance to practise using moles and to work out the formula of water for yourself.

ASSIGNMENT I

Putting information in a table like Table 1 is often not the most striking way to present it. Pie charts or bar charts, for example, can be better.

Draw a pie chart to represent the proportions by mass of the four major constituent elements in the body. Label the fifth 'slice' of the chart to represent the contribution of all the trace and ultra-trace elements.

Now draw another pie chart, this time to represent the percentages of atoms.

Do you think that pie charts provide a better way of seeing and comparing the information in this case?

EL2 *Take two elements ...*

A trace is all you need

Section **EL1** shows that about 99% of your body is made up of only four elements: hydrogen, oxygen, carbon and nitrogen. These elements are obviously vital for life. But the trace and ultra-trace elements, although they make up only the remaining 1% or so of the body, are also essential for good health. You could not live without them!

Table 2 lists the proportions of the trace elements in a 60 kg person. The ultra-trace elements – which include cobalt, copper, iodine, iron, manganese, molybdenum, silicon, vanadium and zinc – are not given because their quantities are so small.

Element	Mass in 60 kg person/g	Percentage of atoms
calcium	780	0.22
sulphur	366	0.13
phosphorus	354	0.13
potassium	126	0.04
chlorine	103	0.03
sodium	61	0.03
magnesium	24	0.01

Table 2 The trace elements in the human body

Figure 2 These foods are all rich sources of calcium compounds — bread and eggs also contain iron compounds, and fish is a good source of iodine compounds

Table 3 shows what some of the trace and ultra-trace elements do. You can see just how essential these elements are for proper body function.

Element	Function
calcium	major component of bone; required in some enzymes
phosphorus	essential for the synthesis of chemicals in the body and for energy transfer
sulphur	required in proteins and other compounds
copper	essential in enzymes involved in oxidation processes
iodine	an essential component of thyroid hormones
iron	contained in haemoglobin and many enzymes
zinc	required for the activity of many enzymes

Table 3 The functions of some trace and ultra-trace elements

The human body is often deficient in iron and calcium. The next section of the unit looks in more detail at the role and chemistry of these elements.

An iron story

The body can easily become deficient in iron, particularly in young teenagers who are growing fairly rapidly. Iron deficiency, or anaemia, can usually be remedied with a course of iron tablets and an alteration in diet.

Iron carries out a vital role in the body: as part of the substance **haemoglobin**, present in blood, it is responsible for the transport of oxygen.

The diagram below shows part of the haemoglobin molecule. It consists of an iron atom at the centre of a ring structure. The ring is the *haem* part of the molecule. Also associated with the central iron atom is the protein, *globin*.

Figure 3 The haemoglobin molecule

Haemoglobin is able to do its job because oxygen molecules become attached to the iron (Fe) atom. Oxygen is not the only substance to behave in this way: carbon monoxide can become similarly attached. Unfortunately, it is attracted more strongly than oxygen. This is why it acts as a poison if it gets into the body: it prevents the haemoglobin from carrying oxygen. One of the reasons why people who smoke are particularly prone to heart disease is that the carbon monoxide they inhale from cigarettes reduces the amount of oxygen their blood can carry. Their hearts therefore have to work much harder to maintain an adequate supply of oxygen to the body.

Once you are 18 years old you can become a blood donor. Because it is inadvisable for people with iron deficiency to give blood, a small sample of blood is always tested first to find the iron concentration. A drop of blood is taken from the donor's thumb and placed in a solution of copper sulphate. The copper sulphate reacts with the haemoglobin to form an insoluble compound, which appears as a white-coloured 'blob' in the solution.

The density of the copper sulphate solution is carefully arranged so that if there is sufficient haemoglobin (and therefore iron) in the blood, the density of the blob is enough to make it sink. If this happens, the person can go on to make a blood donation.

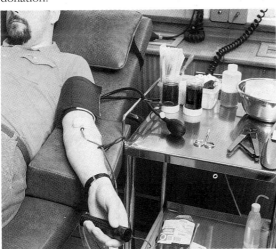

Figure 4 Anyone over 18 years of age can volunteer to become a blood donor

However, if the blob floats there is insufficient haemoglobin in the blood, and the person is not allowed to make a blood donation. A sample of about 10 cm^3 of blood is taken for more detailed analysis from people found to have low haemoglobin levels.

It isn't safe for you to work with samples of blood, but you can work out the concentration of iron in iron tablets in **Activity EL2.1**.

Susan's story

There are several places in the storylines where you can read about people who use chemistry in their jobs. All the stories are about real *people.*
This one is about Susan who works in a medical laboratory where samples of blood are sent for analysis. Susan has been working at the laboratory for 3 years since doing A-levels in Chemistry, Physics and Biology, followed by a degree in Biochemistry. She describes here exactly what happens to blood sent to her for analysis.

Figure 5 Susan relies on chemistry every day in her work at a medical laboratory

"A 10 cm^3 blood sample is sent to our laboratories in a tube which is impregnated with heparin – a substance which stops the blood coagulating. I split the sample into two halves, adding anticoagulant to the first half of the sample to prevent it from clotting, but leaving the second half to clot.

The tests I do on the uncoagulated half are called full blood count (FBC) tests and involve counting the number of red blood cells, the number of white blood cells and the number of platelets. I don't actually count them one by one! An electronic cell counter does the job for me once I have loaded the sample.

The machine also measures the size of the red blood cells. If the cells are smaller than normal, this indicates that the person has anaemia. If, on the other hand, they are bigger than normal, this suggests that the person might have a vitamin deficiency.

I have to leave the second half of the sample to clot. Then the concentration of iron can be measured. To do this I first centrifuge the sample. This separates out the cellular material in the blood from the serum. The serum is a pale straw-coloured liquid, and this is the part I use for the second set of tests. The iron I am looking for is dissolved in this serum. I find the concentration of iron using a colorimeter, a machine which measures the light absorbed by iron in solution. It compares the amount of light absorbed by a solution made up from the serum with the absorption of solutions containing known concentrations of iron.

The results of my tests and those done by my colleagues are then sent back to the patient's doctor. I also have to send a reminder to the patient to go and see the doctor if they require any treatment as a result of having the tests carried out."

A calcium story

Calcium is essential for the healthy development of bones. It is particularly important for a pregnant woman to eat a calcium-rich diet to ensure that her bones remain healthy and her baby's bones are properly formed.

Figure 6 Diet is important during pregnancy, for both the mother and her baby. Among other things, a regular intake of calcium is essential.

Bones containing insufficient calcium are referred to as **demineralised** bones. One of the consequences of people living longer is that a condition called **osteoporosis** is becoming far more common. People with osteoporosis have demineralised bones and tend to suffer from frequent bone fractures and curvature of the spine. The condition is usually observed in women who have passed through the menopause.

An increased intake of calcium can help the condition, and scientists have been trying to develop a technique which would allow them to find out how much of the calcium which is eaten is taken up by the bloodstream and becomes part of the bones. One way is to use a **tracer technique**. Patients are given a *meal* containing a radioactive calcium isotope, and the amount of radioactive calcium which is then absorbed into the bloodstream from the gut is measured.

ASSIGNMENT 2

a What sort of measurements do you think it would be necessary to make on patients if they received treatment involving a radioactive tracer?

b Suggest why there are advantages in using a *short-lived* radioactive isotope of calcium.

c Suggest what might be the disadvantages of using a short-lived isotope.

Good study habits, right from the start, are invaluable to your success in this course. **Activity EL2.2** will help you to take better notes – an important aspect of study skills.

However, radioactive isotopes can be dangerous and scientists have been working with strontium, an element very similar to calcium, to develop an alternative technique. The approach developed from observations made in the 1960s that some children had strontium in their bones. The quantities were small, but were still much larger than normal.

The strontium was present as the radioactive isotope strontium-90, a product of nuclear fission. Its uptake into children's bones was thought to result from the increased atmospheric concentration of strontium-90 which accompanied the testing of nuclear weapons in the 1950s.

It revealed a very important fact for scientists, which is that strontium is taken up into bones during their formation as well as calcium. Normal, non-radioactive strontium can be analysed far more easily than calcium because strontium compounds give out a characteristic red light when they are placed in a flame. The intensity of this red light is a measure of how much strontium is present.

Scientists can therefore use *non-radioactive* strontium to detect the rate at which strontium is absorbed into the blood from the gut. They found that the rate of uptake of strontium was the same as the rate at which calcium was absorbed in tracer experiments. Using strontium is far safer than using a radioactive calcium isotope.

The ability to monitor patterns of absorption of calcium through the use of non-radioactive strontium should now lead to a greater understanding of calcium deficiencies and improve the treatment of bone disorders such as osteoporosis.

Activity EL2.3 can help you to find out more about the chemistry of calcium and strontium and their compounds, together with two other elements – magnesium and barium – and their compounds.

EL3 Looking for patterns in elements

When the elements were being discovered, and more was being learned about their properties, chemists looked for patterns in the information they had assembled.

You have seen that there are close similarities between calcium and strontium. If you have done **Activity EL2.3** you will be able to add magnesium and barium to them to make a 'family' of four elements. Your earlier studies probably introduced you to two other 'families' – lithium, sodium and potassium, and fluorine, chlorine, bromine and iodine.

Figure 7 shows you the historical pattern of the discovery of elements.

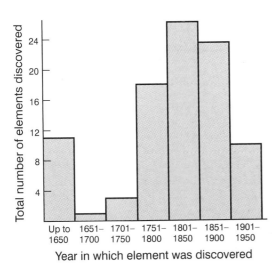

Figure 7 Historical pattern of the discovery of elements – many were discovered in the 19th century

Figure 8 An extract from Chemical News, *March 1866*

Fifty-nine of the 92 naturally occurring elements had been discovered by 1850, so the search for patterns among the elements was particularly fruitful in the mid-19th century.

Much of the work was done by Johann Döbereiner and Lothar Meyer in Germany, John Newlands in England, and Dmitri Mendeleev in Russia. These chemists looked at similarities in the chemical reactions of the elements they knew about, and also patterns in physical properties, such as melting points, boiling points and densities.

Reactions to their suggestions were not always favourable. The March 1866 edition of *Chemical News*, a journal of the Chemical Society, shows you what Professor G. F. Foster had to say about Newlands' 'Law of Octaves' (Figure 8). Three of Newlands' symbols will look unfamiliar. They are listed below with their modern equivalents:

- G is now Be
- Di is now Ti
- Ro is now Rh.

PROCEEDINGS OF SOCIETIES

CHEMICAL SOCIETY
Thursday, March 1

Professor A. W. WILLIAMSON, *Ph.D.,* F.R.S., *Vice-President, in the Chair*

Mr. JOHN A. R. NEWLANDS read a paper entitled 'The Law of Octaves, and the Causes of Numerical Relations among the Atomic Weights.' The author claims the discovery of a law according to which the elements analogous in their properties exhibit peculiar relationships, similar to those subsisting in music between a note and its octave. Starting from the atomic weights on Cannizzaro's system, the author arranges the known elements in order of succession, beginning with the lowest atomic weight (hydrogen) and ending with thorium (=231.5); placing, however, nickel and cobalt, platinum and iridium, cerium and lanthanum, &c., in positions of absolute equality or in the same line. The fifty-six elements so arranged are said to form the compass of eight octaves, and the author finds that chlorine, bromine, iodine, and fluorine are thus brought into the same line, or occupy corresponding places in his scale. Nitrogen and phosphorus, oxygen and sulphur, &c.,

are also considered as forming true octaves. The author's supposition will be exemplified in Table II., shown to the meeting, and here subjoined:–

Dr. GLADSTONE made objection on the score of its having been assumed that no elements remain to be discovered. The last few years had brought forth thallium, indium, caesium, and rubidium, and now the finding of one more would throw out the whole system. The speaker believed there was as close an analogy subsisting between the metals named in the last vertical column as in any of the elements standing on the same horizontal line.

Professor G. F. FOSTER humorously inquired of Mr. Newlands whether he had ever examined the elements according to the order of their initial letters? For he believed that any arrangement would present occasional coincidences, but he condemned one which placed so far apart manganese and chromium, or iron from nickel and cobalt.

Mr. NEWLANDS said that he had tried several other schemes before arriving at that now proposed. One founded upon the specific gravity of the elements had altogether failed, and no relation could be worked out of the atomic weights under any other system than that of Cannizzaro.

Table II – Elements arranged in Octaves

H	1	F	8	Cl	15	Co & Ni	22	Br	29	Pd	36	I	42	Pt & Ir	50
Li	2	Na	9	K	16	Cu	23	Rb	30	Ag	37	Ca	44	Os	51
G	3	Mg	10	Ca	17	Zn	24	Sr	31	Cd	38	Ba & V	45	Hg	52
Bo	4	Al	11	Cr	19	Y	25	Ce & La	33	U	40	Ta	46	Tl	53
C	5	Si	12	Ti	18	In	26	Zr	32	Sn	39	W	47	Pb	54
N	6	P	13	Mn	20	As	27	Di & Mo	34	Sb	41	Nb	48	Bi	55
O	7	S	14	Fe	21	Se	28	Ro & Ru	35	Te	43	Au	49	Th	56

	Group I	Group II	Group III	Group IV	Group V	Group VI	Group VII	Group VIII
Period 1	H							
Period 2	Li	Be	B	C	N	O	F	
Period 3	Na	Mg	Al	Si	P	S	Cl	
Period 4	K Cu	Ca Zn	* *	Ti *	V As	Cr Se	Mn Br	Fe, Co Ni
Period 5	Rb Ag	Sr Cd	Y In	Zr Sn	Nb Sb	Mo Te	* I	Ru, Rh Pd

Figure 9 Mendeleev's Periodic Table (the asterisks denote elements which he thought were yet to be discovered)

Just 3 years later, however, Mendeleev's groupings (see Figure 9) were seen as much more credible.

Unlike Newlands, Mendeleev left gaps in his table of elements. These gaps were very important: they allowed for the discovery of new elements. (Look at Dr Gladstone's comments in Figure 8).

Mendeleev was so confident of the basis upon which he had drawn up his table that he made predictions about elements which had yet to be discovered. In 1871, he predicted the properties of an element he called **eka-silicon**, which he was confident would eventually be discovered to fill the gap between silicon and tin in his Periodic Table. Mendeleev's predictions are shown in Table 4. The element was discovered in 1886 and called **germanium**: its properties are in excellent agreement with Mendeleev's predictions.

Property	Prediction
appearance	dark-grey solid
relative atomic mass	72
density	$5.5\,\mathrm{g\,cm^{-3}}$
reaction with water	none
reaction with acid	very little
reaction with alkali	more than with acid
oxide	basic, reacts with acid
chloride	liquid, boiling point $<100\,^{\circ}C$

Table 4 Mendeleev's predictions for the properties of eka-silicon

Figure 10 Dmitri Mendeleev's (1834–1907) ideas form the basis of our modern classification of the elements. In 1934, the centenary of his birth was marked with this 15-m-high version of Mendeleev's Periodic Table, unveiled at the building in St Petersburg where he had worked

The modern Periodic Table is based on the one originally drawn up by Mendeleev. It is one of the most amazingly compact stores of information ever produced: with a copy of the Periodic Table in front of you, and some knowledge of how it was put together, you have thousands of facts at your fingertips!

Chemical Ideas 11.1 tells you more about the modern Periodic Table.

Chemical Ideas 11.2 looks at a typical Group and will allow you to check your results from **Activity EL2.3.**

ASSIGNMENT 3

Table 4 shows some of the predictions Mendeleev made about the properties of eka-silicon. Use reference books to find out about the properties of silicon and tin, and then make your own predictions about the element which would fill the gap between them.

Find out about some of the properties of germanium and see how well these compare with your predictions and Mendeleev's predictions about eka-silicon.

Activity EL3 will help you to organise the material you have come across in Sections **EL1** to **EL3.**

EL4 *Where do the chemical elements come from?*

A star is born

In the beginning, there was hydrogen – and a lot of it! There still is: hydrogen is the most common element in the universe. Humans also contain quite a lot of hydrogen, but we also contain other, heavier elements as well. The theory of the evolution of the stars shows how heavy elements can be formed from lighter ones, and helps to explain the way elements are distributed throughout the universe.

The theory of how stars form is one of the major scientific achievements of this century. It was developed through observation of stars at different stages in their development, studying them as they changed over time.

The two elements whose atoms are most abundant in space are hydrogen and helium. But the atoms are few and far between. There is about one atom per centimetre cube in the space between the stars, compared with over 10^{19} atoms per centimetre cube in the air you are breathing now. With a density of hydrogen atoms in space as low as this, there is almost no chance that hydrogen atoms will come together to form hydrogen molecules.

However, in some regions between the stars called **interstellar gas clouds**, there may be up to 100 atoms per cm^3. The gas clouds also contain **dust** – debris from earlier stars which have been spread out in space.

Interstellar gas clouds are held together by gravitational forces. Within the gas clouds are regions where the gravitational field makes the cloud contract in on itself, and the gases become compressed. 'Clumps' of denser gas are formed.

The densest part of the 'clump' is its centre. Here the gases are most compressed and become very hot, up to 10 million °C. Such temperatures are high enough to trigger nuclear reactions.

Nuclear reactions are different from chemical reactions. Whereas in chemical reactions atoms are *reorganised* into new arrangements, in nuclear reactions the atoms *change* from one element to another.

One nuclear reaction that takes place in the centre of 'clumps' is **fusion**, when lighter nuclei are fused together to form heavier nuclei. Massive quantities of energy are needed to overcome the repulsions between the positive charges on the two nuclei, but in the centre of stars, where temperatures can reach hundreds of millions of degrees, fusion is common.

The nuclei of hydrogen atoms present in the gas cloud join together by nuclear fusion and the hydrogen turns into helium. The process releases vast quantities of energy, which causes the dense gas cloud to glow. Here are two examples of reactions which take place in the Sun:

$$^1_1H + ^2_1H \rightarrow ^3_2He$$
$$^2_1H + ^3_1H \rightarrow ^4_2He + ^1_0n$$

Notice that atomic numbers and mass numbers must balance in a nuclear equation.

Chemical Ideas 2.1 provides you with information about the structure of atoms. This will help you with your study of this section.

Activity EL4.1 will enable you to find out how our current model of the atom developed.

The nuclear reactions also generate a hot wind which drives away some of the dust and gas, leaving behind the new star. This is often surrounded by planets which have condensed out of the remaining dust cloud.

Heavyweight stars

What happens next to a star depends on its mass. All stars turn hydrogen into helium by nuclear fusion. This process occurs fastest in the heaviest stars because their centres are the hottest and the most compressed. These heavyweight stars have very dramatic lives. The temperatures and pressures at the centre of the star are so great that further fusion reactions take place to produce elements heavier than helium.

Figure 11 The glow of star formation in the Orion nebula

Layers of elements form within the star, with the heaviest elements near the centre where it is hottest and where the most advanced fusion can take place.

Figure 12 shows an example of the composition of the core of a typical heavyweight star after a few million years – long enough for extensive fusion to have taken place.

Figure 12 A model of the core of a typical heavyweight star

The element at the centre of the core is iron. When iron nuclei fuse they do not release energy but they *absorb* it. When the core of a heavyweight star reaches the stage where it contains mainly iron, it becomes unstable and explodes. These explosions are called **supernovae** – the most violent events in the universe. As a result of the supernova, the elements in the star are dispersed into the universe as clouds of dust and gas, and so the life cycle begins again.

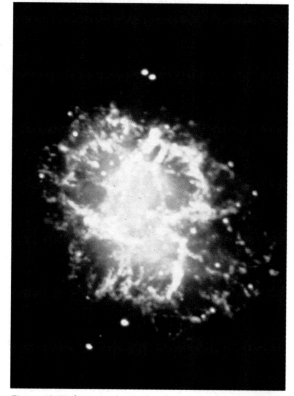

Figure 13 Violence in the Crab nebula – scientists believe that such pictures are evidence of a supernova

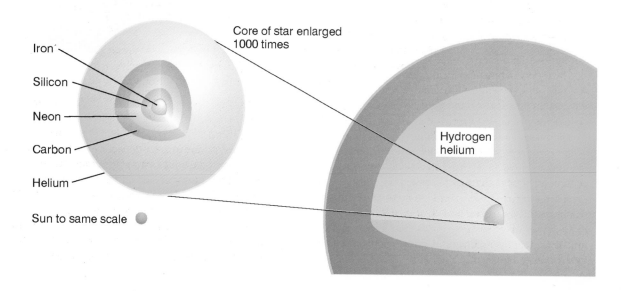

Iron

Silicon

Neon

Carbon

Helium

Core of star enlarged 1000 times

Hydrogen helium

Sun to same scale

ASSIGNMENT 4

Identify the isotopes which are missing from the following nuclear equations:

a $^{12}_{6}C + ? \rightarrow {}^{16}_{8}O$

b $^{14}_{7}N + {}^{1}_{1}H \rightarrow ?$

c $^{7}_{3}Li + ? \rightarrow {}^{4}_{2}He + {}^{4}_{2}He$

The Sun – a lightweight among stars

The Sun is a **lightweight** star: it is not as hot as most other stars and will last longer than heavyweight stars. It will keep on shining until all the hydrogen has been used up and the core stops producing energy: there will be no supernova. Once the hydrogen is used up, the Sun will expand into a **red giant**, swallowing up the planets Mercury and Venus. The oceans on Earth will start to boil and eventually it too will be engulfed by the Sun. The good news for Earth is that the Sun still has an estimated 5000 million years' supply of hydrogen left!

As red giants get bigger, they also become unstable, and the outer gases drift off into space, leaving behind a small core called a **white dwarf**, about one-hundredth of the size of the original star.

How do we know so much about outer space?

The work of chemists has made a vital contribution to the understanding of the origin, structure and composition of our universe. To do this, they have used one of the most powerful analytical tools available today – **spectroscopy**.

Many different spectroscopic techniques exist (others are discussed in the **What's in a Medicine?** storyline), but all are based on one very important scientific principle – under the right conditions a substance can be made to **absorb** (take in) or **emit** (give out) **electromagnetic radiation** in a way which is characteristic of that substance.

If we analyse this electromagnetic radiation (such as ultra-violet light, visible light or radio waves) we can learn a lot about a substance. Sometimes we just want to know what it is. At other times we want to find out very detailed information about it, such as its structure and the way its atoms are held together. Figure 14 shows how visible light can be analysed using a spectrograph.

Absorption spectra

The glowing regions of all stars emit light of all frequencies between the ultra-violet and the infra-red parts of the electromagnetic spectrum. The Sun emits mainly visible light; its surface (**photosphere**) glows like an object at about 6000 K. Some stars are cooler than the Sun; others are much hotter, reaching temperatures as high as 40 000 K and emitting mainly ultra-violet radiation.

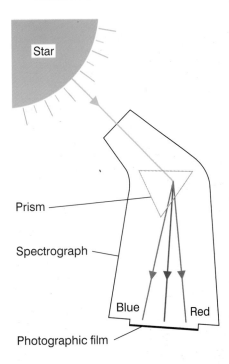

Figure 14 The frequencies in a beam of light can be analysed using a spectrograph

Outside the star's photosphere is a region called the chromosphere (see Figure 15). The chromosphere contains ions, atoms and, in cooler stars, small molecules. These particles absorb some of the light which is emitted from the glowing photosphere. So when we analyse the light which reaches us from the star, we see that certain frequencies are missing – the ones which have been *absorbed*.

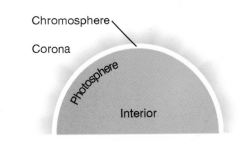

Figure 15 The structure of the Sun

β Centauri is a B-type star (a type of very hot star). The spectrum of the visible light reaching us from β Centauri, in other words the star's visible **absorption spectrum**, is illustrated in Figure 16 (overleaf). You can clearly see the **absorption lines**. Because these correspond to the frequencies which are missing, they appear as black lines on the bright background of light emitted from the star. The absorption lines in β Centauri's spectrum arise only from hydrogen atoms and helium atoms. These are the only atoms able to absorb visible light at the very high temperature of β Centauri.

B-type star

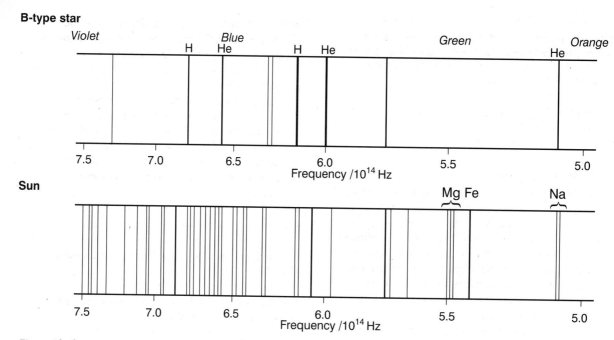

Figure 16 Absorption spectra of a B-type star (eg β Centauri) and the Sun

For comparison, the Sun's absorption spectrum is also shown in Figure 16. Because the Sun is at a lower temperature, different particles are able to absorb visible light. For example, lines from sodium, iron and magnesium can be seen. The Sun's chromosphere consists mainly of hydrogen and helium but, at the temperature of the Sun, these do not absorb visible light.

Emission spectra
When the atoms, molecules and ions around stars absorb electromagnetic radiation, they are raised to higher energy states called **excited states**. The particles can lose their extra energy by emitting radiation. The resulting **emission spectra** can also be detected on Earth.

During a total solar eclipse, the glow of the Sun's photosphere is completely blocked out by the Moon. The light being *emitted* by the chromosphere is all that can be seen, and it is then that the presence of hydrogen and helium is revealed. Hydrogen atoms dominate the chromosphere's *emission spectrum*, but a helium emission line can also be seen. Helium gets its name from *helios*, the Greek word for the Sun. The previously unknown element was first detected in the chromosphere during the eclipse of 1868.

Careful and detailed study of all the types of radiation received on Earth from outer space has allowed a picture to be built up of part of the chemical composition of the universe. More recently, it has been possible to add to this picture by sending up space probes (such as those used in the Voyager missions) fitted with a variety of spectroscopic devices.

ASSIGNMENT 5

The spectrum of the light received on Earth from the white dwarf star Sirius is shown below.

Compare this spectrum with those in Figure 16 and name *five* elements which the spectrum shows are present in Sirius.

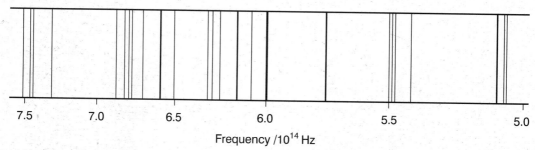

Figure 17 The absorption spectrum of the star Sirius

Chemical Ideas 6.1 will help you to find out more about the information chemists can obtain from spectra. This information includes the arrangements of electrons in shells which is described in. **Chemical Ideas 2.3**.

In **Activity EL4.2** you can look at the emission spectra of some elements for yourself.

Our solar system

Our solar system probably condensed from a huge gas cloud which gradually contracted under the force of gravity. As rings of gas and dust condensed around the Sun, the planets were formed. This material originated from a supernova and therefore contained a range of elements. The non-volatile elements condensed near to the Sun, where temperatures were greatest, while the more volatile elements condensed further away from the Sun at lower temperatures.

So, our solar system is made up of small, dense, rocky planets near to the Sun, and giant fluid planets further away from the Sun. Conditions on all the planets are very different and some of their chemistry seems very unusual when compared with our experiences on Earth. Figure 18 illustrates how unusual some of the chemistry is.

Does this mean then that the composition of the Earth is fixed to just that blend of elements which condensed around the Sun all those billions of years ago? The answer is no. Some of the atoms which formed the Earth were unstable, and began breaking down into atoms of other elements by **radioactive decay**.

That process is still going on today. Now we are also able to produce our own unstable atoms and usefully apply their radioactive decay.

You can learn more about radioactive decay in **Chemical Ideas 2.2**.

Activity EL4.3 introduces you to a current issue concerned with radioactive decay in the UK.

Figure 18 Did you know …?

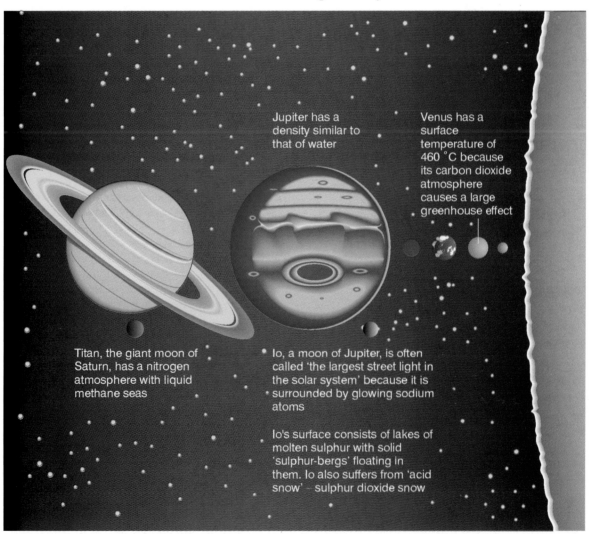

Jupiter has a density similar to that of water

Venus has a surface temperature of 460 °C because its carbon dioxide atmosphere causes a large greenhouse effect

Titan, the giant moon of Saturn, has a nitrogen atmosphere with liquid methane seas

Io, a moon of Jupiter, is often called 'the largest street light in the solar system' because it is surrounded by glowing sodium atoms

Io's surface consists of lakes of molten sulphur with solid 'sulphur-bergs' floating in them. Io also suffers from 'acid snow' – sulphur dioxide snow

Monatomics	Diatomics	Triatomics	Tetra-atomics	Penta-atomics
C^+	H_2	H_2O	NH_3	HCOOH
Ca^{2+}	OH	H_2S	H_2CO	H_2C_2O
H^+	CO	HCN	HNCO	NH_2CN
	CN	HNC	HNCS	HC_3N
	CS	C_2S	C_3N	C_4H
	NS	SO_2	HOCN	CH_2NH
	SO	OCS	$HOCO^+$	CH_4
	SiO	N_2H^+	C_3O	
	SiS	HCS^+		
	C_2	HCO^+		
	CH^+	NaOH		
	NO	HNO		
		HOC^+		

Hexa-atomics	Hepta-atomics	Octa-atomics	Nona-atomics	Others
CH_3OH	CH_3CHO	$HCOOCH_3$	CH_3CH_2OH	HC_9N
NH_2CHO	CH_3NH_2		CH_3OCH_3	$HC_{11}N$
CH_3CN	H_2CCHCN		CH_3CH_2CN	
CH_3SH	CH_3C_2H		HC_7N	
CH_2CCH			CH_3C_3CH	

Table 5 Some chemical species in the interstellar medium

EL5 *The molecules of life*

Chemicals between the stars

You have heard a lot about atoms so far, but humans are made up of molecules and some ions rather than single atoms. So what are the molecules of life, and how did they come into existence?

In the **interstellar medium (ISM)** – the space between stars which contains clouds of gas and dust – there are many chemical species. They form when individual atoms in the ISM happen to meet and bond to one another. Table 5 shows some of these; some will look familiar, but many will look strange.

Chemical Ideas 3.1 tells you about the ways in which elements can combine with each other.

Many of the substances in Table 5 can be described as **organic** species. This means that they contain carbon atoms bonded to elements other than just oxygen.

You should notice something familiar about the elements in these species – they are the elements which are the major constituents of the human body.

Where did the molecules of life come from?

Some scientists have suggested that the molecules in the ISM were the building blocks which reacted together to make the molecules which form the basis of life on Earth. They believe that the energy needed to make these reactions take place came from ultra-violet radiation, X-rays and cosmic rays, and closer to Earth from lightning flashes.

In 1950 an American scientist, Stanley Miller, put methane (CH_4), ammonia (NH_3), carbon dioxide (CO_2) and water – simple molecules like those present in the ISM – into a flask and heated them. He also subjected the mixture to an electrical discharge to simulate the effect of lightning. On analysing the products, Miller found that some of the reaction mixture had been converted into amino acids. Amino acids are the building blocks of proteins, which are formed from long chains of amino acids linked together.

In a separate experiment Leslie Orgel, another scientist in America, made a very dilute solution of ammonia and hydrogen cyanide (HCN) and froze it for several days. When he analysed the 'ice' he identified amino acids and the compound adenine. Adenine is one of four compounds which, together with

Figure 19 Stanley Miller used this apparatus to make amino acids from simple molecules

phosphate units and a sugar called deoxyribose, make up DNA (deoxyribonucleic acid) – the substance which contains the genetic code for reproduction.

Both Miller and Orgel showed that molecules like those in the ISM could react together, under conditions similar to the ones which existed during the early history of the Earth, to form some of the molecules of life. Their experiments give added weight to the suggestion that life on Earth has its origin in molecules from outer space.

You can take a more detailed look at proteins, DNA and other 'molecules of life' later in the course, in the **Engineering Proteins** storyline.

EL6 *Summary*

You began this unit by looking at the elements present in human beings. Next, you looked in more detail at the chemistry of two of the elements found in the body. Having come across a number of different elements, you then found out about the way in which chemists developed a system for classifying the elements. You then went on to consider the origins of all these elements. Finally you came back to humans and found out why you are made of particular elements and how they came to be combined together in this way.

Activity EL6 will help you to check the notes you have made on Sections **EL4** and **EL5**.

DEVELOPING FUELS

Why a unit on DEVELOPING FUELS?

This unit tells the story of petrol: what it is and how it is made. It also describes the work of chemists in improving fuels for motor vehicles, and in searching for and developing alternative fuels for the future.

To achieve this, some fundamental chemistry is introduced. There are two main areas. First it is important to understand where the energy comes from when a fuel burns. This leads to a study of enthalpy changes in chemical reactions, the use of energy cycles, and the relationship between energy changes and the making and breaking of chemical bonds. Secondly, the unit provides an introduction to organic chemistry. Alkanes are studied in detail, and other homologous series such as alcohols and ethers are mentioned.

Isomerism is looked at in connection with octane ratings of petrol, and simple ideas about catalysis arise out of the use of catalytic converters to control exhaust emissions. There is also a brief qualitative introduction to entropy, which follows from a consideration of why the liquid components of a petrol blend mix together. All these topics will be developed and used in later units.

Overview of chemical principles

In this unit you will learn more about ...

ideas you will probably have come across in your earlier studies

- balancing equations
- simple organic chemistry and homologous series
- fractional distillation of crude oil
- combustion of alkanes
- exothermic reactions
- catalysis

ideas introduced in the **Elements of Life** storyline

- moles
- empirical and molecular formulae
- covalent bonding
- polar bonds

... as well as learning new ideas about

- calculating reacting quantities using a balanced chemical equation
- enthalpy changes
- energy cycles
- bond energies
- nomenclature of organic compounds
- properties of alkanes
- isomerism
- alcohols and ethers
- entropy
- molar volumes of gases.

DF1 *Petrol is popular...*

Why don't we all drive electric vehicles? After all, they are clean, quiet and cause no exhaust pollution. Despite these advantages, out of the UK's 30 000 electric vehicles, 27 000 are milk-floats!

One problem with electric vehicles is their poor performance. This is mainly because of the heavy batteries they have to carry around. When were you last overtaken by a milk-float?

Another problem is that it takes so long to recharge their batteries. An electric vehicle has to be recharged overnight for several hours. Electrical energy trickles into the batteries at a rate of about 55 joules per second (55 W).

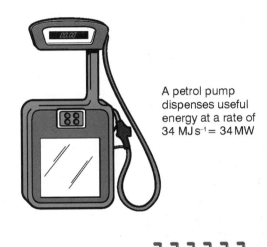

A petrol pump dispenses useful energy at a rate of 34 MJ s⁻¹ = 34 MW

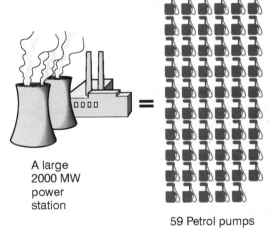

A large 2000 MW power station

59 Petrol pumps

Figure 2 Just 59 petrol pumps can match the power output of a large power station

Figure 1 This is what car parks for electric cars may look like in the future – while the driver is out shopping or at work, the car can be 'filled up'

Now compare this with the rate at which you can fill up a petrol-engined car with its source of energy. A petrol pump delivers petrol at about 1 litre per second, and a litre of petrol transfers 34 000 000 J of energy when you burn it. So the petrol pump replaces the car's energy supply over 600 000 times faster than the battery charger. These numbers are illustrated in a different way in Figure 2.

Petrol is a highly concentrated energy source. Couple that with the ease and cheapness of building petrol engines, and it's not surprising that petrol is popular.

. . . . . *but there are problems*

One problem with petrol is that it's a finite resource, because crude oil supplies are limited. They probably won't last more than about another 100 years.

We need crude oil for more than petrol alone. Crude oil provides the starting materials or **feedstocks** for the petrochemicals industry. For example, it is needed for making synthetic fibres, detergents and pharmaceuticals. As we use up supplies, oil products may become too valuable to burn in car engines.

In **Activity DF1.1** you can look at some of the possibilities for replacing petrol.

Another problem is pollution. Petrol produces carbon dioxide when it burns, and that's a major contributor to the greenhouse effect (see **The Atmosphere** storyline, Section **A6**). Petrol also produces other kinds of polluting emissions, as you'll see later in this unit.

So there's a real need to improve the performance of petrol in car engines so that it burns as cleanly and efficiently as possible – and to find suitable fuels to replace petrol for road transport in the future. How chemists and chemistry can help is one of the major themes of this unit.

First, though, we need to look at the chemistry behind combustion, and ask where the energy comes from when a fuel burns.

You will need to find out how to deal with energy changes in chemistry. **Chemical Ideas 4.1** will help you with this.

You will need to use balanced equations and chemical calculations with confidence throughout your course. If you feel in need of revision, **Chemical Ideas 1.2** and **1.3** will help.

In **Activities DF1.2** and **DF1.3** you can measure the energy changes involved when fuels burn.

DF2 *Getting energy from fuels*

The role of oxygen

Even the crude experimental method in **Activity DF1.2** shows that different fuels have different enthalpy changes of combustion. Let's compare five important fuels – look at Figure 3.

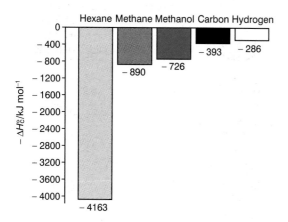

Figure 3 Standard enthalpy changes of combustion for some important fuels

Note that the enthalpy changes are *negative* – this is because during combustion the reactants *lose* energy to their surroundings.

You can see that the enthalpy changes of combustion vary widely. Why should this be? What decides how much energy you get when you burn a mole of a fuel?

We think of fuels as energy sources, but they can't release any energy until they have combined with oxygen. So really we should think of *fuel–oxygen systems* as the energy sources. As you can see in **Chemical Ideas 4.2**, when substances burn the energy released comes as bonds with oxygen are formed.

Chemical Ideas 4.2 will tell you about making and breaking bonds.

ASSIGNMENT 1

a Write down balanced equations for the complete combustion of methane (CH_4), hexane (C_6H_{14}) and methanol (CH_3OH).

b Use the ideas of bond making and bond breaking to explain the following. (Think in terms of the bonds that have to be broken and the new bonds that have to be made when the fuel burns in oxygen.)

 i Why is $\Delta H^{\ominus}_c$ for methane so much less negative than $\Delta H^{\ominus}_c$ for hexane?

 ii Why is $\Delta H^{\ominus}_c$ for methanol less negative than $\Delta H^{\ominus}_c$ for methane? After all, they both have the same number of C and H atoms.

The enthalpy change of combustion of a fuel depends on two things. First, there is the *number* of bonds to be broken and made – and that depends on the size of the molecule involved. That's why larger molecules like hexane have a higher $\Delta H^{\ominus}_c$ than smaller ones like methane.

But $\Delta H^{\ominus}_c$ also depends on the *type* of bonds involved. Let's take your answer to **b(ii)** in **Assignment 1** a bit further. The equations on the next page show the bonds involved in the burning of methane and methanol. The products are the same, but the key difference is that *methanol already has an O–H bond*. In other words, one of the bonds to oxygen is already made – unlike with methane, where all the new bonds have to be made, starting from scratch. Another way of looking at this is to say that methanol is already partly oxidised.

The energy released during combustion comes from the making of bonds to oxygen. If methanol already has one bond made, it will give out less energy when it burns.

(a) Combustion of methane

$$CH_4 + 2O_2 \longrightarrow CO_2 + 2H_2O$$

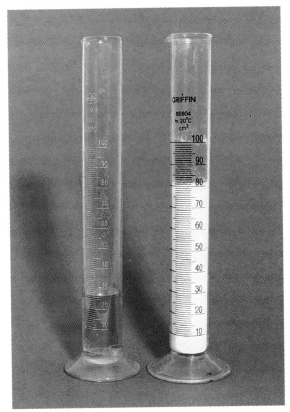

(b) Combustion of methanol

$$CH_3OH + 1\tfrac{1}{2}O_2 \longrightarrow CO_2 + 2H_2O$$

As a general rule, the more oxygen a fuel has in its molecule, the less energy it will give out when one mole of it burns. Oxygenated fuels like alcohols and ethers are less energy-rich than hydrocarbon fuels. However, that's not to say that they are poor fuels. In some ways oxygenated fuels are better, because they are less polluting than hydrocarbons, and they often have a high octane number. More about all this later.

You can use the idea of bond breaking and making by designing a spreadsheet to calculate $\Delta H_c^{\ominus}$ in **Activity DF2.1**.

Important news for slimmers

When you eat too much of an energy food, the excess energy gets stored in your body as fat. The more energy-rich the food, the more fattening it is.

Compare a carbohydrate like glucose with a fat like olive oil. Here are the formulae:

glucose	$C_6H_{12}O_6$
glyceryl trioleate	$C_{57}H_{104}O_6$
(the main constituent of olive oil)	

Per carbon atom, glucose is much more oxygenated than olive oil, so it is much *less* energy-rich. From 1 gram of a carbohydrate like glucose you can get about 17 kJ. From 1 gram of a fat like olive oil you can get about 39 kJ. Gram for gram, fats are more than twice as fattening as carbohydrates.

Alcohol is neither a fat nor a carbohydrate – but it too is bad news for slimmers. In fact there is a whole series of related compounds called **alcohols**, but the

Figure 4 Fats and oils are more energy-rich than carbohydrates – the oil on the left will provide the same quantity of energy as the glucose on the right

particular alcohol present in drinks is ethanol, C_2H_5OH. The same substance is used as an alternative to petrol for cars in some countries. It burns in the car engine releasing energy – and it also releases energy when metabolised in the body (Figure 5).

$\frac{1}{2}$ pint of beer or lager

1 single measure of spirits

1 glass of wine

Each provide about 250 kJ, equivalent to $1\frac{1}{2}$ slices of bread

Figure 5 Alcohol can be fattening

But be thankful that you are not a potato. Humans store energy in fat, but potatoes store it in starch. To store a given amount of energy, you need to have more than twice the mass of starch compared with fat. Think how oversize *that* would make you!

Figure 6 How are these foods made to be less fattening?

Carrying fuels around

For a practical fuel, the enthalpy change of combustion may not be the most important thing to consider. What really matters is the **energy density** – how much energy you get per kilogram of fuel. After all, you have to carry the stuff around with you. We can work this out from the enthalpy change of combustion, using the relative molecular mass. We've done this for five fuels and the results are in Table 1.

Figure 7 The energy density of coal is relatively low – but it is a lot higher than for wood

ASSIGNMENT 2

Look at the values for energy density of the different fuels in Table 1.

a On the basis of energy density, which is the best fuel in the table? What are the practical difficulties involved in using this particular fuel?

b Compare hydrogen and hexane. Explain why hydrogen has the higher energy density, even though it has the lower enthalpy change of combustion.

c Here are some data for octane, C_8H_{18}, and decane, $C_{10}H_{22}$, both of which are components of petrol:

	$\Delta H^{\ominus}_{c, 298}$ /kJ mol^{-1}	Relative molecular mass
octane, C_8H_{18}	−5470	114
decane, $C_{10}H_{22}$	−6778	142

Use the data to calculate the energy density for each of these compounds.

Compare your two answers. How do they compare with the values of energy density given for the fuels in Table 1?

It is important that you make notes as you work through each section. **Activity DF2.2** will help you to check that your notes cover the main points in Sections **DF1** and **DF2**.

This might be a good time to review progress in your preparations for your presentation in **Activity DF1.1**. The work you have covered so far may include some useful information about the fuel you have been allocated.

Later in this unit we will come back to some of the fuels that may replace petrol in the future. But for now, let's look more closely at petrol itself.

DF3 *Focus on petrol*

"Sorry I'm late, the car wouldn't start ..."

What do you blame if the car won't start on a cold morning? Almost certainly the car itself – probably not the driver and certainly not the petrol. Yet the right petrol is actually very important.

Fuel	Formula	Standard enthalpy change of combustion, $\Delta H^{\ominus}_{c, 298}$/kJ mol^{-1}	Relative molecular mass	Energy density (energy transferred on burning 1 kg of fuel)/kJ kg^{-1}
hexane	$C_6H_{14}(l)$	−4163	86	−48 400
methane	$CH_4(g)$	−890	16	−55 600
methanol	$CH_3OH(l)$	−726	32	−22 700
carbon	$C(s)$	−393	12	−32 800
hydrogen	$H_2(g)$	−286	2	−143 000

Table 1 Energy densities of some important fuels

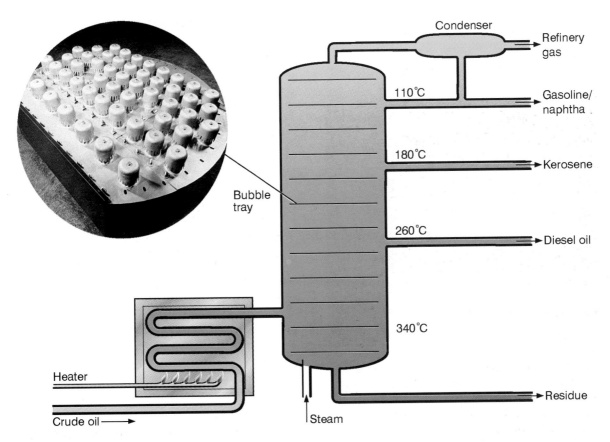

Figure 8 Primary fractional distillation of crude oil

What is petrol?

Petrol is a complex mixture of at least 100 different compounds, mostly hydrocarbons. The main source of petrol is the *gasoline fraction* obtained from the primary distillation of crude oil in a fractionating column. Usually this fraction accounts for 15%–30% of the crude oil. It is a mixture of liquids, mostly **alkanes** with between five and 10 carbon atoms, and boils in the range 20 °C–180 °C.

Table 2 Fractions obtained from the fractional distillation of crude oil

You can find out more about alkanes in **Chemical Ideas 12.1**.

The gasoline fraction is in great demand. Some of it goes to refineries to be used for producing motor fuels. The rest is used in the manufacture of organic chemicals – this part of the gasoline fraction is called **naphtha**.

You can find information about the other fractions produced in the distillation of crude oil in Figure 8 and Table 2.

Name of fraction	Boiling range/°C	Composition	% Crude oil	Use
refinery gas	<20	C_1–C_4	1–2	gaseous fuels and blending with petrol feedstock for organic chemicals
gasoline/naphtha	20–180	C_5–C_{10}	15–30	petrol for cars (gasoline) production of organic chemicals (naphtha)
kerosene (paraffin)	160–250	C_{10}–C_{16}	10–15	jet fuel heating fuel
diesel oil	220–370	C_{13}–C_{25}	15–20	diesel fuel heating fuel
residue	>370	>C_{25}	40–50	fuel oil (eg power stations) lubricating oils and waxes bitumen or asphalt for roads and roofing

Figure 9 The Athabasca oil sands in Canada: a large reserve of crude oil, soaked into sands

In **Activity DF3.1** you can investigate how physical properties change along the alkane series.

The '*straight-run*' gasoline from the primary distillation makes poor petrol. The job of a refinery is to convert it into useful petrol components with the right composition and properties. To do this, the structure of the alkanes present must be modified in various ways. In addition, the heavier fractions, kerosene and diesel oil, are 'cracked' to produce smaller molecules for use as extra petrol components.

The residue can be used to make petrol too, but first it is distilled again, this time under reduced pressure, in **vacuum distillation**. This avoids the high temperatures that would be needed for distillation at atmospheric pressure, since such temperatures would tend to crack the hydrocarbons. The more volatile oils distil over, leaving behind a tarry residue. The fuel oils obtained can be used in power stations or ships' boilers – or cracked to produce more petrol.

As a result of these processes in the refinery, the final petrol contains not only alkanes but other types of hydrocarbons as well – such as **cycloalkanes** which contain rings, **alkenes** which contain a C=C double bond, and **aromatic hydrocarbons** which contain a benzene ring.

You can find out more about these other types of hydrocarbons in **Chemical Ideas 12.1**, **12.2** and **12.3**.

Vacuum distillation

This is a technique for distilling a liquid which decomposes when heated to its boiling point. Distillation cannot be carried out at atmospheric pressure, but if the external pressure is reduced the boiling point can be brought below the decomposition temperature.

ASSIGNMENT 3

a Which fraction from the primary distillation of crude oil would be most likely to contain the following hydrocarbons?

i $C_{35}H_{72}$

ii C_4H_{10}

iii $C_{20}H_{42}$

iv C_8H_{18}

b What type of hydrocarbon is each of the above? Explain your answer.

c The following hydrocarbons are all found in petrol. In each case, draw out one possible structural formula and state the type of hydrocarbon.

i C_7H_8

ii C_4H_8

iii C_5H_{12}

Winter and summer petrol

About 30%–40% of each barrel of crude oil goes to make petrol. But you can see that it's not as simple as just distilling off the right bit at the refinery and sending it to the petrol stations. Petrol has to be blended to get the right properties. One important property is the **volatility**.

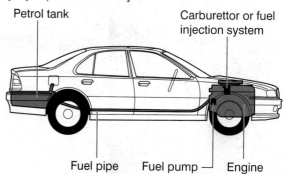

Figure 10 The fuel supply system. When you start a car engine, the fuel pump sucks petrol out of the petrol tank and pushes it to the carburettor. The carburettor partially vaporises the petrol, mixes it with air and sends it to the cylinders in the car engine (nowadays the carburettor is often replaced by an electronic fuel injection system)

In a car engine, a mixture of petrol vapour and air is ignited in a cylinder. The vapour–air mixture is made in the carburettor (see Figure 10). When the weather is very cold, the petrol is difficult to vaporise, so the car is difficult to start.

To get over this problem, petrol companies make different blends for different times of a year. In winter, they put more volatile components in the petrol so it vaporises more readily. This means putting in more of the hydrocarbons with small molecules, such as butane and pentane.

On the other hand, in hot weather you don't want too many of these more volatile components, or the petrol would vaporise too easily. For one thing, you'd lose petrol from your tank by evaporation – a process which is costly and polluting. Also, if the fuel vaporises too readily, pockets of vapour form in the fuel supply system. The fuel pump then delivers a mixture of liquid and vapour to the carburettor instead of mainly liquid. This means that not enough fuel gets through to keep the engine running. It's called *vapour lock*.

Any petrol is a blend of hydrocarbons of high, medium and low volatility. The colder the climate, the more volatile are the components added to the blend. Petrol companies change their blend four times a year – and you don't even notice. But you'd notice if they didn't!

You can compare the volatility of winter and summer blends of petrol in **Activity DF3.2**.

Figure 11 In what way will the petrol blend in Alaska be different from that in Australia?

ASSIGNMENT 4

Petrol blenders talk about the 'front-end' (high volatility), 'mid-range' and 'tail-end' (low volatility) components of a blend.

a What differences will there be between
  i a winter and a spring blend for the UK?
  ii a summer blend for Spain and a summer blend for The Netherlands?

b Use the Data Sheets to look up the densities of some alkanes.
  i How does the density of alkanes change as their molecular mass increases?
  ii Which will have the greater mass at a given temperature: 1 litre of petrol bought in The Netherlands or 1 litre bought in Spain? Explain your answer.

c 'Spanish people get a better bargain than Dutch people when they buy petrol.' Discuss.

The problem of knocking

Another important property which blenders must take into account is the **octane** rating of the petrol (see box). This is a measure of the tendency of the petrol to cause a problem known as '**knock**'.

Octane numbers

The tendency of a fuel to auto-ignite is measured by its **octane number**. 2,2,4-Trimethylpentane (which used to be called 'iso-octane' – hence the name of the scale) is a branched alkane with a low tendency to auto-ignite. It is given an octane number of 100. Heptane, a straight-chain alkane, auto-ignites easily and is given an octane number of 0.

The octane number of any fuel is the percentage of 2,2,4-trimethylpentane in a mixture of 2,2,4-trimethylpentane and heptane which knocks at the same compression ratio as the given fuel. For example, four-star petrol has an octane number of 97 and knocks at the same compression ratio as a mixture of 97% 2,2,4-trimethylpentane and 3% heptane.

2,2,4-trimethylpentane — low tendency to auto-ignition scores 100

$CH_3 - CH_2 - CH_2 - CH_2 - CH_2 - CH_2 - CH_3$

heptane — high tendency to auto-ignition scores 0

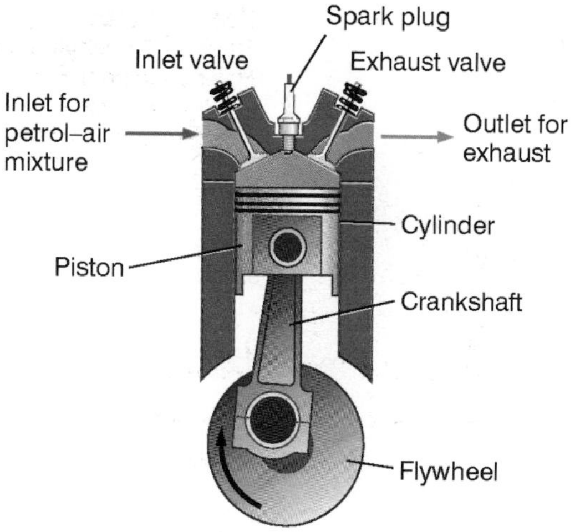

Spark plug

Inlet valve   Exhaust valve

Inlet for
petrol–air →
mixture

Outlet for
→ exhaust

—— Cylinder

Piston —

—— Crankshaft

—— Flywheel

*Figure 12 How a four-stroke petrol engine works. The
compression stroke is shown here. The piston compresses the
petrol–air mixture, then a spark makes the mixture explode,
pushing the piston down and turning the crankshaft*

In a petrol engine, the petrol–air mixture has to
ignite at the right time, usually just before the piston
reaches the top of the cylinder.

Look at Figure 12. As the fuel–air mixture is
compressed it heats up and the more it is compressed
the hotter it gets. Modern cars achieve greater
efficiency than in the past by using *higher compression
ratios*, often compressing the gases in the cylinder by
about a factor of 10.

Many hydrocarbons **auto-ignite** under these
conditions. The fuel–air mixture catches fire as it is
compressed. When this happens, *two* explosions occur:
one due to the compression and another when the
spark occurs. This produces a 'knocking' or 'pinking'
sound in the engine. The thrust from the expanding
gases is no longer occurring at the proper time so
engine performance is lowered, and the inside of the
combustion cylinder can be damaged.

*Figure 13 Auto-ignition is damaging in petrol engines, but
in diesel engines it's an advantage. Diesels have no spark
plugs – they use high compression to make the mixture of
diesel fuel and air auto-ignite*

The auto-ignition of hydrocarbons is explored in **Activity DF3.3**.

ASSIGNMENT 5

Andrew's story

*Andrew works in the research laboratories of a
large oil company. He left school 3 years ago with
A-levels in Chemistry, Physics and Biology.*

"I work as part of a group of scientists. Our research
is aimed at understanding and improving the
performance of fuels in motor vehicles. Part of my
job is to analyse samples of petrol to help other
members of the group with their particular projects.
This may involve analysing individual petrol
blending components – or carrying out pre-race
checks of Formula 1 racing fuels.

I use a technique called **gas–liquid chromatography
(g.l.c.)** to separate and identify the components of a
particular petrol. There may be as many as 300
different compounds present, so I use a computer to
help analyse the results.

A gas–liquid chromatograph contains a long narrow
tube called a **column**, which is packed with inert
solid particles coated with a liquid. The column is
usually wound into a coil to save space, and is kept
at a controlled temperature inside an oven.

When a sample of petrol is injected into the gas
chromatograph, the sample vaporises and is carried
along the column in a stream of gas (usually
nitrogen or a noble gas). The different hydrocarbons
travel along the column at different speeds
depending partly on their volatility and partly on
how well they dissolve in the liquid in the column,
so they emerge from the end at different times. A
detector records each compound as it leaves the
column and a recorder traces out a series of peaks.

Here is the gas chromatogram of a premium-grade
petrol (Figure 14). Each peak corresponds to a
particular hydrocarbon, and the area under each
peak tells us the amount of each hydrocarbon
present.

Each compound contributes to the overall properties
of the fuel, such as volatility and octane quality.
Once we know the composition of a fuel, we can
predict how it will behave in a car engine.

My work is extremely varied and the use of modern
instrumental techniques is challenging and
rewarding. During my time here I have continued
with my studies, completing an HNC course in
Chemistry. I am now studying part-time for a degree
in Applied Chemistry."

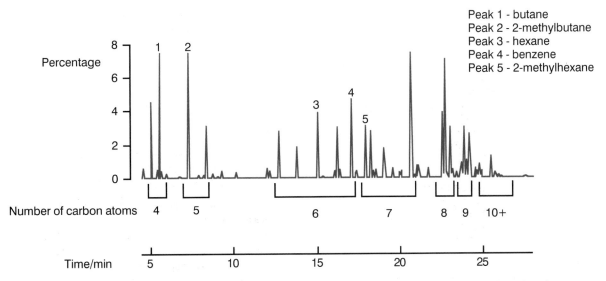

Peak 1 - butane
Peak 2 - 2-methylbutane
Peak 3 - hexane
Peak 4 - benzene
Peak 5 - 2-methylhexane

Figure 14 Gas chromatogram of a premium-grade petrol (eg 2-methylhexane took about 18 min to travel along the column)

Assignment 5: Questions

a Apart from chemists, what other scientists and technologists might Andrew's team include?

b Look at the gas chromatogram in Figure 14.
  i There are two peaks corresponding to four carbon atoms. One is due to butane; what do you think the other is due to?
  ii How does the number of carbon atoms affect how long it takes a compound to travel along the column? Suggest a reason for your answer.
  iii How would the chromatogram change if the column were longer?

You will find out more about gas chromatography and how it is used in **Colour by Design** and **Medicines by Design**.

DF4 *Making petrol – getting the right octane rating*

Different cars have different compression ratios. High performance engines usually have a high compression ratio, and they need a high octane fuel – otherwise there would be knocking and the engine would suffer. There are two ways of dealing with the problem of knock. One is to put special additives in the petrol which discourage auto-ignition. The other is to blend high-octane compounds in with the ordinary petrol.

Look – no lead

Anti-knock additives are substances which reduce the tendency of alkanes to auto-ignite. They increase the octane rating of the petrol.

Since the 1920s, small amounts of lead compounds have been used as economical and effective anti-knock additives. Exactly how they work is still not fully understood, but they help to prevent the reactions which cause knocking.

However, concern over environmental effects has led to a gradual phasing-out of leaded petrol. For one thing, the lead compounds present in the exhaust fumes are toxic. They also poison the metal catalysts in the catalytic converters installed to reduce the levels of other pollutants in exhaust fumes.

Rather than developing alternative lead-free additives, the petrol companies have turned their attention to using refining and blending to get high octane ratings without using lead.

Refining and blending

The hydrocarbons which give the best performance in a petrol engine are not the ones which are most plentiful in crude oil. So it is the job of the refinery to 'doctor' the hydrocarbons to suit our needs.

Mostly, it is a case of getting the right kind of alkane – although other types of hydrocarbons and some oxygenated compounds are also important, as you'll see later.

Which alkanes?

The structure of an alkane has an important influence on its tendency to auto-ignite – in other words, on its octane number. In general, the shorter the alkane chain, the higher the octane number. Short-chain alkanes are also more volatile, of course, so they can be used both to increase the octane number and to improve cold-starting. Even gaseous alkanes like butane can be used – they just dissolve in the petrol.

The idea of isomerism is important in this section. You can find out about it in **Chemical Ideas 3.4**.

You can make models of alkane isomers and practise naming them in **Activity DF4.1**.

But the petrol blenders are limited in the proportion of short-chain alkanes they can include in the blend. Too much and the petrol blend would be *too* volatile.

The other factor that affects octane number is the *degree of branching* in the alkane chain. Quite simply, the more branched the chain, the higher the octane number.

Crude oil contains both straight-chain and branched alkanes. Unfortunately, it does not contain enough of the branched isomers to give it a naturally high octane number. The octane number of 'straight-run' gasoline is about 70.

To get around this, the petrol companies have a number of clever ways to increase the octane number of petrol. They include **isomerisation**, **reforming** and **cracking**.

In **Activity DF4.2** you can look in more detail at the effect of structure on the octane numbers of alkanes.

Isomerisation

Isomerisation basically involves taking straight-chain alkanes, heating them in the presence of a suitable catalyst so the chains break and letting them join together again. When the fragments join again, they are more likely to do so as *branched* rather than as *straight* chains.

Oil refineries do this on a large scale with pentane (C_5H_{12}) and hexane (C_6H_{14}), both products of the distillation of crude oil. It is one important way of increasing the octane quality of petrol.

One isomerisation reaction which can happen with pentane is shown below:

$$CH_3-CH_2-CH_2-CH_2-CH_3 \rightleftharpoons CH_3-\overset{\displaystyle CH_3}{\overset{\displaystyle |}{CH}}-CH_2-CH_3$$

pentane	*2-methylbutane*
octane number 62	octane number 93

Isomerisation reactions like this do not go to completion and a mixture is formed containing all the possible isomers. We say the reaction has come to a **state of equilibrium** when no further change is possible under the reaction conditions. The arrows ($\rightleftharpoons$) indicate that the reaction is reversible and forms an equilibrium mixture.

ASSIGNMENT 6

a Explain why 2-methylbutane is an isomer of pentane.

b A second isomer of pentane is also formed in the isomerisation process. Draw out its structural formula.

c What products might you expect to obtain from the isomerisation of hexane (C_6H_{14})? Draw out the structural formula and give the name of each of your products.

In a modern plant, the isomerisation takes place in the presence of a platinum catalyst. The products then pass over a form of **zeolite** which acts as a **molecular sieve** and separates the straight-chain from the branched isomers (see Figure 31 on p. 36). The straight-chain alkanes are then recycled over the platinum catalyst. Figure 15 gives a flow diagram for the process.

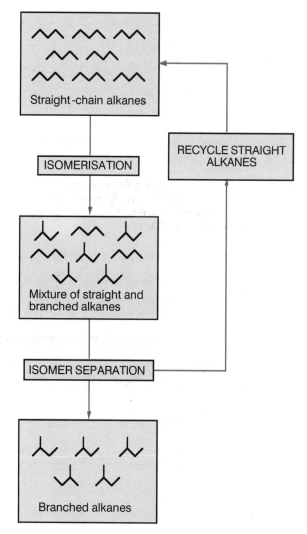

Figure 15 The isomerisation process

You can find out more about zeolites and molecular sieves by making models of zeolites in **Activity DF4.3**.

Cracking: using the whole barrel

Cracking is one of the most important reactions in the petroleum industry. It starts with alkanes that have large molecules and are too big to use in petrol – for example alkanes from the fuel oil fraction. These large molecules are broken down to give alkanes with shorter chains that can be used in petrol. What's more, these shorter-chain alkanes tend to be highly branched, so petrol made by cracking has a higher octane number.

There's another benefit from cracking: it helps solve the supply and demand problem.

Figure 16 illustrates the supply and demand for different fractions of crude oil.

ASSIGNMENT 7

a Demand for petrol exceeds supply. Which of the other fractions would be most suitable for converting to petrol by cracking, in order to meet the shortfall?

b How would the demand figures for *winter* compare with those given in Figure 16, which are for summer?

Figure 16 Supply and demand for different crude oil fractions from the North Sea (the supply figures are given as per cent by mass of crude oil; the demand figures are given as per cent by mass of the total demand)

Cracking: how is it done?

Most of the cracking carried out to produce petrol is done by heating heavy oils in the presence of a catalyst. It is called catalytic cracking or cat cracking for short. The feedstock can be kerosene, diesel oil or the heavier fuel oils from the residue. The molecules in the feedstock can have 25–100 carbon atoms, although most will usually have 30–40 carbon atoms.

Cracking reactions are quite varied. Some of the types of reactions are

• alkanes → branched alkanes + branched alkenes

An example of this is:

$$CH_3-CH_2-CH_2-CH_2-CH_2-CH_2-CH_2-CH_2-CH_2-CH_2-CH_2-CH_3$$

$$CH_3-\underset{\underset{CH_3}{|}}{CH}-CH_2-\underset{\underset{CH_3}{|}}{CH}-CH_3 \qquad CH_2=\underset{\underset{CH_3}{|}}{C}-CH_2-CH_3$$

• alkanes → smaller alkanes + cycloalkanes
• cycloalkanes → alkenes + branched alkenes
• alkenes → smaller alkenes.

The alkenes which are produced are important feedstocks for other parts of the petrochemicals industry.

Cracking always produces many different products, which need to be separated in a fractionating column.

Once again, zeolites play an important role. Type Y zeolite is particularly effective in producing good yields of high octane number products.

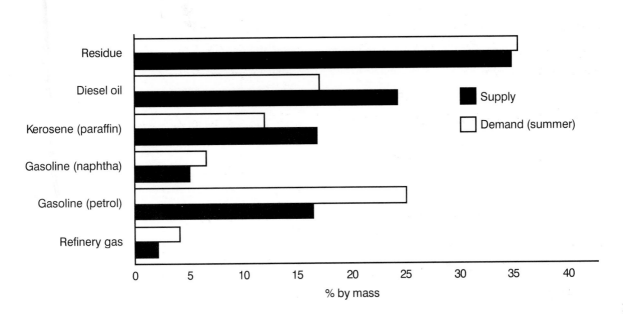

In a modern cat cracker the cracking takes place in a 60-m-high vertical tube about 2 m in diameter (Figure 17). It is called a **riser reactor** because the hot vaporised hydrocarbons and zeolite catalyst are fed into the bottom of the tube and forced upwards by steam. The mixture is a seething **fluidised bed** in which the solid particles flow like a liquid. *Jets of air used. (in suspension)*

It takes the mixture about 2 seconds to flow from the bottom to the top of the tube – so the hydrocarbons are in contact with the catalyst for a very short period of time.

One of the problems with cat cracking is that, in addition to all the reactions you have already met, coke (carbon from the decomposition of hydrocarbon molecules) forms on the catalyst surface so that the catalyst eventually becomes inactive. To overcome this, the powdery catalyst needs to be **regenerated**.

After the riser reactor, the mixture passes into a separator where jets of steam carry away the cracked products leaving behind the solid catalyst. This then goes into the regenerator, where it takes about 10 minutes for the hot coke to burn off in the stream of air which is blown through the regenerator. The catalyst is then reintroduced into the base of the reactor ready to repeat the cycle.

The energy released from the burning coke heats up the catalyst. The catalyst transfers the energy to the feedstock so that cracking can occur without additional heating.

Catalyst acts as a fluidised bed.

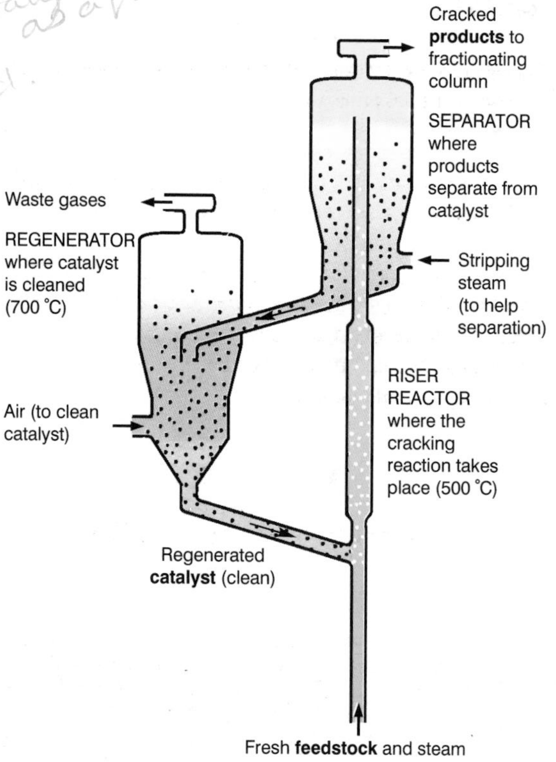

You can try cracking alkanes for yourself in **Activity DF4.4**.

Cat crackers have been in operation since the late 1940s – and have become very flexible and adaptable. They can handle a wide range of different feedstocks. The conditions and catalyst can be varied to give the maximum amount of the desired product – in this case branched alkanes for blending in petrol. Other cat crackers are geared to produce large amounts of ethene ($CH_2=CH_2$), an important raw material for the petrochemicals industry.

ASSIGNMENT 8

The riser reactor uses a fluidised bed of solid catalyst and reactants. Fluidised beds have the following useful properties:

- the solid can flow along pipes
- as the solid can flow, it is easier to make the reaction into a continuous process
- there is very good contact between the gas and the large surface area of the solid catalyst
- energy transfer between the solid and the gas is very efficient.

Suggest why each of these properties is useful or important in the cat cracker.

Cracked **products** to fractionating column

SEPARATOR where products separate from catalyst

Waste gases

REGENERATOR where catalyst is cleaned (700 °C)

← Stripping steam (to help separation)

Air (to clean catalyst) →

RISER REACTOR where the cracking reaction takes place (500 °C)

Regenerated **catalyst** (clean)

↑ Fresh **feedstock** and steam

Figure 17 How a cat cracker works

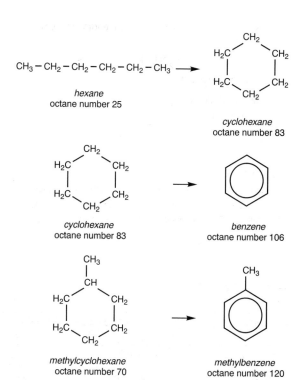

$CH_3 - CH_2 - CH_2 - CH_2 - CH_2 - CH_3 \longrightarrow$

hexane
octane number 25

cyclohexane
octane number 83

cyclohexane
octane number 83

benzene
octane number 106

methylcyclohexane
octane number 70

methylbenzene
octane number 120

Figure 18 Some typical reforming reactions, showing octane numbers of reactants and products

Reforming (Platforming)

Reforming is another trick used by oil refiners to increase the octane quality of petrol components. Reforming involves ring compounds: alkanes are converted to cycloalkanes, and cycloalkanes to aromatic hydrocarbons. Some typical reforming reactions are shown in Figure 18.

These reactions produce hydrogen as well as high octane gasoline components. The hydrogen is a valuable product and is piped away to be used in other refinery processes.

A platinum/rhenium catalyst is often used for reforming – the process is then called *platforming*. There can be £5 million worth of platinum inside one platformer, so it is very important to regenerate the catalyst and keep it in prime working order.

ASSIGNMENT 9

a Using molecular formulae, write out a balanced equation for one of the conversions shown in Figure 18.

b Explain why these reactions are not isomerisations.

c Below is a list of alkanes. For each one, say whether you think

 A It could be used unchanged in petrol

 B It should go through a reforming process before blending to form petrol

 C It should be cracked before blending to form petrol.

 i $CH_3CH_2CH_2CH_2CH_2CH_3$

 ii $CH_3(CH_2)_{15}CH_3$

 iii $(CH_3)_3CCH(CH_3)_2$

 iv $CH_3CH_2CH_2CH_3$

Adding oxygenates

'Oxygenates' is the name the petrol blenders use for fuels containing oxygen in their molecules. Two types of compounds are commonly used: alcohols and ethers (see box).

Alcohols and ethers

Alcohols all have an OH group in their molecule. The best known alcohol is ethanol, commonly called just 'alcohol':

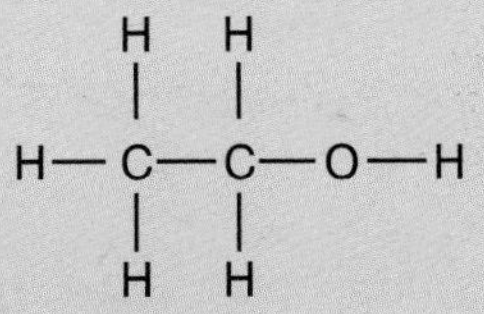

Ethers all have an oxygen atom bonded to two carbons. An example is ethoxyethane (sometimes just called 'ether'):

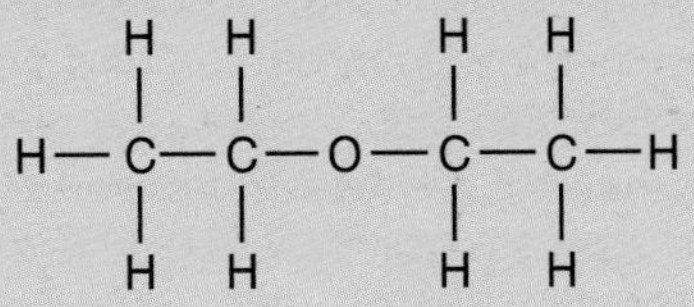

Members of the homologous series of **alcohols** all have an OH group in their molecule. You have already met one example – ethanol, C_2H_5OH (commonly just called 'alcohol'). **Ethers** have an oxygen atom bonded to two carbon atoms, for example ethoxyethane (sometimes just called 'ether'), $CH_3CH_2OCH_2CH_3$.

You can find out more about alcohols and ethers in **Chemical Ideas 13.2**.

You can practise naming alcohols and investigate some of their physical properties in **Activity DF4.5**.

Table 3 shows the oxygenates most commonly used for blending with petrol, together with 'straight-run' gasoline for comparison.

The most commonly used oxygenate is MTBE (MTBE stands for 'methyl tertiary butyl ether', the name that was once used for this compound; its modern systematic name is 2-methoxy-2-methylpropane.)

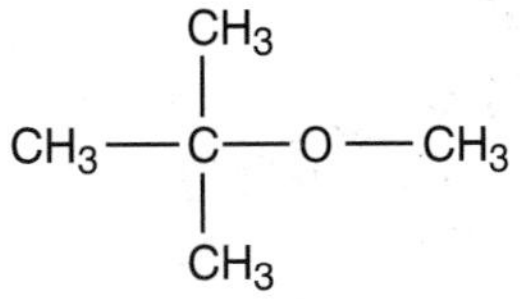

Table 3 Oxygenates commonly used for blending with petrol ('straight-run' gasoline is given for comparison)

Name	Formula	Homologous series	Octane number	Boiling point/°C	Relative cost per litre/pence
methanol	CH_3OH	alcohols	114	65	4.0
ethanol	CH_3CH_2OH	alcohols	111	79	12.0
MTBE	$CH_3OC(CH_3)_3$	ethers	118	55	10.0
'straight-run' gasoline	—	—	70	—	5.0

Figure 19 shows the percentages of MTBE added to different grades of petrol.

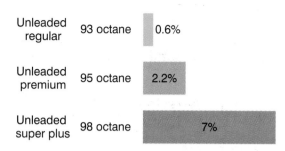

Unleaded regular	93 octane	0.6%
Unleaded premium	95 octane	2.2%
Unleaded super plus	98 octane	7%

Figure 19 Percentages by volume of MTBE typically used in different blends of petrol

There are two advantages to adding oxygenates to petrol. First, they increase the octane number, as you can see from Table 3. Secondly, they tend to cause less pollution when they burn. In particular, levels of carbon monoxide in the exhaust are reduced.

The perfect blend

Figure 21 shows the octane numbers of some of the key ingredients at the petrol blender's disposal.

The blender's job is to produce petrol from these ingredients at minimum cost. Of course, the petrol must meet specifications about volatility, octane number, density, etc. Prices and availability fluctuate and refiners are helped in their decisions by computer models of their refinery. They must take into account not only the prices of crude oil and the final petrol, but prices of their other products from the refinery and energy costs too.

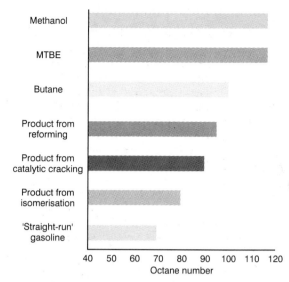

Figure 21 Octane numbers of some of the key ingredients used in petrol blending

Blending is done in batches of around 20 000 000 litres at a time, and can take as long as 20 hours to complete. Thorough mixing is important to give a homogenous liquid.

You can try your hand at blending petrol in **Activity DF4.6**.

You can find out more about the probability of two substances mixing in **Activity DF4.7**.

Activity DF4.8 will help you pull together all the work you have done on petrol so far.

Figure 20 A petrol station in Santos, Brazil. The fuel is a mixture of petrol and ethanol

Why do hydrocarbons mix?

Hydrocarbons are completely miscible with each other and can be blended in any proportions. Have you ever wondered why some liquids mix easily and others, like oil and vinegar, don't mix at all? Mixing of two substances is a natural change – it happens by chance with no external help. The result is an increase in disorder. The idea of disorder or randomness in a system is very important in determining the direction in which changes occur.

We give the amount of disorder in a system a name – **entropy**. When the system gets more disordered, like a pack of cards being shuffled, or two liquids mixing, its entropy increases. Natural changes are always accompanied by an overall increase in entropy.

All substances tend to mix with one another, unless there is something stopping them. In the case of oil and vinegar, there are attractive forces between the particles in vinegar which prevent them mixing with the oil particles.

The idea of entropy is discussed in more detail in **Chemical Ideas 4.3**.

DF5 *Trouble with emissions*

A serious problem

We'll look next at a problem of motor fuels which is causing worldwide concern: exhaust emissions. Figure 22 shows what goes into – and what comes out of – a car engine. The nitrogen oxides, NO and NO_2, are grouped together as NO_x. Similarly, SO_x represents the oxides of sulphur, SO_2 and SO_3, and C_xH_y represents the various hydrocarbons present in the exhaust fumes.

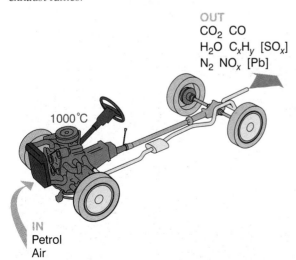

OUT
CO_2 CO
H_2O C_xH_y $[SO_x]$
N_2 NO_x [Pb]

1000°C

IN
Petrol
Air

Figure 22 What goes into – and comes out of – a car engine

The oxides of sulphur in vehicle exhausts come from sulphur compounds in the fuel. In **Activity DF5** you can see how hydrogen is used to remove sulphur from the fuel.

ASSIGNMENT 10

a For each of the substances emitted in the exhaust, as shown in Figure 22, use your knowledge of chemistry to explain where the substance comes from. Write chemical equations where appropriate.

Some will be easier to explain than others! There are two things to bear in mind: the temperature inside a car engine's combustion chamber is about 1000°C, and air is a *mixture* of gases.

b For each of the emissions, say which of the following environmental problems you think it may contribute to:

A Acid rain

B The greenhouse effect

C Damage to the ozone layer

D Toxic effects on humans

E Photochemical smog.

You will need to use your knowledge of air pollution from your earlier studies, or find the information in a textbook.

Unfortunately, these are not the only pollutants caused by motor vehicles. **Ozone** is a *secondary pollutant* formed in sunlight by a series of reactions involving nitrogen oxides (NO_x), hydrocarbons (C_xH_y), oxygen and water vapour. Also produced are irritating and eye-watering compounds formed by oxidation of the hydrocarbons. These reactions all occur in what are known as photochemical smogs.

Figure 23 Photochemical smogs are a problem in Los Angeles, USA

Ozone: friend or foe?

Ozone is a highly reactive substance whose molecules contain three oxygen atoms. Its formula is O_3. In the upper atmosphere (the stratosphere), the presence of ozone is vital because it shields us from harmful solar rays. Concern is growing about the depletion of this layer of ozone brought about by the CFC gases. You will find out more about this in **The Atmosphere**.

Meanwhile, near the ground in the troposphere there is equal concern about *high* levels of ozone. Here it destroys molecules important to many biological processes. It weakens the body's immune system and attacks lung tissue. Ozone, together with hydrocarbons and acid rain, is thought to be responsible for the stunted growth and destruction of many trees in European forests.

Another problem arises because petrol is so volatile. A parked car on a warm day gives off hydrocarbon fumes, mostly butane, from the petrol tank and the carburettor. This is called *evaporative emission* and accounts for about 10% of emissions of volatile organic compounds from vehicles.

Concern about air pollution from motor vehicles is mounting worldwide and many countries are bringing in legislation to limit emissions. The USA has led the way, and cars are put through a rigorous emissions test cycle before they are allowed on the road. Figure 24 shows how emission limits have become increasingly severe.

Tackling the emissions problem

There are two ways of tackling the problem directly. One involves changing the technology of the car engine, including the exhaust system. The other involves changing the fuel used by the car.

Method 1: Changing the engine technology

How much air does a petrol engine need? You can work this out by doing **Assignment 11**.

ASSIGNMENT II

For the purposes of this assignment, assume that petrol is pure heptane, C_7H_{16}.

a Write an equation for the complete combustion of heptane vapour.

b How many moles of oxygen are needed for the combustion of 1 mole of heptane?

c How many moles of C_7H_{16} are there in 1 g of heptane?

d What mass of oxygen is needed to burn 1 g of heptane ($O = 16$)?

e What mass of air is needed to burn 1 g of heptane? (Assume that air is 22% oxygen and 78% nitrogen by *mass*.)

f What *volume* of air (measured at 25 °C and 1 atmosphere pressure) is needed to burn 1 g of heptane? (Assume that 1 mole of oxygen has a volume of 24 dm³ under these conditions and that air is 21% oxygen and 79% nitrogen by *volume*.)

Chemical Ideas 1.4 will help you to carry out calculations involving gases.

The ratio of air to fuel which you worked out in Assignment 11 is the ratio needed to make the petrol burn completely. It is called the **stoichiometric ratio**. (*Stoichiometric* means *involving the exact amounts shown in the chemical equation*.) For an average car engine, the stoichiometric ratio is usually taken to be about 15:1 (by mass).

If you have *less* air than the stoichiometric ratio, it is called a 'rich' mixture, because it's rich in petrol. You burn a rich mixture when you use the choke to start a car on a cold morning. A 'lean' mixture has *more* air than the stoichiometric ratio: it produces less NO_x and CO but the levels of C_xH_y can actually increase (Figure 25). The trouble is, if the mixture is *too* lean, the engine misfires and emissions increase.

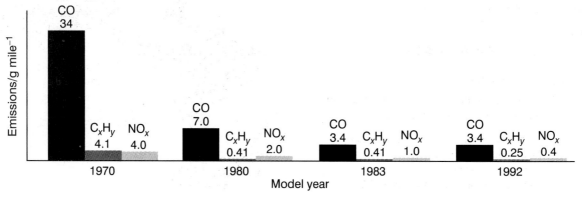

Figure 24 US Federal emission limits for new vehicles have become increasingly severe

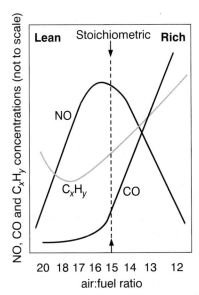

Figure 25 How gases in exhaust emissions vary with the composition of the air–fuel mixture

'Lean-burn' engines use an air:fuel ratio of around 18:1 and have specially designed combustion chambers to get over the problem of misfiring.

Another advantage of a lean-burn engine is that it gives better fuel economy, because you are using less fuel for each firing of the cylinder.

Catalysts can help

Catalysts speed up chemical reactions without getting used up themselves. We can use them to speed up reactions which involve pollutants in car exhausts. Look at these reactions:

$2CO(g) + O_2(g) \rightarrow 2CO_2(g)$ (reaction 1)
$C_7H_{16}(g) + 11O_2(g) \rightarrow 7CO_2(g) + 8H_2O(g)$ (reaction 2)
$2NO(g) + 2CO(g) \rightarrow N_2(g) + 2CO_2(g)$ (reaction 3)

(Here we've used C_7H_{16} as an example of an unburnt hydrocarbon and NO as an example of NO_x).

In these reactions, pollutants are being converted to CO_2, H_2O and N_2, which are all naturally present in the air. These reactons go of their own accord, but under the conditions inside an exhaust system they go too slowly to get rid of the pollutants.

ASSIGNMENT 12

Look at reactions 1–3.

a For each of the pollutants CO, C_xH_y and NO_x, say whether it is being oxidised or reduced.

b Which of these reactions would be important in controlling pollutants from
  i an ordinary engine?
  ii a lean-burn engine? (Look at Figure 25.)

A catalyst made of a precious metal like platinum or rhodium speeds up these reactions in the exhaust system. Such catalysts are used in **catalytic converters**.

You can find out more about catalysts in **Chemical Ideas 10.4**.

A lean-burn engine uses an *oxidation catalyst system* which removes CO and C_xH_y. The exhaust gases are rich in oxygen, so CO and C_xH_y are oxidised to CO_2 and H_2O on the surface of the catalyst. This kind of catalyst system does little to lessen NO_x, because NO_x needs reducing, not oxidising, to turn it to harmless N_2. But that doesn't matter too much in a lean-burn engine, because this type of engine produces less NO_x anyway.

The three-way system

Catalytic converters can be fitted to ordinary engines too. But for an ordinary engine, a simple oxidation catalyst won't do – it wouldn't remove the NO_x. Here, a *three-way catalyst system* is needed, which both oxidises CO and C_xH_y, *and* reduces NO_x. This kind of catalyst system *only* works if the air–petrol mixture is carefully controlled so that it's exactly the stoichiometric mixture for the fuel. If the mixture is too rich, there is not enough oxygen in the exhaust fumes to remove CO and C_xH_y.

This means that cars fitted with three-way catalyst systems need to have oxygen sensors in the exhaust gases, linked back to electronically controlled fuel injection systems. You can see the arrangement in Figure 26.

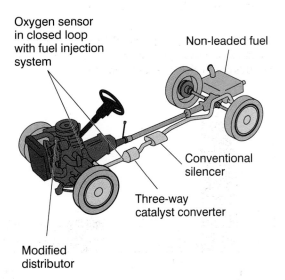

Figure 26 The three-way catalyst system

Figure 27 shows the effect of catalysts on exhaust emissions from ordinary and lean-burn engines. A three-way catalyst system is the most efficient way of simultaneously reducing all three emissions.

All catalytic converters work only when they are hot. A platinum catalyst starts working around 240°C, but by alloying the platinum with rhodium you can get the catalyst to start working at about 150°C. These catalysts are poisoned by lead, so the converters can only be used with lead-free fuel.

The catalyst is used in the form of a fine powder spread over a ceramic support whose surface has a network of tiny holes. The surface area of the catalyst exposed to the exhaust gases is about the same as two or three football fields.

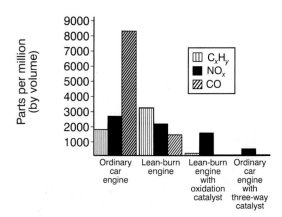

Figure 27 The effect of catalysts on the exhaust emissions from ordinary and lean-burn engines

ASSIGNMENT 13

a Why is it important that catalytic converters start working at as low a temperature as possible?

b What is meant by a *catalyst poison*?

c Why is the catalyst used in the form of a fine powder?

d Suggest a reason why the catalytic converter has eventually to be replaced.

e Catalytic converters convert the pollutants CO, C_xH_y and NO_x into harmless gases. This is still only a partial solution to the emissions problem. Why?

f Why is it possible to fit oxidation catalytic converters to existing cars, but not three-way converters?

Method 2: Changing the fuel

The other approach to tackling the emissions problem is to change the fuel used by cars.

Aromatic hydrocarbons make up as much as 40% of lead-free petrol. Aromatic hydrocarbons may cause higher CO, C_xH_y and NO_x emissions, and some of them may cause cancer. Benzene is the worst, and is strictly controlled, but others may also be controlled in the future.

Butane content too will probably be reduced in the future. Butane is volatile and is responsible for evaporative emissions leading to ozone formation and photochemical smogs.

However, both butane and aromatic hydrocarbons are high octane components of petrol. If they are reduced, their octane quality must be replaced by something else. This is why the petrol companies are looking to the oxygenates as a possible solution.

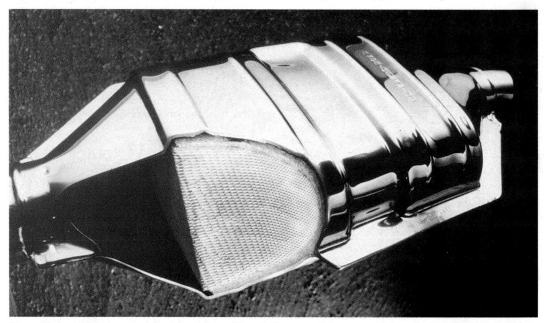

Figure 28 A catalytic converter for a car exhaust. Note the honeycomb structure, giving a high surface area.

The cons

The main problem when using a mixture of methanol and petrol is getting the two liquids to mix. They tend to separate into layers, like oil and vinegar, unless a co-solvent is used. In Germany, a higher alcohol than methanol, called TBA, is mixed with the methanol for this purpose. TBA dissolves in both methanol and petrol.

Another problem is that the petrol–alcohol mixture is **hygroscopic** and absorbs water vapour from the air. The wet methanol corrodes parts of the engine (Figure 30).

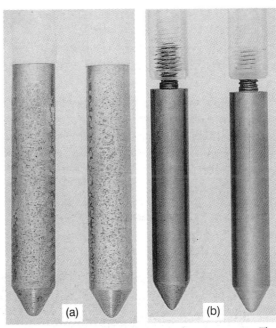

Figure 30 *Methanol absorbs water, making it corrosive. The steel rods in (a) were immersed in petrol containing methanol. Compare them with the rods in (b), which were immersed in normal unleaded petrol*

When the water content reaches a critical level (about 0.5%) two layers separate, giving a layer of petrol sitting on top of a water–alcohol mixture.

Although polluting emissions are reduced, methanol itself is toxic. Long-term exposure can cause blindness and brain damage – that's why 'meths' drinkers go blind. So there is concern over its possible effect on mechanics and petrol-pump attendants at filling stations.

One litre of methanol produces about 40% less energy than 1 litre of petrol. This means larger and heavier fuel tanks and more refuelling trips.

Figure 29 *A methanol plant*

DF6 *Methanol – the key to future fuels?*

The pros

Methanol burns cleanly in a car engine. Its combustion is more complete than that of petrol so emissions, particularly of carbon monoxide, are reduced. Nor does it release carcinogenic benzene vapour or other aromatic hydrocarbons into the air. It has a high octane number (114), and its use requires only small changes to engine and petrol pump design. What's more, it's quite cheap.

So, why don't we use methanol as a fuel? After all, Formula 1 racing drivers have been using it for years. Methanol is less volatile than petrol and less likely to explode in a collision.

In fact, some countries, such as Germany and parts of the USA, have used methanol, but as part of a mixture with petrol.

DF7 *What other solutions are there?*

A combination of new engine design, clever electronics, expensive catalysts and painstaking blending has kept petrol going as a fuel despite all the problems of emission control and changing needs.

At the moment, supplies of crude oil are relatively plentiful and cheap. There is little incentive to change to alternative fuels, which may need new engine technology and major changes to the way the fuel is transported, stored and distributed.

However, the limited crude oil supplies are being used up quickly and we shall have to think seriously about possible alternatives for the future. In the long term, the best solution is to find ways to reduce *all* our energy needs by energy conservation measures such as efficient public transport.

Now is the time for you to present your reports on the prospects for some alternatives to petrol in **Activity DF1.1**. Try to present the most convincing case for your fuel so that it has a fair hearing. You can then discuss the relative merits of each fuel in class and decide on what you think is the most promising way (or ways) forward.

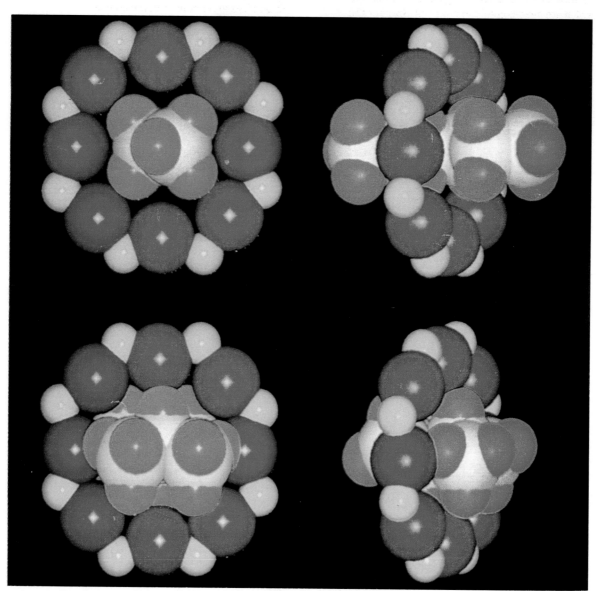

Figure 31 This computer-generated picture shows a molecular sieve in action. In the top pictures, a straight-chain molecule of hexane passes through a molecular sieve. In the bottom pictures, a branched-chain molecule of dimethylbutane cannot pass through. Zeolite molecular sieves are used to separate straight-chain and branched-chain isomers in the isomerisation process (see p. 26).

DF8 *Summary*

This unit began by considering some of the desirable properties of a good fuel, and you found out how petrol is made and how chemists and chemical engineers are helping to develop better fuels for motor vehicles. This means producing fuels which give improved performance and greater fuel economy, so that we use our precious reserves of crude oil as economically as possible. But it is also vital that we drastically reduce the polluting emissions from burning petrol. Quite a challenge!

Petrol is a mixture of hydrocarbons, many of which are alkanes. But the hydrocarbons which give the best performance in the petrol engine are not the ones which are most plentiful in crude oil. So, after the primary distillation of crude oil into fractions, there is a whole range of chemical processes carried out in the refinery to 'doctor' the hydrocarbons to suit our needs.

For some molecules it is enough to rearrange the position of the atoms, but large molecules must be broken down into more useful smaller ones, and some smaller ones are joined together. The final petrol is a blend of many hydrocarbons and possibly some oxygenates too.

In the immediate future, it seems that the use of oxygenates will play a large part in fuel development. However, the story did not end with petrol. Our supplies of crude oil are finite and are needed for more than petrol alone, so you were invited to think about alternative fuels for motor vehicles for the more distant future.

Much of the chemistry you have covered in this unit is fundamental to other areas and you will need to use these ideas in other units in the course.

Activity DF8 will help you to check your notes on this unit.

FROM MINERALS TO ELEMENTS

Why a unit on MINERALS AND ELEMENTS?

The first unit in the course – **The Elements of Life** – told the story of how the elements were formed. The theme is taken further in this unit, which tells how we have learned to win back some elements from the minerals which contain them and turn them into useful substances. One non-metal (bromine) and two metals (copper and tin) are chosen. The elements are not evenly distributed around the world – we are dependent on other countries for our supply. Thus events in other parts of the world can affect our own mineral industry.

The unit introduces three major types of inorganic chemical reaction: acid/base, redox and ionic precipitation. Some important halogen chemistry is covered, and transition metal chemistry is introduced. The concept of amount of substance is extended to include concentrations of solutions.

Overview of chemical principles

In this unit you will learn more about …

ideas you will probably have come across in your earlier studies

- the halogens
- ions in solids and solutions
- dissolving
- acids
- precipitation
- the Periodic Table

ideas introduced in earlier units in this course

- amounts in moles (**Elements of Life**)
- entropy (**Developing Fuels**)
- enthalpy changes (**Developing Fuels**)

… as well as learning new ideas about

- redox reactions
- acids and bases.

FROM MINERALS TO ELEMENTS

M1 *Chemicals from the sea*

The lowest point on Earth

The Dead Sea is the lowest point on Earth, almost 400 m below sea level in the rift valley which runs from East Africa to Syria. It is like a vast evaporating basin: water flows in at the north end from the River Jordan but there is no outflow. The countryside around it is desert and in the scorching heat so much water evaporates that the air is thick with haze, making it hard to see across to the mountains a few kilometres away on the other side. Steady evaporation of the water for thousands of years has resulted in huge accumulations of salts so that the water in the Dead Sea is much denser than usual.

The Dead Sea is such a natural curiosity that surveys of the salt concentration were conducted as early as the 17th century, even though many of the elements in

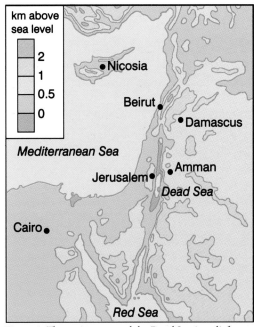

Figure 1 The region around the Dead Sea in relief

Figure 2 The Dead Sea – a natural curiosity

the salts were then unknown. The water contains about $350\,g\,dm^{-3}$ of salts compared with $40\,g\,dm^{-3}$ in water from the oceans. A comparison of the most abundant ions present in Dead Sea water and typical ocean water is shown in Table 1.

Ocean water		Dead Sea water	
Ion	Mass in 1 dm^3 of water/g	Ion	Mass in 1 dm^3 of water/g
Na^+	10.70	Na^+	31.5
K^+	0.39	K^+	6.8
Mg^{2+}	1.29	Mg^{2+}	36.2
Ca^{2+}	0.40	Ca^{2+}	13.4
Cl^-	19.22	Cl^-	183.0
Br^-	0.07	Br^-	5.2
HCO_3^-	0.14	HCO_3^-	trace
SO_4^{2-}	2.51	SO_4^{2-}	0.6

Table 1 Compositions of samples of typical ocean water and Dead Sea water

Estimates suggest that there are 43 billion tonnes of salts in the Dead Sea and a particular feature is the relatively high proportion of bromides.

The sea is the major source of minerals in the region. A chemical industry has grown up around the Dead Sea in Israel and it has become the largest exporter of bromine compounds in the world. The annual production of bromine compounds in Israel exceeds 100 000 tonnes.

ASSIGNMENT I

Dead Sea water is certainly more salty than ocean water, but Table 1 shows that there are differences in ionic composition between the two.

a What do you notice about the abundances of the ions of Group I and Group II in the two samples?

b Compared with ocean water, Dead Sea water has a particularly high proportion of one ion. Which ion is this? How many times more abundant is this ion in Dead Sea water than in ocean water?

Bromine from sea-water

The Dead Sea Works opened at S'dom in Israel on the southwest shore of the Dead Sea in 1934. Extracting minerals from the sea-water starts in shallow evaporation pans where energy from the Sun evaporates the water. Sometimes a dye is added so that more of the Sun's energy is absorbed.

Table 1 gave you the composition of a sample of Dead Sea water in terms of the ions present. If you can't afford the air fare, you can make some artificial Dead Sea water which is very similar to the real thing, by mixing the six compounds listed in Table 2.

Compound	Mass in 1 dm^3 of solution/g
$MgCl_2$	140
$NaCl$	80
$CaCl_2$	40
KCl	13
$MgBr_2$	6
$CaSO_4$	1

Table 2 Recipe for artificial Dead Sea water

What happens when you evaporate Dead Sea water? It's like the reverse of making the artificial solution, and ions will crystallise out together as salts like the ones you put in. These salts have different solubilities and so they will start to crystallise out at different points as the volume of the solution decreases.

Figure 3 Salt evaporation pans in Mauritius

In this case, sodium chloride crystallises out first, then a **double salt** called carnallite ($KCl.MgCl_2.H_2O$), then calcium chloride. The solution which is left is rich in bromide ions.

You can learn more about ionic compounds as solids and in solutions in **Chemical Ideas 5.1**.

Turning bromide ions into bromine is simple chemistry: you can do it in the laboratory by adding chlorine water to a solution containing bromide ions. Industrially it is more complicated than that, and involves some clever chemical engineering, as you can see from Figure 4.

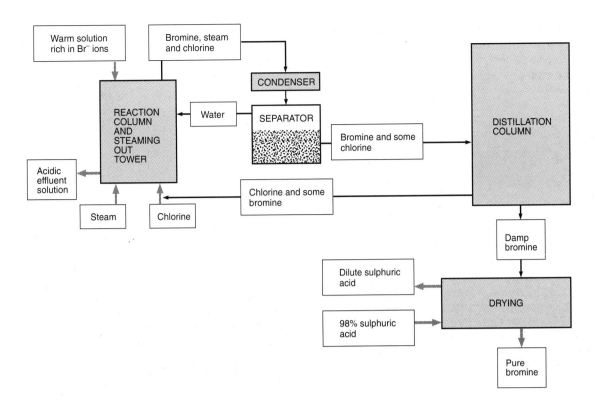

Figure 4 Scheme for industrial bromine manufacture

The partially evaporated Dead Sea water is warmed, then chlorine is bubbled in to displace bromine from the bromide ions. Bromine is volatile (boiling point = 331 K), and bromine vapour is given off with water vapour when steam is blown through the solution. The vapours are then condensed and, as liquid bromine is not very soluble in water, two separate layers form. The dense bromine layer can be easily run off from the water which floats on top. The impure bromine is then distilled and dried.

Half a tonne of chlorine is required to displace each tonne of bromine. The chlorine is made on-site by electrolysis.

The reaction of chlorine molecules with a solution containing bromide ions is an example of a very important category of chemical reaction in which reduction and oxidation take place. Such processes are called **redox reactions**. Many of the reactions of the halogens are redox reactions.

Chemical Ideas 9.1 tells you more about redox reactions.

Activity M1.1 will help your understanding of bromine production.

In **Activity M1.2** you can find out about chlorine production.

Dark, dense and dangerous

Bromine was discovered in 1826 by a French chemist, Jérôme Balard, who later became a professor at the Sorbonne in Paris. His discovery helped Johann Döbereiner spot the idea of 'triads', which was a step on the way to the development of the Periodic Table.

Bromine has a dense and choking vapour – hence its name which is based on a Greek word, *bromos*, meaning *stench*. The liquid produces painful sores if spilled on the skin. You will use bromine several times in this course and you must take great care when you handle it.

Some of the bromine from the Dead Sea Works is transported to Ramat Hovav which is 8 km south of Beersheva, to a factory where bromine-containing compounds are manufactured. The factory used to be just north of Beersheva but the new site was chosen because

- the prevailing wind blows any escaping gases or vapours into the sparsely populated desert
- it is well away from built-up areas
- the underlying geology makes it unlikely that chemical spills will contaminate ground water
- there is a good water supply.

The plant at Ramat Hovav produces calcium bromide, flame retardants which contain bromine, and bromomethane which is used in agriculture as a fumigant to destroy insects and rodent pests. The rest of the Dead Sea bromine is shipped abroad.

Great care has to be taken when transporting bromine. Most of it is carried in lead-lined steel tanks supported in strong metal frames. Each tank holds several tonnes of the element. International regulations control the design and construction of road and rail tankers. The industry's safety record is good but there have been some accidents.

CHEMICAL SCARE SHAKES NEGEV

The driver of the truck that overturned near here early yesterday morning, sending an orange cloud of poisonous bromine gas into the sky over the Arava, said before he died that the accident occurred because he fell asleep at the wheel. The cloud of gas formed by the evaporating bromine, which had a diameter of some 10 kilometres later in the morning, forced scores of residents to leave their homes for several hours. Negev police closed off the road for the day.

According to a senior member of the Dead Sea Works rescue crew, the driver, Yisrael Taib, 32, of Dimona, was trapped when his flatbed truck flipped over on its side at about 5.15 am after rounding a bend some 20 kilometres south of the Arava junction.

Eight people were injured as a result of the accident, most of them rescue workers who tried frantically but in vain to extricate Taib, who was crushed by the steering wheel and the engine block in the mangled cabin.

A senior police officer on the scene praised the rescue crew for the speed with which it reached the spot.

The rescuers arrived shortly after 6 am and worked for several hours, even after a wind change sent the poisonous gas straight towards them.

A safety expert from a major industrial concern in the Negev told *The Jerusalem Post* that the bromine had apparently been packed according to international safety standards, but that yesterday's accident highlighted the need for more careful monitoring of the transportation of dangerous chemicals.

The expert, who sits on a national safety committee, told *The Post* that repeated efforts over the years to have 'black boxes' installed in the cabins of trucks carrying dangerous materials had been thwarted by trucking officials. The expert, who asked not to be identified, conceded that the black boxes wouldn't have prevented yesterday's accident, but would have told safety officials how fast the driver was travelling and how many hours he had been working.

The truck, on its way from the Dead Sea bromine plant south of Beersheva to the port in Eilat, was carrying two containers with over 20 tons of liquid bromine.

They said it was the first accident ever in Israel involving bromine, a deep rust-coloured liquid used in industry, agriculture and medicine. The bromine evaporated quickly in the desert heat. Bromine's boiling point is 59 °C.

Figure 5 Report from The Jerusalem Post

ASSIGNMENT 2

According to *The Jerusalem Post* report (Figure 5), a safety expert recommended more careful monitoring of the transportation of dangerous chemicals. In the light of the report, what do you think the chemical industry does to reduce the risk of injury or death when chemicals such as bromine are transported?

Bromine may once have been just a laboratory curiosity but it is now an important industrial commodity which is manufactured on a large scale. Its most important use is in the production of flame retardants. It is also used in water purification and the manufacture of dyes and agricultural chemicals. Silver bromide is **photosensitive** – an aspect of bromine chemistry which makes modern techniques of photography possible.

Until quite recently the major use of bromine was in the production of a petrol additive which helped to clear out deposits of lead compounds from engines which ran on leaded petrol. This use is less important now that we are able to produce high-grade petrol without lead compounds.

Fears about the transport of such a hazardous chemical as bromine have encouraged the industry to explore other ways of moving bromine around. One suggestion is that bromine should be shipped in the form of calcium bromide, which has a high proportion of bromine. Calcium bromide is supplied in large plastic bags as a 52% solution by mass. It is safe to handle and relatively non-toxic. Unlike the steel tanks, the bags do not have to be returned. Once it has reached its destination, calcium bromide can be reacted to produce bromine and other substances, as needed.

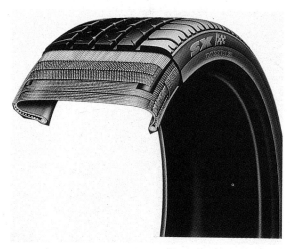

Figure 6 A cut-away section of a radial car tyre: some bromine is used in the manufacture of bromobutyl rubber which forms the airtight lining on the inside of the tyre

Chemical Ideas 11.5 is about the halogens. It will help you to understand and interpret your results when you are doing your experiments.

You can investigate some of the properties of bromine and other halogens and their compounds in **Activity M1.3**.

Activity M1.4 looks in detail at how bromine is handled when it arrives at a chemical plant.

Photography: the almost impossible process

People were aware that silver salts darken on exposure to light as long ago as the 16th century. The darkening is caused by the production of specks of silver metal, but it takes a long time – millions of times longer than you would like to sit for when your photograph is being taken. Fortunately, chemistry can cut down the time needed to take a photograph to just a fraction of a second.

Photographic film is a transparent plastic strip coated with emulsion: a layer of gelatin in which are scattered millions of tiny crystals of silver halides, particularly silver bromide. The emulsion is similar for black and white or colour film. Colour film just has three layers of emulsion, each layer containing a different dye.

When light hits a silver bromide crystal, a bromide ion is converted into a bromine atom and an electron. The electron migrates to the surface of the crystal. The bromine atom is 'trapped' by the gelatin while the electron combines with a silver cation to produce a silver atom.

This process has to happen several times, so that a cluster of a few silver atoms is produced on the surface of the crystal, before the next stage – development – can occur. In development, the film is soaked in a solution of a chemical 'developer'. The silver atom cluster seems to act as a kind of 'conducting bridge' between the developer and the unreacted part of the crystal of silver bromide.

If we represent the developer by the formula DH_2, the reaction between the developer and the silver bromide is

$$DH_2 + 2AgBr \longrightarrow D + 2HBr + 2Ag$$

The end result of developing is that the whole crystal is converted to silver – much more quickly and far more conveniently than if you had relied on light alone.

Next, unreacted AgBr crystals are removed in the fixing process. This leaves behind the dark silver. The more light, the more crystals turn to silver, and the darker the colour. The film is then washed and dried to produce the final negatives.

Several special conditions have to be fulfilled before the little clusters of silver atoms are able to form on silver bromide crystals. It has been estimated that the chances are about 1 : 100 000 000 of finding a substance which satisfies these conditions and which can be used to record photographic images. There are only about 100 000

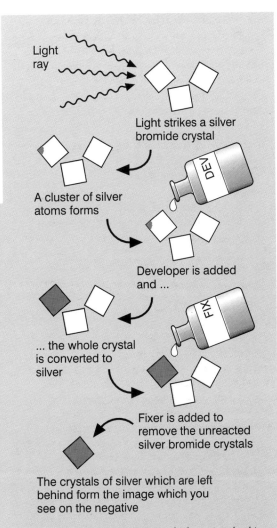

Light strikes a silver bromide crystal

A cluster of silver atoms forms

Developer is added and ...

... the whole crystal is converted to silver

Fixer is added to remove the unreacted silver bromide crystals

The crystals of silver which are left behind form the image which you see on the negative

Figure 7 The chemical changes which are involved in the production of a photographic print

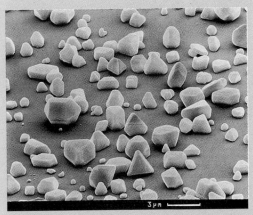

Figure 8 Silver bromide crystals in photographic film

suitable materials to choose from, so the odds against photography being possible are extremely high. We are very lucky that silver bromide exists and it remains the basis of photography despite its high cost.

ASSIGNMENT 3

a **i** Write a half-equation to show the release of an electron when light strikes a bromide ion.

 ii Write a half-equation to show the capture of an electron by a silver ion.

 iii Describe these processes as reduction or oxidation.

b The developing process is a redox reaction.
 i What is the function of the developer?
 ii What happens to the silver ions during developing?
 iii From the point of view of bromide ions, how does developing differ from exposure of the emulsion to light?

M2 *Copper from deep in the ground*

A gift from the Sun?

Copper was probably discovered by chance over 5000 years ago. Potters, using glazes containing highly coloured copper minerals, accidentally reduced the copper compounds with the hot carbon in their fires.

Figure 9 Tools, utensils and coins have been made using copper for thousands of years. This bison from Turkey dates from about 2300 BC and is made of solid copper

Copper could be shaped easily by beating or moulding. Its beautiful appearance – like flames or a burning Sun – made it valuable for ornaments and jewellery. Its durability made it superior to wood and clay for pots and other utensils. The discovery that copper could be alloyed with tin to make bronze – a harder and even more useful and versatile material – gave us the name for a whole era in our history.

Where did it come from?

Copper minerals were formed along with minerals containing silver, lead, iron, zinc, molybdenum, tungsten, tin and other metals, in **hydrothermal deposits**. In other words, they formed from hot water. Deep underground, water is under pressures which are very much greater than atmospheric pressure. It's like a giant pressure cooker, and the high pressures prevent the water boiling. The high temperatures encourage dissolving, and solutions form even though the temperature is well over 100 °C. Many compounds which are insoluble under familiar laboratory conditions are soluble in superheated underground water and some of these compounds can reach high concentrations.

Make sure you understand about concentrations and how to calculate them by working through **Chemical Ideas 1.6**.

In the mineral deposits of southwest England and those you will be finding out about from the USA, hot solutions like these were left over when magma cooled under the Earth's surface. Magma is a molten mixture of rocks, water and other components of the Earth's crust: a kind of 'crustal soup'.

Around 300 million years ago there were great upheavals in the Earth's crust. Magma was forced up under the sandstones, shales and limestones which had been laid down about 50 million years earlier.

Most of the magma solidified to form granite intrusions, leaving hot mineral-rich solutions near the top. The rocks cracked as they cooled, and the solutions streamed out along the cracks. Some were only a fraction of a millimetre wide; others were nearly 1 m across.

Earth's
crust
(solid)

Magma
(liquid)

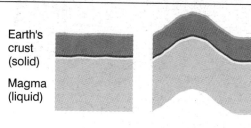

Magma pushes up
the Earth's crust

Granite and hot
solutions form where
magma cools down

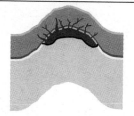

The crust cracks as it cools
and the cracks become filled
with minerals from the hot
solution

Figure 10 How hydrothermal mineral deposits form

The solutions cooled as they came into contact with the colder rocks near the surface and as they moved further away from the hot granite. Minerals began to crystallise. Cassiterite (SnO_2) is one of the first minerals to crystallise in hydrothermal deposits when hot solutions cool. Then a variety of metal sulphides form, such as pyrite (FeS_2), chalcopyrite ($CuFeS_2$), sphalerite (ZnS) and galena (PbS). A vein of minerals which fills a crack in rock is called a **lode**.

In **Activity M2.1** you can look for evidence of these minerals in a sample taken from a lode in The Pennines.

Ancient miners

Chalcopyrite ($CuFeS_2$) is the principal copper-containing mineral in hydrothermal lodes. When the lodes are exposed to air and water, at the Earth's surface, chalcopyrite becomes altered to oxides, hydroxides and carbonates of copper and iron. Four examples are

- cuprite, Cu_2O
- tenorite, CuO
- malachite, $Cu_2(OH)_2CO_3$
- azurite, $Cu_3(OH)_2(CO_3)_2$.

Early civilisations, like the Ancient Egyptians and Phoenicians, could supply their small needs for copper by mining the richest deposits of these altered minerals and reducing them with hot carbon. It has been estimated, for example, that the Egyptians used only 10 000 tonnes of copper in 1500 years.

Sometimes these rich deposits contained as much as 15% by mass of copper. Miners in those days did not know how to process the sulphide materials which lay unaltered 30 m or so below the surface.

But a way had to be found when the surface minerals were used up, and miners were forced to extract the minerals which lay underground. The answer was to roast the sulphide minerals in air. Roasting involves heating in oxygen. A simple example is

$$CuS + 1.5O_2 \rightarrow CuO + SO_2$$

The metal oxide can then be reduced to the metal. More advanced roasting techniques which lead directly to copper metal are used for copper minerals today.

ASSIGNMENT 4

Azurite is a deep blue mineral and was probably used as a glaze by potters thousands of years ago. When it is heated with carbon (such as the charcoal which would have been present in wood fires), copper, carbon dioxide and steam are produced.

a Write a balanced equation for the reaction of azurite with hot carbon.

b Use oxidation states to explain why this reaction is an example of a redox reaction.

c Calculate the maximum mass of copper that could be obtained by heating 1 kg of azurite with carbon.

In **Activities M2.2** and **M2.3** you can process a sample of roasted copper ore and produce some copper from it. The method was once used but has now been replaced by more economical processes. When you have done the activities you will have the opportunity to compare your technique with one which is used in a modern process.

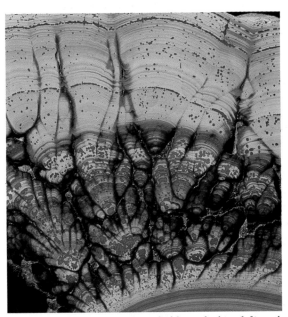

Figure 11 Altered copper minerals, like malachite (left) and azurite (right), often have attractive green or blue colours which are typical of copper compounds

The biggest hole in the world

Towards the end of the 19th century, the demand for copper rose rapidly in response to the need of 'the age of electricity' for wires and other articles. There were not enough rich copper deposits to meet this demand. Deposits with only 0.5%–1% copper in the rock had to be used. One place where this was profitable was at Bingham Canyon in the USA.

Figure 12 Location of Bingham Canyon, Utah, USA

Bingham Canyon is near Salt Lake City in Utah. Copper has been extracted there since 1896. Although the percentage of copper in the rock is small, the total quantity of the mineral is enormous. So it was worth building up a process which could handle the low-grade material and pick out the small proportion of chalcopyrite present. Over 5 000 000 000 tonnes of material have been removed so far.

Development of the technique of **froth flotation** made it possible to separate the chalcopyrite 'needles' from the rock 'haystack' and made mining at Bingham Canyon profitable. The operation was shut down from 1985 to 1988 while it was modernised to fall in line with tighter environmental legislation. The process which is now used is described next.

Getting the copper

Figure 14 describes the Bingham Canyon process in outline. There are four main stages: **mining**, **concentration**, **smelting** and **electrolytic refining**. The scale is huge.

Figure 13 Bingham Canyon mine

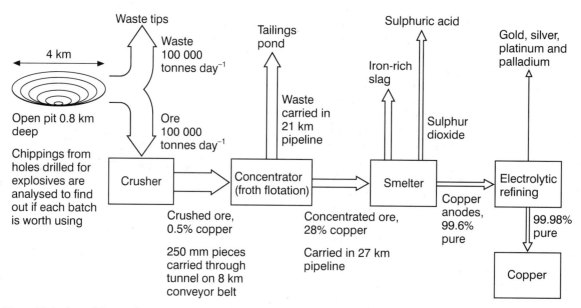

Figure 14 Outline of the Bingham Canyon process

Concentration

The first step is to turn the pieces of rock into a fine powder in a series of *grinding mills*. By doing this, the grains of copper mineral are *liberated* – a large lump of rock made up of lots of crystals of different substances is turned into a mixture of individual tiny crystal grains. **Froth flotation** then separates the grains of copper mineral from the rest of the mixture.

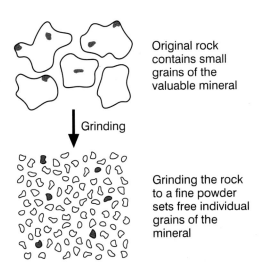

Original rock contains small grains of the valuable mineral

Grinding

Grinding the rock to a fine powder sets free individual grains of the mineral

Figure 15 Liberation of grains: valuable mineral is set free from worthless rock by reducing the size of the lumps

The job that froth flotation has to do is to separate the 0.5% of ground-up rock which is valuable chalcopyrite from the 99.5% which is other material of no value. The minerals are of two different types: chalcopyrite is a sulphide; the others are silicates containing anions made from silicon and oxygen atoms.

In froth flotation, a chemical called a *collector* is added to the water/mineral mixture and binds to the surface of the chalcopyrite grains, giving them a water-repellent, hydrocarbon coating. Detergent is added, and air is then blown into the mixture, causing it to froth. Because they have a water-repellent coating, the chalcopyrite grains become concentrated in the froth and can be removed with it. In this case, the percentage of copper increases from 0.5% to about 30%, producing material in which the copper is nearly 60 times more concentrated than in the ore which is mined. Figure 16 illustrates the froth flotation process.

Froth flotation can be very selective: first one mineral and then others can be removed from quite complicated mixtures.

The *slurry* of copper mineral and water produced from froth flotation is pumped to the *smelter*; the waste slurry is disposed of in a *tailings pond*. Tailings ponds require careful management: in cold countries, the sight of large areas of dirty water is unattractive; in arid Utah, the ponds can dry out and produce dust storms.

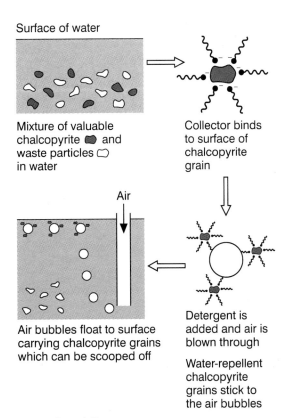

Surface of water

Mixture of valuable chalcopyrite ● and waste particles ○ in water

Collector binds to surface of chalcopyrite grain

Air

Detergent is added and air is blown through

Water-repellent chalcopyrite grains stick to the air bubbles

Air bubbles float to surface carrying chalcopyrite grains which can be scooped off

Figure 16 Froth flotation

Smelting

Production of copper from chalcopyrite concentrate is done in the smelter in a single stage. The overall equation for the process is

$$4CuFeS_2 + 10.5O_2 \rightarrow 4Cu + 2FeO + Fe_2O_3 + 8SO_2$$

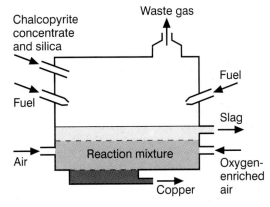

Chalcopyrite concentrate and silica

Waste gas

Fuel

Fuel

Slag

Air

Reaction mixture

Oxygen-enriched air

Copper

Figure 17 A copper smelter

The iron oxides combine with silica (SiO_2), which is also added to the smelter, to form a slag – a low-density crust which floats to the surface. Notice that this process leads directly to copper, not to the copper oxide which is produced in simple roasting. Figure 17 shows details of the smelter.

There is still about 1%–2% sulphur in the copper emerging from the smelter. The sulphur is removed as sulphur dioxide by blowing air through the molten metal. Some copper oxide forms and this is reduced with methane. The copper is then cast into anodes ready for **electrolytic refining**.

Smelting produces large quantities of sulphur dioxide which leads to serious pollution if its release into the atmosphere is not strictly controlled. Breathing air which contains sulphur dioxide causes respiratory damage, and sulphur dioxide is also one of the gases responsible for acid deposition (or 'acid rain' as it is sometimes called). Acid deposition is known to have damaged the ecology of many lakes in parts of Europe, Scandinavia and North America, and to be partly to blame for disease and death among trees in large areas of forest in the same regions.

ASSIGNMENT 5

a Below is a list of some of the environmental hazards which may be associated with mining and mineral processing:

- noise
- rock and solid waste
- dust and smoke
- contaminated water.
- dangerous gases

Set up a table which contains a 5 × 3 grid, and use it to make a list of the hazards which could be associated with each of the following operations: mining, concentrating and smelting.

b What steps could be taken by a responsible mining company to reduce or eliminate the effects of the hazards listed in **a**?

Reading **Chemical Ideas 8.1** will tell you more about acids and their reactions.

The analytical technique of titration is often used in chemistry. In **Activity M2.4** you can work with a solution which is similar to a sample of acid rain, and you can find out the concentration of acid in it.

ASSIGNMENT 6

This assignment makes you think about the waste created at Bingham Canyon each day. The company mines 200 000 tonnes of rock of average density 2.5 tonnes m^{-3} each day. The rock contains 0.5% copper by mass on average.

a What volume of rock is removed each day?

b What is the approximate volume of waste, including tailings, which has to be disposed of each day?

c Which of the stages – mining, concentration and smelting – contribute significantly to the production of waste?

d A large office block built recently in North London has a ground floor area of 1200 m^2 and is 50 m high. Compare the volume of the building with the volume of waste produced each day at Bingham Canyon.

ASSIGNMENT 7

This assignment is about froth flotation which produces a concentrate containing 28% of copper by mass in the form of chalcopyrite ($CuFeS_2$).

a What is the percentage of copper in pure chalcopyrite?

b What is the percentage of chalcopyrite in the concentrate produced by froth flotation?

c Comment on the effectiveness of the technique of froth flotation.

Figure 18 Tall chimneys were built in early attempts to control sulphur dioxide pollution. They reduced local damage, but the pollution still had to fall somewhere and was transferred further afield. Nowadays, there are strict limits on sulphur dioxide emissions from processes like smelting

Electrolytic refining

The copper anodes which are produced from the smelter are 99.6% pure, but this still isn't pure enough for the copper which will be used to conduct electricity. This has to be at least 99.98% pure.

The final purification is done using electrolysis. Figure 19 shows you an illustration of how this is done.

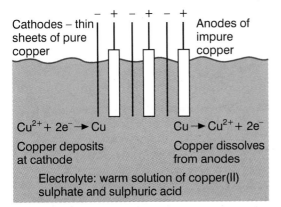

Cathodes – thin sheets of pure copper

Anodes of impure copper

$Cu^{2+} + 2e^- \rightarrow Cu$

Copper deposits at cathode

$Cu \rightarrow Cu^{2+} + 2e^-$

Copper dissolves from anodes

Electrolyte: warm solution of copper(II) sulphate and sulphuric acid

Figure 19 Copper refining

Electrolysis takes about 2 weeks and during this time the cathodes increase in mass from as little as 5 kg to 120 kg. Some of the insoluble impurities are valuable (eg silver and gold) and these are extracted from the sludge which forms. Other impurities are soluble and contaminate the solution, which has to be replaced as electrolysis goes on.

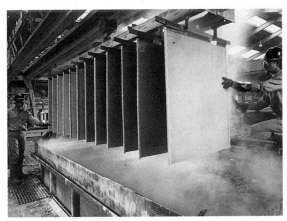

Figure 20 Electrolytic refining of copper

Rock-eating bacteria

Ten per cent of all copper produced in the USA comes from bacteria which 'feed off' chalcopyrite. The bacteria actually make use of the Fe^{2+} and S^{2-} ions rather than the copper in the ore. Bacteria like *Thiobacillus ferro-oxidans* and *Thiobacillus thio-oxidans* obtain the energy they need for life by a series of reactions which involve the oxidation of Fe^{2+} and S^{2-} ions:

$$Fe^{2+} \rightarrow Fe^{3+} + e^-$$
$$S^{2-} + 4H_2O \rightarrow SO_4^{2-} + 8H^+ + 8e^-$$

The micro-organisms do not really 'feed' off the minerals because the ions do not enter the bacteria. Electrons are transported into their cells and are used in *biochemical processes* to reduce oxygen molecules to water. The overall result is that the bacteria convert insoluble chalcopyrite into a solution of iron(III) sulphate and copper(II) sulphate:

$$4CuFeS_2 + 17O_2 + 4H^+ \rightarrow 4Cu^{2+} + 4Fe^{3+} + 8SO_4^{2-} + 2H_2O$$

The optimum conditions for the bacteria are pH 2 and 20 °C–35 °C.

Extracting copper by this process of *bacterial leaching* is cheaper, quieter and less polluting than the smelting process. Unfortunately it is also much slower. It is used at Bingham Canyon on the waste dump. Acidified water is sprayed onto the top surface of the dump. The aerated water then slowly percolates through the pieces of broken rock with their bacterial colonies. The colonies have established themselves naturally – the bacteria are all around us, and are responsible for the brown, iron(III) colour of some streams.

The solutions of copper sulphate produced by bacterial leaching are dilute and impure. The copper needs to be concentrated and separated from other metal ions which are also present. At Bingham Canyon this is done by displacing the copper from solution by using scrap iron to reduce the Cu^{2+} ions. The impure copper is purified further before being turned into anodes for the final electrolysis step.

ASSIGNMENT 8

a The reactions which occur in smelting and bacterial leaching of chalcopyrite are both redox reactions. Explain this by naming the elements which are oxidised and reduced, and describing their changes in oxidation state.

b Minerals like chalcopyrite are often described as reduced ores by the mineral industry. Minerals like malachite are said to be oxidised. Use a chemical explanation to show why, with regard to the anions present, the use of these terms is valid.

Chemical Ideas 4.5 tells you more about dissolving and solutions.

Activity M2.5 investigates some of the ideas about dissolving which you will be reading about.

Although bacterial leaching is only used as a secondary way of producing copper, there are hopes that the method can be used as a primary way of extracting gold. You can find out about this in **Activity M2.6**.

Copper: a vital element

You read about iron in **Elements of Life**. In many ways, copper and iron have similar chemistries. They both belong to a family of elements called **transition metals**. Three important features of transition metals include

- the elements can exist in a variety of oxidation states in their compounds
- the elements and their compounds are often effective catalysts
- their compounds are almost always coloured.

Variable oxidation state

Cuprite (Cu_2O) is copper(I) oxide and tenorite (CuO) is copper(II) oxide. CuO is the black powder used as the starting point for making blue copper(II) sulphate crystals in a school laboratory. You may also be familiar with Cu_2O – it is the red precipitate you see as a positive response to tests for reducing sugars with Benedict's solution or Fehling's solution. Have you noticed what happens when you heat a piece of copper? You get a mixture of red and black colours – Cu_2O and CuO.

The same oxidation states of copper help to keep some molluscs and Crustacea alive. Oxygen is not transported round their bodies by haemoglobin (as in humans) but by haemocyanin – a blue substance which contains copper. The action of haemocyanin depends on the change

$$Cu^{2+} + e^- \rightleftharpoons Cu^+$$

Catalytic properties

Oxygen began to build up in the Earth's atmosphere about 1.5 billion years ago. It was a deadly posion to organisms used to the previously anoxic (without oxygen) environment, and these organisms had to develop substances to protect themselves from the effects of oxygen. One problem was the accumulation of superoxide ions, O_2^-, in cells. Superoxide ions are powerful oxidising agents and cells had to be equipped with an enzyme which could bring about their rapid destruction. The enzyme *superoxide dismutase* contains copper and still protects our cells today.

Copper and its compounds are also important industrial catalysts. For example, ethene is oxidised to ethanal using a catalyst containing copper(II) chloride.

Coloured compounds

Copper compounds are often coloured blue or green as shown in Figure 11.

Using copper

Copper chemistry also plays an essential role in the processes of life, but the everyday uses of copper which are most familiar to us rely on copper's *lack* of chemical reactivity!

Because it does not react with water, even when heated, copper is used for domestic water pipes and hot water cylinders. Copper reacts very slowly with air and retains its untarnished, attractive, metallic appearance when used for objects of art or decoration. Often it is combined with other metals to form **alloys**, for example *bronze* (95% Cu, 5% Sn) and *brass* (70% Cu, 30% Zn).

Our coinage is based on copper: 'copper' coins contain 97% copper mixed with tin and zinc; 'silver' coins are really made from *cupronickel* (75% Cu, 25% Ni).

Pure copper has a high electrical conductivity and is tough – it can be bent and twisted without breaking. That is why it has to be electrolytically refined: tiny quantities of impurity cause it to snap easily or to get dangerously hot when current is passed through it. Almost 60% of all the copper produced is used in electrical applications.

M3 *Mining Cornish tin*

A precarious existence

Cornwall, like Utah, has hydrothermal deposits of copper minerals. But alongside these, the early miners found tin ore (SnO_2). They called it *cassiterite*. At first, tin and copper were alloyed to make bronze. Nowadays, the major use of tin is in the manufacture of tin-plate.

The word *ore* is an economic term. An **ore body** is a mineral deposit which can be mined profitably. When it becomes unprofitable it is called a **mineral reserve**.

Unlike the copper deposits at Bingham Canyon, Cornish tin lies deep underground and is more difficult, expensive and dangerous to extract. The deposits tend to be low grade and their viability depends on many factors.

In the 1960s and 1970s it became possible to separate cassiterite by froth flotation so that a greater percentage of tin could be recovered. Interest in tin mining revived and, as a result, two new mines opened.

It even became economical to extract cassiterite from old tailings dumps. Cornwall was experiencing a minor tin boom. However, during this period, the price of tin had been kept at an artificially high level.

Figure 21 *Cornish tin lies deep underground; lodes were often mined from where they outcropped in the steep cliffs*

Figure 23 *The mineral cassiterite (SnO$_2$)*

In 1985 the price fell sharply and the mines ceased to be profitable. The Cornish tin mines all closed between 1985 and 1990, with devastating effects on the local community.

Mines did not close straight away. Because Cornwall is an area of high unemployment, government funding was made available to help certain mines including Wheal Jane, which eventually closed in March 1990.

The Cornish tin industry has always been subject to slumps and booms. In the early 1800s, alluvial deposits of cassiterite were discovered in Malaysia. These deposits are rich in cassiterite and are easily dredged. In 1828, the *West Briton* newspaper commented:

… at Banca, the tin is near the surface, and the expense of raising it is so small that if it should be brought into unrestricted competition with the Cornish tin, the latter must be driven out of the market.

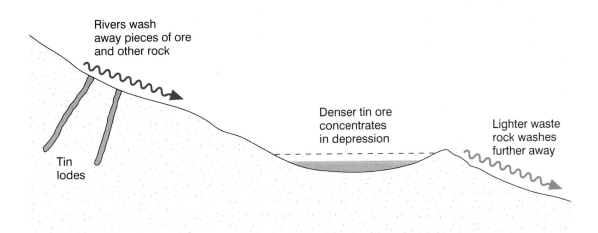

Figure 22 *Formation of an alluvial deposit such as those in Malaysia*

ENGLISH TIN, AND HOW TO COMPETE SUCCESSFULLY WITH AUSTRALIA.

USE DYNAMITE.

Invaluable for BLASTING the HARDEST and WETTEST ROCK; SAFER to USE; and EFFECTS a GREAT SAVING of time and money.

Pamphlets free by post. An experienced man sent underground to give instructions when necessary, free of charge.

Apply, — STEPHEN WILLIAMS, CAMBORNE.

Figure 24 Advert from Mining Journal, *23 October 1875*

But in the 1870s, Malaysia was at war and supplies of tin were cut. The Cornish mines thrived …

Tin mining is going ahead at a tremendous pace …
New mines, and mines which were abandoned during the long and severe depression, when only very large returns of ore would meet working costs, are being set in motion every week in West Cornwall…
                              (*The Times*, 2 December 1871)

Then tin was discovered in Australia. One way for the Cornish mines to compete was to use new technology to reduce mining costs (Figure 24).
     By the end of the 19th century, Cornish tin mining was declining, never to recover its former strength. Malaysian tin was back in production, and rich Bolivian deposits were being mined and transported to the Pacific coast by a new rail link. The numbers of Cornish mines had decreased from several hundred in the early 1870s to just nine by 1897. Miners were forced to seek work abroad – in the USA, Australia and South Africa. Today, descendants of those emigrants can be found all over the world.

An 'odd' metal

Tin is an expensive metal. Table 3 shows you some metal prices from July 1992.
     The biggest use of tin is to make tin-plate: steel coated with a very thin layer of tin, such as is used to make baked-bean cans. It has become increasingly attractive to reclaim the tin from scrap tin-plate as the value of tin has risen.
     The method is quite straightforward – removal of the tin while leaving the iron behind unaffected. Can you work out how to do it?

Metal	Price/£ tonne $^{-1}$
silver	75 000
tin	3694
copper	1395
zinc	727
aluminium	649
lead	434

Table 3 Some metal prices (July 1992)

Most of the elements in the Periodic Table are metals. The non-metals occur in only one part of the Periodic Table – the p-block (Groups 3 to 7 plus Group 0). Tin is an 'odd metal' because it occurs with these non-metals in the p-block. One of its 'chemical relatives' in Group 4 – carbon – is a well-known non-metal.
     Tin shows metallic properties – it conducts electricity, reacts with acids, forms cations, and so on. But it shows non-metallic properties too. For example, it reacts with alkalis. A method which has been successfully used to reclaim tin is based on this 'oddness'. Sodium hydroxide has been used to dissolve away the tin and leave the iron behind.

You can compare some of the properties of the Group 4 elements with other groups in the Periodic Table in **Activity M3**.

M4 *Summary*

In this unit you have learned about the production of three elements (bromine, copper and tin) from their minerals. You have looked, in particular, at some of the chemical aspects of bromine and copper manufacture, both of which rely on redox chemistry. Ideas about redox are also important in explaining many of the important reactions of the halogens.

The processes by which bromine and copper are extracted both involve hazards. In the case of bromine, these arise from the dangerous nature of the element itself. In the case of copper, the production of large quantities of sulphur dioxide at the smelting stage poses a serious problem. Sulphur dioxide is an acidic gas and provides a link with acid/base chemistry.

Most of the bromine and copper compounds in this unit have ionic structures, and much of the chemistry takes place in solution. You have had to learn more about ionic compounds and the process of dissolving, as well as how to calculate concentrations of substances in solution.

Finally, the unit gave you an insight into some aspects of the chemical industry: for example, the quantities of materials which are involved, the emphasis on safety and the importance of economic factors.

Activity M4 will help you to check your notes on this unit.

THE ATMOSPHERE

Why a unit on THE ATMOSPHERE?

The chemical and physical processes going on in the atmosphere have a profound influence on life on Earth. They involve a highly complex system of interrelated reactions, yet much of the underlying chemistry is essentially simple. The focus of this unit is *change*: change in the atmosphere brought about by human activities, and the potential effects on life. Two major problems are explored: the depletion of the ozone layer and the influence of human activities on global warming through the greenhouse effect.

In considering these phenomena, some important chemical principles are introduced and developed. In particular, the effect of radiation on matter, the formation and reactions of radicals and the idea of dynamic equilibrium are introduced, as well as the specific chemistry of species such as oxygen, carbon dioxide, methane and organic halogen compounds that are met with in the context of atmospheric chemistry.

Overview of chemical principles

In this unit you will learn more about …

ideas you will probably have come across in your earlier studies
- the effect of chlorofluorocarbons on the ozone layer
- the greenhouse effect

ideas introduced in earlier units in this course
- the electromagnetic spectrum (**Elements of Life**)
- covalent bonding (**Elements of Life** and **Developing Fuels**)
- the chemistry of simple organic molecules (**Developing Fuels**)
- the use of moles and quantitative chemistry (**Elements of Life**, **Developing Fuels** and **Minerals to Elements**)
- enthalpy changes, energy cycles and bond energies (**Developing Fuels**)
- catalysis (**Developing Fuels**)

… as well as learning new ideas about
- the interaction of matter with electromagnetic radiation
- the formation and reactions of radicals
- the properties of organic halogen compounds
- factors which affect the rate of a reaction
- the nature of dynamic equilibrium.

THE ATMOSPHERE

AI *What's in the air?*

The atmosphere is a relatively thin layer of gas extending about 100 km above the Earth's surface. If the world were a blown-up balloon, the rubber would be thick enough to contain nearly all of the atmosphere. Thin though it is, this layer of gas has an enormous influence on the Earth.

A simplified picture of the lower and middle parts of the atmosphere is shown in Figure 2. The two most chemically important regions are the troposphere and the stratosphere. Note the way that temperature changes with altitude.

The atmosphere becomes less dense the higher you go. In fact, 90% of all the molecules in the atmosphere are in the troposphere. Mixing is easy in the troposphere because hot gases can rise and cold gases can fall. The reverse temperature gradient in the stratosphere means that mixing is much more difficult in a vertical direction. Horizontal circulation, however, is rapid in the stratosphere, particularly around circles of latitude.

Figure 1 The Earth seen from space

Figure 2 The structure of the atmosphere and the change in temperature with altitude

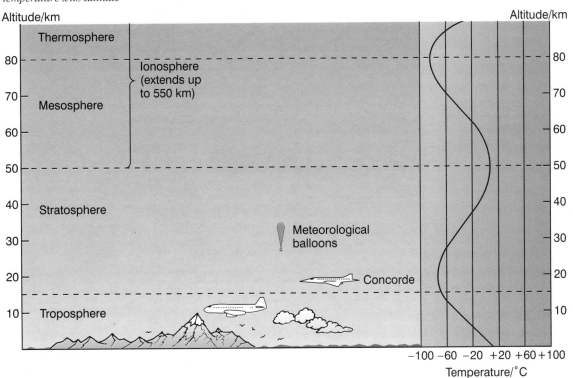

Gas	Concentration (by volume)
	Per cent
nitrogen	78
oxygen	21
argon	1
	Parts per million
carbon dioxide	353*
neon	18.0
helium	5.0
methane	1.7*
krypton	1.1
hydrogen	0.5
dinitrogen oxide, N_2O	0.3*
carbon monoxide	0.1*
xenon	0.09
nitrogen monoxide, NO } NO_x	0.003*
nitrogen dioxide, NO_2	

Table 1 Composition by volume of dry tropospheric air from an unpolluted environment (*variable)

Table 1 shows the average composition by volume of dry air from an unpolluted environment and is typical of the troposphere.

The concentrations of some of these substances are measured in **parts per million (ppm)** by volume. This measure is often used where small concentrations are involved; 353 ppm corresponds to a percentage concentration of 0.0353%.

The atmosphere hasn't always had this composition. The first atmosphere was lost altogether during the upheavals in the early life of the solar system. The next atmosphere consisted of compounds such as carbon dioxide, methane and ammonia which bubbled out of the Earth itself.

Three thousand million years ago there was very little oxygen in the atmosphere. But when the first simple plants appeared, they began to produce oxygen through photosynthesis. For more than 1000 million years very little of this oxygen reached the atmosphere. It was used up as quickly as it formed in oxidising sulphur and iron compounds and other chemicals in the Earth's crust. It wasn't until this process was largely complete that oxygen began to collect in the atmosphere.

When the oxygen concentration reached about 10%, there was enough for the first animals to evolve, using oxygen for respiration. Eventually there was enough respiration and enough other processes going on to remove the oxygen as fast as it formed. Since then, the oxygen concentration has remained at about 21%.

Look again at Table 1. All the gases listed are produced as a result of natural processes. Human activities add more gases to the atmosphere. Some of them, like carbon dioxide, are already present, but we increase their concentration. (These gases are marked by an asterisk in Table 1.) Other gases in the atmosphere, like the chlorofluorocarbons, are *only* produced as a result of human activity.

The first plants

The first plants appeared about 3000 million years ago and were probably single-celled organisms called *cyanobacteria*, or *blue-green bacteria*.

They lived in the surface waters of the oceans under anaerobic conditions, and used sunlight as their energy source to drive the chemical reactions needed to maintain their growth.

Similar organisms are still found on Earth today.

Gases always mix together completely and this natural diffusion process is greatly speeded up by air currents. So in time, pollutant gases spread throughout the atmosphere. Atmospheric pollution is a global problem: it affects us all. In this unit, we shall be looking at two global problems in particular:

- the destruction of the ozone layer
- global warming arising from the greenhouse effect.

ASSIGNMENT I

Use Table 1 to answer the following questions.

a How many parts per million (by volume) of argon are there in a typical sample of tropospheric air?

b In 1 dm^3 of tropospheric air, what is
  i the volume of methane present?
  ii the percentage of methane *molecules* in the sample?

c For each of the gases marked with an asterisk, suggest *one* way in which human activities increase its concentration.

A2 *Screening the Sun*
The sunburn problem

Figure 3 The trend-setting clothes designer Coco Chanel, who set a new fashion for suntanned skin among white-skinned Europeans in the 1920s

Until the 1920s a suntan was something a white-skinned person could not avoid if they had to work outdoors in the Sun. Those who didn't preferred to distinguish themselves by remaining pale. It was the clothes designer Coco Chanel who made sunbathing fashionable. She appeared with a golden tan after a cruise on the yacht belonging to the Duke of Westminster, who was one of the world's wealthiest men.

As we discover more about the effects of the Sun's radiation on the chemical bonds in living material, sunbathing seems less of a good idea.

ASSIGNMENT 2

a Look at the scatterplot in Figure 4. Suggest a reason for the variation of death rate from skin cancer in the USA.

b Skin cancer is more common among office workers than among farmers. Suggest a reason why.

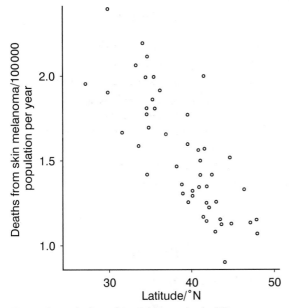

Figure 4 *Deaths from skin melanoma in the USA*

The Sun radiates a wide spectrum of energy. Part of this spectrum corresponds to the energy required to break chemical bonds. Sunlight can therefore break bonds, including those in molecules such as DNA in living material. This can cause damage to genes and lead to skin cancer. On a less serious level, it can damage the proteins of the connective tissue beneath the skin, so that years of exposure to the Sun can make people look wrinkly and leathery. Even brief exposure to the Sun may cause irritation of the blood vessels in the skin, making it look red and sunburnt.

Many of the ideas in this story are linked to the interaction of radiation with matter. **Chemical Ideas 6.2** covers the different ways that radiation and matter can interact.

Chemical sunscreens

The diagram in Figure 5 shows the effect of different parts of the Sun's spectrum on the skin.

You can see that the most damaging region of this spectrum is in the ultra-violet. Fortunately, there are chemicals which absorb much of this radiation.

Have you ever wondered why people don't get sunburnt indoors? You can sit by a window for hours on a sunny day without burning. The glass in the window absorbs the damaging ultra-violet radiation, so it never reaches your skin. (Perspex does let through some ultra-violet, so it is possible to burn through Perspex.)

Chemists have found materials that do a similar job to glass, but can be spread onto the skin. They are called *sunscreens*, and tonnes of them are sold every summer.

But the best sunscreen of all is not made by chemists. It has always been with us. It is the atmosphere.

In **Activity A2.1** you can examine the effect of some substances on radiation from the Sun.

Activity A2.2 investigates the effectiveness of sunscreens.

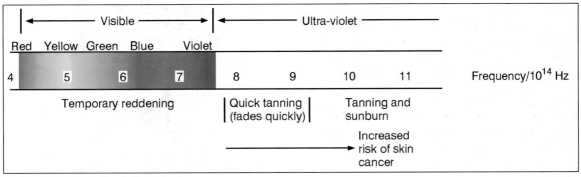

Figure 5 *The effects of sunlight on the skin*

Figure 6 A sunscreen's ability to protect skin is expressed as a 'Sun Protection Factor' or SPF number — SPFs indicate the time it will take for the Sun to produce a certain effect on your skin.

Why is the atmosphere such a good sunscreen?

Certain atmospheric gases absorb ultra-violet radiation strongly. They act as a global sunscreen, preventing much of the Sun's harmful radiation from reaching the Earth.

Most of this absorption goes on in the upper part of the atmosphere, the stratosphere. Particularly important is the gas **ozone**, which absorbs ultra-violet radiation in the region 10.1×10^{14} Hz – 14.0×10^{14} Hz. This is the region which is most damaging to the skin. (Look back at Figure 5 which shows the effect on skin of radiation of different frequencies.) Much of the damaging ultra-violet radiation is absorbed by ozone in the stratosphere.

There is no life in the stratosphere, because the powerful ultra-violet radiation would break down the delicate molecules of living things. Indeed, even simple molecular substances get broken down in the stratosphere. Some of the covalent bonds break to give fragments of molecules (atoms or groups of atoms) called **radicals**.

Higher up in the atmosphere, above the stratosphere, the radiation is powerful enough to knock electrons out of the atoms, molecules and radicals. Ions are produced which lead to the name of that part of the atmosphere – the *ionosphere*.

ASSIGNMENT 3

Look back at Figure 2 on page 55 which shows the different regions of the atmosphere. Suggest the *types* of chemical particles – atoms, molecules, radicals and ions – which can be found in

a the troposphere

b the stratosphere

c the ionosphere.

Activity A2.3 investigates the screening effect of different gases on solar radiation.

A3 *Ozone: A vital sunscreen*

Introducing ozone

Ozone is present in the atmosphere in only tiny amounts, dispersed among other atmospheric gases. If all the ozone in the atmosphere were collected and brought to the Earth's surface at atmospheric pressure, it would form a layer only 3 mm thick.

High up, in the stratosphere, ozone *protects* us by absorbing harmful ultra-violet radiation; however, lower down, in the troposphere, it can be a real nuisance.

Near the ground, ozone causes health problems and is thought to be at least partly responsible for the death of trees in the forests of Northern Europe. It is a very reactive gas and is a powerful oxidising agent. It reacts with many synthetic materials such as plastics, paints and dyes, causing, for example, rubber car tyres to crack.

It isn't really surprising that there is so little ozone in the atmosphere. It reacts so quickly with other substances and gets destroyed. In fact, we might ask why the ozone in the atmosphere hasn't run out. Some reactions must be producing it too.

You can find out more about ozone in **Activity A3.1**.

A lot of the ideas in this part of the story are concerned with radicals. You can find out more about these by studying **Chemical Ideas 6.3**.

How is ozone formed in the atmosphere?

Ozone is formed when an oxygen atom (which is an example of a radical) reacts with a dioxygen molecule:

$$O + O_2 \rightarrow \underset{\text{ozone}}{O_3}$$

One way to make oxygen atoms is by splitting up (**dissociating**) dioxygen molecules. This requires quite a lot of energy – remember that the bond enthalpy of the oxygen–oxygen bond in dioxygen is $+498$ kJ mol^{-1}. In this case the energy can be provided by ultra-violet radiation, or by an electric discharge.

As soon as oxygen atoms have been produced they react with the dioxygen molecules which are always present in the air. You can often smell the sharp odour of ozone near electric motors or photocopiers. The electric discharges happening inside the machine make some of the dioxygen molecules in the air dissociate into atoms. Have you ever noticed the ultra-violet lamps used to kill bacteria in food shops? You can often smell ozone near them too.

World unites on ozone deal

Paul Brown
Environment Correspondent

A worldwide agreement to phase out CFCs and other ozone depleting chemicals by the year 2000 was reached in London last night.

A group of environmentally advanced countries pushed to have the date brought forward to 1997, but were blocked by the United States, the Soviet Union, and Japan. The compromise solution was a 50 per cent reduction by 1995, 85 per cent by 1997, and 100 per cent by 2000. A sub-clause agreed the position would be reviewed in 1992, to see if the timetable could be improved.

The agreement provided for the establishment of a new global front to help the Third World adapt to the changes.

Chris Patten, the Environment Secretary, said: "This is a major step forward in environmental diplomacy. It is a unique agreement bringing together, as it does, the establishment of environmental objectives with provision of funds and the transfer of technology."

It boded well for future global environmental agreements.

Answering criticisms that the agreement still did not go far enough, he said: "We would all like to have stopped CFCs production tomorrow but this was the best agreement that was possible, taking all considerations into account".

Negotiations had run well over the time yesterday as detailed timetables for phasing out chemicals were hammered out for inclusion in the agreement.

There was personal success for Mr Patten, who, as chairman of the conference, redrafted the final document so that both China and India felt they could pledge to sign the Montreal Protocol.

By yesterday, 59 nations had signed and most of the other 39 at the conference were expected to ratify soon.

In spite of ministerial joy at the agreement, there were doubts that the timetable would be quick enough to prevent ozone depletion being a serious problem.

Yesterday's deal meant that CFCs, the main ozone depleter, used in fridges and air conditioning, will go by 2000. Methyl chloroform, a metal cleaning agent, will be banned by 2005.

Much of the argument centred on how quickly individual chemicals could be phased out.

One of the triumphs was getting India and China, with more than one third of the world's population between them, to join. Maneka Gandhi, the Indian Environment Minister, had held out for two days for the transfer of technology from the West to be included in the agreement so India could manufacture CFCs substitutes itself.

Mrs Gandhi said yesterday the agreement now said that if technology was not transferred, that India did not have to stop the manufacture of CFCs. That placed the onus on the West to keep its promises, and on that basis she was prepared to recommend her government to ratify the protocol.

Joe Farman, the British scientist who discovered the hole in the ozone layer, said he feared the agreement was still not stringent enough.

Mr Farman, head of atmospheric dynamics at the British Antarctic Survey, said the ozone hole would go on getting bigger for some time.

Chlorine is currently 3.6 parts per billion in the atmosphere. This would grow to 4.8 parts per billion in 10 years, he said. He calculated this could lead to 18 per cent depletion in ozone in the northern hemisphere during the winter and spring by the year 2000.

Under the agreement, he calculated that it would be 2030 before the chlorine level went down to the 1986 level when the hole was first announced.

Figure 7 Ozone is vital in the stratosphere, but it causes health problems in the lower atmosphere

Some of the ozone in the troposphere is formed in the complex series of reactions taking place in photochemical smogs. These develop in bright sunlight over large cities which are heavily polluted by motor vehicle exhaust fumes (see the **Developing Fuels** storyline). In this case, oxygen atoms are produced by the action of sunlight on the pollutant gas, nitrogen dioxide.

In the stratosphere, oxygen atoms are formed by the **photodissociation** of dioxygen molecules. This happens when dioxygen absorbs ultra-violet radiation of the right frequency.

ASSIGNMENT 4

a What is the bond enthalpy, in *joules per molecule*, of the oxygen–oxygen bond in dioxygen?

b Use the expression $E = h\nu$ to calculate the frequency of radiation that would break this bond.

c What you have calculated is the *minimum* frequency to cause the bond to break. Explain why it is a minimum value.

The reaction can be summarised as:

$$O_2 + h\nu \rightarrow O + O \quad \text{(reaction 1)}$$

In this reaction, $h\nu$ indicates the photon of ultra-violet radiation that is absorbed.

The oxygen atoms produced can do a number of things when they meet another particle and collide with it. The least interesting of these is that the particles just bounce apart again. But even when the oxygen atom collides with a particle it can react with, not every collision results in a reaction.

More interesting is when the oxygen atom sticks onto the particle it collides with. This could be one of three things: O_2, another O or O_3. The three possible outcomes can be represented by reactions 2–4 below:

$$O + O_2 \rightarrow O_3 \qquad \Delta H^\ominus = -100\,\text{kJ mol}^{-1} \text{ (reaction 2)}$$
$$O + O \rightarrow O_2 \qquad \Delta H^\ominus = -498\,\text{kJ mol}^{-1} \text{ (reaction 3)}$$
$$O + O_3 \rightarrow O_2 + O_2 \quad \Delta H^\ominus = -390\,\text{kJ mol}^{-1} \text{ (reaction 4)}$$

Reaction 2 is of course the one which produces ozone.

When the ozone absorbs radiation in the $10.1 \times 10^{14}\,\text{Hz} - 14.0 \times 10^{14}\,\text{Hz}$ region, some molecules undergo photodissociation and split up again:

$$O_3 + h\nu \rightarrow O_2 + O \quad \text{(reaction 5)}$$

It is this reaction which is responsible for the vital screening effect of ozone, since it absorbs the radiation which is responsible for sunburn.

ASSIGNMENT 5

Look at reactions 1–5 on page 59.

a Which reaction or reactions *remove* ozone from the atmosphere?

b Which reaction or reactions absorb ultra-violet radiation?

c Which reaction or reactions are exothermic?

d What relationship is there between
  i reactions 1 and 3?
  ii reactions 2 and 5?

e Explain why this series of reactions has the net effect of using the Sun's ultra-violet radiation to heat the stratosphere, and why the stratosphere is hottest at the top and coolest at the bottom.

Photodissociation and the subsequent reactions of the radicals produced are investigated in **Activities A3.2** and **A3.3**. You cannot use the damaging radiation needed to break down O_2 or O_3, so in the activities you will be working with Br_2 which absorbs light in the visible/near ultra-violet region.

Ozone – here today and gone tomorrow

You can see from reactions 1–5 on page 59 that ozone is being made and destroyed all the time. Left to themselves, these reactions would reach a point where ozone was being made as fast as it was being used up:

rate of producing ozone = rate of destroying ozone

At this point, the concentration of ozone would remain constant. This is called a **steady state**.

It's like the situation in Figure 8 when you are running water into a basin with the plug out of the waste pipe. Before long you get to the point where water is running out as fast as it's running in, and the level of water in the basin stays constant. If you turned the tap on more, the level of the water would rise – but that would make the water run out faster, because of the higher pressure. Before long you would get to a steady state again, but this time with more water in the basin. What would happen if you made the waste pipe larger?

Figure 8 One example of a steady state situation

The water coming out of the tap is like the reactions producing ozone, and the water going down the waste pipe is like the reactions that destroy it.

To estimate the concentration of ozone in the stratosphere, you need to know the **rates** of the reactions that produce and destroy ozone.

Chemists have studied these reactions in the laboratory and are able to write mathematical equations giving the rates of all the reactions involved in producing and destroying ozone. So, for example, taking reactions 1–5, the rate of producing ozone will be the rate of reaction 2. If there is a steady state, this will be balanced by the rate of destruction of ozone: the rate of reaction 4 *plus* that of reaction 5. From these relations chemists can work out what the concentration of ozone *should* be at different altitudes, at different times of day and at different times during the year.

However, when chemists compared their *calculated* concentrations of ozone with *measured* values, they found that the actual concentration of ozone was in fact a good deal *less* than expected.

ASSIGNMENT 6

A number of factors can affect the rate of ozone production and destruction. Remembering that the reactions are taking place in the gas phase and in strong sunlight, suggest *three* factors which could affect the rates of these reactions.

Explain how altering each factor would affect the rate of reaction.

This suggests that the ozone is being removed faster than expected. Going back to the analogy of the basin and the running tap, it's as if the waste pipe had been made larger. But by what?

Activity A3.4 lets you take a look at the variation of dioxygen and ozone concentrations with altitude.

You can read about the factors which affect the rate of a chemical reaction in **Chemical Ideas 10.1**.

What is removing the ozone?

We have seen that ozone is very reactive and reacts with oxygen atoms. But oxygen atoms aren't the only radicals to be found in the stratosphere. There are other radicals which can remove ozone by reacting with it.

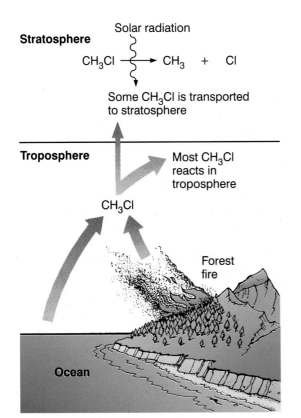

Figure 9 Chloromethane (CH₃Cl) is given off from the oceans and by burning vegetation. It is responsible for the small amounts of naturally produced chlorine in the stratosphere

One important example of a radical which can react in this way is the **chlorine atom** (Cl). Small amounts of chloromethane, CH_3Cl, reach the stratosphere as a result of natural processes (see Figure 9). Once in the stratosphere, chloromethane is split up by solar radiation giving chlorine atoms.

Other chlorine-containing compounds reach the stratosphere, in greater concentrations, as a result of human activities. These also absorb high energy solar radiation and break down to give chlorine atoms.

Chlorine atoms react with ozone like this:

$$Cl + O_3 \rightarrow ClO + O_2 \qquad \text{(reaction 6)}$$

The ClO formed is another reactive radical and can react with oxygen atoms:

$$ClO + O \rightarrow Cl + O_2 \qquad \text{(reaction 7)}$$

So now we have two reactions competing with each other to remove ozone from the stratosphere:

$$O + O_3 \rightarrow O_2 + O_2 \qquad \text{(reaction 4)}$$
and
$$Cl + O_3 \rightarrow ClO + O_2 \qquad \text{(reaction 6)}$$

The concentration of Cl atoms in the stratosphere is much less than the concentration of O atoms. So how significant is reaction 6?

ASSIGNMENT 7

Chlorine atoms are particularly effective at removing ozone. A single Cl atom can remove about 1 million ozone molecules.

Add equations 6 and 7 together to produce the equation for the *overall* reaction caused by chlorine atoms.

Comment on the result. What role are Cl atoms playing in the overall reaction?

It is in situations like this that it is very important for chemists to know something about the *rates* at which reactions occur.

The reaction of O_3 with Cl atoms would not matter much if it took place a lot more slowly than the reaction of O_3 with O atoms.

Chemists measured the rates of these two reactions in the laboratory under different conditions. They showed that, at temperatures and pressures similar to those in the stratosphere, the reaction of O_3 with Cl atoms takes place more than 1500 times *faster* than the reaction of O_3 with O atoms.

Even when they took into account the fact that Cl atoms have a much lower concentration than O atoms in the stratosphere, the chemists still found that the reaction with Cl atoms takes place sufficiently quickly to make a very large contribution to removal of ozone.

What's more, the Cl atoms are regenerated in a **catalytic cycle** (reactions 6 and 7 on this page) and can go on to react with more O_3. So you can see why their effect could be devastating.

ASSIGNMENT 8

There are 50 000 voters in a town. An election is due and the politicians and their helpers are busy canvassing for votes. There are 100 workers for the Orange party and only 2 workers for the Purple party.

These workers operate in different ways. The Orange party workers can convince 10 people per hour to vote for them. Purple party workers can convince 15 000 people per hour to vote for them.

a Does the town end up voting predominantly for the Orange party or for the Purple party?

b This is an analogy for the behaviour of ozone in the atmosphere in the presence of O and Cl atoms. What is represented by
 i voters in the town?
 ii Orange party workers?
 iii Purple party workers?

Competing reactions

Activation enthalpies are very important when *comparing* the rates of two competing reactions taking place under similar conditions. If the activation enthalpy of a reaction is large, only a small proportion of colliding particles will have enough energy to react, so the reaction proceeds slowly. If, however, the activation enthalpy is very small, most of the colliding particles will have sufficient energy to react and the reaction occurs very quickly.

Figure 10 shows the activation enthalpies for the reactions of O atoms and Cl atoms with ozone. The reaction with the lower activation enthalpy (ie O_3 + Cl) will proceed more quickly.

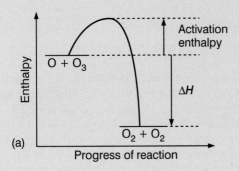

(a)

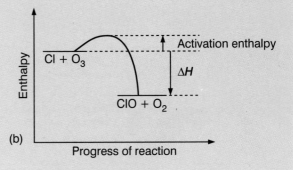

(b)

Other ways ozone is removed

Chlorine atoms aren't the only radicals present in the stratosphere which can destroy ozone in a catalytic cycle in this way.

If we represent the radical by the general symbol X, we can rewrite reactions 6 and 7 on page 61 as:

$$X + O_3 \rightarrow XO + O_2$$
and
$$XO + O \rightarrow X + O_2$$

Overall reaction: $O + O_3 \rightarrow O_2 + O_2$

Two other important radicals which can destroy ozone in this way are described below.

Hydroxyl radicals (HO)

These are formed by the reaction of oxygen atoms with water in the stratosphere. They react with ozone like this:

$$HO + O_3 \rightarrow HO_2 + O_2$$

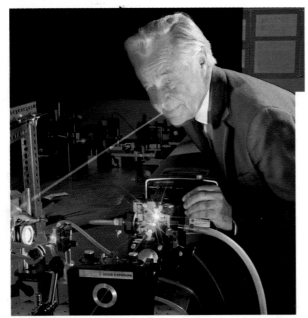

The spectra below were taken in the early days of the technique. They were taken at different times following the flash photolysis of a mixture of chlorine and oxygen. Initially there is no ClO present, but its concentration rises very rapidly after the flash and then decays as it reacts.

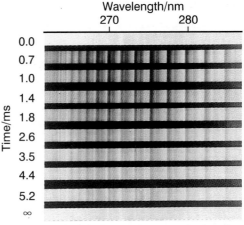

Figure 11 George Porter shared the 1967 Nobel Prize for chemistry for his work on very fast reactions using a technique called **flash photolysis**. *Nowadays, a brief intense flash from a laser starts the reaction. The composition of the mixture is measured spectroscopically with a carefully timed second flash. Reactions which take place in nanoseconds ($1\,ns = 1 \times 10^{-9}\,s$) or even picoseconds ($1\,ps = 1 \times 10^{-12}\,s$) can be studied in this way*

The HO_2 radicals then go on to react with oxygen atoms:

$$HO_2 + O \rightarrow HO + O_2$$

So this is another example of a catalytic cycle, and the HO radicals released can go on to react with more O_3 molecules.

Figure 12 Fatty foods go stale and rancid because of a radical reaction between fats and oxygen in the air. Antioxidants — such as the preservative E320 often added to pastry products — slow down the process by removing the active radicals and interrupting the radical chain reaction

Nitrogen monoxide (NO)

Nitrogen monoxide reacts with ozone to form nitrogen dioxide (NO_2) and dioxygen. Nitrogen dioxide can then react with oxygen atoms to release nitrogen monoxide and dioxygen to complete the catalytic cycle.

NO and NO_2 are both radicals. They are unusual radicals because they are relatively stable and they can be prepared and collected like ordinary molecular substances.

ASSIGNMENT 9

a Write an equation to show the formation of HO radicals from O atoms and water.

b Write equations to show how nitrogen monoxide can destroy ozone in a catalytic cycle.

Nitrogen monoxide in the stratosphere – where does it come from?

Most of the nitrogen monoxide (NO) in the stratosphere is formed as a result of the reaction of dinitrogen oxide (N_2O) with oxygen atoms

$$N_2O + O \rightarrow 2NO$$

Dinitrogen oxide is the most abundant oxide of nitrogen in the atmosphere (see Table 1 on page 56). It is produced by biological reactions on Earth and some is carried up into the stratosphere. Dinitrogen oxide is released by bacteria which break down nitrogen compounds in the soil and also by bacteria in the oceans. But not all comes from natural processes. The increased use of fertilisers contributes to increasing dinitrogen oxide levels.

The radicals mentioned above (Cl, HO and NO) are important, but they are only part of the whole picture. In all, hundreds of reactions have been suggested which affect the gases in the stratosphere.

Many of these reactions have been going on since long before there were humans on Earth. But human activities can have a serious effect on certain key reactions, and so lead to dramatic changes in the concentration of ozone in the stratosphere.

A4 *The CFC story*

For many years, chemists have been concerned that substances put into the atmosphere by human activities may be destroying the ozone layer. In the early 1970s there was concern about high-flying jet aircraft. Jet engines release nitrogen oxides in their exhaust gases: could this make a significant difference to the amount of NO_x ($NO + NO_2$) in the stratosphere and so damage the ozone layer? In the end, it turned out that this wasn't a significant problem – the number of aircraft concerned was then too small to make much difference. (The problem, however, may reappear because large aircraft are being designed in the USA which will fly at supersonic speeds in the stratosphere.)

In 1974 another concern was raised.

To understand some of the ideas and activities in this section you will need to know something about organic halogen compounds. **Chemical Ideas 13.1** gives you an introduction to these.

Sherry Rowland's predictions

Figure 13 Professor Sherwood ('Sherry') F Rowland

Professor Sherry Rowland is the American scientist who, with Dr Mario Molina, predicted back in the early 1970s that chlorofluorocarbons (CFCs) would damage the ozone layer. We talked to him when he visited London, and he described how he made his discovery.

"I originally started looking at the CFC compounds as an interesting *chemical* problem in an environmental setting: whether we could predict from our laboratory knowledge what the fate of the CFCs would be in the Earth's atmosphere. We were not at the beginning thinking of the destruction of the CFCs as an environmental *problem*, but rather as just something that would be happening there.

I've always been attracted to chemical problems – my first research experiment after graduate school involved putting a powdered mixture of lithium carbonate and ordinary glucose in the neutron flux of a nuclear reactor. A nuclear reaction in lithium produces tritium, a radioactive isotope of hydrogen, and I wanted to see if the tritium atoms could replace hydrogen atoms in glucose. (They did – and this led to many further interesting experiments in a field called *hot atom* chemistry.)

With CFCs, we wanted to find out how quickly they would break down in the atmosphere, and by what chemical process. I was working with a young postdoctoral research associate called Mario Molina – this was in 1973 at the University of California at Irvine – and we knew that CFCs are very stable compounds. But how stable? How long could they hang around in the atmosphere? One year or 100 years?

Mario and I looked at all of the processes that could conceivably affect CFCs in the troposphere, and calculated how rapidly such reactions could occur. The answer was very slowly indeed. CFCs remain unreacted for *many decades* – even centuries.

CFC-11   *CFC-12*

So now we knew that CFCs survive unchanged for a very long time. But we also knew that when they eventually reach the stratosphere they must be broken down by the fierce ultra-violet radiation there – everything is! The CFCs contain atoms of chlorine, fluorine and carbon, and their ultra-violet breakdown releases free chlorine atoms.

For example

$CCl_3F \rightarrow CCl_2F + Cl$

So we did some calculations to find out *how many* chlorine atoms would be formed now and in the future, and then asked what would happen to the chlorine atoms. In the stratosphere, we found that chlorine atoms are about a thousand times more likely to react with ozone than with anything else, leaving still another chlorine-containing chemical, chlorine oxide (ClO).

So, once more we asked the same kind of question: what was going to happen to chlorine oxide in the stratosphere? And we found that it would react with oxygen atoms, releasing atomic chlorine again. The two reactions seem to go around in circles – chlorine atoms form chlorine oxide; chlorine oxide forms chlorine atoms – a seemingly endless chain. But with ozone being destroyed at every step! We then calculated how much ozone could be destroyed – each chlorine atom on average destroys about 100 000 molecules of ozone, and mankind has been putting about 1 million tonnes of CFCs into the atmosphere every year since the 1970s.

We couldn't believe the answer! The calculated ozone loss was so high that we thought we must have moved a decimal point by mistake! But we checked very carefully and couldn't find any errors – there really was that much chlorine up there, with much more expected in the future, and the ozone losses would eventually be enormous!

We had started on this problem at the beginning of October 1973, and by mid-December we realised we were onto something very important. When a scientist makes a discovery, the first instinct is to publish it so that other scientists can learn about it, and test the ideas with their own experiments. But the calculated ozone loss was so large that we wanted to be extra certain that no mistake had been made.

So we visited Hal Johnson at the University of California at Berkeley, because he had played a major role in showing how nitrogen oxides from high-flying aircraft – such as Concorde – could affect stratospheric ozone. From Hal we learned that the chlorine chain reaction with ozone had just been discovered, but without a source for chlorine. And we had discovered that the CFCs would be an enormous source of chlorine released directly into the stratosphere!

Now, we were sure that we had discovered something really significant – now it was a major environmental problem. We published our results and conclusions in the scientific journal *Nature*, and waited to see if others could pick holes in them. Many tried – because that's the way science works – but none succeeded. The issue of CFCs and stratospheric ozone had really arrived.

The state of Oregon banned CFCs as propellant gases in aerosols in 1975, and the whole of the USA, as well as Canada, Norway and Sweden, followed in the next 2 or 3 years. Unfortunately, the rest of Europe and Japan did not ban aerosol propellant use, and the other major applications – refrigeration, insulation, cleaning electronics, etc – continued to grow until the appearance of the hole in the Antarctic ozone layer resulted in international action in 1988–1990."

ASSIGNMENT 10

a Rowland and Molina's first question was *how long will chlorofluorocarbons stay in the atmosphere?* Why was it important to know this?

b Why did they not publish their results as soon as they knew how much ozone would be destroyed by chlorine in the stratosphere?

c There is a debate about the value of *pure* scientific research – ie research that has no obvious applications or uses. What does Rowland and Molina's story say about this?

The predictions come true

Science is all about making predictions, then testing them experimentally. The problem with Sherry Rowland's predictions is that they involve a long time scale. What is more, they need a large laboratory to test them: in fact they need the largest laboratory in the world – the Earth's atmosphere.

But in 1985, scientists examining the atmosphere above the Antarctic made a momentous discovery.

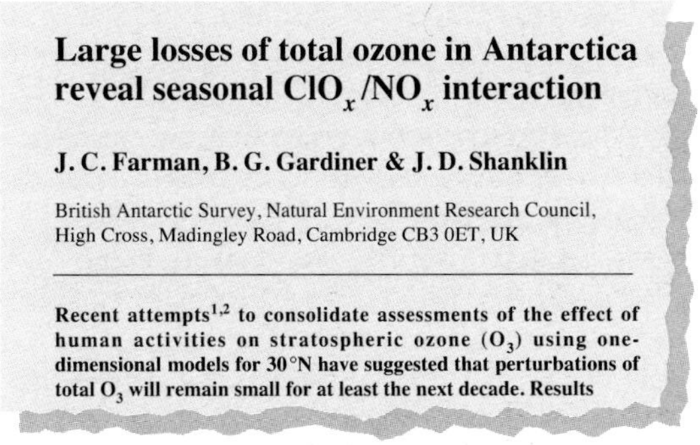

Large losses of total ozone in Antarctica reveal seasonal ClO_x/NO_x interaction

J. C. Farman, B. G. Gardiner & J. D. Shanklin

British Antarctic Survey, Natural Environment Research Council, High Cross, Madingley Road, Cambridge CB3 0ET, UK

Recent attempts[1,2] to consolidate assessments of the effect of human activities on stratospheric ozone (O_3) using one-dimensional models for 30°N have suggested that perturbations of total O_3 will remain small for at least the next decade. Results

Figure 14 The headline-making paper which appeared in the scientific journal Nature *in May 1985, reporting the discovery of a 'hole' in the ozone layer over Antarctica*

Joe Farman's story

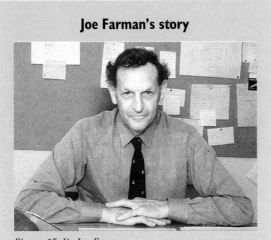

Figure 15 Dr Joe Farman

Dr Joe Farman is the British scientist whose group first discovered the 'hole' in the ozone layer. We went to Cambridge to talk to him, and this is how he described their discovery.

"To stand up and make a fuss you need to have your background secure.

We were measuring ozone concentrations over the Antarctic as part of our work with the British Antarctic Survey. We use ultra-violet spectroscopy: ozone absorbs ultra-violet radiation of a particular frequency. If you measure how strongly the atmosphere is absorbing ultra-violet of that frequency, you can work out the concentration of ozone in that part of the atmosphere. Our measurements started in 1981, and over 2 or 3 years I became convinced that there was something seriously wrong. The concentrations of ozone were much lower than expected, particularly in October, which is the Antarctic spring. In 1984 we put in a new instrument to check our readings, and that gave us confirmation. There really was a 'hole' in the ozone layer.

We were making our measurements from *below*, by looking up into the atmosphere from the Earth's surface at our base in Antarctica. The Americans were making similar measurements, but from *above*: NASA satellites were using ultra-violet spectroscopy to measure ozone concentrations by looking down from above.

So why didn't NASA spot the 'hole' first? The trouble is, NASA satellites make *too many* measurements. They collect enormous quantities of data on all sorts of things, not just ozone concentrations.

Figure 16 The British Antarctic Survey's Halley Base

They can't possibly process all the data, so their computers are programmed to ignore any data that seem impossibly inaccurate. In the case of the ozone measurements, this meant that they ignored most of them, because they were so far out from what was expected. About 80% of the data for October were discarded by the computer because no-one believed ozone concentrations could get that low.

Later, when our own measurements showed the concentration of ozone really was that low, NASA went back and re-examined the discarded data, which confirmed our own measurements.

In 1985 we published our findings in the scientific journal *Nature*. Then it was a matter of convincing the world how serious the problem is. Once a scientist has made a momentous discovery of this kind, there is a duty to tell everyone about it.

To me the real horror is the sheer speed with which it has happened. In 1985 the United Nations published a report saying there was plenty of time to study the ozone problem. At about the same time we published our own results which show that the ozone gets turned over in a period of about 5 *weeks*! We still don't know exactly what the effects of ozone depletion will be, but when you are affecting a system that fast you have to be aware that almost anything could happen.

We may think we understand a lot about the way that nature works, but to my mind we're so ignorant that anything could happen. However good your models are, you have to *keep making measurements* to make sure that nature really does work the way you think.

It's easy to see now, with the benefit of hindsight, where we went wrong with CFCs. The original idea was to look for something *very stable* which would not be flammable, poisonous or corrosive. But the trouble with very stable substances is that they stay around for a long time – and when they do eventually break down they form something *very unstable* and reactive, which is likely to cause trouble."

ASSIGNMENT II

a Explain how concentrations of ozone in the atmosphere are measured.

b Why did NASA discard 80% of their October ozone concentration measurements?

c Joe Farman's group were first aware of the low concentrations of ozone around 1983, but did not publish their findings until 1985. Why did they delay publication?

d Joe Farman gives two reasons why the great stability of CFCs makes them an environmental problem. What are the two reasons?

Figure 17 Helium-filled balloons are sent up into the stratosphere to measure ozone concentrations. A cord almost 10 miles in length attaches the balloon to measuring instruments on the launch vehicle; the cord can be reeled in and out to obtain measurements at different altitudes

Since the mid-1980s, monitoring of ozone concentrations has continued with even greater urgency. Satellite readings and measurements from balloons and high-altitude planes have supported the measurements taken from the ground, and have confirmed the presence of the 'hole' over the Antarctic.

Satellite measurements have also shown that ozone concentrations have gone down in other parts of the globe too. The effect is particularly dramatic in the Antarctic spring (see Figure 18) because of the special weather conditions existing then – but there is evidence of a smaller 'ozone hole' appearing above the Arctic and a general depletion of ozone stretching across northern latitudes, including Canada, the USA and Europe.

CFCs: very handy compounds

In 1930 the American engineer Thomas Midgley demonstrated a new refrigerant to the American Chemical Society. He inhaled a lungful of dichlorodifluoromethane (CCl_2F_2) and used it to blow out a candle.

Midgley was flamboyantly demonstrating two important properties of CCl_2F_2: its lack of toxicity and its lack of flammability. Up to that time, ammonia had been the main refrigerant in use. Ammonia has a convenient boiling point, –33°C, which means it can easily be liquefied by compression. Unfortunately, it is also toxic and very smelly.

Midgley had been asked to find a safe replacement for ammonia, and that meant finding a compound with a similar boiling point but which was very unreactive and therefore safe. He came up with the compound CCl_2F_2.

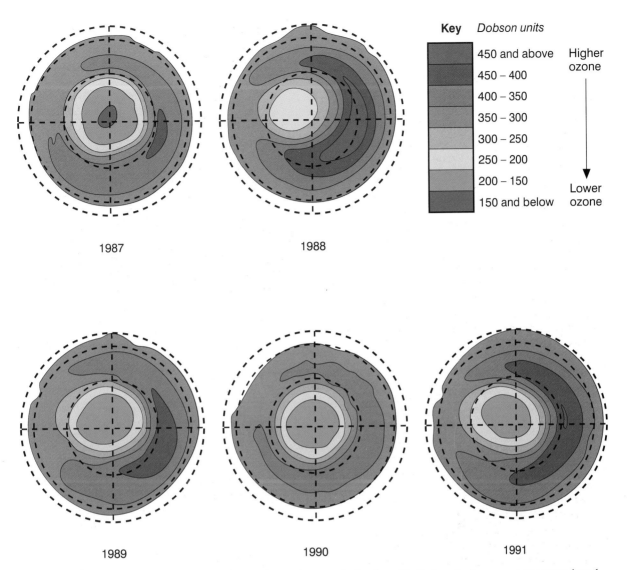

Key *Dobson units*

450 and above   Higher ozone
450 – 400
400 – 350
350 – 300
300 – 250
250 – 200
200 – 150
150 and below   Lower ozone

1987

1988

1989

1990

1991

Figure 18 Mean October values of total ozone (in Dobson units) over the Southern Hemisphere for five consecutive years, based on satellite measurements. (The south pole is at the centre; the equator, 30°S and 60°S latitude circles are shown as dotted circles; Greenwich is at the top.)

The reactions of some halogenoalkanes are investigated in **Activity A4.1.** By extending your results from this activity you should be able to see why Midgley was led to look at CFCs for a refrigerant gas.

CCl_2F_2 belongs to a family of compounds called chlorofluorocarbons (CFCs), which contain chlorine, fluorine and carbon. There are several members of the family, all with different boiling points. That's one of the things that makes them so useful: you can find CFCs with boiling points to suit different applications.

Another useful thing about CFCs is that they are very unreactive, and have low flammability and low toxicity.

You can see the main uses of CFCs in Figure 19 on the next page.

You can make a halogenoalkane in **Activity A4.2.**

Choosing a member of the CFC family for use in a refrigerator is the aim of **Activity A4.3.**

As propellants for aerosols

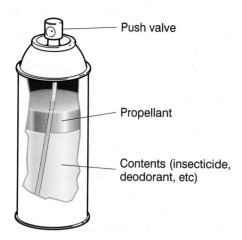

Push valve

Propellant

Contents (insecticide, deodorant, etc)

When the valve opens, the pressure falls inside the can causing the propellant to vaporise. The propellant escapes into the atmosphere along with the other contents of the can.

As blowing agents for making expanded plastics

A volatile CFC is incorporated in the plastic when it is made. The heat given off during the polymerisation reaction vaporises the CFC so it 'blows' tiny bubbles in the plastic making a foam. Inevitably, some of the CFC escapes into the atmosphere during the blowing process, and more escapes when the plastic is finally disposed of.

As refrigerants

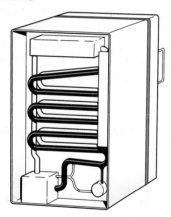

CFCs are used as refrigerants in food refrigerators and air-conditioning units. A total of 55 000 tonnes of CFCs went into the air conditioners of cars in the USA in 1987. Eventually some of these refrigerants end up in the atmosphere, through leakage or when the refrigerator is scrapped.

As cleaning solvents

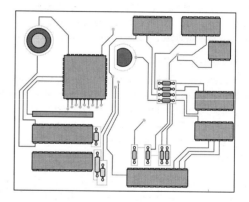

CFCs dissolve grease and are used as solvents in dry-cleaning, cleaning electronic circuits, etc. Some of the solvent escapes into the atmosphere during use.

Figure 19 Everyday applications of CFCs

The trouble with CFCs

When Thomas Midgley and other chemists developed CFCs, they did their job too well. They found a family of compounds that are very unreactive, and this makes them excellent for the jobs just described. The trouble is, they are *too* unreactive.

The estimated lifetimes for CFCs in the troposphere are about 100 years. This gives plenty of time for them to be transported up into the stratosphere – where they are no longer unreactive.

As more became known about the effect of CFCs on ozone in the stratosphere, people began to press for their replacement. This meant that the chemical industry had an important job to do: to find compounds that would replace CFCs, but have no significant damaging effect on the ozone layer.

Activities A4.4 and **A4.5** look at some of the compounds that have been developed for this purpose and how they are manufactured.

Progress has been very rapid. The replacement compounds are hydrochlorofluorocarbons (HCFCs) or hydrofluorocarbons (HFCs). The difference is that these molecules contain H–C bonds and are broken down in the troposphere.

Sadly, they are not a perfect solution. Both CFCs and their replacements are greenhouse gases and contribute to global warming (a problem we shall discuss later in this unit, in Section **A6**). There are fears too that some of the decomposition products may be toxic.

Methane to the rescue

Cl atoms are obviously bad news in the stratosphere. They attack ozone and destroy it. Indeed, they are so reactive that, left to themselves, they would quickly destroy most of the ozone there. Fortunately, they have not done that yet, because there are other molecules in the stratosphere that react with Cl atoms.

Methane, CH_4, is an important example of such a molecule. It is produced on Earth in large quantities by living organisms. Most of the methane released is oxidised in the troposphere, but significant amounts of it are eventually carried up into the stratosphere.

Once in the stratosphere, methane molecules remove chlorine atoms by reacting with them like this:

$$CH_4 + Cl \rightarrow CH_3 + HCl$$

The hydrogen chloride made in this reaction may eventually be carried down into the troposphere where it can be removed in raindrops. This gets rid of some of the troublesome Cl atoms from the stratosphere, although there is not enough methane to stop levels of chlorine rising overall.

Figure 20 Rice paddy fields cover large areas of land and are one of the biggest sources of methane

ASSIGNMENT 12

Here are three reactions involving chlorine atoms from the stratosphere:

$CH_4 + Cl \rightarrow CH_3 + HCl$	(reaction 8)
$Cl + Cl \rightarrow Cl_2$	(reaction 9)
$Cl + Cl_2 \rightarrow Cl_2 + Cl$	(reaction 10)

a For each of these reactions, answer the following questions.

   i Which bond, if any, is broken during the reaction? Use the Data Sheets to find the bond enthalpy of this bond.

   ii What new bond is made during the reaction? Use the Data Sheets to find the bond enthalpy of this bond.

   iii Use the bond enthalpies to find a value for ΔH for the reaction.

b Which of the reactions have the effect of removing chlorine atoms from the stratosphere?

c The energy required to get the bond-breaking/bond-forming processes going in a reaction is called the *activation enthalpy*. Explain why reaction 8 has a much higher activation enthalpy than reaction 9.

d Despite its higher activation enthalpy, reaction 8 normally removes Cl atoms more rapidly than reaction 9. Suggest a reason why.

A5 *How bad is the ozone crisis?*

Ozone is a vital sunscreen gas which protects us from ultra-violet radiation. Removing it from the stratosphere may have serious consequences for the Earth. The trouble is, we do not know just what these will be.

One thing that seems clear is that cases of skin cancer and eye cataracts will increase as ozone is destroyed. It has been estimated that reducing ozone by 10% could cause a 30%–50% increase in skin cancer cases.

Figure 21 Children in New Zealand have to wear hats on school outings in summer, to protect them from harmful ultra-violet radiation

But what about species other than humans? Increased ultra-violet radiation could affect species such as plankton in the oceans. That in turn could affect other organisms involved in the food chain.

And what about the weather? Changes in the amount of radiation reaching the Earth will affect the temperature of the Earth itself, which of course affects the weather.

Governments have gradually realised that it's not worth risking the global experiment that is needed to find the answers to these questions. In 1987, at an international meeting in Montreal, a procedure was agreed for restricting the production and release of CFCs into the atmosphere. Three years later, a second meeting was held in London and the restrictions were tightened to include a *total phase-out of CFCs by the year 2000*. More than 60 countries signed this *revised Montreal Protocol* and a special fund was set up to help developing countries move away from the use of CFCs.

But CFCs are very stable, and they take a long time to travel to the stratosphere. Even after CFCs are phased out in the year 2000, it will be well into the 2000s before the atmosphere returns to the condition it was in before damage to the ozone layer began. Joe Farman calculates that it will not be until 2030 that the amount of ozone-destroying chlorine in the stratosphere goes down to the level it was at when he first discovered the hole over the Antarctic.

ASSIGNMENT 13

The following is an extract from a letter to a newspaper:

"… Ozone is a gas which occurs in the atmosphere in very small quantities. So small, that the total amount, if it were separated from the air and brought to a condition of normal temperature and pressure, would form a layer only a few millimetres high over the whole Earth. The entire atmosphere under the same conditions would reach 8 km.

This tiny amount of ozone absorbs ultra-violet solar energy but is under threat from the CFCs we hear so much about.

If so small a quantity of ozone can produce the protection we require, why can we not manufacture ozone and release it into the atmosphere? …"

What would be your reply to this? Do you think this could be a possible solution?

Figure 22

Figure 23 What objections can you see to Carstairs' solution to the ozone crisis?

Activity A5 should help you to summarise some of the information that has been presented in Sections **A1** to **A5**.

A6 *Trouble in the troposphere*

This story now moves a little nearer to the Earth – to the troposphere, the bottom 15 km or so of the atmosphere. But for the moment we will stick with methane, which in the stratosphere helps remove the chlorine atoms which destroy the ozone layer.

In the troposphere, methane's role has a less helpful side to it. To see why, we need to look at the way the Sun keeps the Earth warm.

How is methane formed?

As humans, we are used to living in an airy world. In particular, we use *aerobic* respiration to oxidise carbohydrates such as glucose to carbon dioxide and water:

$$C_6H_{12}O_6 + 6O_2 \rightarrow 6CO_2 + 6H_2O$$
glucose

But some organisms live in airless places, under *anaerobic* conditions. Instead of turning carbohydrates to CO_2 and water, they turn them to other, less oxidised materials. Yeast is a good example – it converts glucose to ethanol and CO_2.

An important group of bacteria – called *methanogenic bacteria* – work in anaerobic conditions to turn materials such as carbohydrates to methane and other related substances.

Methanogenic bacteria are very common. In fact, you can be pretty sure that wherever carbohydrate is left in anaerobic conditions, methanogenic bacteria will be present, and methane will be produced. Since most biological material contains carbohydrate (or substances that can be converted to carbohydrate), it follows that methane is produced whenever biological material decays anaerobically. This may occur in

- marshes, compost heaps and waste tips, where vegetation rots without air
- rice paddy fields, where water and mud cut off air from rotting vegetation
- biogas digesters where waste material is deliberately kept under anaerobic conditions
- the digestive tracts of animals, where part-digested food is acted on by bacteria (a cow releases about 500 000 cm^3 of methane every day in belches!).

Baked beans are rich in carbohydrate and are notorious for causing methanogenesis in the human intestine. They contain a particular carbohydrate, called raffinose, that doesn't get broken down by normal digestive enzymes. It survives long enough to reach the intestines where is is broken down by methanogenic bacteria.

Methane is one of the most abundant of the trace gases in the troposphere (see Table 1 on page 56), and its concentration is rising. Figure 24 shows the concentrations of methane found by analysing bubbles of air trapped in polar ice.

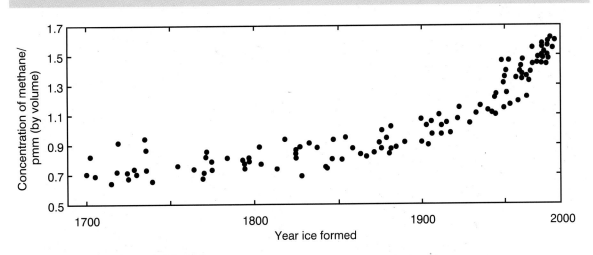

Figure 24 Methane concentrations in air trapped in polar ice samples

ASSIGNMENT 14

Look at the scatterplot in Figure 24.

a The air bubbles were all analysed in 1984. How is it possible to get an estimate of methane concentration in air 300 years ago?

b How has the methane concentration in the air changed over the last 300 years? Suggest reasons for this change.

Radiation in, radiation out

When things get hot, they send out electromagnetic radiation. The hotter the object, the higher the energy of the radiation.

The surface of the Sun has a temperature of about 6000 K, and this means that it radiates energy in the ultra-violet, visible and infra-red regions.

The Earth is heated by the Sun's radiation. Its average surface temperature is about 285 K – a lot cooler than the Sun, but still hot enough to radiate electromagnetic radiation. But at this lower temperature, the energy radiated is mainly in the infra-red region. The situation is illustrated in Figure 25.

The Sun radiates energy around the visible and ultra-violet region. Part of this energy is absorbed by the Earth and its atmosphere, and part is reflected back into space. The part that gets absorbed helps to heat the Earth, and the Earth in turn radiates energy back into space. A steady state is reached, where the Earth is radiating energy as fast as it absorbs it. Under such conditions, illustrated by Figure 26, the average temperature of the Earth remains constant.

As in all steady states, the delicate balance can be disturbed by changes to the system – in particular by changes to the quantities of various atmospheric gases. Methane is one example.

ASSIGNMENT 15

Look at the spectra in Figure 25 which show the ranges and relative intensities of radiation from the Earth and the Sun.

Methane absorbs radiation in the frequency ranges 0.39×10^{14} Hz – 0.46×10^{14} Hz and 0.85×10^{14} Hz – 1.03×10^{14} Hz.

a Will methane absorb the Sun's *incoming* radiation?

b Will methane absorb the Earth's *outgoing* radiation?

c What will be the effect of methane on
  i the balance between incoming and outgoing radiation on Earth?
  ii the temperature of the Earth?

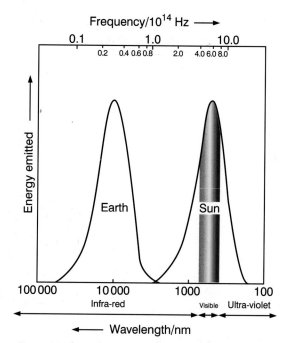

Figure 25 The radiation from the Sun which reaches the outer limits of the atmosphere and the radiation given off from the surface of the Earth (the frequencies and wavelengths are plotted here on a logarithmic scale, so each large division is a factor of 10 greater than the one before)

Methane is an example of a **greenhouse gas**. In effect, it traps some of the Earth's radiation that would otherwise be re-radiated into space. The effect of this is to make the Earth warmer. It's similar to the way glass traps radiation in a greenhouse, heating up the inside. Figure 27 indicates how a greenhouse works, with an attempt to show the relative wavelengths of the radiation involved.

Other gases can behave in this way too. **Activity A6** looks at the absorption characteristics of some atmospheric gases.

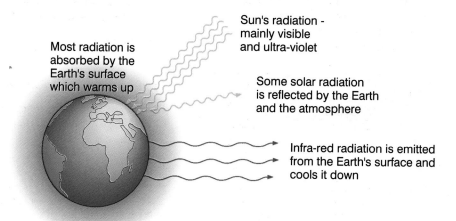

Figure 26 The Earth – input and output of energy

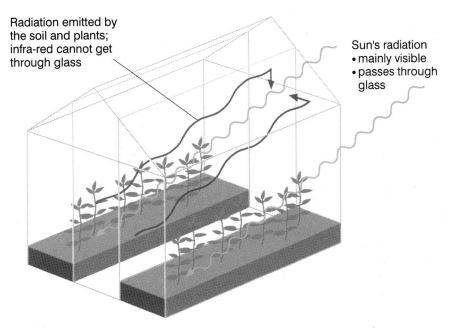

Figure 27 Greenhouse warming

Which other gases have a greenhouse effect?

You should now appreciate that several atmospheric gases absorb infra-red radiation, but not visible or ultra-violet light from the Sun. This means they are greenhouse gases. They let the Sun's visible radiation in, but they stop some of the Earth's infra-red radiation getting out. They contribute to the **greenhouse effect**, which makes the Earth warmer.

Some gases have a more powerful greenhouse effect than others. Table 2 lists some gases, their abundance in the atmosphere and their **greenhouse factors**. The greenhouse factor is a measure of the greenhouse effect caused by the gas, relative to the same amount of carbon dioxide, which is assigned a value of 1. One molecule of methane, for example, has the same effect as about 30 molecules of carbon dioxide.

Gas	Tropospheric abundance (by volume)/%	Greenhouse factor
N_2	78	negligible
O_2	21	negligible
Ar	1	negligible
$H_2O(g)$	1*	0.1
CO_2	3.5×10^{-2}	1
CH_4	1.7×10^{-4}	30
N_2O	3.0×10^{-5}	160
CCl_2F_2	4.8×10^{-8}	25 000
CCl_3F	2.8×10^{-8}	21 000

Table 2 Relative contributions to the greenhouse effect of various gases in the atmosphere (averaged figure)*

ASSIGNMENT 16

Use the data in Table 2 to help with the following questions.

a Bearing in mind both their abundance and the greenhouse factor, list the gases in order of how much they contribute to the total greenhouse effect on Earth.

b Which of these gases are produced in significant amounts by human activities?

c Which gases in **b** would it be most fruitful to tackle in order to control the greenhouse effect?

d Human activities produce a lot of water vapour, but this has very little effect on the net amount of water vapour in the atmosphere. Why?

The greenhouse effect is good for you

Without the greenhouse effect, we would not be here. By trapping some of the Sun's radiation, the atmosphere acts like a blanket: it keeps the average temperature of the Earth high enough to support life.

If we had no atmosphere on Earth, it would be like the Moon – barren and lifeless. The surface of the Moon gets very hot in the day, but is bitterly cold at night. If, on the other hand, the composition of our atmosphere resembled that of our neighbouring planet Venus, the greenhouse effect would make it so hot that life-forms would find it impossible to survive.

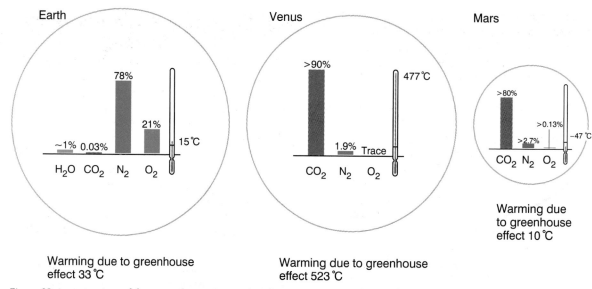

Figure 28 *A comparison of the atmospheres, sizes and surface temperatures of the Earth and its neighbouring planets*

Look at Figure 28 which compares conditions on the surface of the Earth, Venus and Mars. The carbon dioxide atmosphere on Venus is thick and the greenhouse effect is extreme.

Our other neighbouring planet, Mars, has an atmosphere which is mostly carbon dioxide, like that on Venus. But on Mars the atmosphere is very thin. There is only a small greenhouse effect, and so Mars is cold.

We are used to the stable, comfortable temperature on Earth and small changes in that temperature could have a dramatic effect on life.

Is the Earth getting hotter?

About 100 years ago, the Swedish chemist Arrhenius predicted that increasing amounts of carbon dioxide could lead to warming of the Earth. Average temperatures did indeed rise from 1880 to 1940, by about 0.25 °C. But then between 1940 and 1970 they fell again, by 0.2 °C.

So why are we worried today? During the 1970s, measurements of carbon dioxide in the atmosphere began to show a significant increase, and new predictions began to be made about the effect of the carbon dioxide increase on the Earth's climate.

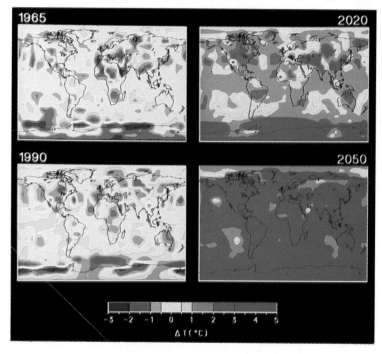

Figure 29 *The global pattern of summer temperature rises as predicted by a NASA climate model, on the basis that the emission of greenhouse gases will continue to increase at current rates*

Making predictions about the climate is very difficult because it involves so many variable factors, many of which are still poorly understood.

The information available is fed into computers to give an overall **mathematical model** of the Earth's climate.

The amount of information needed is enormous. It includes, for example, the concentrations and distribution of the gases in the atmosphere, their predicted lifetimes, and details of how the concentrations are expected to change. Add to this information about variations in the intensity of the Sun's radiation, meteorological data such as air circulation patterns and cloud cover, as well as ocean temperatures and currents, and you can see why powerful computers are needed.

Models are constantly being improved as more reliable information becomes available. Figure 29 shows the global pattern of temperature rises as predicted by a computer model for a doubling in carbon dioxide concentration.

At the time predictions like these were being made, field measurements of the Earth's temperature began to show increases too. Between 1970 and 1990, the Earth's average temperature increased by about 0.4 °C.

Over the last 100 years, the six global-average warmest years have been in the 1980s.

So, is **global warming** really taking place? The climate displays so much natural variation that spotting trends is very difficult. But there is now a great deal of scientific evidence that the Earth is indeed getting warmer, and that this warming is due to human-made emissions of greenhouse gases.

A7 *Keeping the window open*

The two most significant greenhouse gases are carbon dioxide and water. Because they are so abundant in the atmosphere, they absorb a lot of the infra-red radiated by the Earth. Water vapour makes the larger contribution – simply because more of it is present. As Figure 30 shows, carbon dioxide and water absorb in two bands across the Earth's radiation spectrum.

Between these two bands is a 'window' where infra-red radiation can escape without being absorbed. In fact, about 70% of the Earth's radiation escapes into space through this 'window'.

Gases produced by human activities can increase the natural greenhouse effect of the atmosphere. There are two types:

- Gases already naturally present in the atmosphere, which are increased in amount by human activities. Carbon dioxide is an important example. Humans burn fossil fuels, and this increases the amount of carbon dioxide in the atmosphere. This in turn increases the greenhouse effect.

- Gases which are not naturally present in the atmosphere. These gases may absorb radiation in the vital 'window' through which radiation normally escapes into space. CFCs are an example. Although CFCs are only present in the atmosphere in small amounts, they are important because they have a very large greenhouse factor – so each molecule has a big effect.

Figure 30 The Earth's radiation spectrum, showing the regions where CO_2 and H_2O absorb strongly

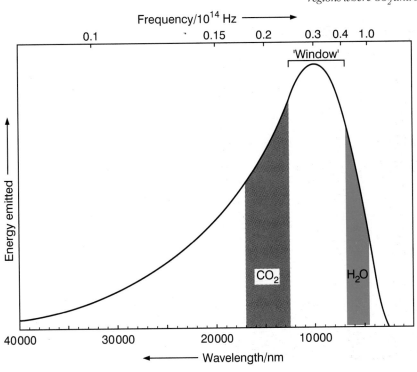

Figure 31 It is difficult to predict accurately the effect of atmospheric water on global warming; water is a greenhouse gas, but water droplets in low clouds tend to block out the Sun and cool the surface of the Earth

Figure 32 The eruption of Mt Pinatubo in the Philippines in June 1991 released enormous clouds of dust and sulphur dioxide, which will lead to some global cooling over the next few years; such events make predictions about climate change even more difficult (the sulphur dioxide released is also expected to lead to some ozone depletion in the stratosphere)

ASSIGNMENT 17

Suppose the average temperature of the Earth increases due to the greenhouse effect.

a What effect will this have on the amount of water vapour in the atmosphere?

b What effect will your answer to **a** have on further global warming?

c Explain why the role of water vapour in global warming is an example of **positive feedback**.

Water is different from other greenhouse gases (see **Assignment 17**). Under most conditions on Earth, water is a liquid, with some vapour associated with it. $H_2O(l)$ and $H_2O(g)$ are quickly interconverted. If human activities such as burning fuels put $H_2O(g)$ into the atmosphere, most of it will condense to $H_2O(l)$ and eventually return to Earth. So in that sense $H_2O(g)$ isn't nearly as much of a greenhouse problem as $CO_2(g)$.

But there are two more things to consider. First, if the Earth *does* get warmer, more $H_2O(g)$ will evaporate from the oceans. That would tend to increase global warming. Second, although $H_2O(g)$ is a greenhouse gas, the droplets of $H_2O(l)$ in clouds tend to block out the Sun, as people living in the UK know well. So more water in the atmosphere *could* work in either direction – to increase or to decrease warming. This is one reason why climate modellers find it so hard to predict what will happen to the Earth's climate in the future.

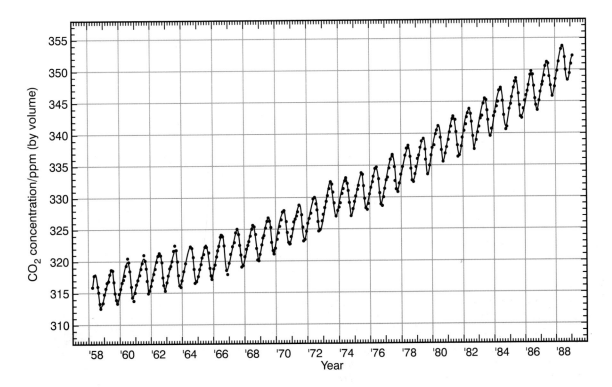

Figure 33 The build up of CO_2 in the atmosphere as recorded at Mauna Loa Observatory, Hawaii

At least half of the expected *increase* in greenhouse effect due to human activities is likely to be caused by carbon dioxide. So control of the greenhouse effect must focus mainly on control of the amount of carbon dioxide we produce.

A8 *Focus on carbon dioxide*

In this section we look more closely at the role of carbon dioxide in the greenhouse effect.

Detecting carbon dioxide

Since carbon dioxide is so crucial in the greenhouse effect, it's important to be able to make accurate measurements of its concentration in the atmosphere. Then we can keep an eye on how its concentration is changing.

The proportion of carbon dioxide in the atmosphere is fairly small – about 0.035%. In your earlier science work you probably used the limewater test to detect carbon dioxide. This test is fine when you want a **qualitative** test and when the concentration of carbon dioxide is fairly large, but it's not nearly sensitive enough to measure the small changes in atmospheric carbon dioxide concentration that occur from year to year. Later in this section you will use a **quantitative** method for measuring carbon dioxide concentration, but even this is not sensitive enough for atmospheric research.

The method most commonly used by researchers is **infra-red spectroscopy**. Carbon dioxide absorbs infra-red radiation – that's the reason for all the trouble. The more carbon dioxide there is, the stronger the absorption.

Using infra-red measurements, it is possible to get an accurate picture of the way carbon dioxide concentration has changed over the years. The graph in Figure 33 shows measurements of atmospheric carbon dioxide concentrations made at Mauna Loa Observatory, situated at an altitude of about 3500 m in Hawaii.

ASSIGNMENT 18

a The graph in Figure 33 shows a zig-zag pattern. What time of year corresponds to
  i the peaks?
  ii the troughs?

b Suggest a reason for this zig-zag pattern.

c What was the average percentage increase in carbon dioxide concentration at Mauna Loa between 1960 and 1984?

d What problems would be involved in making a similar record of carbon dioxide concentration in London?

Where does the carbon dioxide come from – and go to?

The increase in concentration of carbon dioxide in the Earth's atmosphere is due to the increasing use of fossil fuels. Over the last 100 years, the amount of fossil fuels burned has increased by about 4% every year. In 1989 and 1990, 6 Gt of fossil fuels were burned each year.

> 1 Gt = 1 gigatonne = 1×10^9 tonnes

ASSIGNMENT 19

In 1980, the concentration of carbon dioxide in the atmosphere at Mauna Loa (see Figure 33) was 338 ppm (by volume). The *total mass* of carbon dioxide in the atmosphere was estimated to be about 2500 Gt at that time.

Between 1980 and 1984, it is estimated that 20 Gt of fossil fuel were burned throughout the world.

In 1984 the measured percentage of carbon dioxide in the atmosphere at Mauna Loa was found to be 344 ppm (by volume).

Now answer these questions.

a Assume that the 20 Gt of fossil fuel burned between 1980 and 1984 were all carbon (this is a reasonable approximation since the other main element in fossil fuels, hydrogen, has a very low relative atomic mass). Calculate the mass of carbon dioxide formed by burning this mass of fuel.

b Calculate the new total mass of carbon dioxide in the atmosphere in 1984, assuming that the extra carbon dioxide came only from burning fossil fuels.

c By what percentage would you expect the concentration of carbon dioxide in the atmosphere to have increased between 1980 and 1984?

d By what percentage did the concentration of carbon dioxide in the atmosphere actually increase between 1980 and 1984?

e Comment on your answers to questions c and d.

Calculations of the kind you have just done suggest that – judging by the quantity of fossil fuels being burned – the increase in carbon dioxide concentration in the atmosphere *should* have been about *twice* as much as it actually has been. Atmospheric carbon dioxide concentration is not increasing as fast as we might expect. Good news – but where is all the carbon dioxide going?

Oceans soak up carbon dioxide

Oceans cover almost three-quarters of the Earth's surface. Carbon dioxide is fairly soluble in water, so large amounts of atmospheric $CO_2(g)$ dissolve in the oceans.

When carbon dioxide dissolves in water, it forms hydrated CO_2 molecules:

$$CO_2(g) + aq \rightleftharpoons CO_2(aq) \quad \text{(reaction 11)}$$

To understand the chemistry in this section you need an idea of dynamic equilibrium. **Chemical Ideas 7.1** will help you with this.

This is a reversible reaction, as you will know if you have watched what happens when you take the top off a bottle of fizzy drink. However, it is a fairly slow reaction (which is a good thing from the point of view of fizzy drink consumers), and it takes quite a long time for equilibrium to be reached.

The uptake of carbon dioxide by the oceans is quicker than this. Minute marine plants called phytoplankton use up most of the carbon dioxide which goes into the sea. So the concentration of 'free' $CO_2(aq)$ is small and gaseous carbon dioxide is encouraged to dissolve.

A small proportion of the $CO_2(aq)$ (about 0.4%) goes on to react with the water. It forms hydrogencarbonate anions and hydrogen cations:

$$CO_2(aq) + H_2O(l) \rightleftharpoons HCO_3^-(aq) + H^+(aq)$$
$$\text{hydrogencarbonate} \quad \text{(reaction 12)}$$
$$\text{anions}$$

Since $H^+(aq)$ ions are formed, this reaction is responsible for the acidic nature of carbon dioxide. A solution of carbon dioxide in pure water is, however, only weakly acidic. Reaction 12 does not go to completion: an equilibrium is set up with products and reactants both present in solution. Since only 0.4% of the $CO_2(aq)$ reacts, there is very much more $CO_2(aq)$ than $H^+(aq)$ present.

You can investigate some chemical equilibria in **Activity A8.1**.

ASSIGNMENT 20

a What will happen to the position of equilibrium in reaction 11 if the concentration of atmospheric carbon dioxide increases?

b What will be the effect on reaction 12 of the change described in a?

c In Assignment 19 you found that the proportion of atmospheric carbon dioxide was not rising as fast as expected. Suggest a reason for this.

d Do you think carbon dioxide in the oceans and in the atmosphere are actually in equilibrium? Explain your answer.

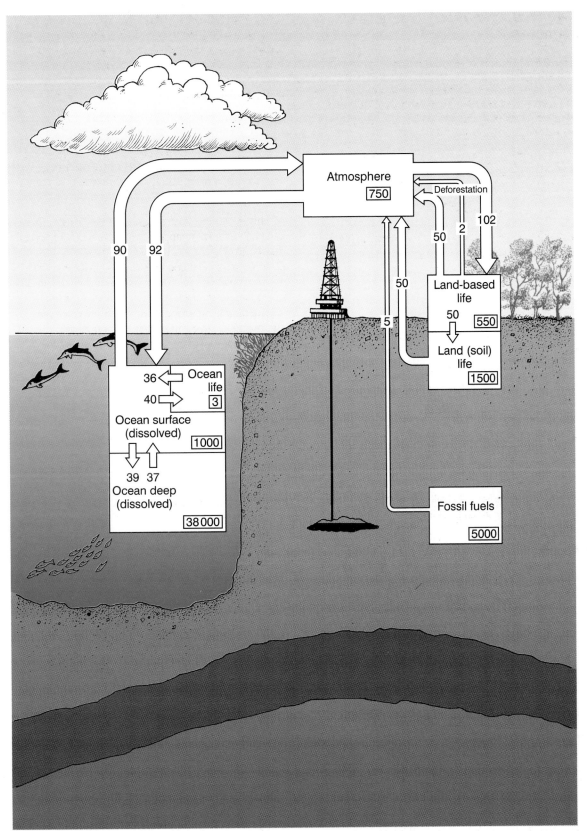

Figure 34 The global carbon cycle. The numbers in boxes are reservoirs, showing the total mass of carbon (in Gt) in a particular part of the cycle; the numbers beside the arrows are fluxes, showing the rate of movement of carbon from one reservoir to another (in Gt year⁻¹)

Since the pH of a solution is related to the concentration of H^+(aq) ions present, reactions 11 and 12 link together the quantity of CO_2 in the air and the pH of water which is in contact with it.

In **Activity A8.2** you can use pH measurements to investigate the rate at which solutions of carbon dioxide lose their gas.

By measuring pH in a situation like this we should therefore be able to deduce from it the concentration of atmospheric carbon dioxide.

Activity A8.3 allows you to measure some carbon dioxide concentrations in samples of air.

The global carbon cycle

The oceans are just one part – a very important part – of the carbon cycle which puts carbon dioxide into the atmosphere and takes it out again. Figure 34 shows the circulation of carbon in the *biosphere*, and the quantities involved. Have a look at the diagram and answer the questions in **Assignment 21**.

Biosphere

The biosphere comprises those parts of the Earth inhabited by living organisms or *biota*. It includes parts of the atmosphere, the oceans and the Earth's surface.

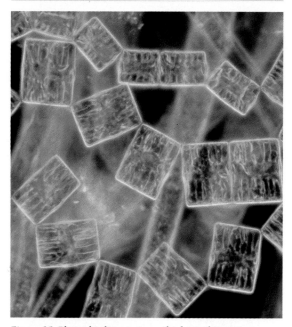

Figure 35 Phytoplankton act as a 'biological pump', removing CO_2 from the atmosphere and transporting organic carbon compounds from surface waters to deeper layers as a 'rain' of dead and decaying organisms. This is balanced by upward transport of carbon by deeper water which is richer in CO_2 than surface water

ASSIGNMENT 21

Look at the global carbon cycle in Figure 34 on p. 79.

a i What is the total mass of carbon passing *into* the atmosphere per year?
  ii What is the total mass of carbon passing *out* of the atmosphere per year?
  iii What is the net change in the mass of carbon in the atmosphere per year?

b Of the various processes that release carbon dioxide into and absorb carbon dioxide from the atmosphere, which do you think are likely to show significant changes over the next 50 years?

c Which single process removes carbon dioxide from the atmosphere at the greatest rate?

d The *residence time* for a reservoir is the average time that carbon spends in that reservoir. It is a measure of how fast carbon atoms are 'turned over' in the reservoir. You can calculate average residence times by dividing the size of the reservoir by the size of the flux. This gives the residence time in years. (Where the ingoing and outgoing fluxes are different, use the outgoing flux to calculate the residence time.)

Calculate the residence time for carbon in
i the atmosphere
ii land-based life
iii ocean life.

Suggest reasons for any difference between **ii** and **iii**. What is the significance for global change of the residence time in the atmosphere?

A9 *Coping with carbon*

It is estimated that in the middle of the 19th century, before the Industrial Revolution had really started pumping carbon dioxide into the atmosphere, the atmospheric concentration of carbon dioxide was 270 ppm. By the early 1990s it was 353 ppm. By the 2080s it will probably have doubled from its pre-Industrial Revolution value to 540 ppm.

The increase in atmospheric carbon dioxide is a serious problem which will have far-reaching effects on the world's climate.

It is thought that the doubling of carbon dioxide concentration will cause an average temperature increase of about 2 °C. If you take into account the other greenhouse gases like methane and CFCs, which are also increasing in concentration, this 2 °C rise will probably be with us by the 2030s – within the lifetime of most people reading this. Although 2 °C may not sound much, it will be enough to have a dramatic effect on the global climate.

'So this is your response to global warming?'

Figure 36

A10 *Summary*

In this unit you have looked at two problems in atmospheric chemistry: the destruction of the ozone layer and an increase in the greenhouse effect leading to global warming. These are problems that affect the whole world.

Ozone depletion is a *stratospheric problem*. At its centre is the idea of the absorption of radiation by gas molecules. Dangerous effects arise from the increased transmission of ultra-violet light through the atmosphere as ozone molecules are destroyed by radical reactions in the stratosphere.

The mechanisms of many chemical processes in the stratosphere require an understanding of radicals and their reactions. Chlorine radicals produced from CFCs have been an example here, and you also studied some other halogen compounds and their chemistry.

The greenhouse effect is a *tropospheric phenomenon*. Again it arises from the absorption of radiation by gas molecules. You have focussed on the role of carbon dioxide and the need to monitor and detect its concentration. This led you to the key idea of chemical equilibrium and its importance in determining the point of balance in some chemical processes.

Activity A10 should help you to get your notes in order at the end of the unit.

The science of the effects of carbon dioxide in an atmosphere, which is what has been presented in this unit, is fairly well known. We are far less certain about the extent to which these effects will occur, the role of other processes and the overall balance which will emerge.

One of the predicted results of global warming is a rise in the mean sea level because of the thermal expansion of water and the melting of some land ice.

Modelling our future climate is extremely difficult. There are people who believe we are heading for disaster from accelerating global warming fuelled by positive feedback. Others believe the Earth will develop ways of compensating for any serious departure from equilibrium.

Reducing the rate of increase of carbon dioxide in the atmosphere is a major challenge for the world as we move towards the 21st century. In **Activity A9** you can investigate some of the possible approaches to solving the problem.

THE POLYMER REVOLUTION

Why a unit on THE POLYMER REVOLUTION?

This unit is intended to operate on three levels. First, it provides some essential information about polymers and polymerisation processes. Through this, you are introduced to alkenes and their reactions, geometric isomerism and ideas about intermolecular forces. You will also learn to recognise carboxylic acids and some of their derivatives.

Second, the unit should enhance your awareness of some aspects of the development of polymers, how they are used in the present day world and the contribution they could make to life in the future. New polymers have ranges of properties which are not available in traditional materials, but their unique properties can lead to problems as well as benefits.

Third, a very important theme which runs through the entire unit is the relationship between the properties of a substance and its structure and bonding. This relationship helps to explain the properties of polymers and is used by scientists in designing polymers for particular applications.

Overview of chemical principles

In your earlier studies, you will probably have come across ideas about

- polymerisation
- how the structure of a substance determines its properties.

In this unit you will learn more about …

- the chemistry of organic molecules (**Developing Fuels** and **The Atmosphere**)
- isomerism (**Developing Fuels**)
- reaction mechanisms (**The Atmosphere**)
- free radicals (**The Atmosphere**)
- covalent bonds (**Elements of Life**, **Developing Fuels** and **The Atmosphere**)

… as well as learning new ideas about

- polymers and polymerisation
- reactions of alkenes
- geometric isomerism
- carboxylic acids and their derivatives
- intermolecular forces
- the relationship between the properties of a substance and its structure and bonding.

THE POLYMER REVANUE REVOLUTION

PR1 *Designer polymers*

Producing a perfect copy

If you had lived in medieval times and visited a monastery, you might have found that one of the most important rooms was the one in which monks made copies of religious documents, painstakingly copying out the original by hand.

Fortunately, today we don't have to copy out by hand everything we want duplicates of: we can use a photocopier. Unlike some of the medieval bibles, the results are not works of art, but they are very good copies and it is almost impossible to tell the difference between the copy and the original. You probably accept this as a normal, everyday fact. But do you know how the photocopier works?

At the heart of the photocopying process is a photoreceptor surface which is sensitive to light. In many machines, the photoreceptor is in the form of a metal drum coated with a very thin layer (about 10^{-5} m thick) of a special polymer called *poly(vinyl carbazole)*.

The polymer is made from a compound, vinyl carbazole, with the chemical structure

vinyl carbazole

A remarkable property of poly(vinyl carbazole) is that it exhibits **photoconductivity** – it conducts electricity much better when light shines on it than when it is in the dark.

Figure 1 Part of a decorative initial letter in the Lindisfarne Gospels, written by Northumbrian monks in the late 7th or 8th century; religious documents like this were laboriously copied by hand

In a photocopier, the surface of the drum is first given an electrostatic charge so that the polymer becomes charged. The interesting behaviour starts when light shines on the drum. If it is in the light, the polymer becomes conducting and so its charge disappears. But if it is in the dark, the polymer retains most of its charge.

A piece of paper with a picture on it is laid on a glass plate and illuminated, so that an *image* of the picture is projected onto the drum.

Can you imagine what happens? The polymer stays charged where there were dark areas in the picture, but loses its charge where the picture was white. So an electrically charged image of the picture is held on the drum.

You can follow the stages involved in producing a photocopy by looking at Figure 2.

Something new

There are many other 'designer polymers' with useful properties. Take *poly(1,1-difluoroethene)*: it's **piezoelectric**, that is it generates electricity when it is bent or twisted. If a sheet of poly(1,1-difluoroethene) is made to shake and wobble by a sound wave, the electrical signals can be processed and the sound wave detected. In reverse, electrical signals sent to a piece of this polymer can make it wobble and act as a type of loudspeaker.

In this unit you will learn about a dissolving polymer – *poly(ethenol)*; a polymer – *Kevlar* – which is about as strong as steel but five times lighter; and *PEEK* – a heat-resistant polymer. You will also make some *poly(pyrrole)* – a plastic which conducts electricity.

Figure 2 How a photocopier works

1 Charge drum

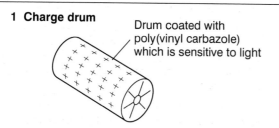

Drum coated with poly(vinyl carbazole) which is sensitive to light

The surface of the drum is given a positive electrical charge.

2 Project image onto drum

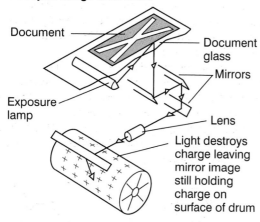

Document — Document glass — Mirrors — Exposure lamp — Lens

Light destroys charge leaving mirror image still holding charge on surface of drum

The document to be photocopied is placed face-down on the document glass. When the start button is pressed, the document is exposed to a light which scans across its surface, and an image of the document is projected through a system of lenses and mirrors onto the surface of the drum.

3 Develop image

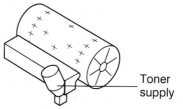

Toner supply

Negatively charged ink powder or toner is dusted over the drum. It sticks to the areas where there is a charge, so an exact copy of the document is held on the drum.

4 Transfer image to paper

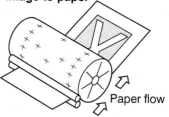

Paper flow

A sheet of ordinary paper is now passed across the surface of the drum. A charge below the paper attracts toner from the drum to the paper.

5 Fuse image to paper

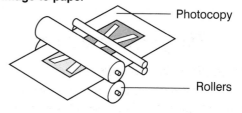

Photocopy

Rollers

Hot rollers fuse the image to the paper to produce an exact photocopy of the original document.

What is a polymer?

A **polymer** molecule is a long molecule made up from lots of small molecules called **monomers**.

If all the monomer molecules are the same, and they are represented by the letter A, an A–A polymer forms:

-- A + A + A + A -- → -- –A–A–A–A– --

Poly(ethene) and pvc are examples of A–A polymers.

If two different monomers are used, an A–B polymer is formed, in which A and B monomers alternate along the chain:

-- A + B + A + B -- → -- –A–B–A–B– --

Nylon-6,6 and polyesters are examples of this type of A–B polymer.

Writing out the long chain in a polymer molecule is very time consuming – we need a shorthand version. See how this is done for poly(propene):

$$-CH_2-CH-CH_2-CH-CH_2-CH-$$
$$\quad\quad\quad |\quad\quad\quad\quad |\quad\quad\quad\quad |$$
$$\quad\quad\quad CH_3\quad\quad CH_3\quad\quad CH_3$$

In the chain, the same basic unit is continually repeated, so the chain can be abbreviated to:

$$\left(\!\!\begin{array}{c} CH_2-CH- \\ | \\ CH_3 \end{array}\!\!\right)_n$$

where n is a very large number.

Fibres, plastics and elastomers

Polymer properties vary widely. Polymers which are soft and springy, which can be deformed and then go back to their original shape, are called **elastomers**. Rubber is an elastomer.

Poly(ethene) is not so springy and when it is deformed it tends to stay out of shape, undergoing permanent or plastic deformation. Substances like this are called **plastics**.

Stronger polymers, which do not deform easily, are just what you want for making clothing materials: some can be made into strong, thin threads which can then be woven together. These polymers, like nylon, are called **fibres**.

Poly(propene) is on the edge of the plastic–fibre boundary – it can be used as a plastic like poly(ethene), but it can also be made into a fibre for use in carpets.

All these polymers have properties which are not possessed by any single natural material, and this gives them some fascinating applications. Making them poses many chemical and technological problems. Chemists have to develop ways of making the required quantities of starting compounds at a reasonable cost, and have to combine them together in the right way to produce a usable material; engineers have to understand how to use and process the polymers.

Some early polymers were discovered almost by accident. But as our knowledge and understanding of the polymerisation process and the properties of polymers have grown, the creation of new polymers has become more systematic. This unit shows you how our knowledge of polymers and the processes which produce them has developed.

Before you go any further, it will help you to become familiar with some facts, figures and applications for the more widely used plastics. You can do this in **Activity PR1**.

PR2 *The polythene story*

An accidental discovery

Imperial Chemical Industries (ICI) was formed in 1926 by the amalgamation of a number of smaller chemical companies. The prime aim of the merger was to form a strong competitor to the huge German chemical company IG Farben.

To understand this section you will need to know about a compound called **ethene** and some of its relatives in the series of compounds known as the **alkenes**. **Chemical Ideas 12.2** contains the information you will need.

In 1930 Eric Fawcett, who was working for ICI, got the go-ahead to carry out research at high pressures and temperatures aimed at producing new dyestuffs. His results were disappointing and his project was eventually abandoned.

The team then moved into the field of high-pressure gas reactions and was joined by Reginald Gibson. On Friday 24 March 1933, Gibson and Fawcett carried out a reaction between ethene and benzaldehyde using a pressure of about 2000 atm. They were hoping to make the two chemicals add together to produce a ketone:

benzaldehyde   *ethene*

They left the mixture to react over the weekend, but their apparatus leaked and at one point they had to add extra ethene.

They opened the vessel on the following Monday and found a white waxy solid. When they analysed it they found that it had an empirical formula CH_2. They were not always able to obtain the same results from their experiment: sometimes they got the white solid, on other occasions they had less success, and sometimes their mixture exploded leaving them with just soot.

The work was halted in July 1933 because of the irreproducible and dangerous nature of the reaction.

Learning to control the process

In December 1935 the work was restarted. Fawcett and Gibson found that they could control the heat given out during the reaction if they added cold ethene at the correct rate. This kept the mixture cooler and prevented an explosion. They also found that they could control the reaction rate and relative molecular mass of the solid formed by varying the pressure.

Figure 3 An early advert for polythene

A month later they had enough of the material to show that it could be melted, moulded and used as an insulator.

Most crucial of all was the identification of the role of oxygen in the process, by Michael Perrin who took charge of the programme in 1935. If no oxygen is present, the polymerisation cannot occur. Too much oxygen causes the reaction to run out of control. The trick is to add just enough oxygen. The leak in Fawcett and Gibson's original apparatus had accidentally let in a small amount of oxygen. Without this, the discovery of poly(ethene) might not have been made. It was also Perrin who showed that even if the benzaldehyde is left out of the reaction mixture, the polymer still forms.

Poly(ethene) is an example of an addition polymer. You can find out more about the formation of polymers like poly(ethene) in the section on addition polymerisation in **Chemical Ideas 12.2.**

Poly(ethene) – or polythene as it is commonly called – is tough and durable, and has excellent electrical insulating properties. Unlike rubber which had previously been used for insulating cables, poly(ethene) is not adversely affected by weather or water.

It also has almost no tendency to absorb electrical signals. Its first important use was for insulating a telephone cable laid between the UK mainland and the Isle of Wight in 1939. Its unique electrical properties were again essential during the Second World War in the development of radar.

If you have never made an addition polymer you can do so in **Activity PR2.1**. You will make some poly(phenylethene) – better known as **polystyrene**.

Figure 4 Poly(ethene) was essential in the development of radar equipment in the Second World War

The first poly(ethene) washing-up bowls appeared in the shops in 1948, and were soon followed by carrier bags, squeezy bottles and sandwich bags. Sadly, poly(ethene) and some other early polymer materials were overexploited. They were used for all manner of novelties and as cheap but poor substitutes for many natural materials. This gave *plastic* a bad name – the word is often used to describe something which looks cheap and does not last. The reputation still sticks, as an undeserved slur on many of today's excellent materials.

ASSIGNMENT I

a Write an equation for the formation of poly(ethene) from ethene.

b Draw the structural formula of part of a poly(ethene) chain. Explain why poly(ethene) can be thought of as a very large alkane.

c Explain why polymerisation of ethene does not occur when there is no oxygen present, but with too much it gets out of control.

A bonus of being big

A polymer molecule is just a very big molecule. This seems obvious now, but the idea wasn't proposed until 1922 and it met with considerable criticism for the rest of that decade. Since the large molecules in a polymer are chemically similar to much smaller ones, it should be possible to predict many of the polymer's properties from the properties of substances which contain the smaller molecules.

Poly(ethene) is the simplest polymer from a chemical point of view, containing only singly bonded carbon and hydrogen atoms. It should behave like an alkane of high relative molecular mass – and in many ways it does. It burns well, and tends not to react with acids or alkalis. Poly(ethene), like all polymer materials, is a mixture of similar molecules, rather than a pure compound, because different numbers of monomers join together in the chain-building process before polymerisation stops. Therefore, poly(ethene) does not melt sharply: it softens and melts over a temperature range. However, this happens roughly where you would expect it to for a very large alkane.

In contrast, poly(ethene)'s mechanical properties are completely unlike those of similar but smaller molecules.

At this point you need to understand about the attractions which arise between poly(ethene) molecules. These attractions (which result from a type of *induced dipole force*) arise between **all** molecules and are described in **Chemical Ideas 5.2**.

Chemical Ideas 5.4 explains the factors, such as chain length, which affect the physical properties of polymers.

Activity PR2.2 provides you with a very tangible example of how the introduction of forces between polymer chains makes a material stronger.

PR3 *Towards high density polymers*

Karl Ziegler

The poly(ethene) produced by Fawcett and Gibson was what we would today call **low density poly(ethene) (ldpe)**. Although they had some control over the product of their polymerisation process, the low density poly(ethene) they made was still quite messy at a molecular level. The polymer chains were extensively branched. This makes it impossible for the chains to fit together in an organised way: they coil around randomly taking up a lot of room, and hence lower the density of the material.

This relatively disorganised and open structure also lowers the strength of the poly(ethene). The next major advance in poly(ethene) production came with the development of **high density poly(ethene) (hdpe)** which resulted from discoveries made by Karl Ziegler.

The German scientist Karl Ziegler was born in Helsa, near Kassel, in 1898. Encouraged to work hard by his father, the young Ziegler set up a chemical laboratory at home, where he became so advanced in his chemistry studies that he was allowed to omit the first year of his degree course.

At the age of 23 he became a professor and started on a research path which was to have a great influence on the future development of polymerisation processes.

Figure 5 Karl Ziegler

Ziegler catalysts

Ziegler was studying the catalytic effects of **organometallic** compounds. These are compounds which contain covalent metal–carbon bonds. Strange things happened in some of his experiments when he was using an aluminium organometallic compound.

He tracked down the unexpected behaviour to tiny traces of nickel compounds left over as impurities in his apparatus after cleaning. His research group then tried putting as many different transition metal salts as possible with the alkylaluminium compound to see what would happen.

In 1953 Ziegler, with his colleagues Holzkamp and Breil, found that adding titanium compounds easily led to the production of very long chain polymers. Simply passing ethene at atmospheric pressure into a solution of a tiny amount of $TiCl_4$ and $(C_2H_5)_3Al$ in a liquid alkane caused the immediate production of poly(ethene).

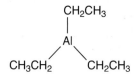

Figure 6 The structure of triethylaluminium, $(C_2H_5)_3Al$

So, like Fawcett and Gibson's discovery of poly(ethene), Ziegler's achievements began accidentally with an impurity.

The poly(ethene) which Ziegler produced had an average relative molecular mass of 3 000 000 with very little branching along the polymer chain. The chains could therefore pack more closely than those made by the original high-pressure process. In this form the poly(ethene) is said to be **crystalline**. This gives the polymer its higher density and greater strength. Figure 7 shows an illustration of how poly(ethene) chains might be packed in hdpe.

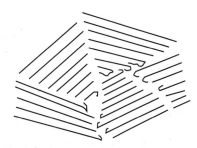

Figure 7 Chain packing in hdpe. When the polymer chains are aligned and packed closely together, the material is said to be crystalline

High density poly(ethene) is often used to make washing-up bowls, water tanks and piping. It is strong and can easily be moulded into complicated shapes: car petrol tanks, for example, can be made to fit neatly into the spaces under the car, something which was impossible with metal tanks. Hdpe is not as easily deformed by heat as ldpe and an early use was as Tupperware food storage containers. The ability to retain shape during heating means that hdpe articles can be heat-sterilised, making hdpe an important material for hospital equipment such as buckets and bed-pans.

Figure 8 Piping and many containers are made from hdpe

ASSIGNMENT 2

Some data for low density and high density poly(ethene) are given in the table below. Use this information to answer the questions which follow.

	Density/ g cm^{-3}	Tensile strength/ MPa	Elongation at fracture/ %	Price/ £ kg^{-1} (1990)
ldpe	0.92	15	600	0.42
hdpe	0.96	29	350	0.49

a Will either polymer sink in water?

b Why is the tensile strength lower for ldpe than for hdpe?

c Use the data to explain the different uses of ldpe and hdpe.

d Suggest why hdpe is more expensive than ldpe.

Ziegler patented hdpe. As a result he became a multimillionaire, and on his 70th birthday he gave $10 million to support further research at the Max Planck Institute where he worked.

Natta and stereoregular polymerisation

Giulio Natta was born in Imperia, Italy, in 1903. He studied chemical engineering at the Milan Polytechnic Institute, and after working at various universities he returned to Milan in 1938 to become Professor of Industrial Chemistry.

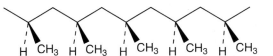

isotactic poly(propene)

Regular structure, so it's crystalline
and tough - like hdpe

Used in sheet and film form for
packaging and containers; used
to make fibres for carpets

atactic poly(propene)

Irregular structure: chains loosely
held, so it's soft and flexible

Used to make roofing materials,
sealants and other weatherproof
coatings

Figure 9 Isotactic and atactic poly(propene)

Natta was convinced that alkylaluminium catalysts were the key to making **stereoregular polymers** – polymers with a regular structure.

In March 1954 he used Ziegler's catalyst to polymerise propene. His reaction mixture contained two forms of poly(propene) – a **crystalline** form and an **amorphous** (non-crystalline) form. He was able to separate them.

In the crystalline form, the methyl groups all have the same orientation along the polymer chain. Natta called this the **isotactic** form. (Iso means *the same* – as in isotope or isobar.) In the amorphous polymer, the methyl groups are randomly orientated and this was called the **atactic** form.

Figure 9 tells you more about these two forms of poly(propene).

Natta went on to develop new catalysts which allowed the polymer molecule to grow outward from the catalyst surface like a growing hair (see Figure 11). These catalysts, known as **Ziegler–Natta catalysts**, have allowed chemists to tailormake specialist polymers with precise properties.

Figure 10 Isotactic poly(propene) is one of the plastics used to make this toy. Its strength and rigidity, combined with its lightness and ease of moulding, make it ideal for this application

The enormous contribution of both Ziegler and Natta to chemistry was rewarded when they jointly received the Nobel Prize for Chemistry in 1963.

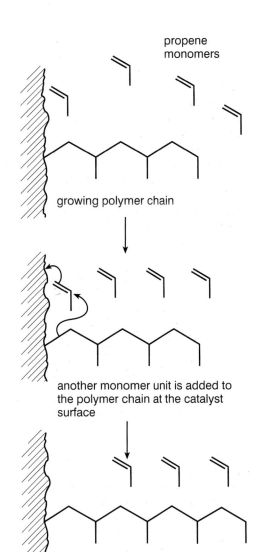

propene monomers

catalyst surface

growing polymer chain

another monomer unit is added to the polymer chain at the catalyst surface

the polymer chain is ready to grow again

Figure 11 Poly(propene) chain growing from a catalyst surface

PR4 *Conducting polymers – breaking the rules*

Conducting polymers bring us almost up to the present day in the story of addition polymers. Several kinds of conducting polymer have been made, but so far their properties have not been exploited. When they are we shall probably see the next significant step forward in the applications of plastics in our lives.

Figure 12 Polymers protect you from lethal electric shocks every time you use electricity. Most polymers are excellent insulators because they have covalent molecular structures. So a conducting polymer is a surprise

ASSIGNMENT 3

On 8 January 1982 *The Wall Street Journal* stated:
"If you had a stable conducting plastic, the number of uses you could ferret out would be astonishing."

Conducting polymers are light, so they are likely to be used in situations where saving weight is important. Suggest some of the situations in which a conducting plastic could be used to good effect.

Before you go any further you will need to have some understanding of two areas of chemistry which may be new to you. **Geometric isomerism** is a phenomenon which arises in alkenes and a number of other types of compound. **Alkynes** are a family of hydrocarbons in which there is a triple carbon to carbon bond.

You can read about geometric isomerism in **Chemical Ideas 3.5**.

Alkynes

Alkynes form a class of unsaturated hydrocarbons. They differ from the alkenes by the presence of a $C≡C$ triple bond instead of a $C=C$ double bond.

Ethyne, the simplest alkyne, has the structure $H—C≡C—H$.

Other alkynes are

propyne $CH_3—C≡C—H$

but-1-yne $CH_3CH_2—C≡C—H$

pent-2-yne $CH_3CH_2—C≡C—CH_3$

Alkynes are named in a similar way to alkenes, but with the suffix -yne instead of -ene.

Ethyne is a linear molecule. There are two groups of electrons around each carbon atom and these are furthest apart when the bond angle is 180°. It may help to make models of some of these alkynes.

ASSIGNMENT 4

a Name the alkynes with the following structures:

i $CH_3—CH_2—C≡C—CH_2—CH_3$

ii $CH_3—CH—C≡C—CH_2—CH_3$
    with CH_3 substituent below the CH

iii (benzene ring)$—C≡C—CH_3$

b Draw structures for the following alkynes:
  i but-2-yne
  ii diphenylethyne
  iii dimethylpent-2-yne.

When ethyne molecules polymerise, the product, poly(ethyne), is a molecule which contains alternating single and double bonds. There is more than one form of this polymer because geometric isomerism causes there to be two ways in which the double bonds can be arranged relative to one another. The structures of two forms of poly(ethyne) are shown in Figure 13; however, of course, mixed *cis* and *trans* arrangements are also possible.

Research chemists in Natta's laboratory first made a mixture of these two forms in 1955. In 1971 Hideki Shirakawa and Sakuji Ikeda at the Tokyo Institute of Technology found that, when they directed a stream of ethyne onto the surface of a solution of a Ziegler–Natta catalyst at −78 °C, only the red *cis*-poly(ethyne) formed.

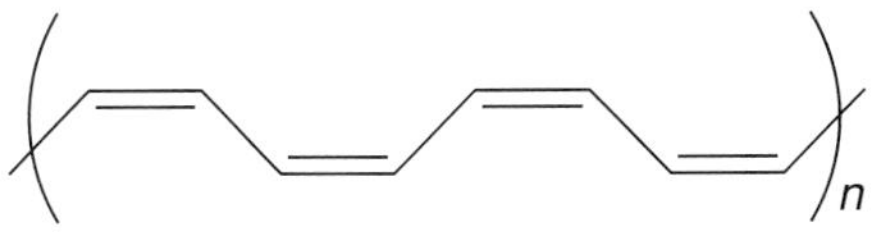

cis-poly(ethyne)

red

unstable; converts to the more
stable *trans* form when warmed

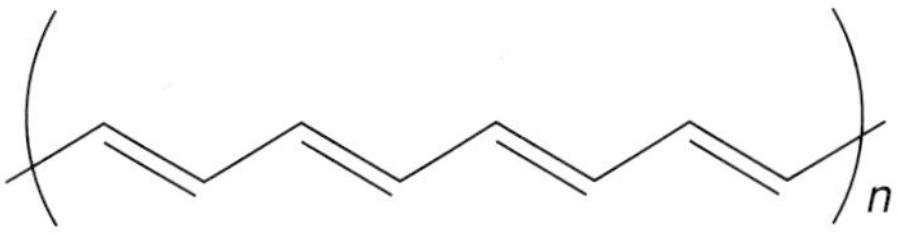

Figure 13 The structures of two forms of poly(ethyne)

trans-poly(ethyne)

blue

the stable form of the polymer

One of Shirakawa's graduate students then repeated
the process, but with catalyst smeared over the inside
walls of a glass reaction vessel. A red film of the *cis*-
polymer again formed, but this time when the film
warmed up it turned silver instead of blue. The student
had made a mistake and used one-thousand-times too
much catalyst. Once again, a mistake was going to lead
to the development of a new polymer.

The graduate student didn't realise the significance of
his discovery. But Alan MacDiarmid did when he visited
Shirakawa's laboratory in 1976. He had been trying to
make metal substitutes at the University of Pennsylvania.
The silvery film became a target for investigation.

Success came a year later. If the silvery material is
'doped' with iodine, a metallic golden sheet forms
which conducts electricity 1 000 000 000 times better
than previous forms of poly(ethyne).

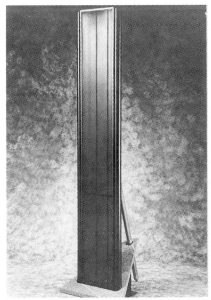

*Figure 14 A conducting polymer is used as the membrane in
this high-performance loudspeaker*

Other monomers can be used to produce conducting polymers.
You can make and test your own conducting polymer in
Activity PR4. The activity also contains an explanation of why
polymers such as poly(ethyne) conduct electricity.

PR5 *The invention of nylon*

Wallace Carothers

Carothers joined the US chemical company Du Pont in
1928. He led a team investigating the production of
polymers that might be used as fibres. This was around
the time when scientists were beginning to understand
more about the structure of polymers, so Carothers
had a scientific basis for his work.

Before you read this section, it will be helpful for you to find
out how to recognise and name carboxylic acids, by reading
Chemical Ideas 13.3.

It was already known that wool and silk have
protein structures, and are polymers involving the
peptide linkage —CONH—. Chemists had also
begun to discover that many natural fibres are
composed of molecules which are very long and
narrow – like the fibres themselves. Figure 15 shows
part of a protein chain in a silk fibre.

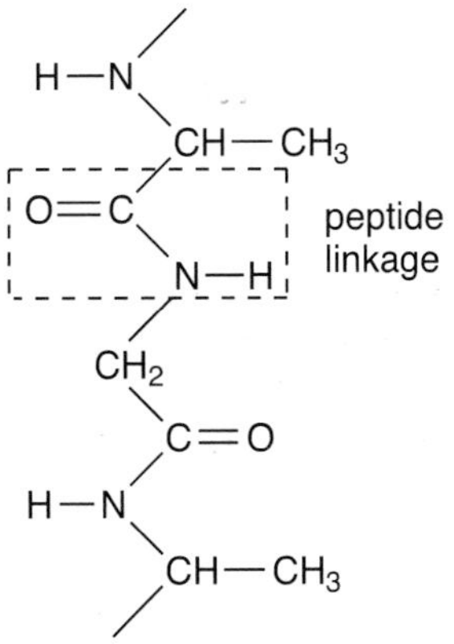

Figure 15 Part of a protein chain in silk

Carothers did not make his discoveries by accident;
he set about systematically trying to create new
polymers. In one series of experiments he decided to
try to make synthetic polymers in which the polymer
molecules were built up in a similar way to the protein
chains in silk and wool. Instead of using amino acids
(the starting materials for proteins), Carothers began
with amines and carboxylic acids.

Amines are organic compounds which contain the —NH_2 functional group. When an —NH_2 group reacts with the —COOH group in a carboxylic acid, an **amide** group —CONH— is formed. In the process, a molecule of water is eliminated. Reactions of this type are known as **condensation reactions**.

carboxylic   amide   amide
acid   group

+H_2O

Figure 16 Nylon replaced silk as the fibre used for parachutes in the Second World War

Carothers used *di*amines and *di*carboxylic acids which contained reactive groups in *two* places in their molecules, so they could link together to form a chain. In this way he was able to make polymers in which monomer units were linked together by amide groups. The process is called **condensation polymerisation** because the individual steps are condensation reactions.

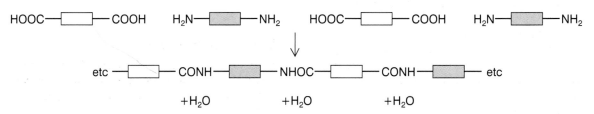

Examples of a diamine and a dicarboxylic acid that can be made to polymerise in this way are

- $H_2NCH_2CH_2CH_2CH_2CH_2CH_2NH_2$ 1,6-diaminohexane
- $HOOCCH_2CH_2CH_2CH_2COOH$ hexanedioic acid.

Because the group linking the monomer groups together is an amide group, these polymers are called **polyamides**. More usually, though, they are known as **nylons**.

The —CONH— group is also found in proteins where it joins amino acids together. You can see this in the structure of the silk protein chain in Figure 15. In this case the secondary amide group is given the special name **peptide group**.

The industrial preparation of nylon from a diamine and a dicarboxylic acid is quite slow. It is easier to demonstrate the process in the laboratory if an **acid chloride** derivative of the acid is used: 1,6-diaminohexane and decanedioyl dichloride react readily and the equation is

$nH_2N(CH_2)_6NH_2$ + $nClCO(CH_2)_8COCl$ →
1,6-diaminohexane   decanedioyl chloride

—$[NH(CH_2)_6$—NH—CO—$(CH_2)_8CO]_n$— + $2nHCl$

Naming nylons

A nylon is named according to the number of carbon atoms in the monomers. If two monomers are used, then the first digit indicates the number of carbon atoms in the diamine and the second digit indicates the number of carbon atoms in the acid. So nylon-6,6 is made from 1,6-diaminohexane and hexanedioic acid. Nylon-6,10 is made from 1,6-diaminohexane and decanedioic acid. This is illustrated below:

- 1,6-diamino*hex*ane + *hex*anedioic acid → nylon-6,6
- 1,6-diamino*hex*ane + *dec*anedioic acid → nylon-6,10

It is also possible to make nylon from a single monomer containing an amine group at one end and an acid group at the other, eg nylon-6 is —$[NH$—$(CH_2)_5$—$CO]_n$— and is made from molecules of $H_2N(CH_2)_5COOH$.

Another important group of condensation polymers are the **polyesters**. These are made by condensation reactions between dicarboxylic acids and *diols*, which have an OH group at each end of their molecule. The monomers are linked together by ester groups (see **Chemical Ideas 13.5**).

Carothers discovered nylon in the spring of 1935, and decided that the best type of nylon to develop would be nylon-5,10. However, Elmer Bolton, the new director of research at Du Pont, argued that nylon-6,6 (formed from 1,6-diaminohexane and hexanedioic acid) was a better material to develop. It is insoluble in common solvents, has a melting point of 263 °C, and can be made from raw materials based on the relatively abundant substance benzene. Bolton said that nylon-6,6 had the best balance of properties and manufacturing cost of the polyamides then known.

If you did not make a nylon in an earlier chemistry or science course, **Activity PR 5.1** allows you to make some nylon-6,10.

In **Activity PR5.2** you can take some nylon molecules apart again.

In 1938 the first product using nylon, 'Dr West's Miracle Toothbrush', appeared. Nylon stockings were seen for the first time in 1939. Most of the nylon produced at this time was used in place of silk for parachute material, so nylon stockings did not become generally available in Britain until the end of the Second World War.

Sadly, Wallace Carothers was not to see the development of his invention. He had been troubled with periods of mental depression since his youth. Despite his success with nylon, and other inventions such as neoprene (the first commercially successful synthetic rubber), he felt that he had not accomplished much and had run out of new ideas.

His unhappiness was compounded by the death of his favourite sister, and on 29 April 1937 he checked into a Philadelphia hotel room and died after drinking a cocktail of lemon juice laced with potassium cyanide.

He was 41. His daughter Jane was born 7 months later.

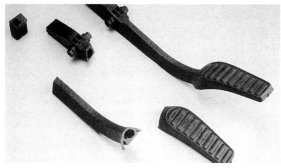

Figure 17 Nylon machine parts

ASSIGNMENT 5

a Name the nylons which contain the following repeating units:

  i —HN—$(CH_2)_6$—NHCO—$(CH_2)_3$—CO—

  ii —HN—$(CH_2)_9$—NHCO—$(CH_2)_7$—CO—

  iii —HN—$(CH_2)_4$—NHCO—$(CH_2)_2$—CO—

b Write out the repeating units and give the names for the polymers formed from the following molecules:

  i $HOOC(CH_2)_5NH_2$

  ii $H_2N(CH_2)_5NH_2$ and $HOOC(CH_2)_5COOH$.

c Nylon-6,8 can be formed by the reaction of a diamine with a diacid dichloride.

  i Write down the structures of the two monomers.

  ii What small molecule is lost when the monomers react?

  iii Draw the structure of the repeating unit in nylon-6,8.

Plastic machine parts

You know that nylon is widely used as a fibre, but it is also a very important **engineering plastic** – a material which can be used in place of a metal in things like machine parts.

Its usefulness arises from its excellent combination of strength, toughness, rigidity and abrasion resistance, as well as its chemical unreactivity in many environments. As an engineering material it is far superior to poly(ethene) or poly(propene). The polymer chains in nylon need only be about half as long as hdpe chains to show the same strength. The more powerful intermolecular forces which act between nylon chains are the source of this increased strength.

At this point it will be helpful to read **Chemical Ideas 5.3** to learn about the intermolecular forces responsible for nylon's strength.

Activities PR5.3 and **PR5.4** will help to illustrate the ideas you are reading about.

In and out of fashion

Towards the end of the 1970s, people's tastes were moving away from nylon clothes and back towards the look and softer feel of natural fibres.

One of the problems with nylon fibres is that they are **hydrophobic** – they repel water. The nylon fabrics produced did not absorb moisture, and did not allow water vapour to escape through the weave. This made them rather sweaty and uncomfortable to wear (although, of course, the hydrophobicity of nylon could be used to advantage in such clothes as swimsuits and waterproof cagoules).

Chemical companies were facing a big downturn in the demand for their nylon, bringing major financial losses, but the high cost of developing a completely new polymer on the scale necessary to replace nylon was too high. To make things worse, the machines which had been specifically designed for making nylon fabrics could not be used for cotton or other natural fibres.

ICI's answer to this problem was to redevelop their nylon so that it bore a much closer resemblance to natural fibres. The first steps were to slim down the thickness of the nylon filament to the equivalent of cotton, and to add a delustrant to the fibre to reduce the shiny appearance. The major breakthrough came when they developed a process for changing the shape and texture of the nylon yarn. They were able to create a large number of loops along the nylon filaments by blowing bundles of them apart with high-pressure air.

The new fibre was called *Tactel*. When the fibre is woven, the loops give the material a softness and texture similar to cotton.

Further refinement of the Tactel family of yarns has led to fabrics which are waterproof but which 'breathe'. For example, very fine yarns have been developed which allow water *vapour* to escape through the weave but do not allow *liquid* water in. Material made from these yarns is ideal for lightweight raincoats and ski-wear.

The solution to the problem of falling demand for nylon was not chemical – it did not involve the creation of a new polymer to suit the new fashion – but *technological*. It involved discovering new ways of handling the existing polymer to produce materials of the type people wanted.

PR6 *Kevlar*

The first aramids

After the invention of nylon, chemists began to make sense of the relationship between a polymer's structure and its properties. They were able to predict strengths for particular structures, and research was directed at inventing a 'super fibre'. In the early 1960s, Du Pont were looking for a fibre with the 'heat resistance of asbestos and the stiffness of glass'.

Figure 18 Tactel fabrics 'breathe' but remain waterproof

The aromatic polyamides seemed promising candidates: the planar aromatic rings should result in rigid polymer chains and, because the ratio of carbon to hydrogen is high, they require relatively large concentrations of oxygen before they burn.

The first polymeric aromatic amide – **aramid** – was made from 3-aminobenzoic acid. The polymer could be made into fibres and was fire-resistant, but it was not particularly strong. The zig-zag nature of the chains prevented the molecules from aligning themselves properly.

A polymer was needed which had straighter chains, and which could be made from readily available and reasonably cheap starting materials. An example is shown in Figure 19.

This substance turned out to have all the right properties except one. The problem was its insolubility, which made it precipitate out of solution before long polymer chains had been able to grow.

The only suitable solvent seemed to be concentrated sulphuric acid. The company engineers were not impressed! However, the remarkable properties of the 'super fibre' were enough to encourage investment in a plant which uses concentrated sulphuric acid as a solvent. The polymeric material produced was called *Kevlar*.

Figure 19 The molecular structure of Kevlar

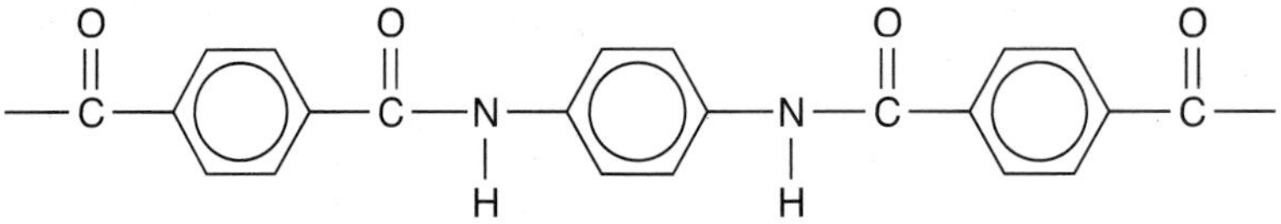

The flat molecules are held together by hydrogen bonds to form a sheet

Fibre axis

ASSIGNMENT 6

a Draw out a small section of the structure of the polymer which would be made from 3-aminobenzoic acid.

b The intermolecular forces in Kevlar are disrupted by concentrated sulphuric acid. That is why it dissolves. How do you think the forces are affected?

c Kevlar fibres are produced by squirting the solution in concentrated sulphuric acid into water. Suggest why the polymer precipitates out when the solution is diluted in this way.

Why is Kevlar so strong?

Kevlar is a fibre which is fire-resistant, extremely strong and flexible. It also has a low density because it is made from light atoms: carbon, hydrogen, oxygen and nitrogen. Weight for weight, Kevlar is around five times stronger than steel! One of its early uses was to replace steel cords in car tyres: the Kevlar tyres are lighter and last longer than steel-reinforced tyres.

Kevlar is strong because of the way the rigid, linear molecules are packed together. The chains line up parallel to one another, held together by hydrogen bonds. This leads to sheets of molecules. The sheets then stack together regularly around the fibre axis to give an almost perfectly ordered structure. This is illustrated in Figure 20.

The important thing to realise about Kevlar is that it adopts this crystalline structure because of the way the polymer is processed to produce the fibre. And this is a consequence of the work put in by the Du Pont team.

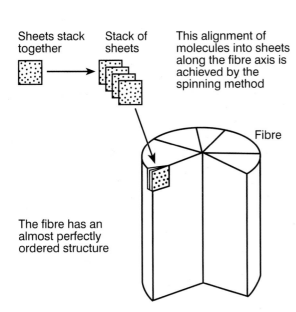

Sheets stack together → Stack of sheets → This alignment of molecules into sheets along the fibre axis is achieved by the spinning method

Fibre

The fibre has an almost perfectly ordered structure

Figure 20 An illustration of the crystalline structure of Kevlar

Figure 21 Leading racing motorcyclists wear protective suits containing Kevlar (the small photo shows Kevlar fibres). The polymer's abrasion resistance is better than leather, the traditional material

Developing a market for Kevlar

A full-scale commercial plant for the production of Kevlar required an investment of $400 million. It was therefore essential that there would be a market for the product. Although Kevlar has some remarkable properties it could not simply replace existing materials. Detailed market development had to take place alongside technical development. In other words, new uses had to be found for the new polymer.

Many uses have now been developed in addition to replacing steel in tyres. Kevlar ropes have 20 times the strength of steel ropes of the same weight. They last longer too. A stiffer form of Kevlar is used in aircraft wings, where its strength combined with its low density is important. And it's ideal for making bullet-proof vests and jackets for fencers.

You can compare models and structures for Kevlar and a nylon in **Activity PR6.**

PR7 *Taking temperature into account*

PEEK

The story of PEEK begins in the early 1960s when John Rose, a chemist at University College London, moved to the Plastics Division of ICI. He was put in charge of a team which had a brief to develop new polymers.

Rose decided to investigate high temperature materials. He knew that these would need to have high melting points and also be resistant to oxidation. For these reasons, he decided that his new polymers would have to be based on aromatic compounds.

The team tried to join aromatic units together in as many ways as possible. They had to develop new types of reactions and solve many other problems along the way. They also had to look for monomers which were reasonably cheap to make.

Out of all this came PEEK. Its structure is shown in Figure 22.

Figure 22 The equation for the formation of poly(ether-ether-ketone), PEEK

Although it is expensive, the very wide range of applications of PEEK made it worth developing.

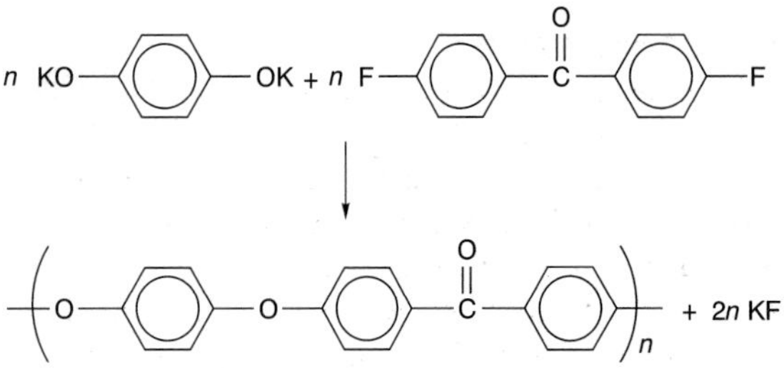

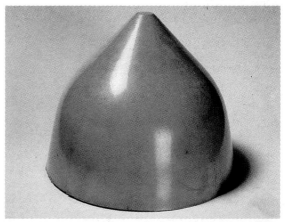

Figure 23 PEEK is a polymer which can withstand very high temperatures. For example, it is used to make plastic kettles and for the nose-cones of missiles (shown here). Polymers have been used for some time in the passenger compartments of cars and airliners, but PEEK is used inside the engines *where it is really hot*

You can find out more about the way polymers are affected by temperature in **Chemical Ideas 5.4**.

Activity PR7 looks at the effect of temperature on an everyday substance – bubble gum.

Mixing it

In this unit, you have by no means come across all the polymers which are available to manufacturers. But suppose you have a particular application in mind. Even a full list would not contain enough substances to allow you to be sure of finding one with just the properties you were seeking. You can bet that at some point you would say, "What we need is something like X but which behaves a bit like Y."

These days, it is far less expensive to modify existing polymer materials than to develop new ones. So, often, well-known polymers are combined to produce new materials which show some of the properties of the individual components. For example, sheets of different polymers can be stacked together to form *laminates*, or polymers can be mixed to produce *composites*.

It is also possible to mix things at a molecular level and to make *polymer alloys*, in which polymers are mixed when molten to give a new material with the desired properties, or to make *copolymers*, or to add *plasticisers*.

You can read more about copolymers and plasticisers in **Chemical Ideas 5.4**.

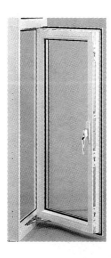

Figure 24 Unplasticised pvc (upvc) is used for making replacement window frames. The more flexible, plasticised form is used for gutters and drainpipes

PR8 *Throwing it away ... or not?*

Is there a problem?

Figure 25 shows some average figures for solid household waste in EC countries. Quantities are given as percentages by mass of total waste.

Much of our waste is disposed of by dumping in landfill sites, but sites are getting harder to find and waste disposal is becoming more expensive. Alternatives to dumping, such as recycling or incineration, and the use of degradable plastics, are beginning to look more satisfactory and more economical.

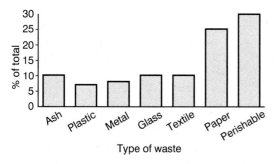

Figure 25 Types of household waste in EC countries

ASSIGNMENT 7

a Suggest why plastic waste is seen as a problem when it accounts for only about 7% of EC solid household waste by mass.

b The cost of disposing of solid waste in Tokyo is about £200 per tonne; in New York City it is about £80 per tonne. In a typical non-urban UK site the cost is around £10 per tonne. Suggest why it costs so much to get rid of waste in these two cities.

Degradable plastics

Most plastics are not degradable because decomposer organisms (bacteria and fungi) do not have the enzymes needed to break them down. There are two important categories of degradable plastic.

1 **Biopolymers.** These are polymers made by living organisms, which decomposers are able to break down.
2 Synthetic plastics which are designed to break down naturally. Three types are commonly used:

- polymers which break down in sunlight – **photodegradable** plastics
- **synthetic biodegradable** plastics which are broken down by bacteria
- **dissolving plastics** which dissolve in water.

Biopolymers

Poly(hydroxybutanoate), or PHB, is a natural polyester made by certain bacteria and used by them as a source of energy. Micro-organisms found in the soil, and in streams and the sea, are able to break the polymer down. PHB degradation in the environment is usually complete within 9 months. But there is a price to pay: PHB is about 15 times more expensive than poly(ethene).

Figure 26 Bottles made from biodegradable plastic, in various stages of degradation

---

Activity PR8.1 is based on an article about the biopolymer poly(hydroxybutanoate), or PHB, which is marketed by ZENECA as *Biopol*.

Photodegradability

Carbonyl groups (C=O) absorb radiation in the wavelength range 270–360 nm (about 10^{15} Hz frequency). This corresponds to light in the near ultra-violet region of the spectrum. These groups can be incorporated into polymer chains to act as energy trappers. The trapped energy causes fission of bonds in the neighbourhood of the carbonyl group, and the polymer chain breaks down into short fragments which can then biodegrade.

_____ **ASSIGNMENT 8** _____

a Suggest some suitable uses for photodegradable polymers.

b Suggest some situations where their use would be unsuitable.

c What happens to a photodegradable polymer if it is disposed of by landfill?

Synthetic biodegradable plastics

Some plastic bags are made of poly(ethene) which has starch granules encapsulated in it. The starch is digested by micro-organisms in the soil when the plastic bag is buried. The bag then breaks up into very small pieces of leftover poly(ethene) which have a large surface area and which therefore biodegrade more quickly.

Dissolving plastics

If soiled laundry from a hospital is mishandled, there is a risk of infection. The risk can be avoided by making the laundry bags out of a dissolving plastic. The dirty linen is safely contained until the bag is placed in the wash – then the bag dissolves and the washing is let out.

The dissolving plastic which is used is poly(ethenol). It is a new synthetic polymer, made from another polymer, poly(ethenyl ethanoate), by the process illustrated in Figure 27.

The extent of reaction can be controlled by adjusting either the temperature or the reaction time. The plastic's solubility depends on the percentage of acid groups which have been removed. Table 1 shows how the two are related. Different solubilities give the plastic different uses.

% of OH groups	Solubility in water
100–99	insoluble
99–97	soluble in hot water
96–90	soluble in warm water
below 90	soluble in cold water

Table 1 Solubility of poly(ethenol)

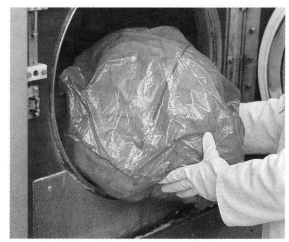

Figure 28 This hospital laundry bag has a section made of dissolving plastic, which dissolves in the washing machine to release the dirty washing

_____ **ASSIGNMENT 9** _____

a What type of intermolecular bonding will there be between the chains of poly(ethenol)?

b Explain why nearly pure poly(ethenol) is insoluble even in hot water.

c How is the intermolecular bonding in this polymer affected if ethanoate groups are still present?

d Explain the effect on solubility of increasing the number of ester groups in the polymer.

e Hospital laundry bags are made from the form of the polymer which is soluble in only hot water. Suggest why this form is chosen.

f Suggest some other uses for poly(ethenol) film.

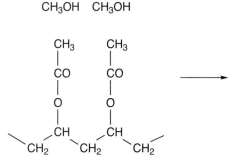

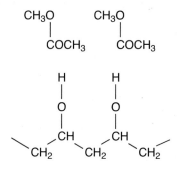

methanol reacts with
poly(ethenyl ethanoate)

some of the acid groups on
the side chains of the polymer
are removed and molecules of the
new ester, methyl ethanoate, are formed

Figure 27 Formation of poly(ethenol) by ester exchange

Dissolving polymers have another medical use – as sutures or stitches in surgery.

Many materials can be used for the suture thread. Once the surgeon has chosen to use soluble thread, a decision is made about how quickly it should dissolve and the appropriate poly(ethenol) is selected.

You can study the behaviour of poly(ethenol) in **Activity PR8.2**.

Degrade or recycle?

Making any object, including a plastic one, requires energy. Some of the energy is needed to make the material – in this case a polymer – and the rest is required for fabrication (turning the polymer into the finished article).

Table 2 takes some familiar objects as examples, and shows how the energy used in production is divided between making the plastic and fabricating the object.

Object	Energy used/%	
	Plastic	Fabrication
5-litre container (pvc)	85	15
5-litre container (hdpe)	90	10
5-litre container (lpde)	94	6
Meat tray (polystyrene)	83	17

Table 2 Energy used in the production of some everyday objects

Most of the energy is used to make the plastics, so from these data alone you would conclude that recycling was worthwhile from the point of view of saving energy.

The situation is not as simple as recycling glass. Most glass is of only one type and comes in only three colours. Even so, it is often only economical to recycle glass if the disposer goes to the bottle bank as part of a normal journey. It is not economical if a special journey is made.

How much does it cost to collect and sort the plastic waste? And what can recycled plastic be used for? There are many applications for which its use is inappropriate. For example, most people do not like the idea of having their food wrapped in recycled plastic.

However, there are 60 companies in the UK which, between them, recycle about 150 000 tonnes of polymers per year. Two-thirds of the recycled plastic comes from industrial waste, and most of this is 'pure' plastic, eg unplasticised pvc from the makers of window frames, and old milk crates and car battery cases which are made from poly(propene).

It is not yet economical to recycle mixed plastics from domestic waste. When it is, it would be nice if we could go back to today's plastic waste to sort and recycle that too. That will not be possible if we spread our plastics around in landfill sites with all our other waste. So perhaps we should bury plastic waste separately so that future generations have a resource which might be worth recovering.

ASSIGNMENT 10

a What problems might there be in operating a 'plastic bank' system for collecting household plastic waste, compared with a 'bottle bank'?

b Use the data given below for ldpe, hdpe and pvc to devise a scheme for separating these plastics. Present your solution in the form of a flow chart.

Polymer	Density/g cm^{-3}
ldpe	0.92
hdpe	0.96
pvc	1.40

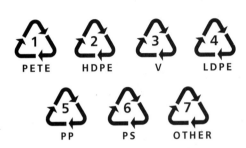

Figure 29 Recycling symbols help people to sort plastics into categories. These symbols are used throughout the USA and are appearing on items within the EC

PR9 Summary

In this unit you have seen how our ideas about polymers and their structures have developed. As a result of this development, chemists have learned how to build up simple molecules into very large polymer chains. The polymers they have produced are new materials with unique sets of properties not possessed by any natural substances.

You have learned about addition and condensation polymerisation, and how the properties of polymers depend on their structures and the intermolecular forces between the chains. Hydrogen bonds, dipole–dipole forces and induced dipole forces are important in this context.

Two classes of organic compounds – alkenes and alkynes – have been important to the development of this story, as has been the phenomenon of geometric isomerism. You have also learned about carboxylic acids, and looked at their reactions with amines.

Finally, you have considered some environmental issues connected with the disposal and recycling of plastics.

Activity PR9 allows you to check that your notes cover the important chemistry contained in this unit.

WHAT'S IN A MEDICINE?

Why a unit on WHAT'S IN A MEDICINE?

This unit introduces the importance of the pharmaceutical industry, both to the personal health of the individual and the financial health of the nation. Through a study of aspirin it illustrates many of the principal activities involved in the development of a medicine. Finally, it considers the problems of development and safety testing.

During the unit, you will study the application of instrumental methods for determining the structure of molecules, and practise extraction of a natural product, organic synthesis and the use of test-tube reactions to identify functional groups. The chemistry of alcohols, phenols and carboxylic acids is studied in some detail and there is an experimental investigation of the conditions necessary for esterification.

Overview of chemical principles

In this unit you will learn more about …

ideas introduced in earlier units in this course
- atomic spectroscopy (**Elements of Life**)
- the electromagnetic spectrum (**Elements of Life**)
- homologous series of organic compounds (**Developing Fuels**)
- alcohols (**Developing Fuels**)
- the interaction of radiation with molecules (**The Atmosphere**)

… as well as learning new ideas about
- molecular structure determination
- mass spectrometry
- infra-red spectroscopy
- nuclear magnetic resonance spectroscopy
- phenols
- carboxylic acids
- esters.

WM1 *The development of modern ideas about medicines*

This unit is about medicines and the pharmaceutical industry. Many pharmaceuticals are complex compounds, but in this unit we focus on the chemistry of a simple and familiar substance – aspirin.

The active ingredients of **medicines** are **drugs** – substances which alter the way your body works. If your body is already working normally the drug will not be beneficial, and if the drug throws the body a long way off balance it may even be a **poison**. When your body is working wrongly a medicine prevents things getting worse and can help bring about a cure, for example when you take aspirin or penicillin. Not all drugs are medicines: alcohol and nicotine are not medicines but they are certainly drugs. Some drugs, eg opium, may or may not be medicines depending on your state of health.

The study of drugs and their action is called **pharmacology**; the art and science of making and dispensing medicines is called **pharmacy**.

People have been using medicines for thousands of years – most of that time with no idea how they worked. Their effectiveness was discovered by trial and error, and sometimes there were disastrous mistakes.

Today's medicines are increasingly designed to have specific effects, something which is becoming easier as we learn more about the body's chemistry and begin to understand the intricate detail of the complex molecules from which we are made. Work at this level comes into the field of **molecular pharmacology** and you will gain a little insight into this in a later unit, **Medicines by Design**.

Activity WM1 tells you about the importance of the UK pharmaceutical industry and also introduces you to medicines used by a very different kind of society in the Amazonian forest.

WM2 *Medicines from nature*

Modern pharmacy has its origins in folklore, and the history of medicine abounds with herbal and folk remedies. Many of these can be explained in present-day terms and the modern pharmaceutical industry investigates 'old wive's tales' to see if they lead to important new medicines.

One such tale is the 'Doctrine of Signatures' which proposes that illnesses can often be cured by plants which are associated with them. A simple example is the use of dock leaves (which grow near nettles) to attempt to cure nettle stings. However, they have not been found to have any scientific validity here.

Figure 1 Feverfew has been used since ancient times for the treatment of migraine; research in the 1970s confirmed that it was an effective medicine for this disorder

Medicines from willow bark

Marshy ground was thought to breed fevers, and so the bark and leaves of willow trees which often grew there were tried as a remedy against fever.

In 400 BC, Hippocrates recommended a brew of willow leaves to ease the pain of childbirth, and in 1763 The Reverend Stone, an English clergyman, used a willow bark brew to reduce fevers.

He argued by the 'Doctrine of Signatures': 'As this tree delights in a moist or wet soil, where agues chiefly abound, I could not help applying the general maxim, that many remedies lie not far off from their causes.'

The 'Doctrine of Signatures' is no longer a current pharmaceutical theory, but it is now known that there is a compound in willow bark and leaves which does have an effect in curing fevers.

Figure 2 Extracts from willow trees have been used in medicine for thousands of years

'Culpeper's Herbal'

Nicholas Culpeper (1616–1654) rose to fame in the wave of enthusiasm for astrological botany which swept England in the 17th century. He believed that plants were 'owned' by certain planets, stars, etc. He also believed that the celestial bodies were the causes of diseases, and that illness could be cured by administering a plant 'owned' by an opposing body, or sometimes by a sympathetic body.

His *Herbal* has been published since 1640 under many titles and contains many references like the following one for the willow.

Willow tree

The leaves bruised with pepper, and drank in wine, help in the wind-colic.

It grows 60–70 feet (18–21 m) high, has a rough bark and narrow, sharp-pointed leaves on its whitish grey branches. It produces yellow male and green female catkins. Also called the white willow.

Where to find it: *Beside running streams and in other moist places.*

Flowering time: *Spring*

Astrology: *The Moon owns it.*

Medicinal virtues: *The leaves, bark and seeds are used to staunch the bleeding of wounds and other fluxes of blood in man or woman. The decoction helps to stay vomiting and also thin, hot, sharp salt distillations from the head upon the lungs, causing consumption.*

Water gathered from the willow when it flowers, by slitting the bark, is good for dimness of sight or films that grow over the eyes. If drank it provokes the urine, and clears the face and skin from spots and discolourings. The decoction of the leaves, or bark in wine, takes away scurf and dandruff, if used as a wash.

Modern uses: *The bark of the willow contains salicin from which aspirin is derived. Herbalists use the bark and leaves as an astringent tonic and as a preventive treatment against diseases that are apt to recur, such as malaria.*

The decoction, made by boiling 1 oz (28 g) of bark in 1 pt (568 ml) of water until the mixture measures 1 pt (568 ml) is given in doses of 1–2 fl oz (28–56 ml) for fevers, diarrhoea and dysentery. The powdered root can be taken in sweetened water in doses of one teaspoonful. An infusion of the leaves – 1 oz (28 g) to 1 pt (568 ml) of boiling water – is a useful digestive tonic.

Figure 3 Nicholas Culpeper the 17th-century herbalist

The substance extracted in the recipe you have just read has no pharmacological effect by itself. The body converts it by hydrolysis and oxidation into the active chemical.

Figure 4 Sixteenth-century herb gathering

In **Activity WM2** you can produce some of the fever-curing chemical by hydrolysing and oxidising an extract of willow bark.

WM3 *Identifying the active chemical in willow bark*

In **Activity WM2** you saw how thin layer chromatography could be used to show that the pharmacologically active chemical in willow bark is possibly salicylic acid. (It has been shown that this is indeed the compound, and the acid is named after the Latin name for willow: **salix**.)

How can we find out the chemical structure of compounds like salicylic acid? One way is to use chemical reactions, and in this section you will learn how chemical tests reveal the presence of particular functional groups in salicylic acid.

Some —OH group chemistry

A knowledge of some relatively simple test-tube experiments can often be used effectively in the identification of unknown substances. For example, you may already know about the use of bromine solutions for detecting double bonds between carbon atoms in alkenes.

Three chemical tests are particularly helpful in providing clues about the structure of salicylic acid.

1. An aqueous solution of the compound is weakly acidic.
2. Salicylic acid reacts with alcohols (like ethanol) to produce compounds called esters. Esters have strong odours, often of fruit or flowers.
3. A neutral solution of iron(III) chloride turns an intense pink colour when salicylic acid is added.

Tests 1 and 2 are characteristic of **carboxylic acids** (compounds containing the —COOH functional group); test 3 indicates the presence of a **phenol** group (an —OH group attached to a benzene ring).

In **Chemical Ideas 13.4** you can find out about the behaviour of the —OH group in an alcohol, a phenol and a carboxylic acid.

Activity WM3 allows you to investigate the behaviour of —OH groups in alcohols, phenols and carboxylic acids.

WM4 *Instrumental analysis*
Making use of infra-red spectroscopy

Although chemical tests provide evidence for the presence of carboxylic acid and phenol groups in salicylic acid, instrumental techniques are today's most efficient research tools. In this section you will learn about three frequently used instrumental techniques:

- mass spectrometry
- infra-red (i.r.) spectroscopy
- nuclear magnetic resonance (n.m.r.) spectroscopy.

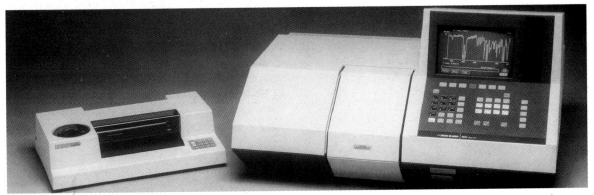

Figure 5 An i.r. spectrophotometer: the sample is inserted in the chamber in the centre of the machine; the spectrum can be viewed on the screen, or a trace can be drawn out by the chart recorder on the left

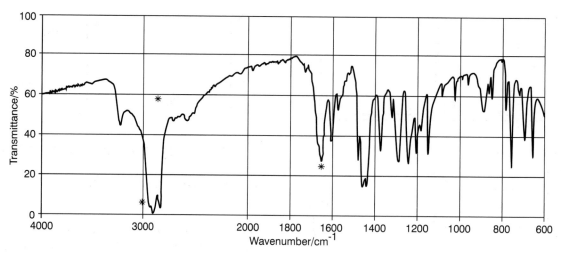

Figure 6 The i.r. spectrum of salicylic acid

One of the very first things which would be done with any unidentified, new substance is to record its **infra-red (i.r.) spectrum**. Figure 6 shows the i.r. spectrum of salicylic acid.

Chemical Ideas 6.7 tells you about infra-red spectroscopy.

An i.r. spectrum measures the extent to which electromagnetic radiation in part of the i.r. region is transmitted through a sample of a substance. The frequency ranges which are absorbed provide important clues about the functional groups which are present. The functional groups absorb at similar frequencies in many different compounds so an absorption pattern provides a kind of fingerprint of the molecule.

The i.r. spectrum of salicylic acid shows clear evidence of the presence of the C=O and —OH groups.

ASSIGNMENT I

Examine the i.r. spectrum of salicylic acid shown in Figure 6. Compare the absorptions marked by an asterisk (*) with the characteristic absorption bands of the different functional groups listed in **Chemical Ideas 6.7**, and suggest which groupings could be responsible.

Do these groupings correspond to what you know of the formula for this compound?

Evidence from n.m.r spectroscopy

A second instrumental technique which would be applied to an unidentified compound is **nuclear magnetic resonance (n.m.r.) spectroscopy**. This investigates the different chemical environments in which the nuclei of one particular element are situated.

Often this element is hydrogen. The nucleus of a hydrogen atom consists of just one proton, and the proton n.m.r. spectrum for salicylic acid is shown in Figure 7. The spectrum shows that salicylic acid contains

- one proton in a —COOH environment
- one proton in a phenolic —OH environment
- four protons attached to a benzene ring.

In this case, the n.m.r. spectrum is quite complicated because all six hydrogen atom nuclei are in different environments in the molecule, and five of them give signals which are close together. Although n.m.r. spectroscopy is of limited value in this case, it provides a powerful technique for determination of the structure of many organic compounds.

You can learn more about n.m.r spectroscopy by working through **Chemical Ideas 6.8**.

The n.m.r. spectrum in Figure 7(a) is a high-resolution spectrum: to explain this in full would be beyond the scope of this unit. The spectrum in Figure 7(b) represents a low-resolution spectrum: information is lost in such a spectrum, but it is much simpler and the positions of the signals still tell us about the environments of the hydrogen atoms.

A combination of i.r. and n.m.r. spectroscopy shows that salicylic acid has an —OH group and a —COOH group both attached to a benzene ring; in other words, a better name for salicylic acid is hydroxybenzoic acid. However, there are three possible isomeric hydroxybenzoic acids: 2-hydroxybenzoic acid, 3-hydroxybenzoic acid and 4-hydroxybenzoic acid. A decision about which isomer salicylic acid is can be made by analysis of the **mass spectrum** of salicylic acid.

(a)

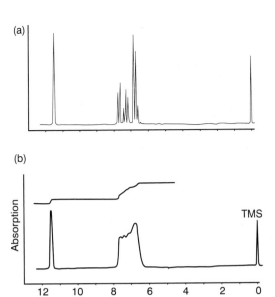

(b)

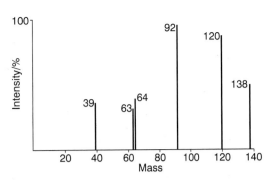

Figure 8 *The mass spectrum of salicylic acid*

Figure 7 The proton n.m.r. spectrum of salicylic acid (the signal labelled TMS is made by a reference compound called tetramethylsilane)

ASSIGNMENT 2

Examine the structure of 2-hydroxybenzoic acid shown below. Explain why the following hydrogen atom nuclei are in different environments within the molecule:

a hydrogen atoms 1 and 6

b hydrogen atoms 3 and 4.

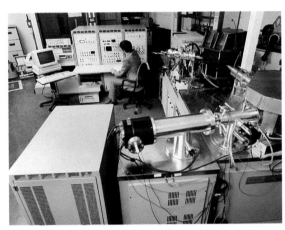

2-hydroxybenzoic acid

The mass spectrum of salicylic acid

Figure 8 shows the mass spectrum of salicylic acid. Chemists can use information contained in spectra like this to find the structures of compounds.

The mass spectrum shows signals which correspond to positively charged ions formed from the parent compound, and fragment ions into which it has broken down. The parent ion signal at mass=138 confirms that the substance has an empirical formula of $C_7H_6O_3$.

The way in which a parent ion breaks down is characteristic of that compound. In this case, comparison with a database of known mass spectra

identifies salicylic acid as 2-hydroxybenzoic acid. Thinking about the way that the 3-hydroxybenzoic acid and the 4-hydroxybenzoic acid isomers would break down also leads to the conclusion that these isomers could not form some of the fragments observed in the mass spectrum of salicylic acid.

Chemical Ideas 6.9 provides you with an introduction to mass spectrometry.

Figure 9 *A modern mass spectrometer*

Activities WM4.1 and **WM4.2** use accurate M_r values, isotope peaks and a database to lead you to the formula of salicylic acid. You can work through **Activity WM4.1** if the mass spectrometer computer programs are available, or **Activity WM4.2** if they are not. Both activities show you how chemists can use fragmentation patterns to deduce or confirm a molecular structure.

Drawing the evidence together

1. Chemical tests showed the presence of a phenolic —OH group and a carboxylic acid —COOH group.
2. Infra-red spectroscopy showed that the —OH and —C=O groups were certainly present.

3. Nuclear magnetic resonance spectroscopy confirmed that there were hydrogen atoms in three types of environment: —COOH, —OH attached directly to a benzene ring and —H attached directly to a benzene ring.

4. Mass spectrometry showed that salicylic acid was the same compound as that stored in the database as 2-hydroxybenzoic acid. The structure of 2-hydroxybenzoic acid is

5. The mass spectrum fragmentation pattern showed that the structure could not be

or

WM5 *The synthesis of salicylic acid and aspirin*

Medicines which are 'natural products', ie those which come directly from plants, may be difficult to obtain when needed. The supply may be seasonal, may depend on weather conditions and may be liable to contamination.

Chemists, therefore, do not want to rely on willow trees as their source of 2-hydroxybenzoic acid. Once the chemical structure of the active compound in a plant is known, chemists can instead begin to search for ways of producing it artificially.

Simple inorganic substances, such as aluminium chloride, can be synthesised directly from their elements, but larger, more complex molecules cannot be made directly in this way. Instead, chemists search for a compound which is already known, and which has a similar structure to the required compound and can be modified.

The compound phenol was already well known in the pharmaceutical industry – it has germicidal properties. It was also readily available as a product from heating coal in gas-works. Its molecular structure differs from that of 2-hydroxybenzoic acid by only one functional group. The problem in synthesis is to introduce this extra group in the right position and without disrupting the rest of the molecule.

ASSIGNMENT 3

Compare the structural formulae of the starting and finishing compounds

and

What extra atoms have to be added?

Refer to an organic chemistry textbook to find out the conditions needed to bring about this change.

In this particular case, by careful control of the conditions, carbon dioxide can be combined directly with phenol to give 2-hydroxybenzoic acid. This general method is known as the Kolbe synthesis (details can be found in many organic chemistry textbooks) and an industrial version of it was developed by the German chemist Felix Hofmann. Thus synthetic 2-hydroxybenzoic acid of reliable purity became available and it was marketed by the chemical company Bayer.

Figure 10 Felix Hofmann who first synthesised 2-hydroxybenzoic acid and aspirin

Synthetic 2-hydroxybenzoic acid was widely used for curing fevers and suppressing pain, but reports began to accumulate of irritating effects on the mouth, gullet and stomach. Clearly the new wonder medicine had unpleasant side-effects. Chemists had a new problem – could they modify the structure to reduce the irritating effects, whilst still retaining the beneficial ones?

Hofmann prepared a range of compounds by making slight modifications to the structure of 2-hydroxybenzoic acid. His father was a sufferer from chronic rheumatism and Hofmann tried out each of the new preparations on him to test the effects. This was a bit more primitive than modern testing of medicines. It is not recorded what Hofmann senior thought of all this, but he survived long enough for his son to prepare, in 1898, a derivative which was as effective as 2-hydroxybenzoic acid and much less unpleasant to use.

The effective product was 2-ethanoylhydroxybenzoic acid (or acetylsalicylic acid). This is known as *aspirin*.

Aspirin belongs to a class of compounds known as **esters**, and Hofmann used the process of **esterification** to produce aspirin. **Chemical Ideas 13.5** tells you about esters and esterification.

Activity WM5 allows you to investigate the conditions which are necessary for converting 2-hydroxybenzoic acid into aspirin.

*Figure 11 Meadowsweet (*Spiraea ulmaria*), from which salicylic acid was first extracted in 1835; aspirin got its name from 'a' for acetyl (an older word for ethanoyl) and 'spirin' for spirsaüre (the German word for salicylic acid)*

WM6 *Delivering the product*

Protecting the discovery

To develop a new medicine costs an enormous amount of money. The price charged by the pharmaceutical company must be sufficient not only to cover the costs of production and marketing, but also to recover the development costs. If other companies could simply copy the medicine, they would be able to sell it at much lower prices. This is where **patents** become important.

When a pharmaceutical company discovers a new medicine, it takes out patents to protect the discovery. Patents only apply to one country, so several patents must be taken out to prevent companies in other countries manufacturing the medicine. When the medicine is approved, the pharmaceutical company markets it under a trade name or *brand name*. Patents only last for a specific amount of time, but while the patent is in force, no other company can manufacture the medicine in that country.

Pharmaceuticals are usually complex compounds with long and unwieldy chemical names. For convenience they are known by shorter, trivial names. These are called 'generic' names in the pharmaceutical business.

So most pharmaceuticals have three names:

- their chemical name
- their generic name
- their brand name.

An example is the compound 2-(4-(2-methylpropyl)phenyl) propanoic acid, known by the generic name *ibuprofen*, and marketed as Brufen (by Boots), Lidifen (by Berk) and Motrin (by Upjohn).

By the time a patent runs out, the company which discovered the medicine will hopefully have sold enough of it to cover its development costs. Afterwards, any company can produce and sell the medicine – usually under its own, new brand name. That's why there are so many ibuprofen tablets around.

In 1899, when the Bayer company in Germany first decided to market 2-ethanoylhydroxybenzoic acid, it was not a new compound, so the compound itself could not be protected by patents. However, the company patented the process by which it was made and also sought copyright for the trade name *Aspirin* in as many countries as possible.

The trade protection lasted until the First World War, when other countries were no longer able to obtain aspirin from Germany. American firms were restrained by the patent agreements from producing it and UK chemists were busy with the war effort, but an Australian pharmacist, George Nicholas, developed a process for producing a 'soluble' form of the medicine and marketed this under the new trade name *Aspro*. As part of war reparations, the German rights to the trade name Aspirin were given up in the UK and Commonwealth countries.

Figure 12 Early advertising for Aspirin in The Netherlands; the slogan on the vehicle means "Aspirin conquers every pain"

Because there are no development costs, the new brands can be made more cheaply than the original one. Currently, the Government encourages doctors to prescribe some medicines by their generic name. The pharmacist is then free to dispense the cheapest brand – which helps to keep health service costs down.

ASSIGNMENT 4

Some common brand-name medicines are:
Seldane, Triludan, Calpol, Nurofen, Ventolin, Algesal, Opticrom, Otrivine, Betnovate, Beconase.

See if you have any of these at home and try to find their generic names from the packets, bottles, etc.

Different ways of buying aspirin

The *Monthly Index of Medical Specialities (MIMS)* recently listed over 75 brand name **analgesics** (pain-relieving medicines) of which 14 contained aspirin. Worldwide, there are over 200 analgesic formulations which contain aspirin.

There are so many because

- the medicine may come in different forms, eg solids, soluble substances and syrups
- other compounds may be present to help relieve other symptoms which occur along with the one being treated
- there may be other substances present to help the action of the principal compound
- for all these different formulations, and aspirin itself, there are many companies each producing their own brand-name equivalent.

Many forms of aspirin are 'over-the-counter' medicines for which you do not need a prescription. In **Activity WM6.1** you can carry out a survey of the aspirin products.

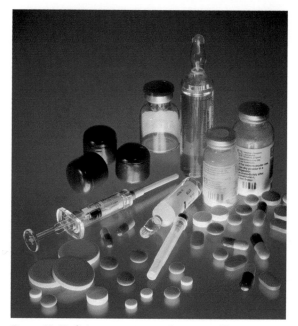

Figure 13 Medicines come in a wide variety of forms

Manufacturers need to analyse samples from each batch of a medicine to ensure that it has been properly blended and each tablet contains exactly the stated amount of active ingredient.

More critically, because these medicines are so easily available and widely used, many households keep some permanently in stock. These are not always safely stored and are sometimes kept unlabelled. Each year many thousands of cases of accidental poisoning occur. Hospital analysts need techniques for establishing quickly which compounds – and how much – are present in tablets, so that the correct treatment can be given.

In **Activity WM6.2** you can try to identify aspirin and some other compounds in commonly available medicinal preparations.

In **Activity WM6.3** you can perform an aspirin assay, in other words an experiment to find out the amount of aspirin in a medicine.

The safety of aspirin

People tend to think of aspirin as a safe medicine, because it is so familiar. But like all medicines, it is only safe if taken in the recommended dose. The lethal dose of aspirin is 30 g for an adult of average size. A typical aspirin tablet contains 0.3 g of aspirin, so 100 tablets could be a lethal dose. Unpleasant symptoms would be experienced with far fewer tablets than this. The recommended dose of aspirin is no more than 12 tablets a day, and it is not recommended at all for children under 12 years old.

ASSIGNMENT 5

It is important to know the recommended doses of medicines and to keep within those doses. Look at the medicines you have at home, and any others which you may take occasionally, and make a note of the recommended dose of each. Remember that there are several aspirin-containing medicines, so that taking one will affect how much you can take of another.

WM7 *Development and safety testing of medicines*

This section is linked to **Activity WM7.1**. You will find it helpful to look at the activity before beginning to read the interview.

An interview

A great deal of time, money and effort is spent by the pharmaceutical industry in discovering and developing new medicines. This is illustrated in the following interview with Martin Joseph, formerly a project leader in the Development Section of ZENECA Pharmaceuticals at Alderley Park, Cheshire.

"I began by asking Martin Joseph to tell me about ZENECA Pharmaceuticals.

'ZENECA Pharmaceuticals is an international business. It has over 3300 employees engaged in research and development (R & D) and they work in many countries throughout the world, including the major markets of the USA, France, Germany, Italy and Japan.'

Figure 14 The ZENECA Pharmaceuticals site at Alderley Park, Cheshire

And that all adds up to a sizeable research budget?

'We will spend over £300 million on R & D in 1993. What you have to remember is that very few new compounds survive the course. Approximately 10 000 new chemicals (we call them 'new chemical entities') are synthesised every year by ZENECA research chemists. All of these are evaluated for their potential usefulness in the treatment of diseases. We are also constantly looking for novel compounds, at various stages of development, by entering into licence agreements with other companies.'

But most of them fall by the wayside?

'Yes, the road from test tube to treatment is very long, very expensive and the odds against reaching the destination are very high. The chances of success are between one in 10 000 and one in 20 000. The cost of bringing any single major new drug to the world market is typically between £50 million and £100 million, but is as high as £250 million when you take into account the failures during development.'

Where is all the money spent? Which are the most expensive bits?

'The research phase absorbs about one-third of the cost and might last from 4 to 10 years. Then development to the point of launch consumes the remaining two-thirds over about 7 years.'

So some of the teams working on new products must accept that their research may come to nothing?

'Not to nothing, but that no new product will result. Yes, that's a hard fact of life in the pharmaceuticals business.'

Where is it all leading at the moment? What are the trends in drug development?

'For about 40 years the pharmaceutical industry has made steady progress in improving therapy in most major disease areas. That means reducing mortality, aiding diagnosis and improving the quality of life by controlling the symptoms of many chronic diseases. It is in that last category that most new medicines find application. They benefit patients by improving their sense of wellbeing and the quality of their lives. There has been a steady increase in R & D expenditure by the pharmaceutical industry as the research targets have become more difficult, development has become more complex, and more and more data is required.'

And has the increase in R & D expenditure led to more new medicines becoming available to patients?

'Quite the reverse. The number of new chemical entities launched worldwide has fallen dramatically from approximately 100 in 1960 to 37 in 1983. Overall, the number of new chemical entities approved has remained fairly constant for the past two decades.

The main reason for the downward trend is that companies are turning their attention to more complex, chronic diseases. In addition, regulatory requirements have become increasingly demanding. In all developed countries the control of the safety, efficacy and quality of new pharmaceuticals is monitored both by the manufacturers themselves and by regulatory authorities.'

And does that stem from major disasters like thalidomide?

'Yes. After the discovery of the effects of thalidomide in the early 1960s a voluntary committee was established in the UK and named after its Chairman, Sir Derek Dunlop. The committee's recommendations were incorporated into the Medicines Act in 1968, and the Licensing Authority and its advisory body – the Committee on Safety of Medicines – were established to police the new Act. The principal effect of this has been to extend the time taken from discovery to the launch of a major new drug.

For example, in 1960 this process might have been expected to take approximately 3 years. Today the average development period is 14 years, although the industry is actively seeking ways of reducing these times without compromising safety.'

And time is money?

'Yes, if the development is prolonged the cost of individual projects increases and the cost of failures also increases.'

Can you put an approximate figure on the total cost of developing a new chemical entity?

'The figure is currently between £50 million and £100 million. If we add an element for projects which are terminated prematurely, then the figure rises to nearer £250 million.'

Is that why profits on the successful drugs must be high?

'Yes, we must achieve adequate sales and profit level in order to continue to finance future pharmaceutical innovation.'

So let's recap. An enormous amount of groundwork is necessary before the first chemicals are mixed in the test tube. The programme must be planned, the literature searched, patents checked, biological testing methods established and the right staff identified or recruited.

'Yes, and that last factor can be the most important. We then need diligence, patience, skill and an element of luck when searching for potential candidate drugs. A lot of new chemicals are synthesised, tested, their molecular structures modified and then retested and so on until finally a compound is identified which fulfils the criteria for full development.'

And when do you start to consider safety aspects?

'Very early indeed. Safety assessment is a major factor in the development of a new drug and some preliminary tests are necessary before any substantial investment is made.'

Does this involve tests on animals?

'It does. Regrettably it is not possible in the present state of knowledge to discover or develop new medicines without using animals. The law requires that the potential toxicity of new drugs be assessed in animals before they may be given to man and that the safety of the industry's workers is similarly protected. The law also provides for the protection of animals so all experiments are conducted under Licences and Certificates issued by the Home Office.

However, it would be irresponsible and illegal to give medicines to people or produce new chemicals without conducting the fullest and most reliable testing possible. It is very unlikely that the malformations caused by thalidomide would remain undetected by the detailed safety evaluations performed today.

In addition to those tests performed to see how well the new medicine does its job, each chemical is tested widely for side-effects.'

Presumably at the start of development you will only have tiny quantities of the new compound available?

'It is quite likely that only some tens of grams of compound will have been made. Synthesis, in the research laboratories, frequently involves materials and methods you couldn't use in full-scale manufacture. Substantial changes in the synthetic routes are often necessary before sufficient bulk drug can be made for development and eventual sale; for the major development activities several hundred kilograms of bulk drug are needed. The process must be able to provide a drug of adequate purity which will remain stable during processing, and at an acceptable cost. Sometimes provision of specialist plant and facilities may be necessary.'

Note that the medicine you have been looking at closely in this unit, aspirin, did not go through all the safety testing described here, because it was developed long before all these safety procedures were established. But aspirin has been known for so long and so widely that its use is accepted by most people – provided the recommended dosage isn't exceeded.

Which medicine to develop?

In **Activity WM7.1** you saw how expensive it is to develop a medicine from discovery right through to marketing. A firm will have wasted millions of pounds if it produces a medicine which does not catch on! Very careful decisions have to be made at several stages to ensure that the medicine is both safe and commercially viable.

Activity WM7.2 gives you a chance to experience decision-making like that involved when a pharmaceutical company considers which medicine should be developed.

Figure 15 Pharmaceutical research has to be carried out in conditions of safety and cleanliness

WM8 *Summary*

In this unit you have learned about some of the chemistry associated with the pharmaceutical industry using one familiar, important medicine – aspirin – as an example. The analytical techniques of mass spectrometry, infra-red spectroscopy and nuclear magnetic resonance spectroscopy allow us to identify the compound which is responsible for its pharmacological activity.

Knowledge of the chemical reactions of organic functional groups gives us the power to construct molecules of compounds which are essential for our wellbeing from readily available starting materials. You experienced something of the scale, complexity and costs involved in the production of a medicine for mass use.

Activity WM8 will help you to check your notes on this unit.

USING SUNLIGHT

Why a unit on USING SUNLIGHT?

This unit explores the ways in which solar energy can be harnessed to provide energy for our use. It starts by examining the conversion of sunlight to chemical energy by photosynthesis, and then moves on to discuss ways of using solar energy to produce electricity or fuels for people in the future.

During this unit some fundamental chemistry is introduced. The main areas looked at are the interaction of atoms, molecules and ions with visible and ultra-violet radiation, and the detailed study of redox reactions. This leads to a deeper understanding of how photosynthesis starts and the possibilities of using processes similar to photosynthesis to obtain a fuel directly from sunlight.

Solar cells are studied in order to understand how they work, and also to consider whether photovoltaic electricity could be used on a larger scale in the future. The possibility of using hydrogen as a fuel is considered in some detail.

In **Colour by Design** the origin of colour is investigated in more detail. Redox reactions are met again in **The Steel Story** and **Aspects of Agriculture**.

Overview of chemical principles

In this unit you will learn more about ...

ideas you will probably have come across in your earlier studies
- photosynthesis
- batteries and dry cells
- oxidation and reduction
- electrolysis

ideas introduced in earlier units in this course
- electromagnetic radiation (**Elements of Life**)
- the interaction of radiation with matter (**The Atmosphere**)
- radical reactions (**The Atmosphere**)
- redox reactions (**Minerals to Elements**)
- alternatives to petrol (**Developing Fuels**)

... as well as learning new ideas about
- the importance of solar energy and how we might make more use of it to supply our energy needs
- interactions of visible and ultra-violet radiation with matter
- the role of chlorophyll in photosynthesis
- redox reactions and electrochemical cells
- predicting the direction a redox reaction can take
- using photochemistry to make hydrogen from water
- how solar cells work
- how fuel cells work
- hydrogen as a possible fuel for the future.

USING SUNLIGHT

US1 *The Sun: sustainer of life*

Without the Sun life on Earth could not exist. We need its regular input of energy to maintain the Earth's surface temperature and to drive the chemical reactions essential for life.

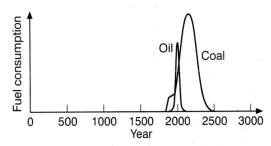

... has a mass of 2×10^{30} kg

... is 5000 million years old

... is 150 million km from Earth

... has a surface temperature of 6400 K

... has a core temperature of 14 million K

... is composed mainly of hydrogen

Figure 1 Our Sun

The Sun's energy can bring about photochemical reactions. In the stratosphere it produces oxygen atoms from dioxygen molecules and these in turn react with other dioxygen molecules to form ozone, O_3. Much of the high-energy solar radiation is absorbed in the stratosphere by molecules of dioxygen and ozone. Although the radiation reaching the troposphere is less energetic, it is enough for other types of photochemical processes to take place, for example **photosynthesis**.

Using solar energy

Most of our energy needs today are met by the products of past photosynthesis – coal, oil, gas and wood. Since there are limited resources of fossil fuels, other sources of energy will be needed in the next century. These include nuclear and solar energy. In this unit we shall look at some ways of using solar energy. These are summarised briefly in Figure 3.

Oil

Coal

Fuel consumption

0   500   1000   1500   2000   2500   3000
Year

Figure 2 Past and projected rates of world consumption of oil and coal: the use of fossil fuels will decline in the future as supplies run out

Figure 3 A summary of this unit

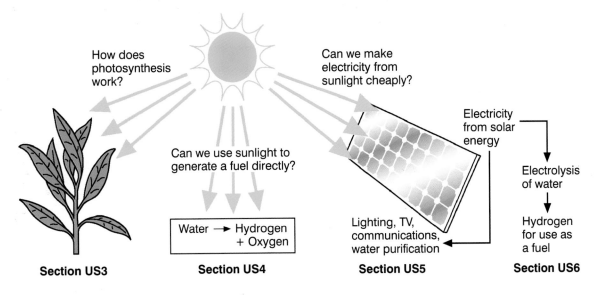

How does photosynthesis work?

Can we make electricity from sunlight cheaply?

Can we use sunlight to generate a fuel directly?

Water → Hydrogen + Oxygen

Electricity from solar energy

Electrolysis of water

Lighting, TV, communications, water purification

Hydrogen for use as a fuel

Section US3   **Section US4**   **Section US5**   **Section US6**

ASSIGNMENT 1

The powerful Sun

The following estimates have been made:

- the incidence of solar radiation on the Earth's surface is 3×10^{24} J per year
- the known reserves of fossil fuels are 3×10^{22} J
- the world's energy needs are 3×10^{20} J per year.

a How many days does it take the Sun to deliver 3×10^{22} J of energy to the Earth's surface?

b What percentage of the Earth's surface would need to be covered by solar collectors operating at 10% efficiency if the world's energy needs were to be met solely by the Sun?

It would seem that only a small area of the Earth's surface would need to be set aside in order to trap all the energy we need.

Using sunlight in photosynthesis

Water and carbon dioxide react together in the presence of sunlight and chlorophyll in green plants to produce oxygen and glucose:

$$6H_2O + 6CO_2 \rightarrow C_6H_{12}O_6 + 6O_2$$
$$\text{glucose}$$

Glucose is a carbohydrate. It is stored in green plants in the form of starch, another carbohydrate, which is insoluble in water. Starch is made up of glucose units joined together in long chains. Carbohydrates are fuels. Thus, the energy of sunlight is stored.

The maximum conversion of incident solar energy achievable at present in agriculture is only about 2% – 3%. How can we improve on this?

One way would be to improve the efficiency of plant growth. Another way would be to develop chemical systems which imitate natural plant photosynthesis.

To do either requires a detailed understanding of the chemistry of photosynthesis. A large number of scientists – chemists, biologists and physicists – are investigating the processes involved, many of which are among the fastest known to us. Some of the chemistry of the light-dependent stage of photosynthesis is developed in Section **US3**.

ASSIGNMENT 2

It has been estimated that if the energy delivered to the Earth's surface by the Sun in 1 day was all converted to carbohydrate, the amount of carbohydrate produced would be enough to feed the population of the world for 1 year.

Give three reasons why only a very small proportion of the Sun's energy is converted into carbohydrate.

Figure 4 The energy of sunlight is converted to chemical energy in the leaves of green plants

Using sunlight to make other fuels

A variety of fuels can be obtained from plants, such as vegetable oils and sugars which can be converted into alcohol. But this involves first growing the plants, and then transporting bulky plant material for processing.

Much research has been done on finding ways to make a gaseous or liquid fuel directly, using sunlight as the source of energy. Such fuels would be useful because they are more easily transported than plants.

We shall explore the feasibility of direct photochemical production of one such fuel (hydrogen from water) in Section **US4**.

ASSIGNMENT 3

The Sun's energy can be stored in a fuel such as hydrogen. The energy is released when hydrogen is burned in air.

a Write an equation for the combustion of hydrogen.

b Explain where the energy released during combustion comes from.

c Use bond enthalpies from the Data Sheets to work out the enthalpy change of combustion of hydrogen.

d Hydrogen is a clean fuel and almost no pollutants are produced. Suggest one possible pollutant and explain how it might be formed in the combustion process.

Using sunlight to produce electricity

Many watches and calculators depend on sunlight in order to work. They use technology which converts sunlight into electricity – the **photovoltaic cell**. These cells will be described in Section **US5**.

There are several problems in producing electricity from sunlight. Sunlight gets scattered by clouds, and absorbed by gases in the atmosphere. This reduces the intensity of the radiation reaching the Earth's surface. Figure 5 shows the intensity of solar radiation arriving at the Earth's surface. Sunlight also varies in intensity depending on the time of day, season, latitude and local weather conditions. And of course the Sun shines only by day.

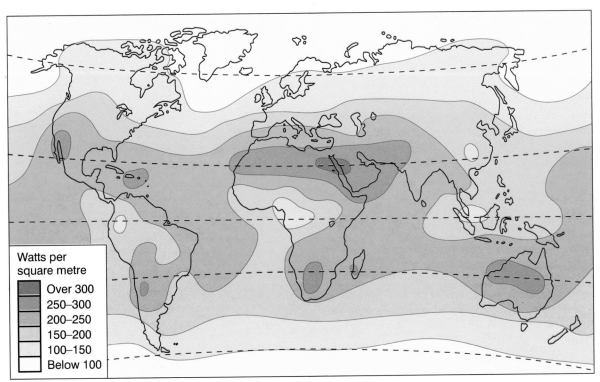

Figure 5 *The intensity of solar radiation at the Earth's surface, in watts per square metre, averaged day and night over a full year*

Watts per square metre

- Over 300
- 250–300
- 200–250
- 150–200
- 100–150
- Below 100

If we try to generate electricity directly from sunlight, then large areas may need to be covered with solar collectors. This would be necessary so that enough excess electricity is produced on sunny days to be stored and used at night and on cloudy days.

So, although solar energy is free, the cost of collecting and using it is high. The goal of harnessing that great source of energy, our Sun, remains a difficult one.

In the words of Lord Porter:

This is a great challenge, certainly the greatest of all challenges to photochemistry and perhaps to the whole of chemistry at this time.

___ **ASSIGNMENT 4** ___

Look at Figure 5.

a Identify the regions which get the most intense solar radiation.

b Suggest why the region near the equator does not get the most intense sunlight.

US2 *Exciting light*

Photosynthesis needs sunlight. Like most natural processes its chemistry is complex and involves a number of stages. Before trying to develop a deeper understanding of photosynthesis, and in particular the role that light plays, we will look at some important processes which involve light and the changes which can occur when substances absorb light.

George Porter

Lord Porter shared the Nobel Prize for Chemistry in 1967 for his work on very fast chemical reactions (see **The Atmosphere** storyline, Section **A3**). This allowed the study of unstable chemical species which exist for only tiny fractions of a second. His interest in fast reactions led him to look at photosynthesis, where the initial reactions occur in less than one-billionth of a second. Some of his most recent research has involved using sunlight to produce hydrogen from water.

Colours around us

We are surrounded by colours. The visible light from the Sun is called white light, but it can be split into light of different colours, as you can see when you look at a rainbow.

Most of the colour we see around us is due to substances which *absorb* light from the visible region of the spectrum. That is, they absorb photons of light with energies corresponding to the visible region. Photons of different energies within this region are perceived by us as different colours.

But colour can also be produced in a different way by a process called **fluorescence**. Some molecules absorb ultra-violet or visible radiation and re-emit visible light of a lower frequency. You can see them in action in highlighter pens, and in some clothing under disco lights.

You can find out more about how colours arise in **Chemical Ideas 6.4**.

You can observe fluorescence in **Activity US2.1**.

The appearance of white products, such as fabrics and plastics, can be improved by adding fluorescent compounds to them called **optical brighteners**. Some materials become yellow with age and some, like many polymers, may contain traces of yellow impurities. The blue or violet light emitted by the optical brighteners when they fluoresce overcomes the yellow tinge of the product. The surfaces also appear brighter because more visible light reaches the eye.

Activity US2.2 allows you to explore one application of optical brighteners.

Figure 6 *Fluorescent compounds are used in reflective clothing to make the wearers more clearly visible*

Photochemical reactions

Sometimes the absorption of light energy can cause a bond in the molecule to break. Then the reaction is said to be **photochemical**.

You can review these ideas in **Chemical Ideas 6.3**.

You may have investigated the photodissociation of bromine and the reactions of radicals in **Activities A3.2** and **A3.3**.

The bromination of alkanes is a photochemical reaction. It involves the homolytic fission of the Br–Br bond in bromine, followed by reactions involving radicals.

ASSIGNMENT 5

a Use $E = h\nu$ to calculate the range of energies of photons corresponding to the ultra-violet region, assuming a wavelength range of 320 nm–380 nm (velocity of light = frequency × wavelength).

b Look up the Br–Br bond enthalpy in the Data Sheets. Remember that the values of bond enthalpies are given per mole of bonds. Calculate the minimum energy needed to break one Br–Br bond to produce Br atoms:

$$Br_2(g) \rightarrow Br(g) + Br(g)$$

c Compare the values obtained in parts **a** and **b**. Is it feasible that the bromination of hexane is initiated by ultra-violet radiation?

Photochemical reactions can also take place in solutions, and may involve ions. Some of these are redox reactions in which electrons are transferred from one species to another. More detailed explanations of how redox reactions occur are given later in this unit.

In **Activity US2.3** you can study the photochemical reduction of iron(III) ions.

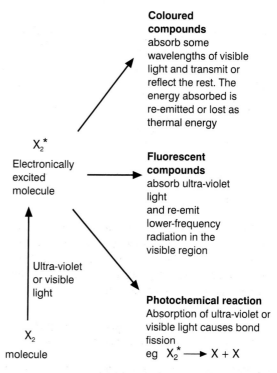

Coloured compounds absorb some wavelengths of visible light and transmit or reflect the rest. The energy absorbed is re-emitted or lost as thermal energy

X_2^*
Electronically excited molecule

Fluorescent compounds absorb ultra-violet light and re-emit lower-frequency radiation in the visible region

Ultra-violet or visible light

X_2
molecule

Photochemical reaction Absorption of ultra-violet or visible light causes bond fission
eg $X_2^* \longrightarrow X + X$

Figure 7 *A summary of the changes which can occur when a molecule X_2 absorbs ultra-violet or visible light*

US3 *Photosynthesis*

Life on this planet would be impossible without photochemical reactions. Photosynthesis traps energy from the Sun and, in plant leaves, converts water and carbon dioxide into carbohydrates and oxygen. The overall reaction can be written

$$n\mathrm{H_2O} + n\mathrm{CO_2} \xrightarrow{\text{sunlight}} (\mathrm{CH_2O})_n + n\mathrm{O_2}$$

$(\mathrm{CH_2O})$ is the building block from which all carbohydrates, like sugars and starch, are made. Algae, some bacteria and marine micro-organisms can also get their energy directly from sunlight by photosynthesis.

Figure 8 summarises the main points of photosynthesis which you should know from earlier studies.

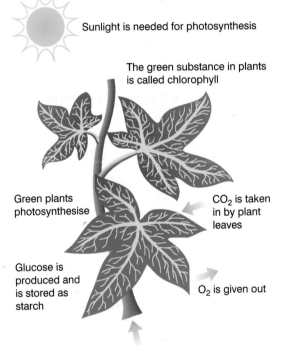

Sunlight is needed for photosynthesis

The green substance in plants is called chlorophyll

Green plants photosynthesise

CO_2 is taken in by plant leaves

Glucose is produced and is stored as starch

O_2 is given out

H_2O is taken up from the soil by plant roots

Figure 8 Photosynthesis

The sunlight which reaches the Earth has a mixture of wavelengths, including those which we perceive as colours. It is the visible radiations that are needed for photosynthesis. However, all the colours of visible light are not equally good at helping photosynthesis to occur.

In **Activity US3.1a** you can investigate how the rate of photosynthesis is affected by the wavelength of light.

Activity US3.1b allows you to study the interactions between chlorophyll and light.

What is the role of chlorophyll?

Chlorophyll appears green because it is absorbing wavelengths that correspond to other colours. If you refer to the colour wheel in Figure 12 of **Chemical Ideas 6.4**, you will see that chlorophyll may be absorbing both red and violet light.

What does chlorophyll do with the energy from this absorbed light? If you shine light on a *solution* of chlorophyll it fluoresces. The chlorophyll molecules in solution are moving randomly, and lose most of the energy they absorb from sunlight by re-emitting it as red light. The fluorescence happens rapidly, within 1×10^{-8} seconds after absorption.

But you do not see plants fluorescing strongly like a chlorophyll solution. In plants, energy is not immediately re-emitted as light. Instead, it is transferred rapidly from excited chlorophyll molecules and used to start a chain of chemical reactions.

Recent research has led to a much better understanding of the first, photochemical, stages of photosynthesis.

Figure 9 These young lettuce plants are being cultivated in greenhouses under sodium vapour lamps

There are many different pigment molecules in plants. You may have separated some of them by chromatography in your earlier studies. By far the most abundant, and the most important, pigment for photosynthesis is **chlorophyll *a***. Its structure is shown in Figure 10 on the next page. Do not worry about how complex it seems: you will not be expected to remember it. But if you look carefully you will see that chlorophyll pigments contain a central magnesium bonded to four nitrogen atoms. The bonding is similar to that between copper ions and ammonia ligands in the complex ion $[\mathrm{Cu(NH_3)_4}]^{2+}$.

The first part of **Chemical Ideas 11.7** provides an introduction to complex ions.

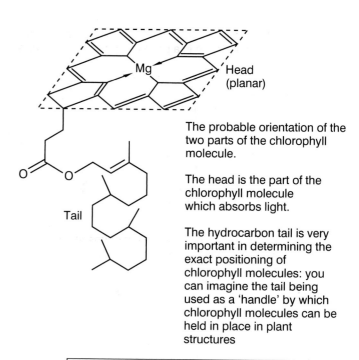

The probable orientation of the two parts of the chlorophyll molecule.

The head is the part of the chlorophyll molecule which absorbs light.

The hydrocarbon tail is very important in determining the exact positioning of chlorophyll molecules: you can imagine the tail being used as a 'handle' by which chlorophyll molecules can be held in place in plant structures

Figure 10 The structure of chlorophyll a (the shaded —CH₃ group is replaced by —CHO in chlorophyll b)

The four nitrogen atoms in chlorophyll are part of a complex organic ring structure arranged round the magnesium. If you look back to the structure of haemoglobin (Figure 3 in the **Elements of Life** storyline) you will see many similarities between the structures of haemoglobin and chlorophyll.

Changes in the energies of electrons in the head section of the chlorophyll molecule enable it to absorb light very strongly, making it such an intense green colour.

Chlorophyll *a* molecules operate in teams. They can be involved in photosynthesis in one of two ways. Most act as **light harvesters**: they absorb light and pass the energy on from one chlorophyll *a* molecule to another until it reaches the **reaction centre**. This consists of a carefully positioned pair of chlorophyll *a* molecules which start the reactions of photosynthesis. The light harvesters and the reaction centre together form a **photosynthetic unit**.

These processes occur in disc-shaped structures called **chloroplasts**. Each leaf cell contains a number of chloroplasts. The photosynthetic units are present in parallel layers of green membranes, seen as dark areas in the cross-section of a chloroplast in Figure 11.

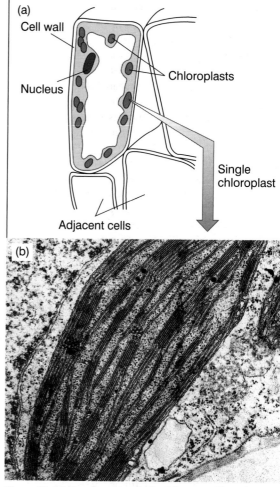

Figure 11 (a) Cross-section of a leaf showing chloroplasts. (b) Cross-section of a single chloroplast (magnified about 15 000 times). The chlorophyll a molecules are embedded in membranes which are arranged in stacks (the dark areas)

The reaction centre contains a special pair of chlorophyll *a* molecules: the two molecules are embedded in a protein support structure and are exactly aligned for reaction

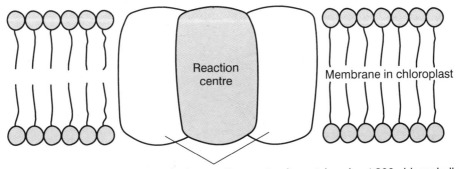

A light-harvesting antenna surrounds the reaction centre; it contains about 300 chlorophyll *a* molecules which absorb light and pass the energy onto the reaction centre

Figure 12 A photosynthetic unit showing the light-harvesting antenna and the reaction centre

Figure 12 shows a photosynthetic unit embedded in a membrane inside the chloroplast. The light-harvesting chlorophyll *a* molecules act like an antenna and funnel sunlight into the reaction centre.

In the light-harvesting antenna the chlorophyll *a* molecules are organised so that they are very close together and transfer of energy between them is very fast – about 10 000 times faster than fluorescence.

The sheer number of pigment molecules involved in light harvesting means that there is a rapid and continuous supply of energy to the reaction centre.

Chlorophyll *a* in the reaction centre uses the energy to start a chemical reaction. The molecules in the reaction centre are fixed in position and arranged so that reaction can occur before the chlorophyll *a* has time to fluoresce and lose its energy.

In a *solution*, however, chlorophyll *a* molecules are not held in specific positions. Transfer of energy between molecules now depends on random collisions. It cannot happen fast enough and fluorescence occurs instead of reaction.

You can revise ideas about redox reactions in **Chemical Ideas 9.1**.

Activity US3.1c gives you a chance to study the kind of reactions which can be initiated by chloroplasts.

How does chlorophyll initiate redox reactions?

Photosynthesis turns carbon dioxide, CO_2, into carbohydrate (CH_2O). Since this is a reduction, a reducing agent is needed. The interactions of chlorophyll *a* with sunlight are designed to make a reducing agent, which we will call A^-.

Photosynthesis in summary

Photosynthesis can be divided into three stages:

- light harvesting
- using light energy to start photochemical redox reactions
- reducing carbon dioxide to $(CH_2O)_n$.

Chlorophyll *a* is involved in the first two stages.

Photosynthesis is a redox reaction. Two half-equations can be written to summarise the reactions of water and carbon dioxide:

$$2H_2O \rightarrow O_2 + 4H^+ + 4e^- \qquad \text{(half-reaction 1)}$$

$$4e^- + 4H^+ + CO_2 \rightarrow (CH_2O) + H_2O$$
$$\text{(half-reaction 2)}$$

The splitting of water in the first half-reaction is an oxidation. The conversion of carbon dioxide to carbohydrate in half-reaction 2 is a reduction. The two half-reactions take place in different parts of the chloroplast.

If you combine the equations for each stage, ie add half-reaction 1 to half-reaction 2, you will obtain the overall equation for photosynthesis:

$$H_2O + CO_2 \rightarrow (CH_2O) + O_2$$

This should really be written as

$$nH_2O + nCO_2 \rightarrow (CH_2O)_n + nO_2$$

Two separate chlorophyll *a* reaction centres have been identified. They are called **photosystem I** and **photosystem II** and each is surrounded by its own team of light harvesters. The two reaction centres operate in a similar way but absorb light of slightly different wavelengths.

They are both embedded in the membrane and are linked together by a chain of reactions in which photosystem II transfers electrons to photosystem I.

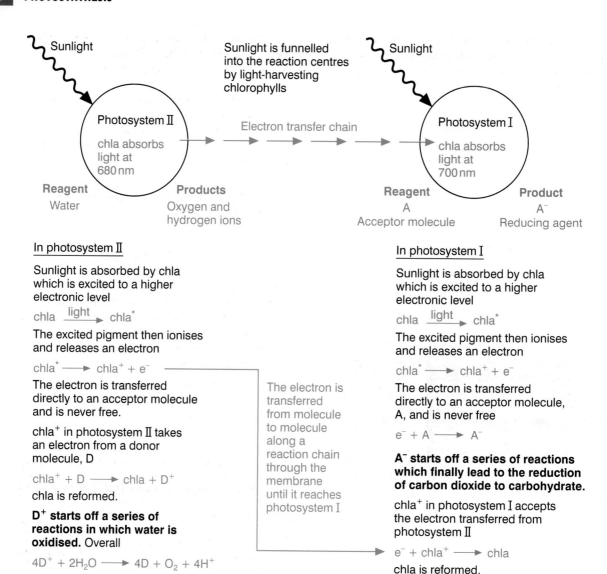

In photosystem II

Sunlight is absorbed by chla which is excited to a higher electronic level

$$chla \xrightarrow{\text{light}} chla^*$$

The excited pigment then ionises and releases an electron

$$chla^* \longrightarrow chla^+ + e^-$$

The electron is transferred directly to an acceptor molecule and is never free.

$chla^+$ in photosystem II takes an electron from a donor molecule, D

$$chla^+ + D \longrightarrow chla + D^+$$

chla is reformed.

D^+ starts off a series of reactions in which water is oxidised. Overall

$$4D^+ + 2H_2O \longrightarrow 4D + O_2 + 4H^+$$

The electron is transferred from molecule to molecule along a reaction chain through the membrane until it reaches photosystem I

In photosystem I

Sunlight is absorbed by chla which is excited to a higher electronic level

$$chla \xrightarrow{\text{light}} chla^*$$

The excited pigment then ionises and releases an electron

$$chla^* \longrightarrow chla^+ + e^-$$

The electron is transferred directly to an acceptor molecule, A, and is never free

$$e^- + A \longrightarrow A^-$$

A^- starts off a series of reactions which finally lead to the reduction of carbon dioxide to carbohydrate.

$chla^+$ in photosystem I accepts the electron transferred from photosystem II

$$e^- + chla^+ \longrightarrow chla$$

chla is reformed.

Figure 13 How photosynthesis is initiated in green plants (chla stands for chlorophyll a; D and A are electron donor and electron acceptor molecules respectively whose structures are not yet known in detail)

The reactions which take place in the two reaction centres are summarised in Figure 13. They start when one of the chlorophyll *a* molecules in the reaction centre becomes excited, and releases an electron. A series of electron transfer reactions begins. The sequence is complicated and you are not expected to recall the details. The events are listed in the columns below the diagram in Figure 13.

Figure 13 shows how the production of oxygen by photosystem II is linked to the production of a reducing agent (A^-) by photosystem I. The reduction of carbon dioxide does not involve light and does not take place in the membrane. The conversion of CO_2 to (CH_2O) is just the start of many different reactions. The carbohydrate produced can be oxidised to release energy (respiration) or used as a starting material to make a whole range of organic molecules needed by plants, such as proteins and fats.

The timescales given in Table 1 show just how rapid the energy transfer is.

Table 1 Timescale of the process in photosynthesis

Photon absorbed; excited chlorophyll formed	10^{-15} seconds	
Electron transfer reactions	$10^{-12} - 10^{-3}$ seconds	
Carbon dioxide reduced and photosynthetic products made	$10^{-3} - 1$ second	These last processes are not directly dependent on light
Use of photosynthetic products by plant	$1 - 10^3$ seconds	

The end products of these reactions provide us with food and warmth: from the materials produced we generate electricity, manufacture clothing, run automobiles – the list could go on and on.

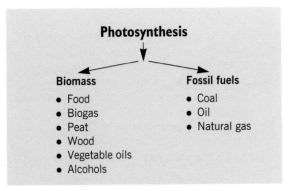

Photosynthesis

Biomass
- Food
- Biogas
- Peat
- Wood
- Vegetable oils
- Alcohols

Fossil fuels
- Coal
- Oil
- Natural gas

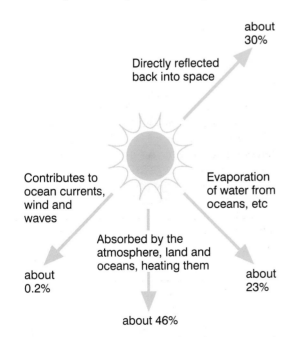

Figure 14 Sugar cane can be grown in sunny countries as an 'energy crop'. The sugar is then fermented to produce ethanol which is used as a fuel for motor vehicles. In Brazil, cars run on a mixture of ethanol and petrol known as gasohol

And yet only a tiny percentage of the solar energy reaching the surface of the Earth is used in photosynthesis – a mere 0.03%. What happens to the rest of it?

We depend for so much on such a tiny percentage of the energy arriving from the Sun. Could we use some of the rest of it to make a fuel for ourselves? What would be a good fuel to make? These questions will be tackled in the next section of this unit.

Activity US3.2 will help you to review some of the important points in the first part of this unit.

ASSIGNMENT 6

We already make use of the Sun's energy in a variety of ways in addition to using the products of photosynthesis. Sometimes we use the Sun's energy directly. Sometimes we generate electricity by methods which are only possible because of energy arriving from the Sun.

Refer to Figure 15 to help you, and list ways in which we make use of the Sun's energy either directly or indirectly.

Directly reflected
back into space
about 30%

Evaporation
of water from
oceans, etc
about 23%

Absorbed by the
atmosphere, land and
oceans, heating them
about 46%

Contributes to
ocean currents,
wind and
waves
about 0.2%

Figure 15 What happens to the energy from the Sun not used in photosynthesis?

All the carbon dioxide on Earth passes through the photosynthetic cycle on average once every 300 years, the oxygen every 2000 years and the water in the oceans every 2 million years

Every carbon atom in your body has been through the photosynthetic cycle many times

The mass of carbon fixed as carbohydrate is 2×10^{11} tonnes per year

Figure 16 Have you thanked a plant today?

US4 *Fuel for the future*

Photosynthesis produces oxygen from water using energy from sunlight, and plants store the energy as carbohydrates. If we could use sunlight to split water into hydrogen and oxygen, we could use the hydrogen as a fuel. The idea is attractive because water is so plentiful, and burning hydrogen produces water again.

To understand this section you need to find out about electrode potentials and electrochemical cells. You can do this by reading **Chemical Ideas 9.2.**

Can sunlight split water and give hydrogen?

We would like to use sunlight to bring about the following redox reaction:

$$H_2O \rightarrow H_2 + \tfrac{1}{2}O_2$$

But this needs a lot of energy. The reverse reaction happens very readily: supply enough energy to a mixture of hydrogen and oxygen – a spark is often enough – and there is an explosion as they react to form water.

In order for a reaction to happen, enough energy must be available for bond breaking, and there must be a pathway by which the reaction can occur. What possible pathways are there for the decomposition of water?

A very small proportion of water molecules is split into ions at room temperature, and the following equilibrium is set up:

$$H_2O \rightleftharpoons H^+ + OH^-$$

But this does not help to produce hydrogen because hydrogen *ions* are produced and not hydrogen *molecules*. There are no changes in oxidation state in the reaction. What we need is a redox reaction. There are two possible pathways.

Radical mechanism

One way to start the reaction would be to break an O–H bond by homolytic fission to form radicals:

$$H–O–H \rightarrow H + OH$$

The hydrogen atom and hydroxyl radical could then continue the reaction by attacking other molecules of water. The O–H bond has a bond enthalpy of $+463\,kJ$ per mole of bonds. To break one O–H bond requires $7.69 \times 10^{-19}\,J$. Light with a wavelength of $258\,nm$ would have just enough energy to cause O–H bonds to break.

ASSIGNMENT 7

Use the relationships below to show that light with a wavelength of 258 nm would have just enough energy to cause O–H bonds to break:

velocity of light = frequency × wavelength

energy = Planck constant × frequency

You will find values for the constants in the Data Sheets.

But light of this wavelength is not absorbed by water. Figure 18 shows the absorption spectrum of water above 120 nm. The longest wavelength of light absorbed which could actually cause O–H bonds in water to break is 185 nm.

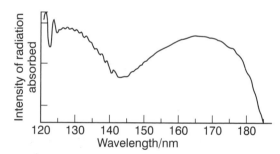

Figure 18 The absorption spectrum of water above 120 nm

Figure 17 The large amounts of water in rivers and oceans suggest that sunlight does not cause water to decompose (which is just as well for the fish!)

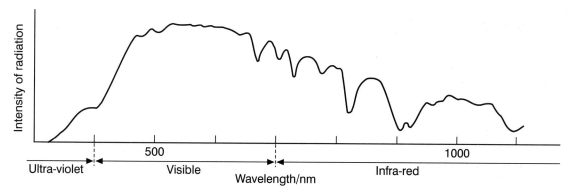

Figure 19 The spectrum of sunlight at the Earth's surface

Figure 19 shows the spectrum of sunlight at the Earth's surface, and you can see that wavelengths below about 300 nm are not present. (If you compare this spectrum with the solar spectra you met in **The Atmosphere** storyline, you will see that there the horizontal axes were marked in increasing frequency units. Here we have used increasing wavelength, which is more common for absorption spectra. But remember, the higher the wavelength of the radiation, the lower its energy.)

So water cannot be decomposed by sunlight alone in a radical reaction because there is not enough energy available to start the reaction.

Only very short wavelength ultra-violet light could bring about the decomposition, or photolysis, of water. When there was no ozone in the atmosphere, sunlight of the required wavelength did reach the Earth's surface. Photolysis of water vapour was the source of the first oxygen in our atmosphere – over 3000 million years ago, before photosynthesis had started.

Ionic mechanism

An alternative mechanism for breaking down water would be an electron transfer process. After all, this is what happens in photosynthesis. A possible first step is an oxidation of water

$$H_2O \rightarrow \tfrac{1}{2}O_2 + 2H^+ + 2e^-$$

followed by the reduction of hydrogen ions

$$2H^+ + 2e^- \rightarrow H_2$$

(In photosynthesis, the reduction step involves carbon dioxide rather than H^+ ions.) The overall reaction is the one we want:

$$H_2O \rightarrow H_2 + \tfrac{1}{2}O_2$$

But is this a feasible mechanism? In order to answer the question we need to be able to predict which direction a redox reaction will take.

In water at pH 7, the values of the electrode potentials for the half-reactions are

$$2H^+ + 2e^- \rightarrow H_2 \qquad\qquad E = -0.42\,V$$
$$\tfrac{1}{2}O_2 + 2H^+ + 2e^- \rightarrow H_2O \qquad E = +0.81\,V$$

Using the technique developed in **Chemical Ideas 9.3**, we find that the redox mechanism for decomposition of water will not work either. Water will not supply electrons to hydrogen ions because the half-reaction

$$\tfrac{1}{2}O_2 + 2H^+ + 2e^- \rightarrow H_2O$$

has a more positive electrode potential than the reaction

$$2H^+ + 2e^- \rightarrow H_2$$

Electrons will not flow away from the more positive potential.

But plants can do it – so why can't we?

Chemical Ideas 9.3 on redox reactions and **Activities US4.1** to **US4.6** will help you to understand how electrode potentials can be used to predict the direction a redox reaction can take.

Can we help sunlight to decompose water?

In plants, chlorophyll plays a key part by using the energy absorbed from sunlight to create substances which can oxidise water in the first stages of photosynthesis.

Can we find a substance which could do the job of chlorophyll? Let's call it substance X.

X must absorb sunlight and be able to make the redox process work.

Electrode potentials at pH 7 for the two half-reactions:

$$2H^+ + 2e^- \rightarrow H_2 \qquad\qquad E = -0.42\,V$$
$$\tfrac{1}{2}O_2 + 2H^+ + 2e^- \rightarrow H_2O \qquad E = +0.81\,V$$

To get the two half-reactions to take place, we need a reducing agent with an electrode potential less positive than –0.42 V, and an oxidising agent with an electrode potential more positive than +0.81 V.

Light absorption can change electrode potentials. If X is the reducing agent then raising one of its electrons to a higher energy level makes it easier for X to give that electron away. So the electronically excited state of X, represented by X*, is a better reducing agent than X.

In terms of electrode potentials

$$X^+ + e^- \rightarrow X \qquad \text{(reaction 3)}$$
$$X^+ + e^- \rightarrow X^* \qquad \text{(reaction 4)}$$

reaction 4 has a less positive potential than reaction 3.

So we are looking for a substance X which is a good absorber of sunlight. X^+ needs to be able to oxidise water, and its excited state, X*, must be able to reduce hydrogen ions. This is summarised in Figure 20.

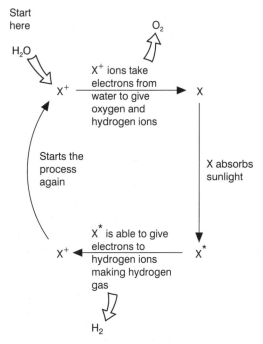

Figure 20 A photochemist's dream

Activity US4.7 will help you to understand how X can cause the decomposition of water and should be done at this stage.

This would mean that we could use water as the source of hydrogen, which is a fuel. On burning hydrogen, water is produced, with no carbon dioxide or sulphur dioxide to cause problems. We would then have a sustainable supply of a non-polluting fuel.

The theory looks good. The problem is to find X. It *must* give two redox half-reactions with suitable *E* values, and be water soluble. Ideally it should also be reasonably cheap and readily available. And the reactions must occur rapidly.

Some of the most successful research so far on decomposing water in this way is based on complexes of ruthenium, a transition metal in Period 5 of the Periodic Table. In this case

- X is a complex of Ru^{2+}
- X^+ is a complex of Ru^{3+}.

The process does work, with additional catalysts added to the system to make the reactions happen fast enough. The best systems generate hydrogen efficiently – but sadly for only a short time (about 4 hours). One of the problems with this type of water-splitting system is that back-reactions tend to occur and the products change back into reactants.

How do plants do it?

To prevent products changing back into reactants, plants have a beautifully designed arrangement of molecules. Electrons are transferred rapidly away from the positively charged ions created. Whisking the electrons away like this stops back-reactions from happening.

The structure of a reaction centre and the way in which electrons are transferred away from it are shown in Figure 21.

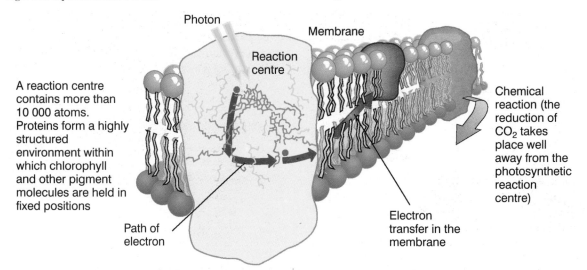

Figure 21 The reaction centre in photosynthesising bacteria: the first stages of photosynthesis occur here

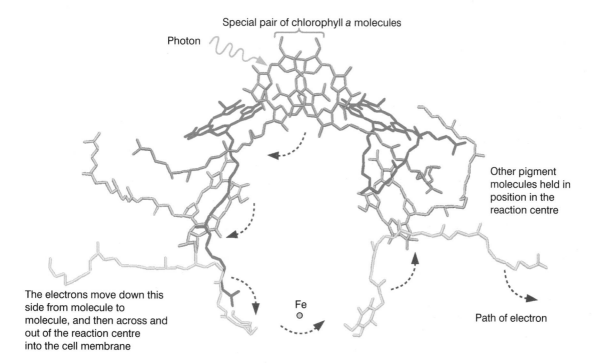

Special pair of chlorophyll *a* molecules

Photon

Other pigment molecules held in position in the reaction centre

The electrons move down this side from molecule to molecule, and then across and out of the reaction centre into the cell membrane

Fe

Path of electron

Figure 22 A computer image showing the arrangement of pigment molecules in a reaction centre

In Figure 22 the arrangement of pigment molecules in the reaction centre is shown in more detail. When electrons leave the *special pair* of chlorophyll *a* molecules which react, they move from one pigment molecule to the next down one side of the structure. They then move out of the reaction centre to take part in the later stages of photosynthesis.

Meanwhile, electrons are donated to the special pair of chlorophyll *a* molecules from molecules outside the reaction centre. These donor molecules become positively charged. In this way, positively charged ions are created at one surface of the membrane, and electrons are transferred to the other surface of the membrane.

Compare this elaborate structure with what happens when we try to use sunlight to make hydrogen from water. In solution, molecules are moving randomly and there is no way to stop the reactions going backwards. When these unwanted reactions occur, energy is transferred to the solution by heating instead of being used to make the redox processes work.

Why reinvent the wheel? Chemists are now looking at other ways to mimic photosynthesis and use the knack that plants have developed over millions of years. In the future, practical water-splitting systems may well be developed.

Figure 23 Three German scientists (from right to left) Robert Huber, Johann Deisenhofer and Hartmut Michel were awarded the 1988 Nobel Prize for Chemistry for determining the detailed structure of a bacterial photosynthetic reaction centre. They worked out the structure using X-ray crystallography. The arrangement in plants is thought to be similar

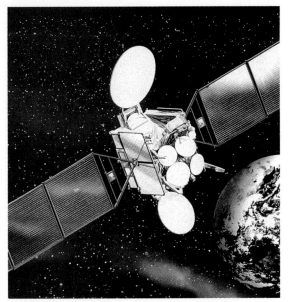

Figure 24 This Intelsat 7 communications satellite is powered by solar panels, which need no maintenance and provide a reliable source of energy

US5 *Solar cells*

Another way to use sunlight is to generate electricity directly. You may have seen or used solar-powered calculators or watches. They depend on the **photovoltaic effect**: when sunlight shines on some materials a small voltage or current can be generated.

Photovoltaic cells, commonly called solar cells, made their first real impact in space exploration where cost was not a major concern.

In the 1970s a combination of factors began to direct solar cell research towards our needs on Earth. These factors included the unstable political situation in the oil-rich countries of the Middle East and the oil crisis of the mid-seventies, together with a growing awareness that fossil fuel resources are limited.

More recently interest has been enhanced by concerns over urban air pollution, acid rain, global warming and risks from the use of nuclear fuels.

Semiconductors

Electrons in atoms are in definite, well-separated energy levels. But when atoms come together to form a solid, the levels group into *energy bands*.

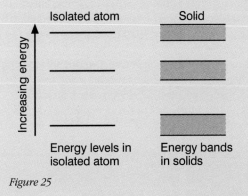

Figure 25

Figure 26

Electrons cannot move through the solid unless there are vacancies to move into, so only electrons in partially filled bands are free to move and conduct electricity. In semiconductors and insulators the bands are either completely filled or completely empty. In order to move, an electron would have to be excited into a higher, unfilled band.

In insulators, the energy gap is very large and the material does not conduct, but in semiconductors the energy gap is small. At room temperature some electrons will have enough energy to move out of the highest occupied band into the lowest unfilled band. Both bands are then partially filled and this allows some movement of electrons. If more energy is provided, then more electrons can move into the higher band, and the conductivity increases.

In contrast, metals are good conductors of electricity, even at low temperatures. Here the highest band occupied by electrons is only partially filled.

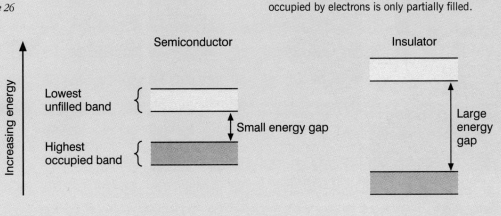

How do solar cells work?

Solar cells are made from **semiconductor** materials. This is a special class of materials which share a key property: they become better conductors as their temperature rises. This is the opposite of the behaviour of metals.

Silicon is the most widely used semiconductor. It is a Group 4 element, and in crystals each atom is joined to four others in a structure similar to diamond. Each silicon atom forms four single covalent bonds.

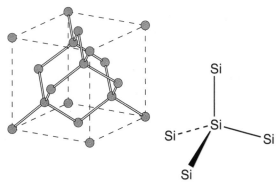

Figure 27 The silicon crystal structure and the arrangement of bonds around a central silicon atom

ASSIGNMENT 8

Draw a dot and cross diagram showing the bonding around one central silicon atom. Do not worry about the surrounding atoms. Show outer electrons only.

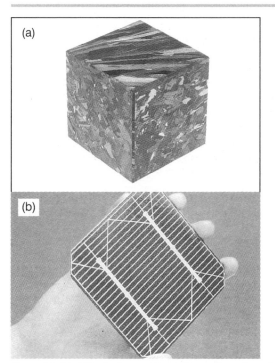

Figure 28 (a) A block of pure silicon; (b) a solar cell made from wafers of silicon about 350 μm thick

The conductivity of silicon increases as the temperature rises. It also increases if silicon is exposed to light.

Silicon absorbs sunlight. You can compare the absorption spectrum of silicon with the solar spectrum at the Earth's surface in Figure 29.

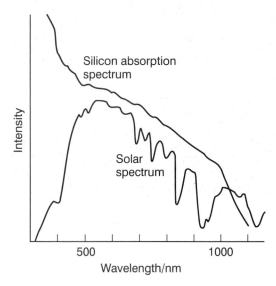

Figure 29 The absorption spectrum of silicon compared with the solar spectrum at the Earth's surface

When photons with enough energy are absorbed, electrons can move into the lowest unfilled band, leaving vacancies in the lower band (Figure 30).

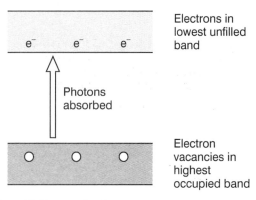

Figure 30 Photoconduction

The electrons move around randomly in the lowest unfilled band. They will eventually fall back into vacant sites in the lower band, giving out energy – unless there is some way of stopping them.

In a solar cell this is done by creating an electric field at a junction between two types of silicon semiconductor, called **n-type** and **p-type** semiconductors.

n-type and p-type semiconductors

The properties of silicon semiconductors are altered by **doping**. This involves adding carefully controlled amounts of impurity atoms. If phosphorus is added then it must form four bonds with silicon in order to fit into the lattice. The structure of the material is unaltered, except that at a few points there are phosphorus atoms rather than silicon.

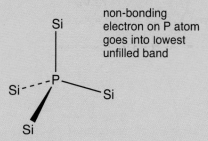

non-bonding electron on P atom goes into lowest unfilled band

But phosphorus has five outer electrons rather than four. The extra electron contributed by each impurity phosphorus atom must occupy the lowest unfilled band. This makes the silicon a better conductor and an **n-type** semiconductor is created.

Another type of semiconductor is produced when boron is added to silicon. Boron is in Group 3 and has only three outer electrons. This means that the highest occupied band is not completely filled and the conductivity of the material is increased.

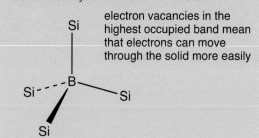

electron vacancies in the highest occupied band mean that electrons can move through the solid more easily

Adding boron makes the silicon into a **p-type** semiconductor.

(Sometimes the electron vacancies in the highest occupied band are called 'positive holes' because they lack negative electrons. The movement of electrons in one direction is equivalent to the movement of 'positive holes' in the opposite direction.)

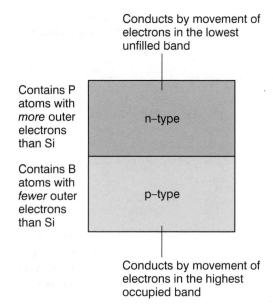

Conducts by movement of electrons in the lowest unfilled band

Contains P atoms with *more* outer electrons than Si — n-type

Contains B atoms with *fewer* outer electrons than Si — p-type

Conducts by movement of electrons in the highest occupied band

Figure 31 Conduction by n-type and p-type semiconductors

Look at Figure 31 which summarises the different ways in which n-type and p-type semiconductors conduct electricity. What will happen at the junction between the two?

At the junction, there are electron vacancies in the highest occupied band in the p-type material, and mobile electrons in the lowest unfilled band of the n-type material.

So electrons move across the junction from the n-type material into the p-type material. This creates a separation of charges on each side of the junction, which prevents further movement of electrons. This is shown in Figure 32.

It is important to remember that n-type and p-type semiconductors are electrically neutral *overall*. The p–n junction merely separates the charges.

In a solar cell, a thin wafer of silicon is used and two layers are created in it (Figure 33). One part per thousand of phosphorus is added to a very thin top layer, and one part per million of boron to the thicker bottom layer.

Figure 32 Formation of an electric field at a p–n junction

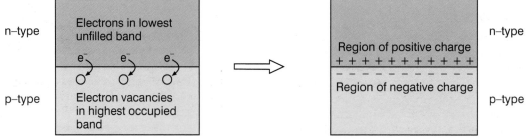

Movement of electrons across p–n junction...   ...creates an electric field across the junction

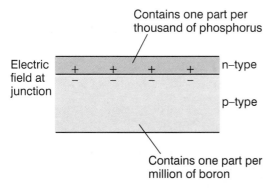

Figure 33 *A p–n junction in a solar cell*

Now if sunlight falls on the thin layer of n-type material, electrons are excited to the lowest unfilled band. They are repelled away from the junction by the electric field and move towards the upper surface of the silicon wafer (Figure 34).

This leaves behind vacancies in the highest occupied band in the n-type material, and electrons move across the junction from the highest occupied band of the p-type material.

If the upper and lower surfaces of the wafer are connected through an external circuit as in Figure 35, then electrons will flow from the top surface to the bottom surface to restore the balance of charge. The energy of sunlight has been converted directly into electricity.

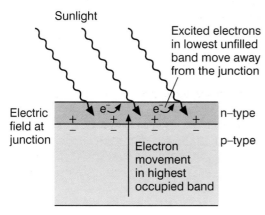

Figure 34 *The effect of light on a solar cell*

Using solar cells

A typical silicon solar cell is shown in cross-section in Figure 36. It has an anti-reflectant coating over the upper surface of a wafer-thin crystal of silicon. When the Sun shines on it, the cell produces a small voltage and current. The current is collected by strips of metal on the upper surface of the cell, and fed into an external circuit which is connected to a metallic layer on the base of the cell.

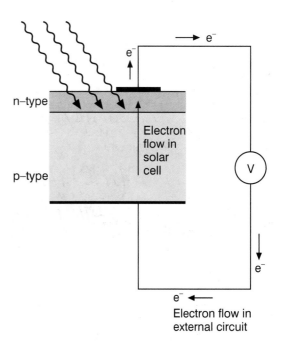

Figure 35 *A silicon solar cell producing electric current in an external circuit*

A typical silicon cell has an area of $100\,cm^3$ and gives $3\,A$ and $0.5\,V$ in full sunlight, so large panels are needed to generate significant amounts of power. Cells are connected in series and mounted in a **solar module**, which gives about $12\,V$ d.c. Modules are constructed to withstand exposure to weather and sunlight, and to remain in use for at least 20 years.

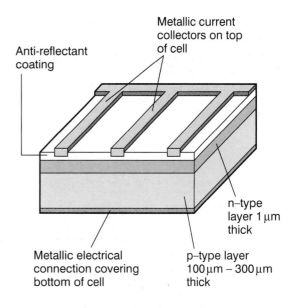

Figure 36 *Cross-section of part of a solar cell*

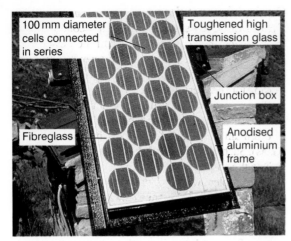

Figure 37 Solar modules connected to form an array: each module has a power output of about 38 W in good sunlight

Modules can be connected together to give larger photovoltaic systems (see Figure 38). Batteries can be used if the electricity needs to be stored.

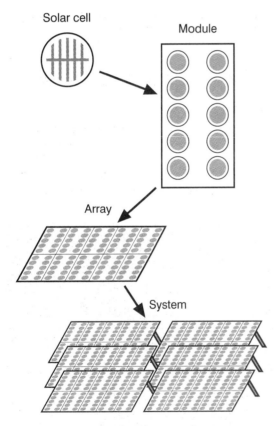

Figure 38 Components of a photovoltaic system

So photovoltaic cells are a non-polluting source of electricity: there is no noise, there are no moving parts and minimal maintenance is needed. Central power stations are not required, and so photovoltaic systems can be located near users. They can operate on any scale from portable modules to multimegawatt power plants.

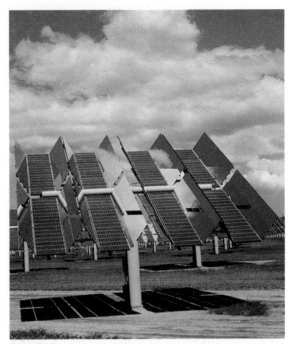

Figure 39 A photovoltaic power plant in California, USA

Year	Cost/$ MJ^{-1}
1970	16.7
1980	0.42
1990	about 0.14

Table 2 Cost of photovoltaic electricity to the consumer

The limiting factor is cost, although this is decreasing rapidly. Table 2 shows how the cost of photovoltaic electricity to the consumer has dropped in the USA in the last two decades. (In 1990, the cost of electricity from coal-fired stations was about 0.017 $ MJ^{-1}.)

In **Activity US5.1** you can examine some of the costs involved in solar cell production.

Pilot photovoltaic plants have been set up in many countries. So far, only about 4% of the electricity they produce is fed into national grids; the rest is used locally. But this is expected to change. By the end of the century, it is likely that over 20% of the photovoltaic electricity produced worldwide will be fed into national grid systems.

Marketing photovoltaic power

People deciding on which kind of power station to build will not opt for photovoltaic power if it is much more expensive than other power sources.

ASSIGNMENT 9

Costs in terms of money are not the only factors to take into account when choosing energy sources. What other costs should be considered?

How would taking these into account affect the competitiveness of photovoltaic electricity?

At 1990 costs, photovoltaic power is often the best choice where electricity is needed far away from where it is being generated. It is used, for example, to power telecommunications systems, to protect remote pipelines against corrosion, and in the electrification of isolated homes. By 1995 it should be possible to reduce the cost to two-thirds of the 1990 value. Photovoltaic power could then become the best choice for water-pumping systems, or the electrification of whole villages.

Figure 40 A solar-powered water pumping system in Thailand

If the cost can be reduced below this then it becomes a good choice for power supplies to whole islands, and there are many sunny islands in the world.

At a cost of half the 1990 value, photovoltaic power could be cheap enough to a compete with other power sources in some countries for supplying electricity to national grids to cover peaks in demand. In the USA, for example, peaks in demand used to occur on cold winter evenings, but now occur around 4 pm on hot sunny days, when refrigerators and air-conditioners are in maximum use. Photovoltaic power generation would be at its maximum at this time and the energy would not need to be stored.

It's an interesting thought – people switching on solar power to keep cool, because the Sun is making them too hot!

Getting the cost down

If photovoltaic power is to make a major contribution to our needs, then costs need to fall further. One avenue of research is in trying to increase the efficiency of energy conversion in solar cells; another is in looking for cheaper materials.

Work is progressing well in developing thin-film solar cells based on semiconductors other than silicon, eg cadmium telluride (CdTe) and gallium arsenide (GaAs). Such films use much less material, and could reduce the cost of solar electricity.

One problem with solar energy is that the Sun does not shine all the time. We need a way of storing the energy. Photovoltaic energy is usually stored in lead–acid or nickel–cadmium batteries. An alternative means of storage is to use the electricity to generate chemical fuels, and the most promising fuel produced this way is hydrogen.

You will find out more about thin-film solar cells in **Activity US5.2**.

If you have a suitable solar cell available you can produce hydrogen from water in **Activity US5.3**.

US6 *The hydrogen economy*

Why hydrogen?

People who favour a hydrogen economy see water as a plentiful source of hydrogen. If hydrogen could be extracted from water without consuming fossil fuels it would reduce our dependence on these fuels, and help to reduce the amount of carbon dioxide released into the atmosphere.

Figure 41 This car is powered by hydrogen

Hydrogen could be distributed as we now distribute natural gas, and burned as a heating fuel, or used in internal combustion engines, or converted into electricity in a **fuel cell**.

But how can we make the hydrogen? The most likely large-scale method of producing hydrogen seems to be by electrolysis of water, obtaining the energy needed for this from some renewable source, such as solar cells. But why produce electricity and then use it to make hydrogen? There are two major advantages:

- hydrogen can be stored
- it can be used in the internal combustion engine.

A possible scheme is shown in Figure 42. It may seem a rather indirect way of producing hydrogen compared with the approach in Section **US4**, but all the technologies needed already exist. We have large-scale electrolysis plants for other purposes, large storage tanks, and a network of gas pipelines.

In **Activity US6.1** you can investigate the possibility of using hydrogen as a fuel for motor vehicles.

You can investigate how fuel cells work in **Activity US6.2**.

The hydrogen economy would use hydrogen as a way of storing and distributing energy. If systems are costed over whole lifetime use in terms of money and energy, then distributing hydrogen by pipeline may be cheaper than transmitting electricity.

Locally, fuel cells could be used to generate electricity on a small scale where it is needed, and where photovoltaic systems are not practical.

In **Chemical Ideas 1.5** you can find out how to use the ideal gas equation to carry out calculations on compressing hydrogen for transport and storage.

Figure 42 Hydrogen production in the future

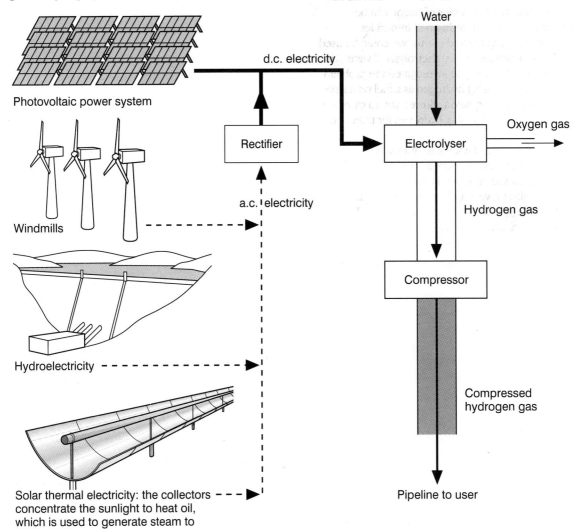

US7 *Summary*

In this unit you have studied some of the ways we could use the energy income from the Sun, rather than consuming our energy capital. Many other methods are also being explored. Green plants make use of solar energy to convert carbon dioxide and water into glucose and oxygen in a complex process called photosynthesis. In the first part of the unit you studied the first stage of photosynthesis, which takes place in strategically positioned reaction centres in the chloroplasts. This allowed you to extend your knowledge of the changes which can take place when substances interact with visible and ultra-violet radiation.

You then looked at the possibilities of setting up similar systems outside plants to obtain a fuel directly from sunlight. This led to a detailed study of redox reactions.

Another way of using sunlight is to generate electricity directly using photovoltaic cells. This introduced you to Group 4 semiconductors and you found out how the properties of silicon can be modified by the careful addition of impurities.

The electricity generated in this way could be used to generate hydrogen by the electrolysis of water. In the last part of the unit you investigated the problems and advantages of using hydrogen as a fuel on a large scale. The ideal gas equation allowed you to carry out calculations on compressing hydrogen for transport and storage.

Our main source of energy is ultimately from nuclear reactions. But we have a choice of reactors. We could build nuclear reactors on Earth, with all the attendant risks, or we could use that nuclear fusion reactor which already works, which is safe and which is 150 000 000 km away – the Sun.

Activity US7 will help you to check your notes at the end of this unit.

ENGINEERING PROTEINS

Why a unit on ENGINEERING PROTEINS?

This unit introduces you to proteins – one of the most versatile classes of chemicals found in all living things. Through the example of insulin – a hormone crucially important for life – you learn about the structures of proteins, their synthesis in cells, and how chemists are able to modify their structure and function: the technique of protein engineering. The unit ends by looking at enzymes – another vitally important class of proteins.

To understand how proteins are formed, you need to know about amino acids, and in that sense the unit carries forward your study of organic chemistry. But explanations of the structures and behaviour of proteins and other macromolecules found in cells are based on physical chemical ideas: in particular, molecular shape and intermolecular bonding, and chemical equilibrium. Studying the behaviour of enzymes also provides an opportunity to extend your chemical knowledge, this time about the rates of chemical reactions.

Overview of chemical principles

In this unit you will learn more about …

ideas introduced in earlier units in this course
- covalent bonding (**Elements of Life** and **Developing Fuels**)
- amines and amides (**The Polymer Revolution**)
- condensation (**The Polymer Revolution**)
- chemical equilibrium (**The Atmosphere**)
- the rates of chemical reactions (**The Atmosphere**)

… as well as learning new ideas about
- the shapes of molecules
- optical isomerism
- amino acids
- protein structure
- protein biosynthesis, DNA and RNA
- molecular recognition
- genetic engineering
- the effect of changes in concentration on a chemical equilibrium, and the use of K_c
- enzymes
- rate equations, reaction orders and half-lives.

EP1 *Christopher's story*

This story is based on an idea by Professor Guy Dodson and work done by his research group at the University of York. It is written for Christopher Altendorfer and William Lockhart.

Just another day

Christopher is 11 years old. Just over 2 years ago he suddenly became very ill; he was taken into hospital where tests showed that he had developed *diabetes*.

About one person in 400 develops this kind of diabetes – juvenile onset diabetes – when they are quite young.

For some reason, possibly as a result of an earlier viral infection, Christopher's pancreas had stopped producing a *hormone*: **insulin**. Hormones are chemicals which regulate the rate at which we carry out our body activities. Insulin controls the uptake of glucose and some other sugars by our cells. Without insulin, Christopher's cells could not absorb glucose, and its concentration in his blood was building up. Untreated, he would have died within a few weeks.

Today, Christopher looks like any other 11-year-old boy. He goes to school; he rides his bike; he swims. In fact, he's very fit because he has to take regular exercise and eat a healthy diet. No sweets or cakes; no sugary drinks. But for most people who produce no insulin of their own, a carefully controlled diet is not enough. They must take insulin, by injection, usually twice a day.

Figure 1 Christopher needs regular injections of insulin so that the cells in his body can absorb glucose

The morning regime goes like this. The first thing he does is to test his blood-sugar level. He pricks his finger, puts a drop of blood onto a strip of test paper and places the test paper into a machine. After a few seconds he reads the digital display and writes the figure into a notebook. This isn't part of the treatment; it's part of the monitoring process which helps him to keep his blood-sugar level within certain limits. The reading tells him how successfully he is balancing his insulin dose, his food intake and his exercise. Every few months, he sends his log books to the hospital to be checked. It's a way of encouraging him to be sensible, but Christopher doesn't need much encouragement – he remembers how he felt 2 years ago.

After the blood test, Christopher goes to the fridge and takes out two bottles of insulin. With the help of his mother, he mixes himself a dose and injects the insulin into a fold of skin below his ribs; from there it will act more quickly than from, say, an arm. Then, however hungry he might be, he must wait half an hour before he eats his breakfast. At first sight Christopher's breakfast looks like anyone else's. But there is always a measured amount of carbohydrate – cereal or bread perhaps – always fruit, and never any sugar. He puts sugar-free sweetener in his tea and on his cereal, and he has his own special jam.

Figure 2 Christopher's typical breakfast

Perhaps the most unusual thing about Christopher's day is the frequency and regularity of his meals. He eats breakfast, lunch and dinner, and those meals are interspersed with snacks. Whilst he is growing, this suits him fine: he says he's always hungry anyway! It may not be quite so easy when he's grown up, and it's certainly difficult to keep eating when he's ill.

Half an hour before his evening meal, he gives himself another injection of insulin. Whatever he's doing, he must stop for that. Life can get exciting: one Sunday morning, Christopher's mother dropped one of the insulin bottles on the kitchen floor and it broke. She phoned the local pharmacist who came out specially to open the shop. As long as Christopher gets his twice-daily dose of insulin, he remains fit and well. Without insulin, he would die. The pharmacist took the situation very seriously.

More about insulin

Insulin is a hormone, and a **protein**. Many hormones are proteins (for example human growth hormone) but there are others, like the sex hormones, which are not.

The name *protein* (meaning 'first thing') was coined by Berzelius in 1838. He had little idea what proteins were, but he recognised their importance because they were so widespread in living things.

Proteins are big molecules with relative molecular masses up to about 100 000. They play a key role in almost every structure and activity of a living organism. That's why they are regarded as among the most important constituents of our bodies.

Insulin was first isolated in 1921 by two young scientists, F G Banting and C H Best, working in Toronto. Only 1 year later it became available for the treatment of diabetes in the form of a preparation extracted from the pancreas of pigs or cows. Before then, diabetes was frequently fatal, and diabetics spent their numbered days living miserable lives on starvation diets which were designed to contain as little sugar or starch as possible. Vegetables which had been boiled three or four times and agar jelly (a protein) were standard fare.

Figure 4 Protein in the form of collagen is an important part of animal skins – leather is made of animal skin, so consists partly of protein

Injections of insulin have transformed the situation. Today we don't even need to use pig or beef insulin – we have synthetic human insulin available from the biochemical industry. But the treatment still doesn't mimic natural insulin production as in non-diabetic people.

Splitting the six-pack

What happens to insulin levels when we eat? Figure 5 shows how the concentration of insulin in the blood of a non-diabetic person would be expected to behave after a meal.

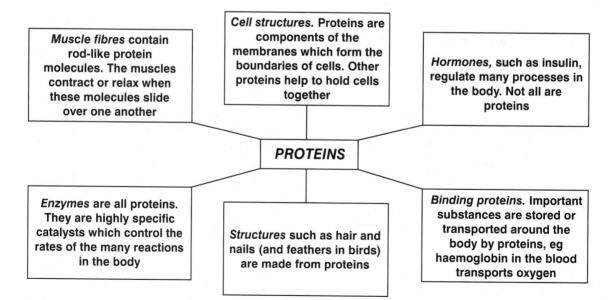

Muscle fibres contain rod-like protein molecules. The muscles contract or relax when these molecules slide over one another

Cell structures. Proteins are components of the membranes which form the boundaries of cells. Other proteins help to hold cells together

Hormones, such as insulin, regulate many processes in the body. Not all are proteins

PROTEINS

Enzymes are all proteins. They are highly specific catalysts which control the rates of the many reactions in the body

Structures such as hair and nails (and feathers in birds) are made from proteins

Binding proteins. Important substances are stored or transported around the body by proteins, eg haemoglobin in the blood transports oxygen

Figure 3 Proteins perform other functions in our bodies in addition to acting as hormones

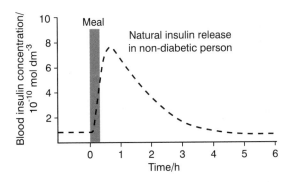

Figure 5 Insulin levels in the blood of a non-diabetic person

Notice four points about this graph:

- a concentration as low as 10^{-10} mol dm^{-3} of insulin in the blood can have profound physiological effects
- there is a low-level, 'background' concentration of insulin in the body, even when food is not being digested
- insulin release follows rapidly after eating
- the insulin level peaks soon after eating and then falls off, eventually reaching the 'background' level.

We don't just make insulin when we eat: we make it all the time, and it is stored in special cells in the body. It is not stored in the form of individual molecules, but as **hexamers** – six molecules clustered together because of interactions between their surfaces.

When the concentration of glucose in the blood rises, insulin hexamers are released into the bloodstream. This makes the insulin solution very dilute, and the hexamers burst apart. The monomers are then quickly carried to where they are needed.

Why does Christopher have to wait for half an hour between his insulin injection and his meal? Figure 6 shows how his blood insulin concentration might vary. (Also shown, for easy comparison, is the curve from Figure 5 for a non-diabetic person.)

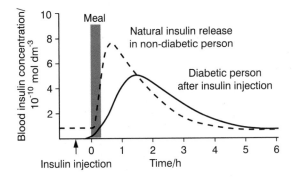

Figure 6 Insulin levels in the blood of a diabetic person following an insulin injection (injections also contain a slow-acting form of insulin which produces an effect for up to 12 hours; after that the insulin level falls to zero)

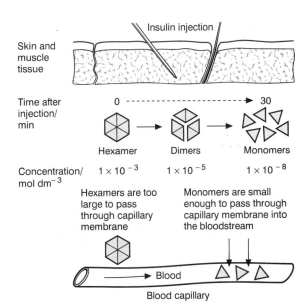

Figure 7 Injecting insulin

Christopher doesn't have a store of insulin which special cells can release directly into his bloodstream. He has to inject hexamers just under his skin, and they are too big to pass immediately through the capillary membranes into his blood. They have to spread out at the injection site and become diluted before they can break up into dimers and monomers which can diffuse away. This takes time. That's why Christopher has to inject his insulin half an hour before he starts to eat.

Christopher uses two bottles to prepare his dose because his injection is a mixture of two types of insulin. One has been prepared so that it breaks down easily and produces an effect close to the rapid response of normally produced insulin; the other breaks down slowly and gives him a low-level insulin concentration which is not permanent but which does last for up to 12 hours.

Christopher's injection is an improvement on the early preparations but, even so, the two curves in Figure 6 are clearly different. Because the insulin levels are different, diabetic people will still have unusual blood glucose levels, and this can lead to complications and illness later in life. That's why Christopher also has to be so careful about his diet.

But the big difference, of course, is that normal insulin release switches on and off every time we eat – our insulin levels fit in with our food intake. It's the other way round for Christopher: his meals have to be planned around his levels of injected insulin.

To help Christopher further and make his injections mimic natural insulin release more closely, the half-hour time delay during which hexamers begin to break down needs to be eliminated. That would mean injecting insulin monomers which can get straight into the bloodstream: Christopher could then have injections along with his meal. Life would be closer to normal – and so would his blood-sugar levels.

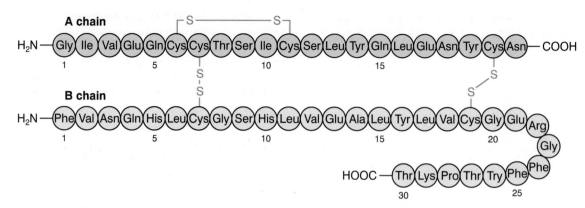

Figure 9 Human insulin

Insulin monomers can be made. Clinical trials of the new form of the hormone began in 1987 and the results so far are encouraging.

Before monomeric insulin could be made, scientists needed a thorough understanding of the protein's structure and function. This required contributions over many years from many areas of science. In particular, scientists needed to know

- the composition and structure of insulin
- the shape of the monomer and the regions of the molecule which interact to form dimers and hexamers
- the types of intermolecular interaction which occur in the hexamer
- how to modify the monomer proteins to prevent them sticking together.

Figure 8 Christopher injects insulin hexamers into the tissues just below his skin; it takes about half an hour for the hexamers to diffuse apart, split into monomers and enter his bloodstream

Modifying the structure of a protein is called **protein engineering**. In this unit you will find out about one way of making and modifying proteins using **genetic engineering** – but first you need to know more about proteins and how they are made in the body.

EP2 *Protein building*

Amino acids: the building blocks of proteins

Figure 9 illustrates the composition of a molecule of human insulin.

The abbreviations in circles represent the **α-amino acids** which have combined to form insulin. There are two short chains of these amino acid residues – the parts of the original molecules which are joined together to form the protein. All the proteins in the world are made from just 20 α-amino acids which have the same general structure as shown in Figure 10.

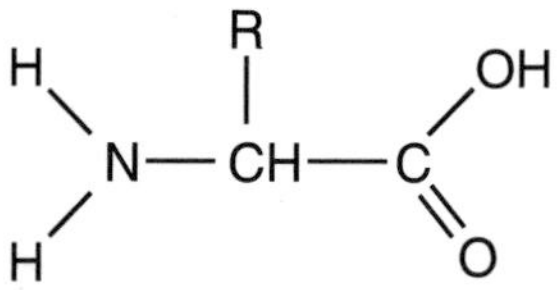

$$\underset{H}{\overset{H}{N}}-\underset{R}{\overset{|}{CH}}-\underset{\parallel O}{C}-OH$$

The amino group (–NH$_2$) and the carboxylic acid group (–COOH) are both attached to the same carbon atom: the α-carbon. That is why they are called α-amino acids.

Figure 10 General structure of α-amino acids

You can read about the reactions of carboxylic acids in **Chemical Ideas 13.4**.

You can learn more about amines and amino acids in **Chemical Ideas 13.7**.

The 20 amino acids which occur in proteins each have a different side chain, labelled R. Table 1 shows the structures of these R groups and the names of the amino acids, together with their abbreviated symbols.

In all of us, even adults who have stopped growing, proteins need to be continuously replaced. This is obvious when your hair and your nails grow after they have been cut. It is also important that hormones and some enzymes (like the digestive enzymes) are made when needed, then destroyed once they have done their job, so that they do not go on producing their effects after the need has passed.

Table 1 The 20 amino acids which make up proteins (for clarity, the whole amino acid has been drawn out in the case of proline)

Amino acid	Abbreviation	R group	Amino acid	Abbreviation	R group
glycine	Gly	—H	cysteine	Cys	—CH₂—SH
alanine	Ala	—CH₃	methionine	Met	—CH₂—CH₂—S—CH₃
valine	Val	—CH(CH₃)CH₃	aspartic acid	Asp	—CH₂—C(=O)OH
leucine	Leu	—CH₂—CH(CH₃)CH₃	glutamic acid	Glu	—CH₂—CH₂—C(=O)OH
isoleucine	Ile	—CH(CH₂—CH₃)CH₃	asparagine	Asn	—CH₂—C(=O)NH₂
phenylalanine	Phe	—CH₂—(phenyl ring)	glutamine	Gln	—CH₂—CH₂—C(=O)NH₂
proline	Pro	(pyrrolidine ring: HN–CH–COOH)	tyrosine	Tyr	—CH₂—(phenol ring)—OH
tryptophan	Trp	(indole ring with CH₂)	histidine	His	—CH₂—(imidazole ring: HN, N)
serine	Ser	—CH₂—OH	lysine	Lys	—CH₂—CH₂—CH₂—CH₂—NH₂
threonine	Thr	—CH(CH₃)OH	arginine	Arg	—CH₂—CH₂—CH₂—NH—C(=NH)NH₂

We replace our proteins from the food we eat, but we do not need to eat proteins which are identical to the ones being replaced. We do not need to eat human hair or finger nails to grow our own! In fact, we don't even have to eat animal protein; we can supply our needs by eating plants.

Activity EP2.1 allows you to investigate the reactions of amines and amino acids.

This is because our bodies break proteins down into their constituent 'building blocks' – amino acids. Eight of these are usually classified as *essential amino acids* – our bodies cannot synthesise them: we must take them in as food. The other 12 can be made from carbohydrate and other amino acids in the body.

The amino acids are then reassembled to make our own collection of proteins. For each of us, this collection is unique: most of your proteins will be identical to those found in other humans, but some will be different. Human proteins are also different from the proteins of other animals. However, in some cases very similar proteins are found not just throughout the animal kingdom but in plants and micro-organisms as well: for example, the enzymes which oxidise glucose in cells' metabolism.

All these millions of proteins are built up from the same small number of amino acids. What makes each protein different is the order in which the amino acids are joined to one another. This is called the **primary structure** of the protein. You have already seen the primary structure of human insulin in Figure 9.

In **Activity EP2.2** you can break down aspartame and identify its amino acid components.

Figure 11 The artificial sweetener aspartame *is made from a combination of two amino acids; it is not a sugar and so it can be used by diabetics*

ASSIGNMENT I

The amino acids in Table 1 are grouped according to key features of their R groups: for example, whether their side chains are polar and will interact strongly with water, or whether they are non-polar and will disrupt water's intermolecular bonding. Use the abbreviated symbols for the amino acids to answer the questions below.

a List four amino acids in each case which you think have
  i non-polar side chains
  ii polar side chains
  iii ionisable groups on their side chain.

b Look at the structures of leucine and isoleucine. Explain why isoleucine is so named.

c List one amino acid in each case in which the R group contains
  i a primary alcohol group
  ii a secondary alcohol group
  iii a phenol group
  iv a carboxylic acid group.

Making peptides

When amino acids combine to form a protein like insulin, the carboxylic acid group on one amino acid joins on to the amino group on the next, and a molecule of water is lost from between them. This type of process is called a **condensation**, and the –CONH– group which links the amino acid residues in the product is called a **peptide link**. Two amino acids joined in this way make a *dipeptide*.

two amino acids
(R and R' represent different side chains)
produce a dipeptide

H_2O

peptide link

You met amides and condensation reactions in **The Polymer Revolution** storyline, Section **PR5**.

The same group can be formed between any carboxylic acid and any amine, but in this more general case it is usually referred to as a **secondary amide group** (or more simply an **amide group**).

CH$_3$—C(OH)(=O)—N(H)(H)—CH$_2$—CH$_3$

secondary amide group
linking ethanoic acid
and propylamine residues

H$_2$O

CH$_3$—C(=O)—N(H)—CH$_2$—CH$_3$

Chemists cannot make amino acids react together directly. They have to make the –COOH group more reactive: for example, by turning it into an acyl (acid) chloride. To make proteins, they also need to take into account another property of amino acids.

Amino acid molecules are not flat: they have a three-dimensional shape based upon the tetrahedral arrangement of the four bonds around the α-carbon atom. When we look at them properly in this way, all the amino acids in Table 1, with the exception of glycine, exist in *two* isomeric forms known as **D** or **L optical isomers**. Proteins are built up from only the L isomers.

You can learn more about the shapes of molecules by reading **Chemical Ideas 3.3**.

Chemical Ideas 3.6 tells you more about optical isomerism.

Cells are able to build up proteins directly from amino acids, and only the L amino acids react. That's why chemists are learning how to use bacterial and yeast cells to make proteins – in many ways it's better than using traditional techniques.

As a chemist you would need three things before you could synthesise a protein in the laboratory:

- a set of instructions for the protein – in other words, something which told you its primary structure
- supplies of the pure amino acids ready for you to use in the appropriate steps
- a way of making the amino and carboxylic acid groups react with one another more easily.

Representing amino acid sequences

The dipeptide obtained by condensing the carboxylic acid group of glycine with the amino group of alanine has the structure

H$_2$N—CH(H)—CO—NH—CH(CH$_3$)—COOH

This dipeptide would be abbreviated to **Gly Ala**. The convention of reading peptide groups in the direction with the free NH$_2$ group on the left is very important if the amino acid sequence is to be read unambiguously.

If we look at how a cell makes its proteins we can see a close parallel with what the chemist would do.

ASSIGNMENT 2

a Draw the structure of the dipeptide Ala Gly.

b In the tripeptide Ser Gly Ala, which amino acid has an unreacted
  i NH$_2$ group?
  ii COOH group?

Balloons can be used to give quite good illustrations of molecular shapes. You can try using them like this in **Activity EP2.3**.

In **Activity EP2.4** you can build models for some amino acids and investigate optical isomerism further.

Activity EP2.5 illustrates one way your body can recognise the different D and L forms of a molecule.

Activity EP2.6 helps you to summarise what you have read so far in Section **EP2**.

How cells make proteins

The instructions specifying the primary structure of insulin are carried by molecules of a **ribonucleic acid (RNA)**. There are many different RNA molecules. **Messenger RNA** (or **mRNA**) molecules provide a code which tells the cell which amino acids to put together, in which order, to make a protein. Just as there are many different proteins, so there are many different mRNA molecules.

The amino acids which the cell has to use are not in separate containers as they would be in the laboratory: they are dissolved and mixed together in the fluid within the cell. **Transfer RNA** (or **tRNA**) molecules play a similar role to the person who separates the amino acids for you at the chemical supplier. They select and separate the amino acids needed for protein synthesis.

The cell has a different tRNA for each different amino acid. It also has a set of enzymes which recognise the tRNA and its corresponding amino acid. The enzymes catalyse the formation of an ester bond between the carboxylic acid group of the amino acid and an –OH group on the tRNA. Once the enzyme has joined the amino acid to the tRNA, the resulting complex can diffuse to the place where the protein is being made.

Figure 12 shows that RNA molecules consist of strands formed from **ribose** sugar molecules and **phosphate** groups. One of four **bases** is attached to each ribose unit. The order of bases shown in Figure 12 is for illustration only: the sequence is different in different RNA molecules.

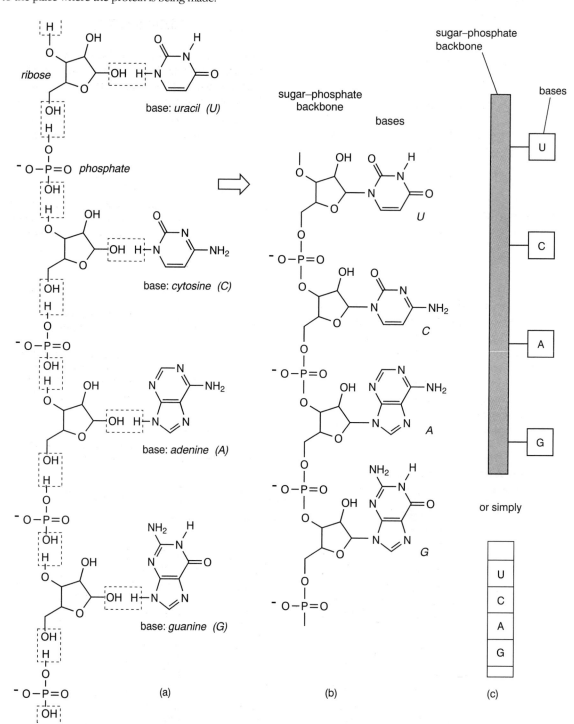

Figure 12 *Representations of the structure of RNA: (a) how groups join together; (b) a skeletal formula; and (c) two simpler ways of showing the structure*

It is the bases which form the code for protein synthesis and we can regard the sugar–phosphate strand as just a 'backbone' on which they are held. Two simpler ways of depicting RNA are also shown in Figure 12.

The cell's catalyst for protein production is a small particle called a **ribosome**. This contains a third type of ribonucleic acid, **ribosomal RNA (or rRNA)** bound to protein molecules. When the mRNA and the ribosome have collided in the fluid in the cell, the ribosome moves along the mRNA, rather like a bead on a chain, reading the code, and catalysing the reactions which join the amino acids together.

ASSIGNMENT 3

a In the formation of RNA, what type of reaction is responsible for the linking of
  i the ribose and phosphate?
  ii the ribose and base?

b The skeletal formula of ribose is shown in the illustration of RNA (Figure 12). Draw a full structural formula for ribose.

Cracking the code

How can *four* bases code for *20* amino acids? If a single base told the cell to build an amino acid into a protein, there would need to be 20 different bases. But there are only four bases, so protein building can't be coded by single bases.

Writing the code in pairs of bases isn't enough either – it would only cover 16 amino acids (you should be able to write down 16 different pairs of the four letters U, C, A and G).

In fact, a **triplet code** is needed, where a combination of three bases tells the cell which amino acid to use. There are now more combinations than there are amino acids, so some amino acids are defined by several base triplets. The combinations, or **codons**, are shown in Table 2. Notice that there are also codons which *stop* the protein chain building.

ASSIGNMENT 4

Table 2 shows that for some amino acids only the first *two* bases of the RNA codon are important. The identity of the third base does not matter. Make a list of these amino acids.

For other amino acids, it is important that all *three* bases are correct. Make a list of these amino acids.

tRNA molecules can recognise and bind to the codons on mRNA through **anti-codons**. Base G in the anti-codon specifically recognises base C in the codon (and vice versa). Bases U and A recognise one another similarly. So, for example, anti-codon GUA will bind to codon CAU.

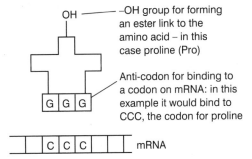

Figure 13 Schematic representation of a tRNA molecule showing the three bases which form the anti-codon

Table 2 The triplet base code used in mRNA

First base	Second base				Third base
	U	C	A	G	
U	UUU Phe	UCU Ser	UAU Tyr	UGU Cys	U
	UUC Phe	UCC Ser	UAC Tyr	UGC Cys	C
	UUA Leu	UCA Ser	UAA Stop	UGA Stop	A
	UUG Leu	UCG Ser	UAG Stop	UGG Trp	G
C	CUU Leu	CCU Pro	CAU His	CGU Arg	U
	CUC Leu	CCC Pro	CAC His	CGC Arg	C
	CUA Leu	CCA Pro	CAA Gln	CGA Arg	A
	CUG Leu	CCG Pro	CAG Gln	CGG Arg	G
A	AUU Ile	ACU Thr	AAU Asn	AGU Ser	U
	AUC Ile	ACC Thr	AAC Asn	AGC Ser	C
	AUA Ile	ACA Thr	AAA Lys	AGA Arg	A
	AUG Met	ACG Thr	AAG Lys	AGG Arg	G
G	GUU Val	GCU Ala	GAU Asp	GGU Gly	U
	GUC Val	GCC Ala	GAC Asp	GGC Gly	C
	GUA Val	GCA Ala	GAA Glu	GGA Gly	A
	GUG Val	GCG Ala	GAG Glu	GGG Gly	G

Figure 14 summarises the roles of the different types of RNA in protein synthesis.

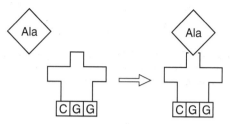

Messenger RNA (mRNA) carries the code for protein synthesis

Transfer RNA (tRNA) collects an amino acid and takes it to the mRNA strand

Ribosomes contain **ribosomal RNA (rRNA)** and catalyse protein synthesis

Figure 14 The roles of the different types of RNA in protein synthesis

Figure 15 shows how the codons on a mRNA molecule are read as they are threaded through the ribosome and 'translated' into a protein chain.

You can think of the ribosome as sliding along the mRNA chain rather like a bead. tRNA molecules, each carrying an amino acid, feed into the front of the ribosome and the protein chain grows from the back.

In recent years, chemists have learned a lot about how molecules recognise one another. The molecules must have shapes which fit neatly together so that groups are placed in the best positions for the formation of intermolecular bonds.

The bases in RNA all have flat shapes, and Figure 16 shows how the correct pairs of bases fit neatly together and place groups in just the right positions for hydrogen bonds to form.

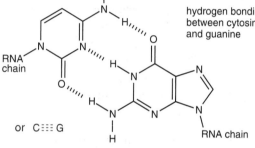

Figure 16 Molecular recognition and bases on RNA (the symbol ::: is used to represent two hydrogen bonds; ::::: represents three hydrogen bonds)

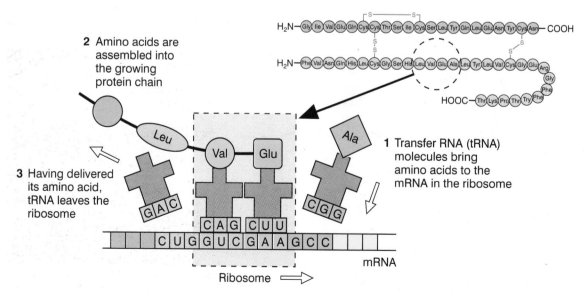

2 Amino acids are assembled into the growing protein chain

3 Having delivered its amino acid, tRNA leaves the ribosome

1 Transfer RNA (tRNA) molecules bring amino acids to the mRNA in the ribosome

Figure 15 Protein synthesis and the reading of codons on mRNA

ASSIGNMENT 5

a Use the codons from Table 2 to predict the peptides which would be obtained if RNA molecules with the following patterns of bases were used:

   i AAAAA …
   ii CGCGCGCG …
   iii UACCUAACU

b Predict the base triplet anti-codons for the amino acids

   i Trp
   ii Asp.

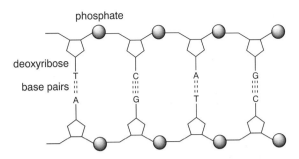

Figure 17 Two DNA strands held together by hydrogen bonds between pairs of bases (again === and ≡≡≡ are used to represent sets of two and three hydrogen bonds)

A permanent record

mRNA is destroyed when production of its corresponding protein is no longer required. It represents a temporary set of instructions for producing a protein. The cell keeps the permanent record in the nucleus in the form of other strand-like molecules known as **deoxyribonucleic acid (DNA)** molecules. DNA and RNA both consist of sugar–phosphate strands with attached bases, but there are important differences:

- the sugar, ribose, in RNA is replaced by deoxyribose in DNA, hence the change of letters from R to D
- the base uracil (U) in RNA is replaced by the base *thymine* (T) in DNA
- two strands of DNA are normally paired off together in the famous *double helix* arrangement proposed in 1953 by Francis Crick and James Watson.

ribose

deoxyribose – note the absence of an OH group

thymine

Crucial to Crick and Watson's double helix model was the understanding that pairs of bases in DNA can form hydrogen bonds together: A with T, and C with G.

The hydrogen bonding interactions between C and G are identical to those which occur between RNA codons and anti-codons. The A === T interaction is similar to that between A and U in RNA: the bases thymine and uracil differ only by the presence of a methyl group in thymine.

Figure 18 shows how the double helix of DNA molecules is held together by hydrogen bonding between the bases.

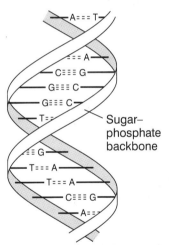

Figure 18 An illustration of the DNA double helix

Sugar–phosphate backbone

Figure 19 Francis Crick (right) and James Watson (left) in 1953 with their model of part of a DNA molecule

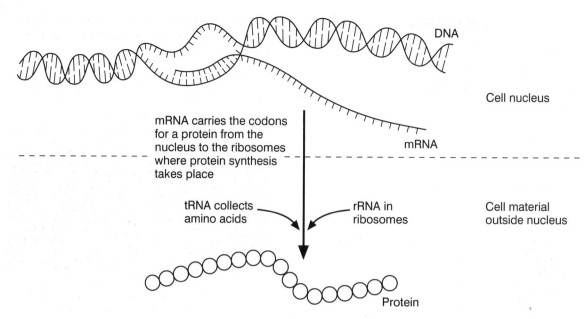

Figure 20 *A summary of protein synthesis in higher organisms*

mRNA carries the codons for a protein from the nucleus to the ribosomes where protein synthesis takes place

DNA

Cell nucleus

mRNA

tRNA collects amino acids

rRNA in ribosomes

Cell material outside nucleus

Protein

In **Activity EP2.7** you can make a model of the DNA double helix.

You can find out about the events leading up to Crick and Watson's breakthrough and read their original paper in **Activity EP2.8**.

When a cell starts protein production, the record in the DNA has to be turned into an RNA message carried by mRNA, which is then 'read' to form the protein as shown in Figure 15.

The full process is summarised in Figure 20.

With only very few exceptions, all cells use the same system, which we can sum up as:

DNA codes for RNA
RNA codes for proteins

Another important contrast between DNA and RNA is that each DNA molecule contains the information for the production of many different mRNA molecules, but each mRNA molecule is a set of instructions for just one protein. A DNA segment responsible for a particular protein is called a **gene**.

The full set of all the genes of an organism its called its **genome**. In 1987 two laboratories produced maps of the genome of the bacterium *Escherichia coli*. The genome consists of about 4.7×10^6 base pairs (see Figure 17) which account for about 300 genes. The bacterium can therefore produce about 300 different proteins.

The human genome consists of about 3.5×10^9 base pairs: between 50 000 and 100 000 genes. We can produce between 50 000 and 100 000 proteins.

Mapping the human genome is an ambitious, and costly, undertaking. The *Human Genome Project* was set up in 1988 to achieve this. It is a vast international venture which is expected to take at least 15 years.

Figure 21 *The Genome Database at John Hopkins University, Baltimore, USA, contains records of all the information collected so far about the human genome*

Every cell in your body contains a full set of genes and so has a DNA molecule which carries, for example, the gene for insulin production. But the gene is only 'switched on' in the special pancreas cells which make insulin.

In addition to very many genes, DNA molecules contain base combinations which start or stop RNA production, as well as regions of 'junk DNA' which appear to have no function – perhaps relics of earlier predecessor organisms.

ASSIGNMENT 6

One strand of DNA in a cell nucleus carries the following sequence of bases: CAGT.

a Write down the corresponding sequence of bases on the mRNA strand which copies from it.

b Write down the corresponding sequence of bases on the other DNA strand in the double helix.

EP3 *Genetic engineering*

Changing genes

How can we make human insulin? You might think it could be done by removing some human pancreas cells, growing them by supplying them with the appropriate amino acid nutrients, and then extracting the insulin. Unfortunately this can't be done: human cells do not grow like this.

But the technology for handling other types of more robust cells, particularly bacterial and yeast cells, is well established. Bacteria can be used to produce chemicals like lactic acid. Brewers have used yeasts for thousands of years to convert sugars into ethanol; more recently, pharmaceuticals like penicillin and oxytetracycline have been made in fermenters using moulds.

In recent years, scientists have learnt how to build human genes into bacterial or yeast cells. These cells can then be used to generate proteins. The insulin gene can be used in this way. The first human insulin was made using the bacterium *E. coli* and became available in 1982. More recently, yeast cells – which more closely resemble human cells – are being used.

Figure 22 Genetically engineered yeast cells are fermented under carefully controlled conditions; the cells multiply rapidly and produce a precursor of insulin, which is converted to human insulin using enzymes

Taking genes from the cells of one type of organism and putting them into the cells of another type of organism is called **genetic engineering** or *recombinant DNA technology*. The details of the method vary according to the gene and the micro-organism: no two processes are identical. Figure 23 represents a generalised approach.

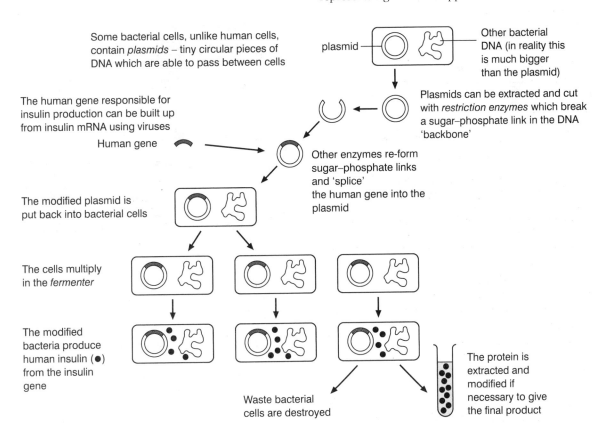

Figure 23 An illustration of the general approach used to produce a sample of insulin using genetic engineering

New genes go out to work

Proteins such as insulin, human growth hormone and factor 8 (the blood clotting agent given to haemophiliacs) are products of genetic engineering. An important advantage of such products is that they are purer than the ones prepared by traditional means. For example, genetically engineered factor 8 removes the risk of haemophiliacs contracting AIDS through blood products from infected donors. But the applications and potential of genetic engineering reach wider than pharmaceuticals.

Vaccines

The body's immune system defends it against virus infection by recognising the protein coating on the outside of the virus. If the coat protein is produced via genetic engineering – minus its dangerous contents – it can be injected into the body to act as a vaccine. Hepatitis B vaccine is produced and works in this way.

Waste management and pollution control

Modified bacteria and fungi, which turn potentially harmful materials into harmless forms, could be used widely by industry and environmental protection agencies. A new oil-digesting 'superbug' has been created which contains a collection of genes from several bacteria. The bacteria have been chosen because they each metabolise different components of crude oil. When the appropriate genes from all the bacteria are combined, the resultant bacterium can break down all the chemicals found in crude oil.

Figure 24 Oil spillages can be treated with oil-digesting bacteria – a product of genetic engineering

Materials

Poly(hydroxybutyrate) is a biodegradable plastic. You might have read about it in **The Polymer Revolution**, **Activity PR8.1.** It is made by the bacterium *Alcaligenes eutrophus*. The gene which leads to the production of poly(hydroxybutyrate) has been placed into another bacterium which bursts open when it is heated. The polymer can then be extracted more easily.

Pest and weed control

Two approaches are being explored in this area.

- Genes for pesticide or herbicide resistance can be transferred into important crop strains. The land is then sprayed to kill off pests or weeds without damage to the crop.
- Some plants produce their own natural pesticides. Genes for producing proteins which are toxic to predatory insects have been introduced into tobacco and tomato plants. This reduces the need for spraying with synthetic pesticides.

Figure 25 Batches of genetically engineered potato seeds at a research laboratory in California. The aim is to produce disease-free potatoes and bring down growers' costs

Selective plant breeding

Genes for enhanced photosynthesis or increased drought resistance can be introduced into plants to enable them to be grown in less sunny or drier climates. A future application might involve giving plants genes which are responsible for nitrogen fixation, thus reducing the need for artificial fertilisers.

EP4 *Proteins in 3-D*

Folded chains

Beef, pig and human insulin all have different primary structures, but they are equally effective at treating diabetes. So scientists need to know about more than just primary structure before they understand how insulin works. One thing they now know is that insulin, like most proteins, has a precise shape which arises from the folding together of the chains. The action of insulin is critically dependent on this shape.

As long as different molecules fold to the same shape, they may have the same action. Chain folding gives proteins their three-dimensional shape; it also places chemical groupings in positions where they can interact most effectively.

Four types of interactions are important in chain folding:

- **instantaneous dipole-induced dipole attractive forces** between non-polar side chains on amino acids like phenylalanine and leucine. The centres of protein molecules tend to contain amino acids like these so that the non-polar groups do not interfere with the hydrogen bonding between the surrounding water molecules.
- **hydrogen bonding** between polar side chains (eg $-CH_2OH$ in serine and $-CH_2CONH_2$ in asparagine), *and* between the peptide groups which link the chain together. If amino acids with these side chains are situated on the outside of proteins, hydrogen bonds can also form to water molecules surrounding the protein.
- **ionic attractions** between ionisable side chains, such as $-CH_2COO^-$ in aspartic acid and $-CH_2CH_2CH_2CH_2NH_3^+$ in lysine.
- **covalent bonding**. The $-SH$ groups on neighbouring cysteine residues can be oxidised to form $-S-S$ links: look back at Figure 9 on p. 138. There are three such links in human insulin; two hold the A and B chains together.

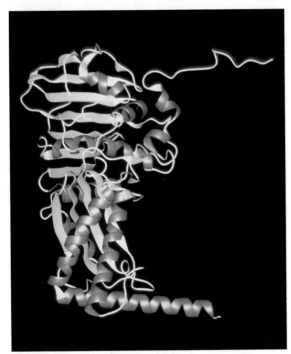

*Figure 26 The tertiary structure of a protein; here the enzyme gyrase is illustrated as a **ribbon diagram**. The helices (in red) and the sheets (in yellow) show up clearly in this representation. The thin white lines represent irregular regions. (Gyrase is involved in the DNA unwinding process)*

You can read about instantaneous dipole-induced dipole forces and hydrogen bonding in **Chemical Ideas 5.2** and **5.3**.

The chains in a protein are often folded or twisted in a regular manner as a result of hydrogen bonding. Two arrangements of the protein chain are common:

- tightly *coiled* into a **helix** where the C=O group of one peptide link forms a hydrogen bond to an N–H group *four* peptide links along the chain
- stretched out into regions of *extended* chain, which lie alongside one another and hydrogen bond to form a **sheet**.

The two components of a protein's shape – helix and sheet – are sometimes referred to as its **secondary structure**.

The chains may fold up further. The overall shape is stabilised by instantaneous dipole-induced dipole attractive forces, by hydrogen bonding, by ionic attractions and by covalent bonding. The overall shape of a protein is sometimes called its **tertiary structure**.

Compare the ribbon diagram of insulin in Figure 27 with Figure 9 on p. 138, which shows its primary structure.

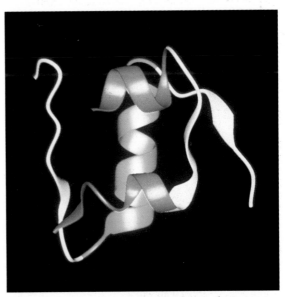

Figure 27 A ribbon diagram showing the two chains in insulin. There are two short helical sections (in red) in the A chain. The B chain contains a helical section (in blue) between amino acids 9 (Ser) and 19 (Cys)

Insulin hexamers

The same ideas about intermolecular interactions help to explain why insulin molecules stick together to form dimers and hexamers. The **space filling model** of the insulin monomer illustrated in Figure 28 on the next page shows that one side of its structure consists mainly of amino acids with non-polar side chains.

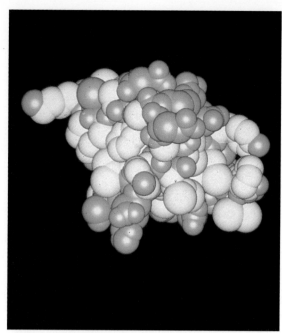

Figure 28 Space filling representation of an insulin monomer: the white spheres represent amino acid residues with non-polar side chains

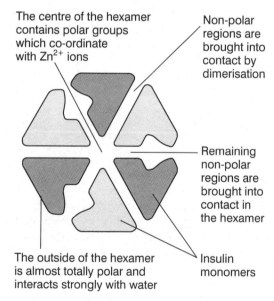

The centre of the hexamer contains polar groups which co-ordinate with Zn^{2+} ions

Non-polar regions are brought into contact by dimerisation

Remaining non-polar regions are brought into contact in the hexamer

The outside of the hexamer is almost totally polar and interacts strongly with water

Insulin monomers

Figure 29 An insulin hexamer

Left exposed to water, this non-polar side of the insulin monomer would disrupt water's hydrogen bonding. The non-polar sides of two insulin monomers come together when a dimer is formed, so the disruption is reduced. Figure 29 shows that a similar thing happens when hexamers form.

The arrangement of several protein sub-units into a bigger unit is sometimes referred to as **quaternary structure**.

So, for insulin, we have

- **primary structure**: the order of amino acid residues
- **secondary structure**: coiling of parts of the chain into a helix or the formation of a region of sheet
- **tertiary structure**: folding of the chain into an insulin monomer
- **quaternary structure**: joining of monomers into a hexamer.

Figures 30 and 31 show a space filling diagram and a skeletal diagram of the insulin hexamer.

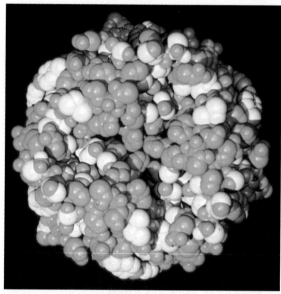

Figure 30 A space filling diagram of the quaternary structure of an insulin hexamer: the white spheres represent amino acid residues with non-polar side chains

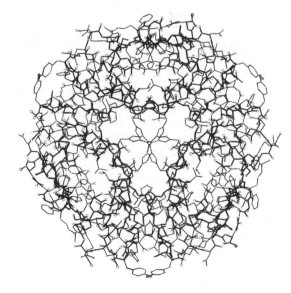

Figure 31 Skeletal diagram of the insulin hexamer

Working out the structure of insulin

Insulin was recognised as a protein in 1928. Its primary structure was revealed in 1955 by Professor Fred Sanger and his team at Cambridge. They broke the protein into shorter bits by hydrolysis, then used chromatography to identify these bits. By piecing together the bits, they eventually worked out the amino acid sequence. Professor Sanger received a Nobel Prize for his work on the amino acid sequencing of proteins and a second Nobel Prize for more recent work on sequencing DNA.

The three-dimensional structure of insulin has been worked out from X-ray diffraction studies carried out by Professor Dorothy Hodgkin's group at Oxford. Professor Hodgkin received a Nobel Prize in 1964 for earlier work, particularly work on the structure of vitamin B_{12} and penicillin. At that time she was only the third woman, after Marie Curie and her daughter Irène Joliot-Curie, to receive a Nobel Prize.

Figure 32 Professor Dorothy Hodgkin with a model of insulin

EP5 *Giving evolution a push*

Insulins that stay single

Insulin monomers are better for diabetics than insulin hexamers because they work faster. So is there a way of injecting monomers rather than hexamers?

The trouble is that the hexamer and its monomers are in dynamic equilibrium:

insulin hexamer	$\rightleftharpoons$	3 insulin dimers	$\rightleftharpoons$	6 insulin monomers
Ins_6	$\rightleftharpoons$	$3Ins_2$	$\rightleftharpoons$	$6Ins$

and the positions of these equilibria depend on the concentration of the insulin in solution. Look back at Figure 7 on p. 137. As hexamers spread out from the injection site, they become diluted and the equilibria shift towards the right.

Insulin monomers are the main form present when the concentration of the solution has fallen from 1×10^{-3} mol dm^{-3} to 1×10^{-8} mol dm^{-3}. But injecting a dilute monomer solution just would not be practicable: the volume of solution needed would be enormous!

You met the idea of chemical equilibrium in **Chemical Ideas 7.1**. You can find out more about the effect of concentration on the position of an equilibrium in **Chemical Ideas 7.2**.

ASSIGNMENT 7

The equilibrium between the insulin hexamer and insulin dimer can be represented as

$$Ins_6 \rightleftharpoons 3Ins_2$$

Write an expression for the equilibrium constant K_c for this reaction.

What are the units of K_c?

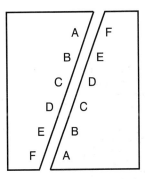

Figure 33 When one of the shapes is turned upside down, the letters (which represent amino acid residues) do not lie in contact with their counterparts on the other shape

A possible solution might be to modify the structure of the insulin monomers to prevent them sticking together so readily. The position of equilibrium for the modified insulin would be much further to the right and the monomers would be stable in more concentrated solutions.

Figure 29 on p. 150 shows that insulin monomers fit together so that chemically identical faces – faces which possess the same amino acid sequences – are in contact. But the monomers are chiral. So, when they form dimers, one of the monomers must be 'upside down' in relation to the other. An individual amino acid residue on one monomer is therefore not in contact with its counterpart on the other monomer. The simple illustration in Figure 33 shows what this means.

A closer look at the amino acid residues on the dimerising surfaces shows that most of them have non-polar side chains, but some are polar or contain ionised groups.

For example, residue B13 (amino acid 13 in the B chain) is a glutamic acid with a negatively charged side chain containing the –COO⁻ group. This is placed next to residue B9 – serine with a polar side chain containing the $-CH_2OH$ group – in the dimer.

Figure 34 Space filling representation of an insulin dimer showing the positions of amino acids serine B9 (in yellow) and glutamic acid B13 (in red)

What would happen if B9 were changed to aspartic acid – another amino acid with a negatively charged side chain? Four negatively charged COO^- groups – two aspartic acid/glutamic acid pairs – would be placed together and the dimer would be blown apart.

Changes like this can be studied without doing experiments, by making use of **computer graphics**. Powerful programs can be used to generate views of the protein structure, like the one in Figure 34, which can be rotated through any angle to study the shape in detail.

Chemists need to know the precise position of every atom in a molecule before they can generate a computer graphics representation of its structure. Information like this is available from **X-ray diffraction studies** on insulin crystals.

Figure 35 Insulin crystals. Protein crystals are often hard to grow; fortunately, insulin produces beautiful crystals

Figure 36 shows plots of blood insulin levels like those which are found in diabetic patients who have received insulin injections. Two curves are shown: for injection of human insulin and for the modified insulin just described with Asp^{B9} – aspartic acid in position B9.

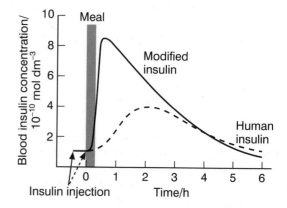

Figure 36 Insulin levels in diabetic patients using human insulin and modified insulin: human insulin is injected 30 min before the meal; modified insulin is injected immediately before the meal

The modified insulin gets into the bloodstream more quickly than injected human insulin because it is monomeric and does not need time to break down into hexamers. Its release more closely resembles normal insulin production.

Designer genes

Changing the amino acid residue at position B9 in insulin from serine to aspartic acid produces monomers which have similar biological activity to human insulin and which act faster after injection. How can the new form – an insulin analogue – be made?

There is no need to join 51 amino acids together by chemical synthesis. We know how cells make proteins, and we can insert insulin genes into yeast or bacteria. All that needs to be done is to alter the human insulin gene so that a codon for serine (eg AGG) is changed to a codon for aspartic acid (eg CTG). Then the yeast or bacterial cells will make the insulin analogue for us.

This really isn't as difficult as it seems – thanks to the remarkable ability of molecules to recognise one another.

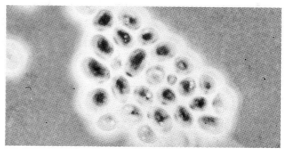

Figure 37 A microscopic factory – the yeast cells used to produce monomeric insulin

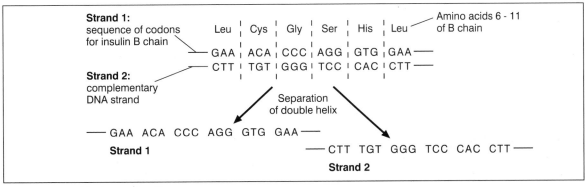

Figure 38 Part of the human insulin gene

Figure 38 shows the part of the insulin gene which tells the cell to join together the six amino acids of the B chain around B9. After genetic engineering this gene would be built into a bacterial plasmid. The plasmid can be 'unzipped' by certain viruses to form two single-stranded DNA molecules.

If chemists synthesise a small piece of DNA with 18 bases in the same sequence as that shown for Strand 1, it will recognise and stick to Strand 2 at precisely the part shown in Figure 38. It will do this because T sticks to A and G sticks to C, *and* because the chance of finding the same sequence of 18 bases anywhere else in the plasmid is, for all practical purposes, zero. The small piece of DNA will be like a 'chemical magnet', only sticking to the right section on the complementary DNA strand.

Normal processes within the cell will build bases onto the ends of the small section of synthetic DNA to complete the double helix and produce a plasmid which is indistinguishable from the one at the start (see Figure 39).

In fact, the chance of finding the 18-base sequence anywhere else on Strand 2 is so unlikely that the cell will tolerate a mistake. If the chemist builds the small piece of DNA with the codon CTG in place of AGG, it will still stick onto the same place – even though two of the bases are wrong. The cell will then complete the double helix as usual. What the chemist has done, of course, is to replace the Ser codon (AGG) by the Asp codon (CTG).

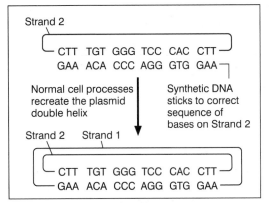

Figure 39 The cell recognises the small piece of synthetic DNA and incorporates it into a plasmid

Figure 40 shows what happens when the bacteria multiply with this new DNA inside them. A new strain of bacterium is produced which carries the gene for producing monomeric insulin – and it all comes about as a result of hydrogen bonding and molecular recognition.

Monomeric insulin has been tried out on patients and the trials have been promising.

Figure 40 The cell tolerates a change to one of the bases in the piece of DNA and incorporates the synthetic DNA into a plasmid – when the cell divides, two different plasmids are formed

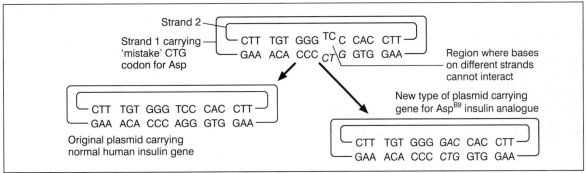

EP6 *Enzymes*

Testing glucose levels

There is a simple test you can do to check whether you are diabetic – although to be really certain you should go and see your GP. You can buy some reagent strips from a pharmacy and test for glucose in your urine. (When glucose builds up to a high level in the blood, it 'spills over' into the urine.)

The fresh reagent strip has a small pink square at one end which turns purple-blue in the presence of glucose. The square is impregnated with four reagents:

- glucose oxidase, an enzyme which catalyses the reaction

  glucose + oxygen →
  gluconic acid + hydrogen peroxide

- an indicator (often orthotoluidine); this is present in its reduced form (XH_2) which is colourless, but it turns into a coloured form (X) when it is oxidised

- peroxidase, an enzyme which catalyses the oxidation of the indicator by hydrogen peroxide

  hydrogen peroxide + XH_2 → water + X

- a buffer: a mixture of chemicals which keeps the reagents at a fixed pH during the test.

If the manufacturer's instruction sheet is available, you will also see that it recommends storing the test strips below 30 °C but not in a refrigerator.

The test strips illustrate *four* important points about enzymes. Enzymes are

1. *catalysts*
2. *highly specific*: for example, the test strips only work with glucose – they give no response with other sugars
3. *sensitive to pH*: many work best at a particular pH and become inactive if the pH becomes too acidic or too alkaline
4. *sensitive to temperature*: many enzymes work best at temperatures close to body temperature; most are destroyed above 60 °C–70 °C.

Figure 41 A simple urine test gives a measure of blood glucose concentration

You can use some glucose test strips with different sugar solutions in **Activity EP6.1**. The activity illustrates the important points about enzyme behaviour.

Active sites

Enzymes are so *specific* because they have a precise tertiary structure which exactly matches the structure of the **substrate** – the molecule which is reacting. It's another example of molecular recognition. Scientists often think of the 'lock and key' analogy, in which the enzyme is the 'lock' and the substrate is the 'key'. There may be lots of related keys, and several may fit into the lock, but only one will work.

The analogy is a good one. Figure 42 shows a space filling model of the enzyme *lysozyme* which catalyses the breakdown of the cell walls of bacteria and helps protect us from infection. There is a cleft in the enzyme surface formed by the way the protein chain folds. The shape of the cleft is tailored for the substrate molecules to fit into. Within the cleft are chemical groups – some of the side chains on the amino acid residues – which bind the substrate and possibly react with it. This region of the enzyme is called its **active site**.

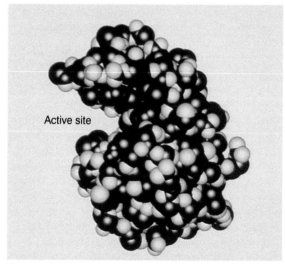

Active site

Figure 42 Space filling model of the enzyme lysozyme, showing the cleft which forms the active site

The bonds which bind the substrate to the active site have to be weak so that the binding can be readily reversed when the products need to leave the active site after the reaction. The bonds are usually hydrogen bonds or interactions between ionic groups. The binding may cause other bonds within the substrate to weaken or it may alter the shape of the substrate so that atoms are brought into contact to help them to react.

After reaction, the product leaves the enzyme which is then free to start again with another molecule of substrate. The whole process is summarised in Figure 43.

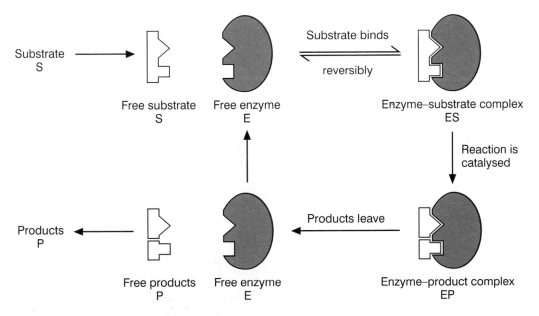

Figure 43 *Illustration of the 'lock and key' model of enzyme catalysis*

This is the simplest model of enzyme catalysis

$$E + S \rightleftharpoons ES \rightarrow EP \rightarrow E + P$$

What happens, of course, is more complex. In many cases, scientists believe that the substrate is not quite a perfect fit, and must alter its shape to fit into the active site. This means that both the substrate and the active site will be in strained arrangements, and this helps the reaction to occur.

***

Activity EP6.2 is a model-building exercise which illustrates the way in which substrate molecules fit onto an enzyme. It also shows how other molecules can *inhibit* the enzyme's action.

Enzymes as catalysts

In a catalysed reaction, reactants need less energy before they can turn into products than they do in an uncatalysed reaction. Their **activation enthalpy** is lower. This is illustrated in Figure 44 for the case of enzymes.

When the activation enthalpy is lower the reaction takes place more quickly.

***

You were introduced to the idea of activation enthalpy in **Chemical Ideas 4.2** and **10.1**. You can learn more about activation enthalpies and the rates at which chemical reactions take place in **Chemical Ideas 10.2**.

***

Figure 44 *Lowering of the activation enthalpy barrier in a catalysed reaction*

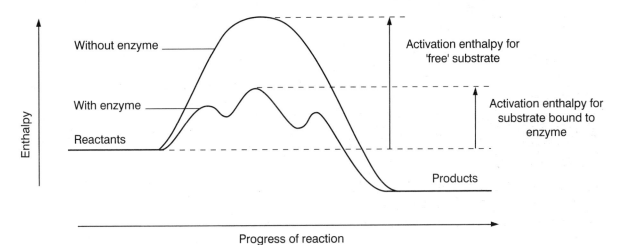

Enzymes are usually only present in minute traces. If the substrate concentration is high enough, all the enzyme molecules will have substrate molecules attached. If the substrate concentration is increased further, no more enzyme–substrate complexes can be formed, and the rate at which substrate molecules pass through the reaction pathway and change into products remains the same. In this situation the reaction rate does not depend on the substrate concentration. Chemists say the reaction is **zero order** with respect to substrate.

When the substrate concentration is low enough, not all enzyme active sites will have a substrate molecule bound to them. The overall reaction rate will now depend upon how frequently enzymes encounter substrates, which will depend upon how much substrate there is – twice as much substrate, twice as many encounters. Reaction rates which depend upon concentrations in this way are called **first-order reactions**.

If the enzyme's active site contains ionisable groups, the enzyme's action will be affected by a change in pH. For example, if there is a –COOH group which acts by donating an H^+ to the substrate, raising the pH will turn it into –COO$^-$ and the enzyme will not be able to work.

The enzyme will also become inactive if its shape is destroyed. Figure 45 illustrates how the active site of an enzyme can be made up from the side chains of amino acids in different parts of the protein molecule. They are held close together by the enzyme's tertiary structure.

If the tertiary structure is broken, the enzyme loses its shape and the side chains are no longer close together. The active site is destroyed and the enzyme is said to be **denatured**.

The tertiary structure is held together by weak dipole-dipole bonds and hydrogen bonds. These can easily be broken by raising the temperature, which causes them to vibrate more vigorously. Ionic interactions holding the tertiary structure together can be broken by changing the pH.

So enzymes are *sensitive* to relatively small changes in *temperature* or *pH*.

Figure 46 The proteins in egg white are denatured when the egg is cooked

In **Activity EP6.3** you can investigate how changing the concentration of the enzyme and the substrate affects the rate of a reaction.

You can study the effect of concentration on reaction rate in **Activity EP6.4** and determine the order of the reaction.

You can investigate enzyme kinetics further in **Activity EP6.5** which uses *urease* as an example.

Enzymes at work

A diabetes test strip uses an enzyme to detect glucose. It is not the only medical application of enzymes. In a 1991 catalogue of 197 medical diagnostic kits and reagents, 54 of them were based on the use of enzymes.

However, medical applications use only small quantities of enzymes. Very much larger amounts are used in the food industry and in the manufacture of washing powders, and almost all of these are *hydrolases* – enzymes which hydrolyse fats, proteins or carbohydrates.

In the food processing industry, two major uses of enzymes are

- producing glucose syrup (used as a sweetener in food products) by breaking down starch with enzymes like α-amylase
- making cheese using rennet enzymes: these break down the milk protein casein and cause the separation of the curds (solid) from the whey (liquid).

Other uses include baking, brewing and fruit processing.

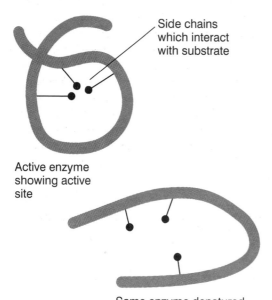

Side chains which interact with substrate

Active enzyme showing active site

Same enzyme denatured

Figure 45

Many biological washing powders contain one or more enzymes to assist in the removal of stains. The enzyme is usually a *protease* to hydrolyse proteins in blood and food, but a *lipase* may also be added to break down fats. More recently, cellulases have been added too. These break down the tiny surface fibres that give older clothes a fluffy, dull look. Protein engineering is being used to make enzymes which are more stable in hot washes, or to create more active enzymes which will do their job at lower temperatures.

Figure 47 Proteases are added to 'biological' detergents to remove protein stains such as grass, blood, egg and sweat

Enzymes are finding applications in wider areas of waste treatment. For example, an enzyme is being used to destroy cyanide ions which are left over after gold extraction or after the production of some polymers. Enzymes can also be used to help break up oil spillages.

Figure 48 Enzymes are important in the production of bread, cheese and wine

EP7 *Summary*

This unit has introduced you to some of the things chemists have found out about proteins and their building blocks, amino acids. Proteins play a wide variety of roles in our bodies: they are molecules of almost infinite diversity, despite all being made by the same type of condensation reaction which results in the formation of a secondary amide group.

This diversity can be explained in terms of

- the sequencing of the different structural units of the 20 naturally occurring α-amino acids (the primary structure)
- the interactions between these units which give proteins their precise three-dimensional shapes (the secondary, tertiary and quaternary structures).

Understanding these points led you into deeper consideration of molecular geometry and intermolecular forces. You also saw how a combination of these factors can lead to specific recognition of one molecule by another – a process which is essential in the building up of proteins according to the information contained in the genes on the DNA molecules stored in the nuclei of cells.

Consideration of one particular protein – the hormone insulin – provided a setting for this chemistry. It also provided an example of how chemists' understanding of proteins has reached a level enabling them to manipulate the processes which go on in a cell, in order to produce new proteins which are modified versions of those we have inherited. Central to this new field of protein engineering are the techniques of computer molecular graphics and recombinant DNA technology. Monomeric insulin is one protein produced by such technology. The dynamic equilibrium which exists between insulin hexamers and monomers led you to study the effect of concentration on chemical equilibrium.

The unit ended with a more general look at one class of proteins – the enzymes – which control the rates at which many of the chemical reactions in our bodies take place. This led to the need to develop a more detailed understanding of catalysis and how reaction rates are affected by the concentrations of chemicals.

Activity EP7 will help you to summarise what you have learned in this unit.

THE STEEL STORY

Why a unit on THE STEEL STORY?

This unit tells the story of the production of steel with emphasis on the redox reactions involved and the huge scale of the process. You will learn about the large variety of steels possible and discover how the composition of a steel is related to the job it has to do.

Looking at the composition of steel leads into a detailed study of the properties of iron and other d-block transition metals. These are the structural metals used by engineers to make things we need in everyday life. The metals and their compounds are also of great importance as catalysts, both in industry and in biological systems. Through this, you are introduced to ideas about electronic structure and the building up of the Periodic Table. The unique chemistry of transition metals is closely related to their electronic structure: these ideas are built on in the remaining parts of the unit.

The story of steel continues with the problems of corrosion. Rusting is introduced as an electrochemical process and various methods of rust prevention are considered. You will use standard electrode potentials to explain observations and make predictions about redox reactions. The problems arising when food is preserved in 'tin' cans leads to an investigation of the chemistry and stereochemistry of metal complexes. Finally, the importance of recycling steel is discussed together with some of the problems which must be overcome.

Overview of chemical principles

In this unit you will learn more about these ideas introduced in earlier units in this course …

- extraction of metals (**From Minerals to Elements**)
- electron energy levels in atoms (**Elements of Life**)
- atomic absorption and emission spectra (**Elements of Life**)
- redox reactions and oxidation numbers (**From Minerals to Elements** and **Using Sunlight**)
- using standard electrode potentials (**Using Sunlight**)
- catalysis (**Developing Fuels** and **Engineering Proteins**)
- isomerism (**Developing Fuels, The Polymer Revolution** and **Engineering Proteins**)
- why compounds are coloured (**Using Sunlight**)

… as well as learning new ideas about

- the nature and production of steel
- how the properties and uses of steel are related to its composition
- the arrangement of electrons in atoms
- the building up of the Periodic Table in terms of electronic structure of the atoms
- the properties of the d-block elements
- complex formation
- the effect of complexing on redox reactions.

SS1 *What is steel?*

There is no one material called steel: just as there are many plastics, so there are thousands of different steels. Steel is the general name given to a large family of **alloys** of iron with carbon and a variety of different elements.

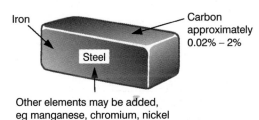

Figure 1 The composition of steel

Even small differences in the composition of the steel have a dramatic effect on its properties. This is particularly true in the case of carbon. Iron containing 4% carbon is extremely brittle and of limited practical use. With 0.1% carbon, however, it is easily drawn into wire form and is ideal for making staples or paper-clips. With 1% carbon, steel is much tougher and harder wearing and is used, for example, to make tools or the wire cord in car tyres.

Alloys

An alloy is a mixture of a metal with one or more other elements. The components are mixed together while molten and allowed to cool to form a uniform solid. The presence of other elements in a metal changes its properties and can often increase its strength. For example, brass is an alloy of copper and zinc and is stronger than either pure metal. Duralumin is used for building aircraft: it is an alloy of aluminium and copper with smaller amounts of magnesium, iron and silicon.

In **Activity SS1** you can find out for yourself how much of one element, manganese, there is in a familiar item such as a paper-clip or staple. Manganese is just one of many elements steelmakers can add to steel to change its properties.

Changing the composition of steel is not the only method steelmakers use to adjust its properties. They can subject the final steel to varying degrees of heating and cooling (heat treatment) and work it by rolling or hammering. All these processes modify the metal structure and affect its properties.

Steel is such a versatile material because both its structure and composition can be adjusted to tailor its properties exactly to the uses you have in mind. The possibilities for variety are almost endless.

In this unit, you will be concerned only with its composition and how this is controlled during manufacture. Not all elements are good news for steelmakers. Even small amounts of phosphorus, sulphur or dissolved gases (such as oxygen, nitrogen and hydrogen) can lead to poor-quality material. Brittle steel is a problem anywhere, but in an oil-rig or oil pipeline in the North Sea it could lead to catastrophe.

ASSIGNMENT 1

Write down the names of 10 items made from steel. Select items which illustrate the wide range of steels available.

Figure 2 One of the many uses for steel

What elements does steel contain?

There may be many different elements present in a steel in addition to iron. A few, such as carbon and silicon, are non-metals but most are metals. Some of the metals commonly added are shown in Table 1.

Metal	Symbol	Metal	Symbol
aluminium	Al	molybdenum	Mo
chromium	Cr	nickel	Ni
cobalt	Co	niobium	Nb
copper	Cu	titanium	Ti
lead	Pb	tungsten	W
manganese	Mn	vanadium	V

Table 1 Metals commonly added to steel

If you look at the positions of these elements in the Periodic Table shown in Figure 3, you will see a clear pattern emerging. Many of the elements present in steel, including iron, are **d-block elements**.

To appreciate why these elements are called d-block elements and to understand their position in the centre of the Periodic Table, you need to know more about the energy levels in atoms and how electrons are arranged in these energy levels.

You can find out about energy levels in atoms by studying **Chemical Ideas 2.4.**

SS2 *How is steel made?*

Making steel on a large scale with the right composition is a highly skilled business, involving sophisticated technology. The chemistry is spectacular!

Starting with blast furnace iron

Nearly all new steel, whatever its final composition, is made from the same starting material. This is impure iron from a blast furnace.

Figure 4 Molten iron is carried to the steelmaking vessel in a ladle

The molten iron has many other elements dissolved in it. The most important are carbon, silicon, manganese, phosphorus and sulphur.

Activity SS2.1 will help you to remember what happens in a blast furnace and understand why the iron produced is so impure.

You can see the composition of a typical sample of blast furnace iron in Table 2.

Element	Fe	C	Si	Mn	P	S
% by mass	94.0	4.42	0.66	0.41	0.085	0.027

Table 2 An analysis of typical blast furnace iron

Metal of this composition is very brittle and has a limited range of uses - who, for example, would buy a hammer which had a head likely to shatter on first impact? The carbon content must be lowered, most of the phosphorus and sulphur removed, and other elements added before the material is allowed to solidify.

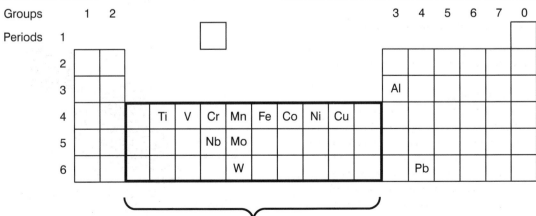

d-block elements

Figure 3 The position in the Periodic Table of the metals commonly present in steel

Figure 5 Iron is extracted from iron ore in a blast furnace

All of this is achieved in the **Basic Oxygen Steelmaking (BOS) process,** in which batches of about 300 tonnes of high-quality steel are made in just 40 minutes. If possible, watch a video of the steelmaking process. You may be fortunate enough to visit a steelworks.

ASSIGNMENT 2

The percentage of carbon by mass in the iron may seem rather low and insignificant (see Table 2). If we look at it in a different way its importance becomes clearer.

Use the information in Table 2 to calculate the relative amount in moles of iron and carbon in blast furnace iron. Neglecting the contributions from the other elements, work out the *percentage of moles* of the two elements, iron and carbon.

Approximately how many atoms of carbon are there in every 100 atoms of product from a blast furnace?

Removing unwanted elements

About 300 tonnes of molten iron from a blast furnace are poured into a huge container called a *ladle*.

Removing sulphur

Sulphur is the first element to be removed. This is done in a separate reduction process before the main steelmaking reactions take place. Several hundred kilograms of powdered magnesium are injected through a vertical tube, called a *lance*, into the molten iron. In a violent exothermic reaction the sulphur is reduced to magnesium sulphide, which floats to the surface and is raked off:

$$Mg + S \rightarrow MgS$$

ASSIGNMENT 3

a Write an ionic equation to show what happens to sulphur during the reaction with magnesium and explain why this process is a reduction.

b Draw a dot–cross diagram to show the bonding in magnesium sulphide.

Removing other elements

Carbon, phosphorus and other elements are removed by direct oxidation with gaseous oxygen (the O in BOS). The equations are shown in Figure 6.

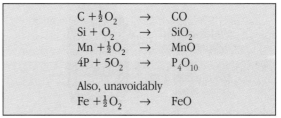

$$C + \tfrac{1}{2}O_2 \rightarrow CO$$
$$Si + O_2 \rightarrow SiO_2$$
$$Mn + \tfrac{1}{2}O_2 \rightarrow MnO$$
$$4P + 5O_2 \rightarrow P_4O_{10}$$

Also, unavoidably
$$Fe + \tfrac{1}{2}O_2 \rightarrow FeO$$

Figure 6 Oxidation reactions in the BOS converter

The huge ladle brings the molten desulphurised iron to the steelmaking vessel or *converter*, which already contains some scrap steel (Figures 4 and 7). Now is the time for some very violent chemistry!

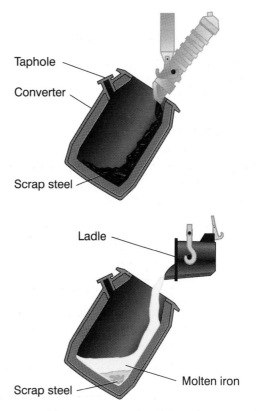

Figure 7 Adding (a) scrap steel and (b) molten iron to the converter

The converter turns into a vertical position and a water-cooled lance gradually inches its way down close to the surface of the iron. A supersonic blast of oxygen under pressure forces its way into the vessel and creates a seething foam of molten metal and gas which is blasted up the walls of the converter (Figure 8). Over the next 20 minutes or so, most of the impurities of carbon, silicon, manganese and phosphorus, as well as some of the iron, are oxidised.

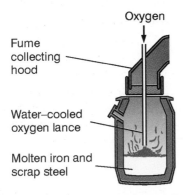

Figure 8 *The oxygen blow*

Look again at the equations in Figure 6. Carbon monoxide escapes as a gas and is collected via a hood over the vessel. The other oxides remain in the converter and must be separated from the molten metal.

The oxides of phosphorus and silicon are acidic and will react with bases to form salts. So, soon after the oxygen blow has started, a mixture of calcium and magnesium oxide (made by heating limestone and dolomite) are added to the converter.

These are basic oxides (the B in BOS) and react with the acidic oxides to form a molten 'slag' which floats to the surface. The oxides of manganese and iron also collect in the slag.

The slag can be separated from the molten metal because the two have different densities and form two layers. You may have used the same principle to separate two immiscible liquids in the laboratory using a separating funnel.

ASSIGNMENT 4

a Suggest how the carbon monoxide collected may be used elsewhere on the plant.

b Apart from economic reasons, why is it not a good idea to release the carbon monoxide into the air?

c When calcium oxide reacts with the acidic oxides SiO_2 and P_4O_{10}, the products are *salts*. Write down possible names and formulae for the two salts formed.

d Explain why CaO is considered to be a basic oxide and P_4O_{10} an acidic oxide.

Keeping track

The process is closely monitored in the control room where a computer models the conditions in the converter. Two minutes before the predicted end of the oxygen blow an automatic sampling device, called a *sublance,* descends into the converter. It measures the temperature and carbon content and removes a sample of metal for analysis.

The computer uses the up-to-date information on temperature and carbon content to predict exactly how much more oxygen is needed to reach the target composition and temperature. The sample withdrawn is rushed to the analysis laboratory to determine the percentages of the elements in the steel.

Measuring the composition

Analytical chemists quickly measure the composition of the steel using *atomic emission spectroscopy*. This involves making the steel sample into an electrode for an electric arc, so that each element present emits a characteristic line spectrum. The intensities of the lines are proportional to the concentration of atoms of each element. At this stage the analysis involves only a few elements, but the method can be used to monitor up to 20 elements.

You can read about atomic emission spectroscopy in **Chemical Ideas 6.1**.

Figure 9 *The progress of the blow is monitored in the control room*

During the oxygen blow the elements are oxidised in a sequence illustrated in Figure 10. When most of the impurities have been removed, some of the iron is also oxidised. This is unavoidable but is kept to a minimum.

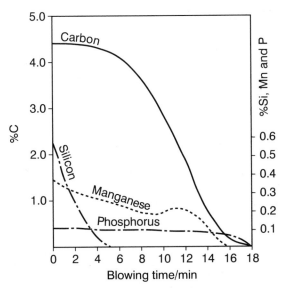

Figure 10 Removal of elements during steelmaking (note that %C and %Si, Mn and P are plotted on different scales; the rise in %Mn after 10 min is because the scrap steel used had a relatively high manganese content)

At the end of the blow, the converter is rotated to pour off the molten steel through a hole near the top into a ladle, and then tilted in the opposite direction to remove the slag (Figure 11).

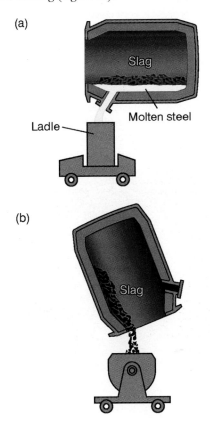

Figure 11 (a) Tapping off the molten steel and (b) removing the slag

ASSIGNMENT 5

During the oxygen blow, the elements in the converter compete for the oxygen. The order of their removal as oxides depends on their affinity for oxygen at the high temperature involved and on the amount of each element present.

Use Figure 10 to answer these questions.

a Which element is the first to be removed?

b Which element is the last to be removed?

c Is this what you would have expected from what you know about the reactivity of these elements with oxygen at lower temperatures?

d At the high temperatures in the converter, sulphur has a similar affinity for oxygen to that of iron. Suggest why it is better to remove most of the sulphur *before* the oxygen blow in a separate process.

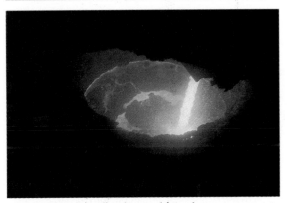

Figure 12 Tapping off molten steel from the converter

Controlling the temperature

Careful control of temperature is a vital part of making steel. At the end of the oxygen blow a temperature of about 1700 °C–1740 °C must be reached. This is the *target tapping temperature*. Higher temperatures waste expensive energy and can cause severe damage to the converter linings. Lower temperatures can be even more costly if the metal solidifies before it is supposed to.

No external heating is necessary. The oxidation reactions are all highly exothermic and generate a tremendous amount of energy. Some of this energy is of course lost to the surroundings. The rest is absorbed in raising the temperature of the converter contents. Some energy is absorbed by the scrap steel (which was added to the converter at the start) as it melts and heats up, maintaining a 'heat balance'. The scrap therefore neatly serves both as a coolant and a source of recycled steel.

Activities SS2.2 to **SS2.4** look more closely at some of the changes which happen during steelmaking.

Meeting the specification

By now the elements which are not wanted – and also some that are – have been removed from the iron. The elements which are wanted have to be put back. The computer model predicts the exact quantity of each substance needed to achieve the **specification** for the particular batch of steel.

Every batch of steel is destined for a particular customer who specifies the requirements for its composition according to its eventual use. This detailed recipe is called the specification for that batch of steel.

ASSIGNMENT 6

It may seem strange to you that elements such as carbon which have just been removed in the converter are now re-added.

a Why do you think the carbon content is adjusted in this way, rather than by stopping the oxygen blow at the appropriate carbon concentration?

Steelmaking is a batch process. It is found to be most cost-effective to produce batches of around 300 tonnes. However, it is possible to make steel by a continuous process.

b Why do you think this is less economical?

Another problem is that excess oxygen dissolves in the metal during the oxygen blow. One way of removing this is to throw ingots of aluminium into the ladle as it is being filled with molten steel from the converter. Aluminium oxide forms and floats to the surface.

Carbon, manganese and silicon, which were removed in the blow, are often added at this stage. Chromium and more aluminium are other common additions. More exotic elements such as niobium, molybdenum and tungsten may also be added. Argon is blown into the liquid steel, using a lance, to stir the mixture and make sure it is uniform.

Throughout the addition processes, the temperature is closely monitored and samples are taken frequently for analysis. With this information the computer constantly updates its predictions.

A final 'trimming' adjusts the concentrations of elements in the steel to the required values and the molten steel is now ready for casting. This may be continuous casting into very long strands of solid metal (Figure 13) or it may be poured into moulds in which it sets into ingots, rather like making ice cubes.

The effects of various elements on the properties of steel are illustrated in **Activity SS2.5.**

Figure 13 Continuous casting of steel into narrow strips of metal

Can steelmaking be improved?

World production of steel continues to rise even though plastics and other man-made materials are taking over the role of steel in some areas. There is a tremendous and growing demand for even higher-quality specialist steels with uniform and consistent compositions.

The BOS process is kept constantly under review and new technology is introduced to produce batches of steel to these very precise specifications as efficiently and economically as possible.

Perhaps the most important changes in the future will be in the use of continuous monitoring by computers and quality measurements at all stages of the process. Computers can alert plant engineers when there are problems and even give advice on possible solutions – or perhaps correct the problem themselves.

Figure 14 This Portuguese fisherman is making a lobster pot from scrap steel cable

As we become more concerned about the environment and recycle more and more steel, larger and more efficient **electric arc furnaces** may take over a greater share of the production. In 1988, 26% of steel worldwide was produced by electric arc furnaces.

The electric arc furnace

An electric arc furnace uses old scrap steel which is melted by the heat generated when a spark is produced between carbon electrodes. Lime is added and the impurities removed as a slag.

By carefully selecting the scrap and making necessary additions, relatively small batches of steel are made to meet given specifications.

ASSIGNMENT 7

Richard's story

Richard works in a steelworks. After doing A-levels in Chemistry, Physics and Maths he took a degree in Chemistry, Analytical Chemistry and Toxicology followed by a PhD in Analytical Chemistry. He is now a year into his first job which he describes below.

"I'm an investigative chemist, or you might call me a chemical trouble-shooter. I work as part of a quality assurance team whose aim it is to ensure that the steel we produce is exactly what the customer wants.

If there is a query about the chemical composition of our steel I may be brought in to investigate the problem. First of all I have to think about how the supposed problem might have arisen. This raises questions like:

- is the analysis method appropriate?
- are the analysis figures accurate?
- are they typical of that batch of steel?
- if there is a real discrepancy, is it a one-off event or could it happen again?
- at what stage in the process could this difficulty occur and why?

Figure 15 Dr Richard Clinch on site at the British Steelworks in Scunthorpe

Out of this thinking comes a hypothesis and a method to test it.

Then it is out of my office, on with the protective clothing and down to the steelmaking plant to supervise the taking of the molten metal samples I need. This could be at 3 pm or 3 am. My luck always seems to favour 3 am!

To analyse the samples I use a combustion analysis instrument for carbon, nitrogen and sulphur, and atomic emission spectroscopy for up to 20 other elements.

Then it is back to thinking. I look at the results and decide if we have a problem. Then I suggest a remedy and meet with production management to discuss the implications.

Back in my office a phone call tells me about the next problem. No two days are the same!"

a In Richard's story, what do you think is meant by
  i a 'hypothesis'?
  ii 'combustion analysis'?

b How do you think nitrogen came to be in the steel?

SS3 *A closer look at the elements in steel*

Understanding the chemistry of d-block elements

To understand how steel behaves when exposed to weathering and what can be done to prevent corrosion, or to understand how fruit juices can affect the inside of a food can, you need to know more about the chemistry of d-block elements.

These elements are sometimes called **transition metals** because they show a transition in properties between the reactive s-block metals and the less reactive metals on the left of the p-block. Their chemistry is very characteristic and is a direct result of their electronic structure.

Chemical Ideas 11.6 tells you about the properties of d-block elements.

Typical chemical properties of transition metals include

- the formation of compounds in a variety of oxidation states
- catalytic activity of the elements and their compounds
- a strong tendency to form complexes
- the formation of coloured compounds.

The elements on the edges of the d-block, such as scandium and zinc, do not show many of these properties and are not usually classed as transition metals.

Figure 16 The oxidation states of vanadium: from left to right, the beakers contain solutions of vanadium in oxidation states +5, +4, +3 and +2

Variable oxidation states

Metals like sodium or magnesium have just one oxidation state in all of their compounds, but transition metals form compounds in a range of oxidation states, many with beautiful and characteristic colours (see Figure 16).

In **Activity SS3.1** you can explore a number of the colourful oxidation states of vanadium and use electrode potentials to make predictions about changes between them.

Catalysis

Another property characteristic of transition metals and their ions is that many can act as catalysts.

For example, iron is the catalyst in the manufacture of ammonia in the Haber process. Nickel is used in the hydrogenation of vegetable oils to make margarine. A platinum–palladium–rhodium mixture (sometimes with other transition metals) is the catalyst in the catalytic converters in car exhaust systems.

Catalysts also play a vital role in biological systems, enabling complex reactions to occur quickly in dilute aqueous solution at moderate temperature and pH – the conditions in a living cell. Many transition metal ions are required by living things in minute but definite quantities. Cobalt, copper, manganese, molybdenum and vanadium are all ultra-trace elements essential for the catalytic activity of various enzymes.

ASSIGNMENT 8

Make a list of some of the catalysts you have met already together with the reactions they catalyse.

How many are transition metals or compounds of transition metals?

You can read about catalysis in **Chemical Ideas 10.4.**

In **Activity SS3.2** you will investigate the catalytic activity of cobalt(II) ions.

(a)

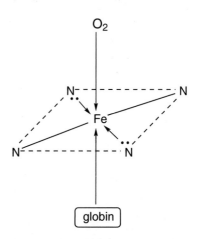

The *porphyrin* ring attaches itself to the central Fe $^{2+}$ ion via its four nitrogen atoms. In doing so it loses two hydrogen ions.

(b)

The nitrogen atoms of the *porphyrin* ring occupy four ligand sites. The other two sites are taken up by the protein, globin (which also binds to the metal through a nitrogen atom), and a molecule of oxygen.

Figure 17 (a) The porphyrin ring system; (b) haemoglobin

Complex chemistry

You may have met the blue complexes of copper(II) ions with water and ammonia ligands in **From Minerals to Elements (Activities M2.2** and **2.3).** Complex formation is a further characteristic property of transition metals.

Typically, a central metal ion is surrounded by six electron-donating ligands, although complexes with two and four ligands are also common.

Iron forms the red complex, haemoglobin, responsible for transporting oxygen in the blood (**Elements of Life** storyline, Section **EL2**). The structure of this complex is shown in Figure 17.

The oxygen molecule is relatively loosely attached to the iron. It is carried around the body in the bloodstream and released from the complex when needed.

You can read more about the chemistry of complexes in **Chemical Ideas 11.7.**

In **Activity SS3.3** you will meet some complexes of d-block elements.

Coloured compounds

The colour of a transition metal compound depends on the oxidation state of the metal ion, the nature of the ligands surrounding it, and the spatial arrangement of these ligands. A wide variety of colours is observed (Table 3).

Gemstone	Colour	Ion present
blue sapphire	blue	V^{3+} or Co^{2+}
emerald	green	Cr^{3+}
topaz	yellow	Fe^{3+}
turquoise	blue-green	Cu^{2+}
amethyst	purple	Mn^{3+}
ruby	red	Cr^{3+}

Table 3 The colours of many gemstones are due to the presence of traces of d-block metal ions

Figure 18 The Rose Window at York Minster: glass is coloured green with either chromium(III) or iron(II); cobalt(II) gives blue glass and copper(II) gives a blue-green colour

d-Block metals can be expensive

The most abundant d-block element in the Earth's crust is iron which is relatively cheap. Some of the other d-block elements, however, can be expensive. The cost of the steel rises if these are used in steelmaking.

For example, stainless steel contains a minimum of 12% chromium (by mass) and usually nickel as well to make it corrosion resistant. A typical stainless steel might contain 74% iron, 18% chromium and 8% nickel. It is as much as five or six times more expensive than ordinary steel and this severely limits its use.

The price of a metal depends on many other factors besides its abundance in the Earth's crust. These include the cost of mining the ore, the ease of extraction of the metal from the ore, the demand for the metal, transport costs and political factors in the countries involved.

Some elements are said to be *strategically critical* because one or two countries have a monopoly over their supply. For example, the Republic of South Africa holds more than 70% of the world's known reserves of chromium, with Zimbabwe having over half of the remainder, whereas most of the world's deposits of molybdenum are found in the USA and Canada.

Activity SS3.4 will help you to check that you have understood the main points in Section **SS3**.

SS4 *Rusting*

A return to nature

Many metals, including iron, occur in the Earth's crust as oxides. This is because the change from a metal to its oxide is an energetically favourable process – in other words, the oxide is more stable than the metal. Indeed, to reverse the process and extract the metal from its ore requires a great deal of energy. No wonder then, that given the opportunity iron tends to re-form its oxide – ie it **rusts**. Rusting is a special name for the **corrosion** of iron.

Figure 19 shows the redox cycle involved when a metal is extracted from its ore and then corrodes.

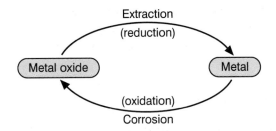

Figure 19 Redox cycle involved in the extraction of metal from oxide ores and subsequent corrosion of the metal

The rusting of steel is a very familiar problem to all car owners. About half of the cars driven gleaming from the showroom just 10 years ago are now on the scrap heap. Some have been written off in accidents, but for most it is rust that has sealed their fate. The iron has simply returned to nature.

Figure 20 Repairing rust damage on a car body

In **Activity SS4.1** you can investigate some of the chemistry involved in rusting and in one method of rust prevention.

Cars rust because the steel they are made from reacts with oxygen and water in the atmosphere. When iron or steel rusts a hydrated form of iron(III) oxide with variable composition ($Fe_2O_3.xH_2O$) is produced. This oxide is permeable to air and water and does not form a protective layer on the metal surface. So the metal continues to corrode under the layers of rust.

Iron and steel will rust whenever they are in contact with moist air, but the rate of rusting is greatly influenced by other factors, such as impurities in the iron, the presence of acids or other electrolytes in the solution in contact with the iron, and the availability of dissolved oxygen in this solution.

What happens during rusting?

Rusting is an electrochemical process. Electrochemical cells are set up in the metal surface, where different areas act as sites of oxidation and reduction.

Two half-reactions involved in rusting are

$$Fe^{2+}(aq) + 2e^- \rightarrow Fe(s) \qquad E^{\ominus} = -0.44\,V$$
$$\tfrac{1}{2}O_2(g) + H_2O(l) + 2e^- \rightarrow 2OH^-(aq) \qquad E^{\ominus} = +0.40\,V$$

The reduction of oxygen to hydroxide ions occurs at the more positive potential, and so electrons flow to this half-cell from the iron half-cell.

You can read about electrochemical cells and electrode potentials in **Chemical Ideas 9.2** and **9.3**.

Figure 21 shows what happens when a drop of water is left in contact with iron or steel.

The concentration of dissolved oxygen in the water drop determines which regions of the metal surface are sites of reduction and which regions are sites of oxidation.

At the edges of the drop, where the concentration of dissolved oxygen in the water is higher, oxygen is reduced to hydroxide ions.

$$\tfrac{1}{2}O_2(g) + H_2O(l) + 2e^- \rightarrow 2OH^-(aq)$$

The electrons needed to reduce the oxygen come from the oxidation of iron at the centre of the water drop, where the concentration of dissolved oxygen is low. The $Fe^{2+}(aq)$ ions pass into solution:

$$Fe(s) \rightarrow Fe^{2+}(aq) + 2e^-$$

The electrons released flow in the metal surface to the edges of the drop.

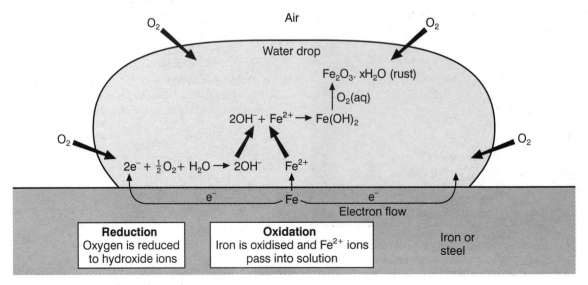

Figure 21 Rusting is an electrochemical process

This explains why corrosion is always greatest at the centre of a water drop or under a layer of paint: these are the regions where the oxygen supply is limited. Here 'pits' are formed where the iron has dissolved away.

Rust forms in a series of secondary processes within the solution, as Fe^{2+} and OH^- ions diffuse away from the metal surface. It does not form as a protective layer in contact with the iron surface.

$$Fe^{2+}(aq) + 2OH^-(aq) \rightarrow Fe(OH)_2(s)$$

$$Fe(OH)_2(s) \xrightarrow{O_2(aq)} Fe_2O_3.xH_2O$$

The electrode potential for the oxygen half-reaction depends on pH, and acid conditions accelerate rusting. Any ionic impurities, eg sodium chloride from salt spray near the sea, will promote rusting by increasing the conductivity of the water.

Great improvements have been made over the last few years in tackling the rust problem in cars. Figure 22 shows the results of a survey carried out in 1988. The percentage of cars with serious rust was relatively low in cars younger than 5–6 years. Seven-year-old cars, however, showed a sudden increase in the incidence of serious rust.

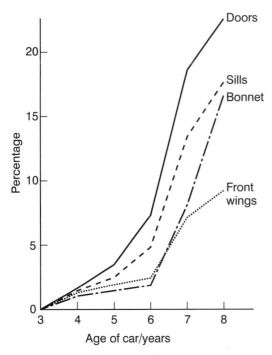

Figure 22 *Percentage of cars with serious rust based on a survey of cars in 1988 (from* Which?, *February 1989)*

This suggests perhaps that the rusting problem may only have been postponed and not eliminated – and reminds us that the best we can hope to do is to slow down the return to nature rather than halt it.

ASSIGNMENT 9

Look at the graph in Figure 22, which shows the percentage of cars between 3 and 8 years old in 1988 with serious rust problems in specified areas.

a List some of the ways used by car manufacturers to protect steel from rusting.

b In which area of the cars were the manufacturers' rust treatments least effective?

c Suggest a reason why this area is difficult to protect.

Keeping nature at bay

The simplest way of protecting steel against rust is to provide a barrier between the metal and the atmosphere. The barrier may be oil, grease or a coat of paint.

Figure 23 *Protecting iron railings from corrosion*

Figure 24 *Early advertising signs were saved from the damaging effects of weather and pollution by a corrosion-resistant coating of vitreous enamel*

A barrier made from an organic polymer is increasingly used. The steel is coated with a plastic film – a colourful and flexible solution to the rusting problem. A quick look around at home will provide a wealth of examples – sink drainers, refrigerator and dishwasher shelves, milk bottle carriers and bicycle baskets.

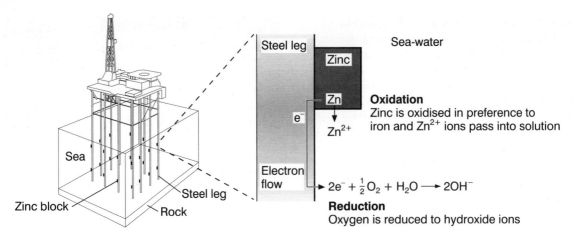

Figure 25 In a North Sea oil-rig sacrificial protection of the steel supports is achieved by using zinc blocks: zinc is oxidised in preference to iron and so protects the steel legs from corrosion

Sometimes iron is covered with a thin layer of another metal. Some car manufacturers make their car bodies from **galvanised** steel. This has a protective coating of zinc. When the galvanised surface is undamaged the zinc layer is protected from corrosion by a firmly adhering layer of zinc oxide.

Even if the coating is scratched the protection is still maintained because the zinc corrodes in preference to the iron. The zinc is being used as a **sacrificial metal**. One of the earliest examples of using a sacrificial metal was suggested by Humphrey Davy in 1824 to protect the metal sheathing on sailing ships from corrosion.

Today blocks of zinc are used to protect North Sea oil-rigs by transferring corrosion from a valuable complex steel structure to a readily replaceable metal lump (see Figure 25).

You can see the reason for this by comparing the standard electrode potentials of the iron and zinc half-cells. Any metal with a more negative $E^{\ominus}$ value than iron could be used as a sacrificial metal.

ASSIGNMENT 10

Use the standard electrode potentials given below to explain why zinc and magnesium, but not tin, can be used as sacrificial metals to protect steel.

Half-reaction	$E^{\ominus}$/V
$Mg^{2+}(aq) + 2e^- \rightarrow Mg(s)$	−2.37
$Zn^{2+}(aq) + 2e^- \rightarrow Zn(s)$	−0.76
$Fe^{2+}(aq) + 2e^- \rightarrow Fe(s)$	−0.44
$Sn^{2+}(aq) + 2e^- \rightarrow Sn(s)$	−0.14

In the sea, conditions are far from standard, but the *order* of electrode potentials for these reactions is not changed.

Stainless steel – the perfect solution?

Many of the steel items you use at home, particularly those which come into regular contact with water – such as the kitchen sink, cutlery and the drum of your washing machine – are made of stainless steel which needs no further protection.

Stainless steel was developed in 1913 by a Sheffield chemist called Harry Brearley. He was investigating the rapid wear of rifle barrels and decided to try a steel containing a high level of chromium to see if this would prolong their life.

Routine analysis of steel at that time involved dissolving it in acid, and here Brearley met an unexpected difficulty. His high-chromium steel would not dissolve. He also noticed that samples of it left lying around the laboratory stayed shiny.

Brearley immediately realised that he had found a steel which would make excellent cutlery. It would not need to be dried carefully after washing or need frequent polishing.

Figure 26 Harry Brearley and some early stainless steel cutlery

He did encounter some prejudice about the idea. One of the foremost cutlers in Sheffield thought the idea 'contrary to nature', while another is said to have remarked that 'rustlessness is not so great a virtue in cutlery, which of necessity must be cleaned after each using'! We now take it for granted that our knives and forks stay shiny and are not attacked by the acids in food.

Stainless steel does not rust because it forms a surface layer of chromium(III) oxide (Cr_2O_3). Unlike rust, this oxide is not hydrated and adheres closely to the metal surface. The oxide layer is invisible to the naked eye, being only a few nanometres thick, and allows the natural brightness of the metal to show through. Even so, it is impervious to air and water and so protects the metal beneath it. Furthermore, if you scratch the surface film it quickly reforms and restores the protection.

Is stainless steel then the perfect solution to the rusting problem? Unfortunately things are not that simple. Stainless steel is expensive and we have to take this into consideration when deciding which steel to use.

In **Activity SS4.2** you can look at the problem of choosing the 'best' steel for a particular job – the exhaust system of a car.

SS5 *What happens inside a 'tin' can?*

A prize-winning invention

Napoleon remarked at the beginning of the 19th century that an army marches on its stomach. His armies were widely separated on campaigns in Russia and Spain. They were severely limited by long supply

brisket, salt	7 lb	oatmeal	3 pints
beer	7 gallons	sugar	6 oz
beef, salt	4 lb	tea	3 oz
pork, salt	2 lb	vinegar	half a pint
pease	2 pints		

Table 4 The weekly allowance of provisions for men serving in His Majesty's ships in 1804

lines from France, and the lack of fresh provisions sapped their fighting strength. Similar problems affected British sailors, whose diet at sea must have taxed the most imaginative naval cook.

Napoleon offered a prize to anyone who could suggest a solution to his food supply problem. In 1812 he awarded 12 000 Francs to a French confectioner, Nicolas Apert, for inventing a method of preserving cooked food by sealing it in an airtight glass jar while it was still hot.

Meat, vegetables and fruit could be kept palatable for long periods of time. Later that year an Englishman, Peter Durand, adapted Apert's method by using a tin-plated iron canister instead of a glass bottle – with obvious advantages. So the tin canister or 'tin can' was born.

In 1824 Captain Sir Edward Parry set out on his third voyage in search of the 'North West Passage' from the Atlantic to the Pacific Ocean, taking with him a good supply of canned food. His aim was to find an Arctic route to India and the Far East. One of his ships became ice-bound and he was forced to abandon it together with a large quantity of stores.

Some of the cans were recovered by Captain Ross in a similar expedition 4 years later (Figure 27). In 1939 one of these cans was opened. After more than a century, the roast veal and gravy inside were still wholesome.

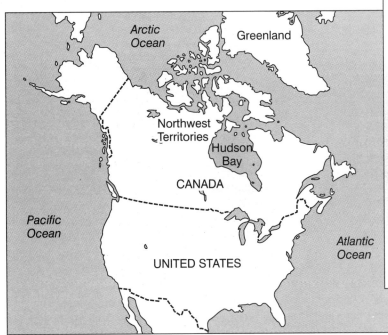

Figure 27 The famous can of veal taken by Parry on his 1824 expedition in search of the 'North West Passage'

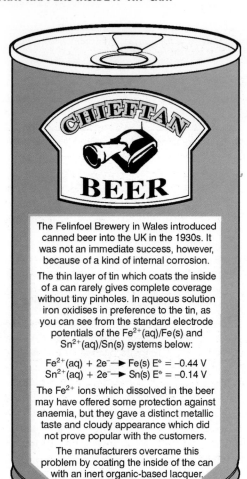

The Felinfoel Brewery in Wales introduced canned beer into the UK in the 1930s. It was not an immediate success, however, because of a kind of internal corrosion.

The thin layer of tin which coats the inside of a can rarely gives complete coverage without tiny pinholes. In aqueous solution iron oxidises in preference to the tin, as you can see from the standard electrode potentials of the $Fe^{2+}(aq)/Fe(s)$ and $Sn^{2+}(aq)/Sn(s)$ systems below:

$$Fe^{2+}(aq) + 2e^- \longrightarrow Fe(s)\ E^\circ = -0.44\ V$$
$$Sn^{2+}(aq) + 2e^- \longrightarrow Sn(s)\ E^\circ = -0.14\ V$$

The Fe^{2+} ions which dissolved in the beer may have offered some protection against anaemia, but they gave a distinct metallic taste and cloudy appearance which did not prove popular with the customers.

The manufacturers overcame this problem by coating the inside of the can with an inert organic-based lacquer.

ASSIGNMENT II

a When preserving food, why is it important that the jar or can is airtight and sealed while the food is still hot?

b Peter Durand used iron plates dipped into molten tin and soldered together to make a container. What was the purpose of the tin?

c What would happen if a tin can were scratched on the outside so that the iron showed through? Refer to the standard electrode potentials in Assignment 10.

d Suggest reasons why it is not a good idea to use zinc instead of tin to coat the can.

Chemistry inside the can

Unfortunately, canning food and drinks can have its problems. Different foods provide different environments inside the can and can affect the way the metal corrodes. Figures 28 and 29 show some of the problems which can arise inside a can.

Figure 28 The chemical environment inside a can of peaches is quite different from that inside a beer can

A can of fruit contains carboxylic acids such as citric acid. The acids are partially dissociated into ions in solution and their anions – such as citrate ions – can form complexes with Sn^{2+} ions. The complexing removes $Sn^{2+}(aq)$ ions from the solution and upsets the equilibrium between $Sn(s)$ and $Sn^{2+}(aq)$ ions. Under these conditions, the relative values of the electrode potentials of the tin and iron half-cells are reversed and the tin is now the more readily oxidised of the metals. So, in the presence of peaches and other fruit, the tin corrodes in preference to the iron.

The Sn^{2+} ions which become part of the food contents are not toxic – nor do they have an adverse effect on the flavour. In fact, they are responsible for some of the tangy taste we expect of canned fruit!

There may, however, be problems if we leave the tin on the shelf too long. As the thin layer of tin is sacrificially oxidised it will eventually be stripped off revealing the steel beneath. The acidic juices will then begin to react with the iron. Peaches are perhaps better eaten sooner rather than later!

Chemical Ideas 9.4 looks at how complexing affects electrode potentials.

Unlike beer and peaches, baked beans were created especially for the can. When they were introduced into the UK from the USA at the turn of the century they were a luxury item. Today nearly 200 billion baked beans are eaten every year, amounting to over 3000 beans for every man, woman and child!

In **Activity SS5** you can make models of some metal complexes to investigate their structure.

SS6 *Recycled steel*

Why recycle?

You saw earlier in the unit that recycled scrap is an integral part of the BOS process. Scrap steel makes up about 18% of every cast of 'new' metal. In the electric arc process for making steel, *only* scrap is used.

Much of the scrap used in steelmaking comes from the steelworks itself – waste from previous batches, miscasts, etc – or from industries which make the steel products. The composition of this type of scrap is well known. In this respect, the steel industry consumes its own waste.

Figure 30 An electric arc furnace recycles scrap steel

Scrap from discarded products, such as cars and washing machines, however, must be carefully graded and selected. Steelmakers need to have a good idea of the content of the scrap metal to avoid adding unwanted elements to the steel. Some of the elements present improve the properties of the steel. For example, many mild steels now contain low concentrations of transition metals such as nickel and chromium from the added scrap. Other elements such as tin and copper can cause problems if incorporated into the 'new' steel.

In the rest of this section you will look at two very different sources of scrap steel and some of the problems of recycling.

Activity SS6.1 looks at one topical issue of recycling.

Beans are rich in proteins which contain sulphur. The high temperature used to sterilise the can contents may cause breakdown of some protein with the evolution of hydrogen sulphide. This breakdown can also occur in the body at lower temperatures with noisy and smelly results! (You may remember from **The Atmosphere** that beans also seem to stimulate the production of methane in the intestine.)

The hydrogen sulphide produced can react with both tin and iron inside a can to form sulphides. The sulphides are black and insoluble, but not toxic. Beans, however, are marketed in a bright orange-red tomato sauce in which a few flakes of black sulphides are not going to put off a hungry consumer.

Tuna fish is rich in protein and so cans of tuna might well suffer from sulphur staining just like baked beans. In this product, however, black specks would clearly be seen as an unwelcome contaminant. The difficulty is neatly overcome by coating the inside of the can with a laquer to which some zinc oxide or carbonate has been added. Now it is insoluble zinc sulphide which is formed, but since zinc sulphide is white rather than black, the stain is almost invisible.

Figure 29 The problem with canning food rich in protein

Recycling used 'tin' cans

Recycling used 'tin' cans involves removing the tin coating from the steel. Recycling has been done for a very long time using the wastage from the tin plating works. Only since the 1980s have attempts been made to extract used 'tin' cans from household waste and recycle them on a large scale.

Shredding the cans and removing unwanted paper and residual food is a vital part of the preparation before detinning. One easy way of cleaning the cans is to burn off the unwanted material: unfortunately, during burning, the tin diffuses into the steel and makes it less useful. Mechanical shredding devices like the one in Figure 31 are now used. After shredding, the steel fragments are picked out magnetically. About 98% of the unwanted material can be removed in this way.

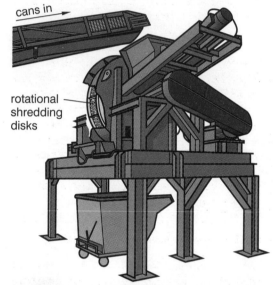

Figure 31 The Cutler Shredder for shredding and cleaning used 'tin' cans: the cans are torn apart between a spinning disc and a cage, which rotate in opposite directions; dirt, labels, lacquer and food scraps are freed in the process and the fragmented cans fall through the holes in the cage

Detinning

Once tin plate has been obtained, the next step is to remove the tin from the surface of the steel. But how? We need to find some difference in the properties of steel and tin which will allow us to do this. Unlike iron, tin is not a d-block metal.

One modern process makes use of the fact that tin but not steel will dissolve in strongly alkaline solutions. The cleaned and shredded tin cans are treated with a hot solution of sodium hydroxide in the presence of an oxidising agent, such as sodium nitrate(V). The tin dissolves as a complex of tin(IV) as shown in the half-equation below:

$$Sn(s) + 6OH^-(aq) \rightarrow [Sn(OH)_6]^{2-}(aq) + 4e^-$$
$$\text{stannate(IV) ion}$$

This equation summarises a complex series of reactions. The tin probably reacts first with the oxidising agent to form tin oxide. Tin oxides are **amphoteric** and dissolve in both acids and alkalis. Here the tin oxide dissolves in alkali to form the stannate(IV) ion.

The steel left behind is rinsed and pressed into bales for transport to a steel plant. The tin can be recovered by electrolysis.

ASSIGNMENT 12

a Would you class tin as an s-, p- or d-block element? Explain your answer.

b Tin oxides are amphoteric, which means they dissolve in both acids and alkalis. Write an equation for the reaction of tin(II) oxide with dilute acid.

You can carry out a detinning process for yourself in **Activity SS6.2** and recover both the steel and some tin.

The steel room

To finish the unit, here's an interesting aspect of recycling steel. The explosion of atomic bombs at Hiroshima and Nagasaki in 1945 increased worldwide atmospheric radiation above the natural background level. Atomic weapon tests and accidents at nuclear power stations have added to the amount of radioactive material in the atmosphere. A small amount of this radioactive material is incorporated into steel during its manufacture.

For most uses of steel, this level of radioactivity is negligible, but there is one exception. In hospitals and other places where radioactive tracer techniques are used (remember **Elements of Life** storyline, Section **EL2**) it is essential that the sensitive detector units are screened from naturally occurring background radiation.

Rooms constructed of 15-cm-thick steel, lined with lead, are built to provide this protection. But such protection is of little value if the steel itself is radioactive. The answer is to use steel manufactured before 1945 and which has not since been subject to radioactive fallout. But where can you get such steel?

At the end of the First World War in 1918, an armistice was signed. As part of this agreement the German fleet was instructed to sail to Scapa Flow, a naval port in the far north of Scotland. Some months later a small number of German sailors who had been left on the ships opened the valves to let in the Atlantic Ocean and deliberately sank the lot.

Now, 70 years later, the ships serve a very peaceful purpose. The pre-atomic age steel from the armoured hulls, decks and ammunition stores of battleships is salvaged and used to build the steel rooms which shield sensitive hospital equipment. Almost a case of turning guns into plough shares!

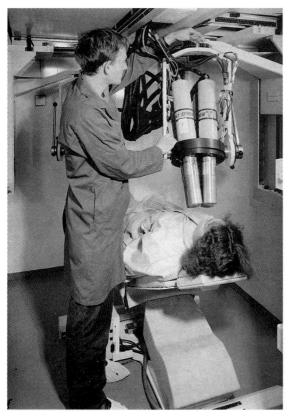

Figure 32 A patient being treated in a steel room in a hospital

SS7 *Summary*

In this unit you have followed the story of steel production from the iron ore fed into the blast furnace to a finished steel product. This is not one story but many. Each starts with iron from the blast furnace but leads to one of a multitude of different steels, each tailored to the job it has to do. Steel production has to be a batch process and must be closely monitored. Recent advances have been aimed at producing higher quality steels to exact specifications, quickly and reliably – and on a huge scale.

Looking at the composition of steel led you into a more detailed study of iron and other d-block metals. These are the structural metals used by engineers to make the things we use in everyday life. The metals and their compounds are also of great importance as catalysts, both in industry and in biological systems. The characteristic properties of d-block metals are closely related to their electronic structure.

The story of steel next led to the problems of corrosion and the inevitable return to nature. Here you found out about the mechanism of rusting as an electrochemical process and what steps can be taken to slow it down. The problems arising when food is preserved in 'tin' cans led to an investigation of the chemistry and stereochemistry of metal complexes.

In the final section, you considered the importance of recycling steel and some of the problems which must be overcome.

Activity SS7 will help you to summarise what you have learned in this unit.

Figure 33 Raising the scuttled German fleet at Scapa Flow, 1928

ASPECTS OF AGRICULTURE

Why a unit on ASPECTS OF AGRICULTURE?

Growing crops for food has long been a major human activity. The rapidly increasing world population means that the need to provide enough food without destroying our environment is one of the biggest challenges facing us.

The chemical and physical processes occurring in soil are highly complex. They involve a number of interrelated reactions. This unit looks at the chemical nature of soil, and at some of the processes which occur as plants grow and decay. It then looks at ways in which a knowledge of these processes can be used to maximise crop yields and ensure our food supply.

Finally, chemical methods of pest control are studied. In particular, the unit covers the development of pesticides which do not persist in the environment, and also explores the applications of some herbicides.

In considering these aspects of agriculture you will apply knowledge and understanding of chemical principles developed earlier in the course. These include ideas about intermolecular forces, reaction kinetics, redox chemistry, chemical equilibrium and the behaviour of functional groups in organic molecules. You will also learn about the structures of alumino-silicate minerals, ion-exchange processes, and some specific chemistry of the elements of Groups 4 and 5. The industrial manufacture of ammonia is covered, and there is a general overview of bonding structure and properties.

Overview of chemical principles

In this unit you will learn more about …

ideas introduced in earlier units in this course
- intermolecular forces (**The Polymer Revolution**)
- the relationship between properties of substances and their structure and bonding (**Elements of Life** and **The Polymer Revolution**)
- redox reactions (**From Minerals to Elements** and **Using Sunlight**)
- reaction kinetics (**The Atmosphere** and **Engineering Proteins**)
- catalysis (**Developing Fuels**, **Engineering Proteins** and **The Steel Story**)
- the behaviour of functional groups in organic molecules (various units)
- chemical equilibrium (**The Atmosphere** and **Engineering Proteins**)

… as well as learning new ideas about
- the chemistry of Group 4 elements
- structures and properties of silicates and clays
- ions in solution and ion-exchange processes
- the redox chemistry of nitrogen and the chemistry of Group 5 elements
- the effects of changes in temperature and pressure on chemical equilibrium
- the selection of optimum conditions for the industrial manufacture of ammonia.

AA
ASPECTS OF AGRICULTURE

AA1 *What do we want from agriculture?*

The impact of agriculture is enormous and has changed the face of the Earth. It is hard to take in the *scale* of agriculture today, as we try to provide food for an ever increasing number of people.

In this unit you will look at the production of crops for food, but remember that agriculture also involves the cultivation of plants such as cotton, grown for fibre, and sugar cane, grown for fuel, and forests producing timber.

As they grow, plants take carbon dioxide from the air into their leaves, and water and nutrients from the soil via their roots. When we harvest crops we disturb the natural nutrient cycles by removing large quantities of plants before the natural processes of decay take place.

Our planet cannot produce an *unlimited* supply of food for its human population. The problem of rapid population growth needs to be tackled, but the challenge to agriculture remains. The ultimate goal is to feed everyone adequately, without harming the environment. This involves producing enough food, of the right kind, in the right place, and at the right time.

How can we increase food production *without* destroying the world's remaining forests and wildernesses? It can be done by making the most efficient use of *existing* agricultural land – particularly by improving crop varieties and planting techniques, and making sensible use of fertilisers and pesticides.

Mistakes have been made. Growing one crop again and again on the same soil can destroy its fertility. Agricultural technology appropriate in one place cannot just be exported to other regions with different soil types and growing conditions.

To avoid repeating past mistakes we need to use knowledge and understanding, gained both from scientific research and from the experience of farmers, to develop sustainable systems of agriculture – that is, agriculture that can go on indefinitely without degrading the environment.

Figure 2 Climate conditions change. The Sahara once provided the Romans with grain, but today the desert is advancing southwards every year.

What do plants need for growth?

The nutrient elements essential for the growth of plants are shown in Table 1.

Elements used in relatively large amounts		Elements used in relatively small amounts
carbon	nitrogen	iron
hydrogen	phosphorus	manganese
oxygen	potassium	boron
	calcium	molybdenum
	magnesium	copper
	sulphur	zinc
		cobalt
		chlorine
mostly from carbon dioxide and water	from soil	

Table 1 Essential nutrient elements and their sources; other minor nutrients (sodium, fluorine, iodine, silicon, strontium and barium) are not needed by all plants

Figure 1 Harvesting wheat in Oxfordshire

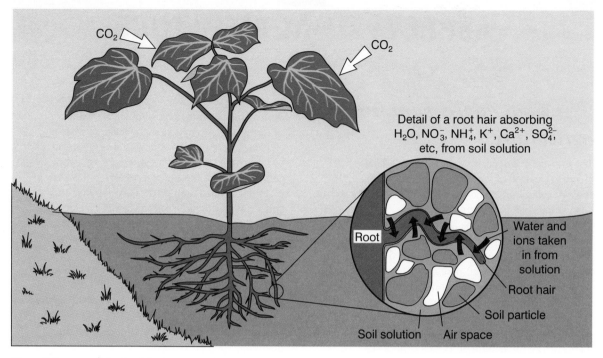

Figure 3 Sources of plant nutrients

The table also shows the importance of soil in making nutrients available to plants

no soil = no food

So what *is* soil, and how does it support plant life?

AA2 *The world at your feet*

The Earth's crust is just 1.5% of the volume of the planet. In this unit we are concerned with the thin layer, typically 1 m–2 m thick, on the top of the crust. This is the soil.

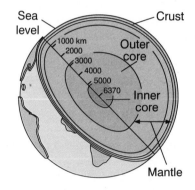

Figure 4 The layers of the Earth

Figure 5 Layers of soil exposed in a road cutting

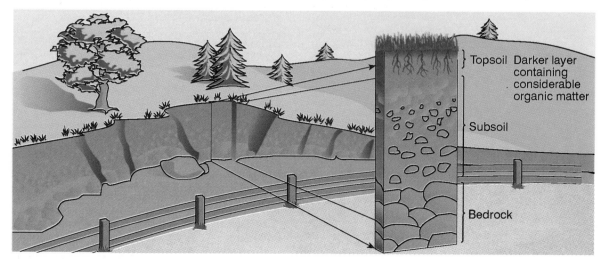

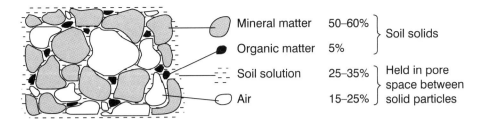

Figure 6 The four major components of soils, showing the approximate proportions by volume for a typical moist soil

Element	% by mass
oxygen	47
silicon	28
aluminium	8
iron	5
calcium, sodium, potassium, magnesium	2–4 each

Table 2 Composition of the Earth's crust by mass

Road cuttings often reveal to us the underlying layers of a soil (see Figure 5). Plants take nutrients and water from the soil which also supports them as they grow.

What is soil?

Soil is a mixture of weathered rock fragments and organic matter. Together they make a porous fabric which can hold both air and water. The approximate proportions by volume for a typical moist soil are shown in Figure 6.

The quantities of air and water in a soil are variable and their proportions are important in determining how well the soil supports plant growth. The minerals play a vital part, both in retaining water and in making nutrient ions available to plants.

Soil minerals are produced by weathering of the rocks which make up the Earth's crust. The fragments of rock and minerals vary enormously in size and are divided into classes by diameter (see Figure 7).

The coarse fragments are relatively inactive chemically. It is the very fine clay fraction which is most active. How is this clay fraction formed?

Size of fraction	Very coarse	Coarse	Fine	Very fine
	Stone, gravel	Sand	Silt	Clay
Diameter/mm	2.0		0.06	0.002

Figure 7 Major size classes of inorganic particles in soil

Weathering

Weathering is the action of wind, rain, frost and sunlight – and nothing on the surface of the Earth's crust escapes it. Weathering breaks up the rocks. It changes their physical and sometimes their chemical composition. It carries away soluble materials and some of the solid fragments as well. But weathering is creative as well as destructive: it makes a soil from the uppermost layers of weathered rock.

Figure 8 summarises the main pathways of weathering in the moderately acid conditions of humid temperate climates. In different climates the rates of the reactions alter, and this alters the composition of the soils. For example, many tropical soils are high in iron and aluminium oxides because the chemical reactions involved in weathering are faster at higher temperatures.

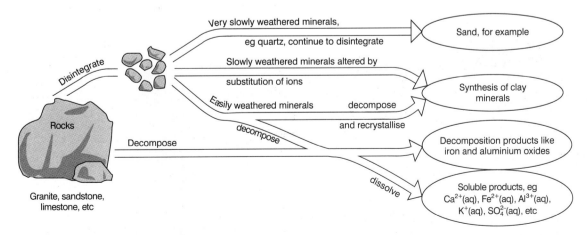

Figure 8 Processes of weathering in moderately acid conditions common in humid temperate climates (granite and sandstone are mixtures of silicate minerals such as quartz, feldspars and micas)

Most chemical reactions take place more quickly at higher temperatures. You can read about the effect of temperature on the rate of a reaction in **Chemical Ideas 10.3**.

In **Activity AA2.1** you can use the 'iodine clock' method to investigate the effect of temperature on the rate of a reaction.

You will need to learn something about the structure of the clay minerals to understand how soils function. But first, something about the rocks from which clay minerals are formed: the **silicates.**

To understand the rest of this section, you will need to read more about the chemistry of silicon, and other Group 4 elements, in **Chemical Ideas 11.3.**

Silicates

An isolated silicate ion SiO_4^{4-} is shown in Figure 9. Each silicon atom is covalently bonded to four oxygens at the corners of a tetrahedron. The silicon atom is at the centre of the tetrahedron and has an oxidation state of $+4$.

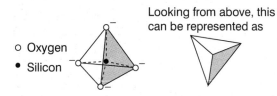

○ Oxygen

● Silicon

Looking from above, this can be represented as

Figure 9 The silicate(IV) ion SiO_4^{4-}

Many minerals in the Earth's crust are silicates, in which SiO_4 tetrahedra are linked by sharing oxygen atoms between adjacent tetrahedra. A simple example is shown in Figure 10. Note that the *unshared* oxygen atoms carry a single negative charge.

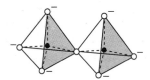

Figure 10 The $Si_2O_7^{6-}$ ion

ASSIGNMENT I

Draw dot and cross diagrams for an isolated SiO_4^{4-} ion and for the ion, $Si_2O_7^{6-}$, made by linking two silicate tetrahedra together. Show clearly the charges on individual oxygens.

Pure quartz is a continuous three-dimensional network of silicon and oxygen atoms, with each oxygen atom shared between two adjacent tetrahedra. (Because all the oxygen atoms are shared, none of them carry a negative charge.) The number of oxygens per silicon is

$$\tfrac{1}{2}+\tfrac{1}{2}+\tfrac{1}{2}+\tfrac{1}{2} = 2$$

and quartz has the overall composition SiO_2. It is very slowly weathered to sand. This type of weathering is a purely physical process.

(a)

(b)

Figure 11 (a) Crystals of quartz, SiO_2; (b) sand is made up of small grains of SiO_2 (the pale brown colour is due to iron impurities)

The silicate tetrahedra can join up in a number of other ways. We will represent a silicate tetrahedron as

looking from above. Remember that the corners represent oxygen atoms. The tetrahedra can join up to form **chains** by sharing two corner oxygens.

Figure 12 A single chain

They can also form double-stranded chains in which two or three oxygens are shared. Asbestos is an example of this kind of arrangement.

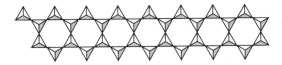

Figure 13 A double-stranded chain

Figure 14 Fibres of asbestos are made up of double-stranded silicate chains

Sheets of silicate tetrahedra can be built up by joining more strands together. These occur in micas and clays.

In sheets like this all the unshared, negatively charged oxygens point in one direction (upwards, out of the plane of the paper in Figure 15). In each silicate tetrahedron one oxygen is wholly owned by a silicon, and the other three are shared. The number of oxygens per silicon is

$$\tfrac{1}{2}+\tfrac{1}{2}+\tfrac{1}{2}+1=\tfrac{5}{2}$$

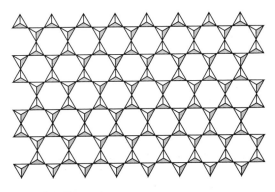

Figure 15 A silicate sheet

Figure 16 Mica is made up of sheets of silicate tetrahedra

In whole numbers, the ratio Si:O is 2:5. The net charge on each Si_2O_5 unit is −2 (each oxygen has an oxidation state of −2 and silicon has an oxidation state of +4). The overall structure of the sheet can be represented as $(Si_2O_5^{2-})_n$.

What balances the negative charge? Many cations such as Na^+, Ca^{2+}, Mg^{2+} and Al^{3+} are held to the silicate sheets to balance the negative charge. Some of these cations fit into the hollows formed by the rings of tetrahedra.

During weathering, aluminium(III) can replace some of the silicon(IV) atoms at the centre of the tetrahedra in the silicate sheets to give a variety of different minerals. When this happens each aluminate tetrahedron has an extra negative charge because the aluminium is in oxidation state +3 compared with silicon's +4. Extra cations are then needed on the surface of the sheet to balance the extra negative charges. The physical properties of the silicate minerals are very dependent on how many Si(IV) atoms are replaced, and therefore how many extra cations are needed.

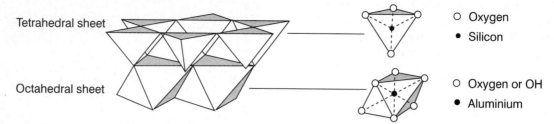

Figure 17 *The sheet structure of clay minerals*

You can find out about the relationship between the properties of a substance and its structure and bonding in **Chemical Ideas 5.6**.

Activity AA2.2 allows you to build models of silicate and clay structures to help you to understand the structures represented in the diagrams in this section.

Clay minerals

Clay minerals contain two different kinds of **sheets:**

- **tetrahedral sheets** based on silicate tetrahedra with varying amounts of Al(III) substituted for Si(IV)
- **octahedral sheets** based mainly on Al^{3+} and/or Mg^{2+} ions surrounded by six oxide or hydroxide ions in an octahedral arrangement. The octahedra link together in the sheet by sharing oxygens (see Figure 17).

These sheets form into **layers** in different ways. Clays are classified into types based on the arrangements of the sheets.

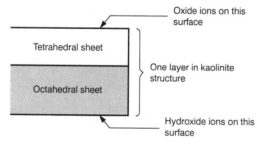

Figure 18 *A layer in kaolinite*

Kaolinite is a common example of a **1:1 type** clay. Each layer in the kaolinite is made up of one tetrahedral and one octahedral sheet.

The layers are held closely together by hydrogen bonding between the hydroxide ions on the surface of the octahedral sheets and the oxide ions on the surface of the tetrahedral sheet in the next layer. Water and cations cannot enter between *the layers* of a crystal of kaolinite, so the crystals do not expand on wetting.

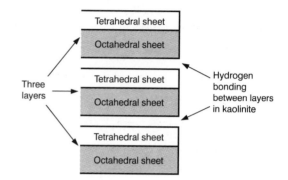

Figure 19 *Hydrogen bonding between the layers in kaolinite*

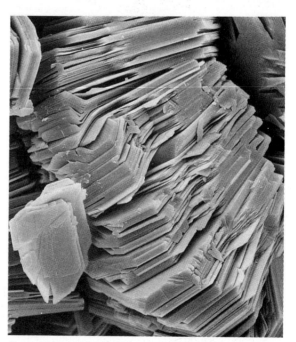

Figure 20 *Scanning electron microscope picture of kaolinite showing the crystalline layer structure*

ASSIGNMENT 2

Kaolinite does not usually expand very much when wetted. Explain why water does not enter between the layers and push them apart.

In **2:1 type** clays an octahedral sheet is sandwiched between two tetrahedral sheets (see Figure 21). **Montmorillonite** and **vermiculite** are examples of this type of mineral and both are common in soils.

There is little attraction between the oxygens at the bottom of one layer and those at the top of the next layer. This means that water and cations can easily enter the interlayer space in 2:1 type minerals.

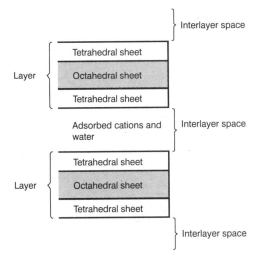

Figure 21 *A 2:1 clay mineral, eg montmorillonite*

When water enters the interlayer space in a clay mineral such as montmorillonite it forces the layers apart and exposes a large internal surface. This internal surface is much greater than the external surface area of the crystals.

	Montmorillonite (2:1 expanding mineral)	Kaolinite (1:1 non-expanding mineral)
total surface area per unit mass/m^2 g^{-1}	700–800	up to 15

Table 3 The total surface areas (internal + external surface areas) of an expanding and a non-expanding mineral

Figure 22 *Modelling clay, containing kaolinite, absorbs comparatively small amounts of water when wet – the water gets between the small plate-like crystals which slide easily over one another, so wet clay is pliable and slippery; however, water cannot penetrate between the layers within a crystal*

In montmorillonite, Mg^{2+} ions substitute for some of the Al^{3+} ions in the octahedral sheet, and Al^{3+} ions substitute for some of the silicon in the tetrahedral sheet. The individual layers of this substance therefore have a high negative charge. In vermiculite, even more aluminium has substituted for silicon so that the negative charge is even higher than in montmorillonite.

A swarm of cations is attracted to both the external and internal surfaces to balance the negative charge (see Figure 23).

These cations are hydrated: each one is surrounded by layers of water molecules. This water held round the clay crystals gives wet clay its characteristic sticky feel.

The cations held to the surfaces of clay minerals are very important for agriculture because they provide a source of nutrient ions for use by plant roots. There is continuous movement of ions between the surfaces of clays and the soil solution in a process called **ion exchange**.

Figure 23 *Exchangeable cations at the inner and outer surfaces of a crystal of a 2:1 clay mineral like montmorillonite*

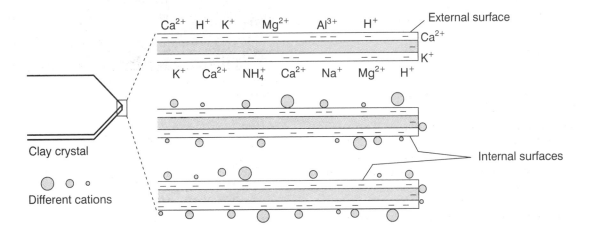

You can investigate the physical properties of some silicate and clay minerals like quartz, mica and vermiculite in **Activity AA2.3.**

Figure 24 Clay soils containing montmorillonite or vermiculite are heavy to plough and dig when wet; when dry, they shrink and crack

Soil organic matter

The organic matter in soil is made up of plant debris, animal remains and excreta, and the products formed by decomposition of all these things. Soil organic matter forms a store from which the next generation of plants will get their nutrients. A variety of organisms living in the soil make use of the debris deposited. During the processes of decomposition, elements in organic compounds are converted into inorganic ions such as ammonium, nitrate(V), sulphate and phosphate ions. This is called **mineralisation.**

Some of the carbon in decomposing organic matter is released into the atmosphere as carbon dioxide. A range of new organic molecules is synthesised to make **humus.** There are many macromolecules in humus with molar masses up to $500\,000\,g\,mol^{-1}$. Major components of humus are esters of carboxylic acids, carboxylic acid derivatives of benzene and phenolic compounds. The following two groups are therefore common:

carboxylic acid group   *phenol group*

Both these groups can lose H^+ ions. If they do then negatively charged groups are left on the molecules in humus. These are able to form ionic bonds with metal cations so that humus can hold a variety of nutrient ions in a similar way to clays.

How are nutrient ions taken up by soils?

Cation exchange

Many of the cations held to the inner and outer surfaces of clay minerals can be replaced by different ions from the soil solution. The process is called **cation exchange**. For example NH_4^+ ions can exchange with Ca^{2+} ions. The balance of charge must be maintained, so two singly charged ions will replace one doubly charged ion.

$$clay–Ca^{2+}(s) + 2NH_4^+(aq) \rightleftharpoons clay–2NH_4^+(s) + Ca^{2+}(aq)$$

The exchange is rapid and reversible. The direction of the exchange reaction depends on the concentrations of the ions involved and on how strongly they are held by the clay.

ASSIGNMENT 3

In a laboratory experiment, a solution of ammonium nitrate(V) is allowed to seep slowly through a sample of a clay soil.

a Describe what happens to the ammonium ions and the nitrate(V) ions.

b Ammonium nitrate(V) is commonly added to soils as a nitrogen fertiliser. Use your answer to **a** to explain why heavy rain can leach out nitrate(V) ions from clay soils more quickly than ammonium ions.

The ability of a clay mineral to exchange ions is measured by its **cation exchange capacity**. This is the amount in moles of exchangeable positive charge (mol_c) held by 1 kg of the mineral. (One mole of singly charged ions is equivalent to half a mole of doubly charged ions or to one-third of a mole of triply charged ions.)

Cation exchange capacities vary widely, depending on the surface area of the mineral, and the number of charges on its inner and outer surfaces.

Substance	Cation exchange capacity/$mol_c\,kg^{-1}$
kaolinite	0.3
montmorillonite	1.0
vermiculite	1.5
humus	1.5–3.0

Table 4 Cation exchange capacities of some clay minerals and humus

Soils vary in the quantities of clay and organic matter which they contain. Typical soil cation exchange capacities are in the range $0.02\,mol_c\,kg^{-1}$–$0.6\,mol_c\,kg^{-1}$.

Plant roots withdraw nutrients from this pool of exchangeable cations. The ions held by the clay or humus are in equilibrium with the free ions in the soil solution. The ions in the soil solution can be absorbed by plant roots, or can be washed away out of the soil by rain, upsetting this equilibrium.

You can find out more about ion exchange by reading **Chemical Ideas 7.5**.

The size of ions in solution is discussed in **Chemical Ideas 3.2**.

In **Activities AA2.4** and **AA2.5** you can investigate ion exchange.

Effect of pH on soil

Under natural conditions H^+ ions from rain, and from plant roots and microbe activity, displace Ca^{2+} and other ions from soil solids. This has two effects: the soil becomes more acidic, and its store of nutrients in the form of exchangeable cations is reduced.

Exchangeable cations are lost for two reasons. Firstly, cations held to the surfaces of the clay layers are replaced by H^+ ions. Secondly, at high pH, weathering of clay minerals takes place more quickly (see Section **AA2**, Figure 8) and aluminium oxide is released into the soil. The surface of the oxide binds H^+ ions, so that it becomes positively charged and repels cations.

The release of aluminium ions from clays at low pH causes another problem. High aluminium concentrations in the soil solution are toxic to crops.

Table 5 shows soil pH values below which plant growth is restricted.

Crop	pH below which growth is restricted
beans	6.0
oats	5.3
potatoes	4.9
wheat	5.5
lettuces	6.1
cabbages	5.4
apples	5.0
blackcurrants	6.0

Table 5 Soil pH values below which plant growth is restricted

How is soil acidity overcome?

Bases such as ground limestone, chalk or basic slag from steelmaking can be added to the surface to make a soil less acidic. The amount of base needed to reach a desired pH depends on the soil's capacity to neutralise alkali. This is called its **buffering capacity.** A clay soil at pH 5 will need more lime to bring its pH to 7 than the same mass of sandy soil. The clay soil has a higher buffering capacity.

As alkali is added to a clay soil, the pH of the soil changes very little at first, and then slowly rises. The soil acts as a **buffer** and is able to resist changes in pH to some extent. It can do this because H^+ ions bound onto the soil solids replace some of the H^+ ions in the soil solution as soon as they are removed.

Figure 25 shows the effect of adding alkali to some clay minerals.

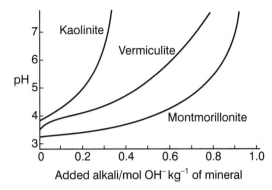

Figure 25 The effect of adding alkali to some clay minerals

Plots like this for different soils allow the **lime requirement** of each soil to be calculated.

ASSIGNMENT 4

Look at Figure 25.

a Which of the three minerals has the lowest buffering capacity?

b Suggest a reason why the mineral you have chosen in **a** should have a lower buffering capacity than the other two.

In **Activity AA2.6** you can measure the pH of a soil, and estimate its buffering capacity and lime requirement.

Figure 26 Farmers add lime to reduce soil acidity

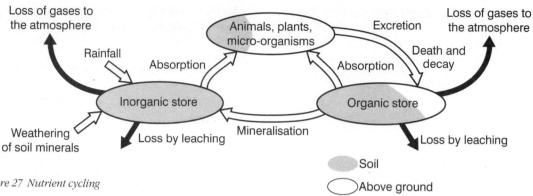

Figure 27 Nutrient cycling

Soil
Above ground

AA3 *How does soil remain fertile?*

How can we grow crops again and again on the same soil without decreasing its fertility?

The fertility of a soil depends on many things, such as the clay and humus content, the moisture content and temperature. It can be damaged by destroying the arrangement of particles and pore spaces in the soil, and by removing too many nutrients.

Nutrient cycling

Apart from carbon dioxide from the air, plants get all their nutrients from the soil (see Section **AA1**, Figure 3). These nutrients are drawn from an **inorganic store** in the soil, and an **organic store** partly on top of and partly in the soil. Elements are cycled continuously between living systems, the organic store and the inorganic store. The general routes are shown in Figure 27.

The organic store is replenished by animal excretions, and by death and decay of living organisms. Micro-organisms act on organic matter and convert it into humus. They also convert it into inorganic ions (mineralisation), producing ammonium, nitrate(V), phosphate and sulphate ions (see Section **AA2**). Weathering of soil and rock minerals releases more ions into the inorganic store.

Nutrients are lost by being leached out of the top layers of soil by rainwater, and nitrogen can be lost by conversion into gases, such as N_2 and N_2O, which disperse into the atmosphere. Figure 28 shows typical values for the total quantities of some elements in different soils.

> **Hectares**
>
> Land areas are conveniently measured in **hectares** (ha).
>
> 1 ha = 1×10^4 m^2 (= 2.47 acres)
>
> A football pitch is about 0.5 hectares. Fields range from about 6 hectares to about 60 hectares.

Only a small fraction of each element in the soil is actually available to plants in the form of ions which can be absorbed through their roots. You can measure the nitrogen content of soil in the form of nitrate(V) and ammonium ions extracted from a known mass of soil. Extraction methods are also used to determine quantities of potassium and phosphate ions. The extracted quantities are used to classify soils as low, medium and high in nutrients present in forms which plants can use. Figures are given for three major nutrients in Table 6.

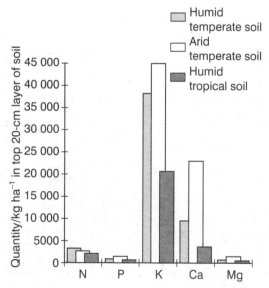

Figure 28 Quantities of some elements present in different soils

Soil range	Nutrient extractable in forms which plants can use/kg ha^{-1} in top 20-cm layer of soil		
	Nitrogen	Potassium	Phosphorus
low	40	0–150	0–23
medium	90	150–600	23–63
high	140	over 600	over 63

Table 6 Nutrients in soils in forms which plants can use

ASSIGNMENT 5

Refer to Table 6 and Figure 28. In a humid temperate soil rated high in nutrients, what percentage of

a the total potassium content

b the total nitrogen content

is in a form which plants can use?

Figure 29 A leaf from (a) a healthy plant and (b) a plant with potassium deficiency

Many crops make severe demands on the ability of the soil to supply nutrients. This makes the rates at which nutrients are interconverted in the cycles very important. The rate of supply of ions to plant roots has to be rapid enough during the peak growing period in May and June to meet the demands of the crops. Crop yields are reduced if there is a shortage of even one nutrient.

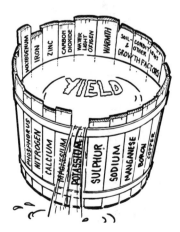

Figure 30 A German chemist, Justus von Liebig, used this barrel to illustrate to his students that a deficiency of any single plant nutrient is enough to limit growth – in the diagram, potassium is the nutrient limiting the yield

In the next section, you will look at one nutrient cycle in more detail.

You can measure the nitrogen content of a soil in **Activity AA3.1.**

The nitrogen cycle

Almost all the nitrogen in soil is present in complex organic compounds and so is not readily available to plants. Various processes convert gaseous nitrogen and organic nitrogen compounds into the soluble ammonium and nitrate(V) ions which plants *can* use. The main processes in the nitrogen cycle are listed below. As you read through, refer to the diagram of the nitrogen cycle in Figure 32 (p. 189).

Chemical Ideas 11.4 gives a summary of the chemistry of nitrogen and other elements in Group 5.

Gains of nitrogen to the soil

Biological fixation Some kinds of bacteria in soil, and in root nodules in legumes, such as peas and beans, can convert nitrogen gas to ammonium ions. A reducing agent is needed to provide the electrons. The half-equation for the reduction is

$$N_2(g) + 8H^+(aq) + 6e^- \rightarrow 2NH_4^+(aq)$$

Other additions to soil nitrogen Lightning, burning of hydrocarbon fuels and natural fires all cause some oxidation of nitrogen in the atmosphere to nitrogen oxides which are carried down to the soil in rainwater. In Europe about $20\,kg\,N\,ha^{-1}$–$40\,kg\,N\,ha^{-1}$ are deposited from the air onto the soil each year. Some of this is in the form of nitrogen oxides and some as ammonium ions which have come from ammonia emitted by animal excreta.

Figure 31 Lightning generates enough energy to convert nitrogen and oxygen in the air to nitrogen monoxide, $N_2 + O_2 \rightarrow 2NO$

Transformations in the soil

Mineralisation Soil bacteria and other micro-organisms break down organic nitrogen compounds into simpler molecules and ions. Any nitrogen not needed by the organisms themselves is released into the soil as ammonium ions:

several steps

organic N $\;\rightarrow\rightarrow\rightarrow\;$ $NH_4^+(aq)$

The NH_4^+ ions are held by clay minerals as exchangeable cations.

A well-drained soil is best for mineralisation, and the reaction is much faster at the higher temperatures of tropical soils. Radioactive labelling with ^{15}N shows that only 1%–3% of soil nitrogen is mineralised each year.

ASSIGNMENT 6

Overall, mineralisation has a first-order rate equation

rate of mineralisation = $k[N]$

where k is the rate constant at a particular temperature and $[N]$ is the quantity of organic nitrogen per hectare in the top 20 cm of soil.

The rate constant k varies from 0.01 yr^{-1} to 0.06 yr^{-1}. For a time interval of 1 year, the quantity of organic nitrogen mineralised in the top 20 cm of soil equals $k[N] \text{ kg ha}^{-1}$.

a Use the above equation to calculate the quantity of nitrogen mineralised in 1 year (in the top 20 cm of 1 ha) in the three soils A, B and C. The soils have different organic nitrogen contents and different temperatures. (Remember, the value of k depends on the temperature.)

Soil	Soil organic nitrogen/kg ha^{-1}	Rate constant k/yr^{-1}
A	1000	0.01
B	2000	0.03
C	2000	0.06

b Refer to Figure 28 on p. 186 for information about the nitrogen content of different types of soil. Think about the factors that affect the rate of mineralisation, and explain why a humid tropical soil has the highest rate of mineralisation.

Nitrification Ammonium ions can be oxidised by certain aerobic bacteria in the soil. The bacteria carry out the reactions as a means of obtaining respiratory energy. The overall process is called nitrification because the end product is the nitrate(V) ion. It occurs in two stages.

Stage 1 $\quad NH_4^+(aq) + 1\frac{1}{2}O_2(g) \rightarrow$
$NO_2^-(aq) + 2H^+(aq) + H_2O(l) + \text{energy}$

The bacteria which do this are called *Nitrosomonas*. The optimum pH is between 7 and 9, and the reaction stops in dry conditions. The nitrate(III), NO_2^-, produced is rapidly oxidised further.

Stage 2 $\quad NO_2^-(aq) + \frac{1}{2}O_2(g) \rightarrow NO_3^-(aq) + \text{energy}$

The bacteria converting nitrate(III) to nitrate(V) are called *Nitrobacter*. They can tolerate dry conditions and higher acidity than *Nitrosomonas*.

Some nitrification occurs in soils at temperatures down to 0 °C, but it ceases in waterlogged soils where the oxygen content is too low.

Losses of nitrogen from the soil

Denitrification Where oxygen content is low, anaerobic bacteria reduce nitrate(V) ions in the sequence:

$$NO_3^-(aq) \rightarrow NO_2^-(aq) \rightarrow NO(g) \rightarrow N_2O(g) \rightarrow N_2(g)$$

In flooded soils, like those used in rice cultivation, losses by denitrification can be high.

Leaching Nitrogen is lost by leaching mainly as the nitrate(V) ion NO_3^- which is not held by clays or humus in temperate soils. The quantities lost depend on the soil structure and the amount of rainfall, as well as the nitrate(V) level in the soil.

Loss of ammonia gas Ammonium ions are converted into ammonia under alkaline conditions in some soils.

Uptake by plants In natural systems the quantity of nitrogen removed per year is relatively small. For example, a coniferous forest takes up 25 kg N ha^{-1} –78 kg N ha^{-1} each year. Crops cultivated to give high yields take up much more nitrogen, 100 kg N ha^{-1} –500 kg N ha^{-1} per year. Soil nitrogen cannot be converted into ammonium ions fast enough to meet this demand, even when the reserves of organic nitrogen are high.

In order to maintain or increase crop yields, nitrogen must be added to the soil in a form that plants can readily use.

In **Activity AA3.2** you can use the information in this section to investigate the nitrogen cycle in more detail.

Adding nutrients

Nutrients are added to soil in two ways:

- as manure from livestock
- as inorganic compounds, either crushed rock or synthesised compounds.

Long-term experiments have been conducted at the Rothamsted Experimental Station in Hertfordshire since 1843, investigating the effects of adding nutrients to the soil. They have shown that yields can be

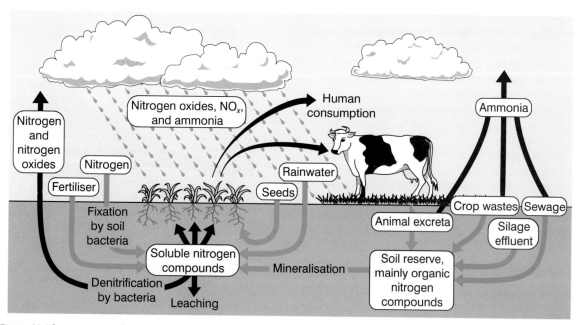

Figure 32 The nitrogen cycle

Figure 33 Famous fields: researchers at Rothamsted Experimental Station study plots set up more than a century ago

	Manure produced/ t yr^{-1}	Nutrient content/kg t^{-1}		
		N	P	K
1 dairy cow	23	4.7	0.6	4.4
10 pigs	21	6.3	1.5	2.9

Table 7 The nutrient content of some farmyard manures

ASSIGNMENT 7

A farmer plans to add 144 kg nitrogen per hectare to a small field of wheat. The area of the field is 7 ha.

a Calculate the total mass of nitrogen needed.

b Calculate the mass of cow manure needed to supply the nitrogen for the field.

increased, and high productivity maintained, by adding nutrients to the soil.

After a century, the application of farmyard manure to plots of land has more than doubled the organic nitrogen content of soil, increasing its nitrogen reserve. In addition, farmyard manure has encouraged flourishing populations of small animals like earthworms, and soil micro-organisms. These assist in converting organic nitrogen into forms usable by plants.

The water content of farmyard manure is high (around 90%–95%), so large quantities of manure have to be used to supply adequate nutrients (see Table 7). Because of the bulk, long-distance transport of manure is uneconomical. Drying processes have been developed, but processing costs are high.

Figure 34 Manure is a good source of nitrogen and other nutrients

While manure is a resource to be used wherever possible it only returns some of the nutrients removed by livestock back to the soil. It cannot *completely replace* nutrients removed in crops and exported from a farm. Another source of nutrient is needed in order to maintain the productivity of the soil.

Long-term experiments as at Rothamsted show that high levels of productivity can also be sustained using inorganic fertilisers.

You can see the increasing importance of inorganic fertilisers over the last 40 years in Figure 35. During this time average grain yields have almost tripled. Today, inorganic fertilisers support about half the world's cereal production. Without them we cannot hope to feed the world.

How is inorganic fertiliser produced?

The raw materials for fertiliser manufacture are

- water
- air
- natural gas
- phosphate rock (calcium phosphate)
- minerals containing potassium chloride
- sulphur.

The range of fertilisers produced includes *ammonium nitrate(V)*, *ammonium sulphate*, *ammonium phosphate*, *urea* ($CO(NH_2)_2$) and *potassium nitrate(V)*. The compounds are sold individually, or mixed to produce a range of products with different N:P:K ratios to meet farmers' needs.

Figure 36 Haber's apparatus for the synthesis of ammonia

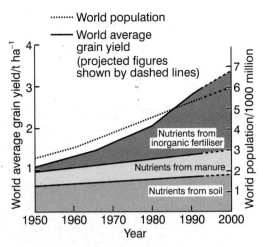

Figure 35 World population figures shown against world trends in grain yields; the shaded areas show estimates of the relative contributions of the different sources of plant nutrients

ASSIGNMENT 8

The major costs involved in distributing and applying nitrogen fertilisers are to do with the mass of material which must be transported for a given mass of nitrogen.

a Calculate the percentages by mass of nitrogen in the three nitrogen fertilisers ammonium nitrate(V), ammonium sulphate and urea. (Make sure that you write the correct formula for each one.)

b List the fertilisers in order of increasing transport costs.

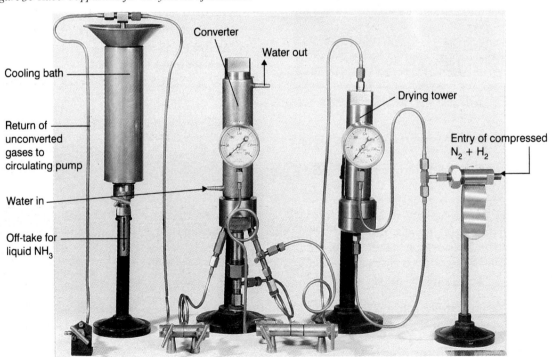

At the heart of fertiliser production is the synthesis of ammonia from nitrogen and hydrogen. The apparatus shown in Figure 36 was used by the German chemist Fritz Haber to develop the method of synthesis, and with it he managed to produce 100 g of ammonia in 1909.

Figure 37 Fritz Haber (1868–1934)

The process was scaled up by Carl Bosch, a chemical engineer employed by BASF (Badische Anilin und Soda Fabrik) near Mannheim in Germany. In 1913 the first industrial plant went into production with a capacity of 30 tonnes of ammonia per day. Modern plants use the same basic design principles, but with capacities of about 1500 tonnes per day.

About 6500 experiments were carried out between 1910 and 1912 to discover an effective catalyst. Today, finely divided iron is used. Small amounts of potassium, aluminium, silicon and magnesium oxides are added to improve its activity.

Both Haber and Bosch were awarded Nobel prizes in chemistry: Haber in 1918 for his academic work, and Bosch in 1931 for inventing and developing the high-pressure technology.

In modern factories the hydrogen is usually made by reacting water with natural gas. Nitrogen from the air is purified and mixed with hydrogen. The heated gases pass over the catalyst where they react to form ammonia:

$$N_2(g) + 3H_2(g) \rightleftharpoons 2NH_3(g)$$

The reaction is reversible. Ammonia produced in the forward reaction can decompose to nitrogen and hydrogen in the reverse reaction. If a mixture of nitrogen and hydrogen is placed in contact with the catalyst and left for a sufficient time then an equilibrium mixture containing all three gases will be obtained.

To investigate how the highest yields can be obtained, nitrogen and hydrogen in the volume ratio 1:3 were mixed and held at different temperatures and pressures. The equilibrium yield of ammonia was recorded. Some results are shown in Table 8.

The equilibrium position depends on the temperature and pressure chosen for the reaction. As you can see from the data in Table 8, the percentage of ammonia in the mixture increases with increasing pressure and falling temperature. Maximum conversion to ammonia is obtained at high pressures and low temperatures.

However, high pressures are very expensive to achieve, and at low temperatures ammonia is produced only very slowly. The reaction conditions chosen are those which give the most economic production of ammonia. It is better to get moderate yields of ammonia rapidly than to wait a long time for a higher yield. Ammonia is separated from unreacted nitrogen and hydrogen which can then be recycled over the catalyst.

Most reactors now operate at pressures between 70 atm and 200 atm, and at temperatures between 400 °C and 600 °C. Energy consumption in modern factories is about 35 MJ for every kilogram of nitrogen converted to ammonia.

Chemical Ideas 7.4 explains how the variation in equilibrium position can be predicted.

You can read about the effect of catalysts on the rate of a reaction in **Chemical Ideas 10.4**.

Pressure/ atm	NH₃ present at equilibrium/%					
	100 °C	200 °C	300 °C	400 °C	500 °C	700 °C
10	–	50.7	14.7	3.9	1.2	0.2
25	91.7	63.6	27.4	8.7	2.9	–
50	94.5	74.0	39.5	15.3	5.6	1.1
100	96.7	81.7	52.5	25.2	10.6	2.2
200	98.4	89.0	66.7	38.8	18.3	–
400	99.4	94.6	79.7	55.4	31.9	–
1000	–	98.3	92.6	79.8	57.5	12.9

Table 8 Volume percentage of NH₃ in equilibrium mixtures in the reaction N₂(g) + 3H₂(g) ⇌ 2NH₃(g)

ASSIGNMENT 9

a The forward reaction in the Haber process is exothermic ($\Delta H^{\circ} = -92\,\text{kJ}\,\text{mol}^{-1}$). Explain how the experimental results in Table 8 are in agreement with Le Chatelier's principle.

b Pick out the conditions of temperature and pressure from those listed in Table 8 which would give
  i the highest yield of ammonia
  ii the fastest rate of conversion to ammonia.

c What practical reasons can you think of for not using very high pressures?

d The boiling points of N_2, H_2 and NH_3 are $-196\,^{\circ}\text{C}$, $-253\,^{\circ}\text{C}$ and $-33\,^{\circ}\text{C}$ respectively. How do you think the ammonia could be separated from unreacted nitrogen and hydrogen?

Figure 38 *The Norsk Hydro NPK fertiliser factory at Glomfjord in Norway*

Saving money and protecting the environment

Fertilisers cost money. Farmers do not want to apply fertiliser nitrogen just to have it leached out of the soil as nitrate(V) ions. To avoid wastage, they need to match the addition of fertiliser to the needs of the crop they are growing. They should also apply it when the crop is most likely to take up the nitrogen. Any excess leached out of the soil could eventually get into drinking water. Concern over nitrate(V) levels in drinking water has led to an EC limit of $50\,\text{mg}\,\text{dm}^{-3}$.

Figure 39 shows the soil nitrate(V) levels during 1 year. Nitrate(V) levels are low in January and February. In spring the rate of mineralisation increases and fertiliser is added. Higher soil nitrate(V) levels result, but the rapidly growing crop takes up nitrogen, and nitrate(V) levels decrease again. After harvesting there is an increase in soil nitrate(V).

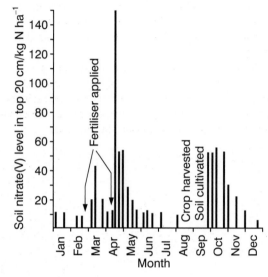

Figure 39 *Soil nitrate(V) levels throughout the year measured at the ZENECA Agrochemicals Research Station at Jealott's Hill*

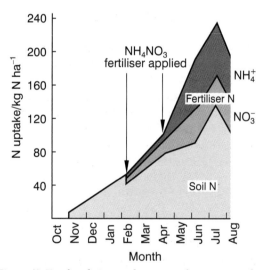

Figure 40 *Uptake of nitrogen by winter wheat measured at the ZENECA Agrochemicals Research Station at Jealott's Hill; the shaded areas show the relative contributions of the three sources of the nitrogen*

Ploughing introduces air into the soil and encourages microbial activity. Warm moist soil in autumn leads to rapid mineralisation of organic matter. Soil nitrate(V) levels rise. As temperatures fall and the soil becomes waterlogged, denitrification causes a decrease in soil nitrate(V) levels. Leaching reduces the levels even further from December onwards.

To reduce the risk of nitrate(V) leaching, winter crops can be grown. Figure 40 shows the uptake of nitrogen by winter wheat. Over $40 \, \text{kg ha}^{-1}$ of soil nitrogen have been absorbed by late February. Ammonium nitrate(V) fertiliser is then applied in two stages to match the needs of the crop. The fertiliser used in this study was labelled with the radioactive ^{15}N isotope so that nitrogen entering the crop could be identified as either soil nitrogen or fertiliser nitrogen. At harvest, $112 \, \text{kg ha}^{-1}$ of soil nitrogen had been taken up by the crop.

Work at Rothamsted has shown that, in plots where no crops have been grown and no fertiliser applied, $45 \, \text{kg ha}^{-1}$ nitrate(V) are leached from the soil each year. This comes from the large reserve of organic nitrogen in soil, converted to nitrate(V) ions by microbes.

Figure 41 Ploughing up grassland releases nitrate(V) ions from the organic nitrogen reserves

ASSIGNMENT 10

In answering these questions you may need to refer to the data in Figures 39 and 40, as well as the nitrogen cycle in Figure 32.

a What effect does ploughing have on the rate of mineralisation of soil organic matter to inorganic ions? Why does it have this effect?

b In uncropped land when do you think the greatest loss of nitrate(V) will occur? What two processes account for this loss? What are the environmental consequences?

c Suggest why denitrification tends to be the most important factor in determining soil nitrate(V) levels in early winter.

d Organic farmers grow crops without the use of any fertilisers or pesticides. However, they must be very careful about when they apply farmyard manure. If applied in the autumn, it can lead to far greater nitrate(V) loss by leaching than inorganic nitrogen fertilisers. Explain why farmyard manure increases the rate of nitrate(V) production.

e 'Catch' crops can be grown between main crops. What do you think they are catching? When should catch crops be ploughed into the soil?

Inorganic fertilisers are designed containing different proportions of nutrients. This makes it easier for farmers to apply just the quantities needed by the crops. If used correctly, inorganic fertilisers can supplement the nutrient levels in the soil, so that high yields of crops can be maintained without damaging the environment.

Activity AA3.3 will help you to think about revising for exams and to draw up your revision timetable.

AA4 *Competition for food*

Other organisms compete with us for the food we grow. This competition can reduce crop yields worldwide by 30%–40%. For example, in the UK, mildew may reduce barley yield by up to 35% and wheat yield by 20%. In the tropics insects such as locusts cause major crop losses (a swarm of locusts can have a mass of 15 000 tonnes and eat a similar mass of food in a day).

Control of diseases and pests is now made easier by a variety of scientific advances, such as the selective breeding of plant species more resistant to attack and chemical control using pesticides.

Figure 42 Some common pests: (a) 'rust' disease; (b) lupin aphids; (c) a cotton bollworm caterpillar; (d) flowering weeds in a crop of wheat

DDT

DDT is an **organochlorine** insecticide (the initials stand for dichloro-diphenyl trichloroethane). It was discovered in 1939 in the laboratories of the Swiss chemical company, Geigy. It has prevented millions of deaths from diseases like typhus (which killed 2 500 000 Russians during the First World War) and malaria (one of the most fatal and debilitating human diseases).

DDT is highly toxic to insects but has very low toxicity to mammals. It is made in a one-stage synthesis from cheap raw materials, which keeps its cost down.

Excellent insecticide though it is, DDT has its disadvantages. It is chemically very stable, and so it accumulates in the environment where it can persist for many years and becomes concentrated up food chains. Its use has been banned in many countries, but, because it is cheaper than newer insecticides, it is still widely used in developing countries.

Some insects have developed a resistance to DDT by increasing their production of enzymes which catalyse the removal of HCl from DDT to give a non-toxic product, DDE.

DDT

removal of HCl by enzymes in mammals and resistant insects

↓

DDE

When the double bond forms in DDE the molecule becomes planar. The change in shape is enough to make DDE biologically inactive because it changes the way in which the molecule interacts with the receptor site in insects.

Pesticides (insecticides, herbicides and fungicides) kill insects which eat our crops, weeds which compete with the crops for soil nutrients, and moulds which rot plants and seeds. Many disease-carrying organisms like mosquitoes are also controlled by pesticides.

While there are undoubted benefits from using pesticides, there can also be problems. Many pesticides can be damaging to human health and to the natural environment if used incorrectly. Organisms other than the target ones can be killed. If these are predators which would eat the pests we wish to destroy, then the pests might actually benefit.

Some older pesticides can remain in the soil, and then build up through food chains, affecting predators like birds and contaminating human food supplies. Pesticides may leach into our water supplies.

Therefore the challenge to the modern agricultural chemist is an enormous one – to find substances which are *specific* to the target organism, which kill at low dosages so that only small amounts need be applied to fields, and which do not persist in the environment or travel into the water supply.

Pests can build up resistance to chemicals, so chemists need to keep finding new products to overcome this.

Figure 43 Pests can develop resistance to chemicals

Many situations require pesticides which act rapidly. Can you think of any? A number of fat-soluble molecules have been discovered which act very rapidly. These are non-polar molecules which dissolve in fatty tissue in the insects, and so can reach their sites of action quickly. But fat-soluble molecules like DDT can accumulate in the fatty tissues of animals and become concentrated up food chains (Table 9).

	Concentration of DDT/mg kg^{-1}
sea-water	3×10^{-6}
fat of plankton	4×10^{-2}
fat of minnows	0.5
fat of needlefish	2
fat of cormorants	25

Table 9 DDT concentrations up a food chain (data from Long Island, USA)

Using pesticides which kill a wide range of pests, for example DDT, can also increase the risk of undesirable side-effects.

The search for a new pesticide

The research and development involved in producing a new product is lengthy and expensive, requiring the collaboration of a great many scientists. Chemists, biologists, toxicologists, chemical engineers and process engineers are all involved.

A large company may invest as much as £100 million each year in research and development, from which only one or two new products may result.

When an interesting compound is discovered which is active against pests, chemists will usually try to improve its activity by making systematic changes to the structure, continually testing and working out the 'best' substitutions in various parts of the molecule.

The compounds are tested on target pests and compared with existing products for potency and for the range of pests affected. The compounds which come out best in laboratory tests may be tried out to see if they will work in real field situations. Then hundreds of field trials are conducted on substances chosen for development.

The successful compound will be judged on a range of factors which will include

- ease of manufacture
- persistence in soil
- cost of the final product
- marketability
- leaching losses into drainage water
- toxicity to humans
- comparison with known compounds
- who owns the patents surrounding the invention.

Patents are important because the company needs to be able to make a profit in return for its investment in research and development.

The pyrethroid story

For many centuries the dried flower heads of a chrysanthemum, *Chrysanthemum cinerariaefolium*, have been used to ward off insects, particularly mosquitoes. The structures of the natural insecticides present in the flower heads were worked out in the 1920s and 1930s. One of them, *pyrethrin 1*, is shown below:

Figure 44 The pyrethrum flower

ASSIGNMENT II

---

a A carbon atom with four different groups attached to it is described as a chiral centre. (If the carbon atom is part of a ring, and the structure of the ring is different on each side of the carbon atom, the ring counts as two different groups.) Copy the structure of pyrethrin 1 and identify the chiral centre(s) by marking them with an asterisk (∗).

b List the functional groups present in pyrethrin 1.

Pyrethrins have some of the qualities of the ideal insecticide. They are powerful against insects but are harmless to mammals under all normal circumstances. However, natural pyrethrins are unstable in light. A photochemical oxidation reaction occurs which means that they are of limited use in agriculture since they break down so quickly.

Michael Elliott spent many years working at Rothamsted on the synthesis of **pyrethroids**, compounds related to natural pyrethrins. He was looking for compounds like the natural compounds which would be active against insects, but more stable in light and air.

He made an important breakthrough in 1977, with the synthesis of *permethrin*, the first pyrethroid sufficiently stable to be used widely in agriculture.

pyrethrin 1

permethrin

A later discovery, *cypermethrin*, is a more active insecticide, so smaller quantities can be applied to achieve the same effect.

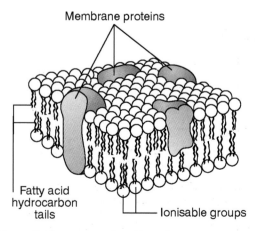

cypermethrin

ASSIGNMENT 12

a Compare permethrin with pyrethrin 1. The changes Elliott made decreased the sensitivity of the molecule to photochemical reactions. List all the changes you can identify.

b Make a model of the cyclopropane ring in permethrin so that you can identify the geometric isomers. The structure shown is *trans*-permethrin. Draw the structure of *cis*-permethrin, and mark on it any chiral centres. (You can read about isomerism in **Chemical Ideas 3.5** and **3.6**.)

How do pyrethroids work?

The compounds are able to penetrate insects very rapidly to reach their site of action. These are sites in the membranes of nerve cells. Cell membranes are made up of a double layer of molecules, aligned with their long hydrocarbon chains inside the membrane and their ionisable groups on the surfaces of the membrane. You can see the structure of a cell membrane in Figure 45.

Proteins embedded in the nerve cell membrane act as channels for the passage of ions in and out of the cells. The channels open and close selectively, so that a difference in the concentration of Na^+ and K^+ ions builds up across nerve cell membranes. This causes an electrical potential difference across the membrane and is vital to the functioning of nerve cells. If the system of transporting ions across the membrane is disrupted the nervous system cannot work properly. You will find out more about the functioning of nerve cells in **Medicines by Design**.

Pyrethroids work because they penetrate the cell membrane and block open the sodium channels. This leads to massive disruption of the nervous system of the insects.

A key factor in the activity of pyrethroids is that they are much more soluble in fats than in water. This means that they can pass readily from the aqueous solution used for spraying into the fatty tissues of the insect. This difference in solubility can be measured as a **partition coefficient**. Partition coefficients are equilibrium constants which measure the ratio of concentrations of a substance dissolved in two immiscible solvents in contact with one another at the same temperature:

$$\text{partition coefficient}, K = \frac{\text{concentration in solvent A}}{\text{concentration in solvent B}}$$

For studies of biologically active substances, the most common measurement is the partition coefficient, K_{ow}, between octan-1-ol (solvent A) and water (solvent B)

$$\text{partition coefficient}, K_{ow} = \frac{\text{concentration in octan-1-ol}}{\text{concentration in water}}$$

If K_{ow} is high the compound will move out of aqueous solution into fatty tissue.

Values of K_{ow} for pyrethroids are very high so $\lg K_{ow}$ is usually quoted. For example, if $K_{ow} = 10^5$, then $\lg K_{ow} = 5$; if $K_{ow} = 10^7$, $\lg K_{ow} = 7$. Pyrethroids with $\lg K_{ow}$ less than 5 are not insecticidal. In active compounds, $\lg K_{ow}$ is usually between 6 and 7, or even higher. In practice, when K_{ow} has been measured for one compound, tables of data can be used to calculate the effect on K_{ow} of changing substituents, so that molecules with the desired properties can be selected.

Concentrations of pyrethroids needed for insecticidal activity can be very low. For example, deltamethrin is active at concentrations as low as 10^{-12} mol dm^{-3} in cell membranes.

Membrane proteins

Fatty acid
hydrocarbon
tails

Ionisable groups

Figure 45 The structure of a cell membrane

deltamethrin

Chemical Ideas 7.3 will tell you more about partition equilibria.

In **Activity AA4.1** you can analyse data for pyrethroids and other pesticides to investigate the link between values of partition coefficients and the concentration of pesticides in living organisms.

What happens to pyrethroids in the environment?

In mammals, pyrethroids are rapidly broken down into polar products, either by oxidation or by hydrolysis of the ester group. These polar products are not attracted to the fatty membranes, but remain in aqueous solution and are excreted before they can reach sensitive sites in the body.

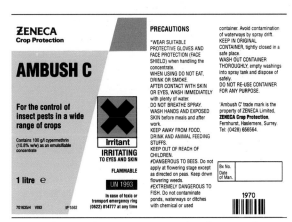

Figure 46 Hazard warning on a pyrethroid insecticide; pyrethroids are toxic to fish, perhaps because they gain direct access, via the gills, to the bloodstream

Commercially available pyrethroids are effective in the field at applications of 200 g ha⁻¹ or less. With the most active compounds, only 20 g ha⁻¹ may be needed. This is much less than the quantities required when using other insecticides like organochlorines, organophosphates and carbamates, for which applications of 1 kg ha⁻¹ are common.

Synthetic pyrethroids persist on crops for 7–30 days. Any pyrethroid residues reaching the soil are attracted into the soil organic matter. Once there they are rapidly hydrolysed and oxidised by routes like those in mammals. The products are inactive polar compounds, so residues of active, non-polar compounds do not build up in the environment.

ASSIGNMENT 13

Permethrin is safe to mammals because enzymes called esterases catalyse the hydrolysis of the ester linkage.

a Look at the structure of permethrin on p. 195, and draw the structural formulae of the hydrolysis products. Explain why these are more soluble than permethrin in water.

b The course of the hydrolysis can be followed by thin layer chromatography. The R_f values in the eluting solvent used in one experiment are shown below:

	Permethrin	Alcohol derivative
R_f value	0.6	0.15

The acid derivative did not move much above the base line.

Describe in outline the procedure you would use to follow the progress of the reaction. Sketch how the chromatograms would look (i) when the hydrolysis reaction was incomplete and (ii) when it had reached completion.

c The hydrolysis of permethrin in the soil is a first-order reaction. Calculate the half-life of permethrin if there is 2% of the insecticide left in the soil 2 months after application. (You may wish to refer to the section on half-lives in **Chemical Ideas 10.2**.)

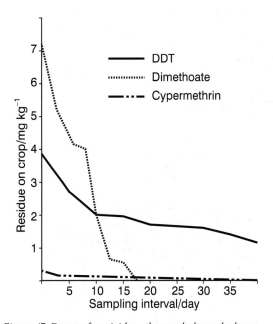

Figure 47 Decay of pesticides – the graph shows the large reduction in pesticide residues on crops when newer pesticides like cypermethrin replace older ones like DDT and dimethoate; less pyrethroid is needed, and it decays faster to inactive products

ASSIGNMENT 14

Tefluthrin, unlike most pyrethroids, retains its activity in the soil. It was developed in 1987 by ICI chemists to combat corn root worm which feeds on the roots of maize.

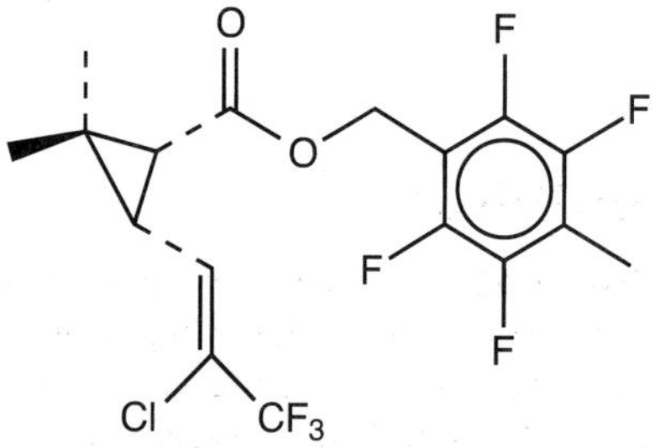

tefluthrin

The compound has a lower boiling point than normal pyrethroids, and so is more volatile. Sufficient molecules vaporise into the air spaces in the soil for the compound to retain its activity long enough to be effective. Larvae take in air from the soil, along with the tefluthrin which gains direct access to their nervous systems.

a What changes would you think of making to a molecule in order to reduce its boiling point? Explain your answer.

b Suggest reasons why the tefluthrin has a lower boiling point than permethrin. (Fluorine atoms can be regarded in this context as similar to hydrogen atoms; a fluorocarbon has a similar boiling point to an alkane with a similar carbon skeleton.)

In **Activity AA4.2** you can discuss what structural features are important in making pyrethroids active against insects.

Herbicides

Herbicides can increase crop yields by destroying weeds. There are two main types of herbicide: **total herbicides** and **selective herbicides**. Total herbicides destroy all green plant material and are used in fields before a crop is planted.

One example of a total herbicide is **paraquat**. Pure paraquat is highly toxic, but in the concentrations applied to kill weeds it is relatively harmless to humans and is rapidly inactivated on contact with soil.

The structure of the paraquat ion is

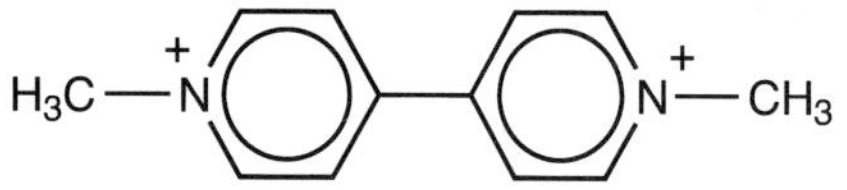

paraquat ion

As soon as the positive paraquat ions contact the soil they are removed by adsorption onto the soil solids. This is a particularly useful property of paraquat because it means that it is inactivated as soon as it reaches the soil. It only kills those plants whose *leaves* it touches.

Adsorption and absorption

Paraquat is deactivated when it comes into contact with soil because it is adsorbed onto the soil solids. A substance is **adsorbed** when it is bound to the *surface* of another substance.

Figure 48 Adsorption

Be careful not to confuse this with **absorption**. In absorption, the absorbed substance diffuses *into the bulk* of another substance. In coloured plastics, for example, dye molecules are absorbed into the bulk of the plastic.

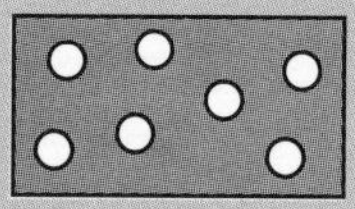

Figure 49 Absorption

Each type of soil is capable of holding irreversibly a particular amount of paraquat. This amount is called the **strong adsorption capacity** of the soil. Some values are given in Table 10. If the paraquat concentration rises above the strong adsorption capacity of the soil, paraquat can be displaced into soil water and can damage growing plants.

Paraquat can be used as an alternative to ploughing as a means of destroying weeds before a crop is sown, but farmers also need to destroy weeds in growing crops without harming the crops themselves. They therefore want a range of selective herbicides.

Some herbicides have been developed which can kill broad-leaved plants without damaging grasses. Others will kill grasses but not broad-leaved crops like soya bean and sugar beet. Some can even control grassy weeds in grass-like crops such as rice, maize and other cereals. Their selectivity depends on differences in metabolism between the plants.

In **Activity AA4.3** you can select appropriate herbicides for particular uses and learn something about their modes of action.

Source	Soil type	Composition			Strong adsorption capacity/ mol kg^{-1}
		% sand	% silt	% clay	
Newark	clay	34	24	42	0.137
Oakham	clay loam	33	37	29	0.047
Jealott's Hill	sandy loam	49	33	18	0.041
Sutton Coldfield	sandy loam	78	15	8	0.0078
Bagshot	loamy sand	85	11	4	0.0019

Table 10 Strong adsorption capacities of some soils

ASSIGNMENT 15

Refer to Table 10. (A loam is a rich soil consisting mainly of clay, sand and humus.)

a How is the strong adsorption capacity of a soil related to soil type?

b You learned about soil solids in Section **AA2**. Use your knowledge to explain the correlation between soil type and strong adsorption capacity.

c What physical method would you use to confirm your suggestions in your answer to **b**?

d What are the implications of the figures in Table 10 for farmers and gardeners in Bagshot?

Figure 50 The herbicide applied here will kill the weeds but leave the cereal crops undamaged

Figure 51 Terrace farming in Nepal; successful agriculture adapts to local conditions

AA5 *Summary*

This unit has introduced you to some of the issues involved in developing and maintaining a system of agriculture which is able to feed the world's rapidly increasing population without damaging the environment.

To understand these issues, you first needed to learn about the composition and structure of soil, in particular the nature of silicate and clay minerals. This led to a more detailed study of Group 4 chemistry and the need to understand the relationship between the properties of a substance and its structure and bonding. Consideration of the weathering processes which produce soil provided a setting in which to learn about the effect of temperature on chemical reactions.

Clay soils can bind positive ions – such as metal ions, NH_4^+ ions and H^+ ions – to the surface of the negatively charged silicate sheets. These exchangeable cations form a pool of nutrients from which plants can draw. This led to a study of ion-exchange reactions and the behaviour of ions in general. Understanding the processes which occur as plants grow and decay is vital to understanding how nutrients are cycled. Central to this is the nitrogen cycle and the redox chemistry of nitrogen.

The use of inorganic fertilisers is vital in maintaining soil fertility and high crop yields. The Haber process for the manufacture of ammonia from nitrogen and hydrogen is the key step in the production of nitrogen fertilisers. An understanding of the effects of temperature and pressure, both on the position of the chemical equilibrium and on the rate of the reaction, is necessary to select the optimum conditions for this process. The use of a catalyst is also important.

In the last section of the unit, you studied some methods of pest control. A study of the action of pyrethroids, modern insecticides which do not persist in the environment, provided a setting in which to learn about partition equilibria.

Activity AA5 will help you to summarise what you have learned in this unit.

COLOUR BY DESIGN

Why a unit on COLOUR BY DESIGN?

Coloured compounds are everywhere. The ability to make synthetic dyes and pigments to colour an enormous variety of things is one of the great achievements of modern chemistry.

The first part of the unit describes work carried out in the Scientific Department of the National Gallery, London, on the conservation of two paintings: *The Incredulity of S. Thomas* painted by Cima da Conegliano in 1504 and *A Wheatfield, with Cypresses* painted by Vincent van Gogh in 1888.

The chemists at the National Gallery use a variety of analytical techniques to investigate pigments and paint media. This provides an ideal setting in which to learn about ultra-violet and visible spectroscopy, atomic emission spectroscopy and gas–liquid chromatography. Analysis of the drying oils used in the 16th-century Italian altarpiece requires an understanding of the structure of oils and fats. This links in well with your previous work on acids, alcohols and esters.

The second part of the unit traces the development of synthetic dyes for cloth. In this part of the unit, you will extend your knowledge of organic chemistry further and learn about the special structure of the benzene ring and the types of reactions arenes undergo.

Finally, the unit provides an opportunity to draw together some ideas you have met earlier to build up a simple theory of colour.

Overview of chemical principles

In this unit you will learn more about …

ideas introduced in earlier units in this course

- why compounds are coloured (**Using Sunlight** and **The Steel Story**)
- the interaction of radiation with matter (**The Atmosphere**, **What's in a Medicine?** and **Using Sunlight**)
- spectroscopy (**What's in a Medicine?**)
- atomic emission spectra (**Elements of Life** and **The Steel Story**)
- aromatic compounds (**Developing Fuels** and several other storylines)
- esters (**The Polymer Revolution** and **What's in a Medicine?**)
- reaction mechanisms (**The Atmosphere** and **The Polymer Revolution**)
- intermolecular forces (**The Polymer Revolution**)

… as well as learning new ideas about

- ultra-violet and visible spectroscopy
- gas–liquid chromatography
- oils and fats
- the structure of benzene and the reactions of arenes
- the chemistry of dyes
- theories of colour.

COLOUR BY DESIGN

CD1 *Ways of making colour*

The natural world is full of colour. Some colours, like the blue of the sky or the colours in a rainbow, are produced by the scattering or refraction of light. But in most cases, colour is due to the presence of *coloured compounds* and arises from the way these compounds interact with light: think of the brightly coloured flowers in a summer garden, the vivid display of a peacock, and the more subdued colours you can find in stones and rocks.

You can remind yourself why some compounds are coloured by reading **Chemical Ideas 6.4**.

From the earliest times people have used the natural substances around them to colour themselves and their possessions. We know that some Neanderthal tribes roaming Europe 180 000 years ago prepared their dead for burial by coating them with *Red Ochre* (iron(III) oxide). For tens of thousands of years, humans made colouring agents from minerals they found in rocks, so the colours produced were mostly dull and earthy. These mineral **pigments** were mixed with oil or mud to form a paste which would stick to surfaces.

This was fine until people learnt to weave and make fabrics. When the paste-like pigments were applied to fabrics, the cloth became stiff and the colouring material soon fell out. Pigments were no good for colouring cloth. Cloth could only be coloured by soaking it in a solution of a **dye**.

Pigments and dyes

The way a coloured substance is used determines whether it is called a **dye** or a **pigment**. You can dye your hair or your clothes, but when you paint a picture you are using pigments.

The main thing to remember is that *dyes are soluble substances whereas pigments are insoluble*.

Pigments can be spread in a surface layer (as in a paint or a printing ink) or mixed into the bulk of a material (as when making a coloured plastic bowl).

Dyes are always incorporated into the bulk of a material and they attach themselves to the molecules of the substance they colour. This attachment can be the result of hydrogen bonding or of weaker intermolecular forces, such as instantaneous dipole-induced dipole forces or other dipole–dipole forces. Sometimes stronger ionic or covalent chemical bonds are involved.

You will find that there is another general distinction. Most dyestuffs are organic compounds. Pigments tend to be inorganic. Inevitably, though, there are exceptions to this rule. The green pigment, chlorophyll, is a complex formed between a large organic molecule and magnesium.

Figure 1 Modern dyes make life very colourful

Many of the early dyes came from crushed berries or plant juices. The early Britons used a blue dye called *woad*, which they extracted from the *Isatis tinctoria* plant. The main coloured component of woad is *Indigo*. The same dye is used today to colour blue denim jeans.

Some dyes came from animals. Mexican dyers around 1000 BC discovered the red dye *Cochineal*. They extracted it from small insects which live on the *Opuntia* cactus. Only female insects produced the dye, and they had to be collected by hand: about 150 000 insects were needed to make 1 kg of dye! It was the Spaniards who brought Cochineal to Europe in 1518 AD. It was used until 1954 to produce the bright red jackets of the Brigade of Guards. You may have eaten it as a food colouring.

Indigo

Cochineal

Until about 100 years ago, dyes and pigments were expensive and colours were mainly for the wealthy. Ordinary people wore clothes dyed with cheap vegetable dyes – the colours were drab and quickly faded.

The great breakthrough came when chemists learnt how to make coloured substances in the laboratory. The starting materials for the new **synthetic** dyes were cheap. They came from **coal tar**, an unwanted by-product of the new coal gas industry. In the second half of the 19th century, as towns and cities were lit up by gas lamps, chemical companies producing dyes from coal tar flourished – and Europe exploded in a riot of colour!

Not only did chemists learn to copy natural colours, but they also used the compounds they obtained from coal tar to make a whole range of entirely new coloured compounds.

Modern colour chemists now have a vast range of coloured substances available to them. They need to understand not only why compounds are coloured, and which structures lead to particular colours, but also how to bind coloured substances to different types of

Figure 2 A late 19th-century dyehouse

Figure 3 A gas holder built by the Imperial Gas Company at Bethnal Green in London. 'Coal gas' was made by heating coal in the absence of air. Coke, coal tar and a liquid rich in ammonia were also produced.

The coal gas industry provided the raw materials for the production of synthetic dyes – and later for the production of pharmaceuticals, plastics, perfumes and explosives. Coal tar was then replaced by oil as the source of organic chemicals.

fibres and surfaces. Once the chemistry is understood, it becomes possible to *design* a coloured molecule for a particular purpose: colour by design.

Many of the advances in colour chemistry have been made as a result of intensive research and painstaking 'trial and error'. Every so often, though, an important step forward seems to happen by chance.

In **Activity CD1** you can produce coloured compounds by a variety of different processes.

ASSIGNMENT 1

a Look carefully at the structure of Cochineal on p. 202. Make a list of the different functional groups in the molecule, giving the name and formula of each.

b What structural feature present in both Indigo and Cochineal do you think could be responsible for their colours?

CD2 *The Monastral Blue story*

A chance observation

Monastral Blue is one of the best blue pigments ever made. It is widely used to colour plastics, printing inks, paints and enamels because it gives a very pure blue. The paint on most blue cars, for example, contains Monastral Blue. Its discovery arose from a chance observation at a Scottish dyeworks. Fortunately, the people who made the observation took the trouble to investigate further.

Figure 4 Monastral Blue is the pigment in the blue paint on this classic steam locomotive

In 1928 in Grangemouth, Scotland, the firm Scottish Dyers (which later became part of ICI) was making phthalimide, a compound needed for dye manufacture.

In this process, a white substance, phthalic anhydride, is melted in a glass-lined iron vessel, and ammonia is passed into it:

ammonia(g) + phthalic anhydride(l) → phthalimide(l)

The product, too, is white, but on this occasion they found that some batches contained traces of a blue substance. The blue compound seemed to have formed where the reaction mixture came into contact with a part of the vessel where the lining was damaged.

Later, when the blue substance was analysed, all samples were found to contain 12.6% iron. The structure of the blue substance, although complex, was interesting for a number of reasons – not least because it was closely related to that of some naturally occurring substances called **porphyrins**.

Also chlorophyll + haemoglobin.

At first it was thought that the new blue compound, named **iron phthalocyanine**, would be of academic interest only, but further investigation suggested that it may be a useful blue pigment.

Porphyrins everywhere

You have already met some important examples of coloured substances which contain porphyrin ring systems. *Haemoglobin* is responsible for the red colour of blood and is involved in transporting oxygen around the body (see **Elements of Life**, Section **EL2** and **The Steel Story**, Section **SS3**). *Chlorophyll a* gives leaves their green colour and is responsible for harvesting light and initiating photosynthesis (see **Using Sunlight**, Section **US3**).

ASSIGNMENT 2

Read the account of the discovery of iron phthalocyanine in the previous column.

a Why did the blue pigment form?

b What is the significance of the fact that *all* samples of the blue pigment contained 12.6% iron?

The structure of the blue compound

The blue compound is made up of large flat molecules. Each molecule contains a 16-membered ring of alternating carbon and nitrogen atoms, with an iron atom at the centre. Look carefully at Figure 5 which shows the structure of iron phthalocyanine. Make sure that you can pick out the 16-membered ring surrounding the iron atom.

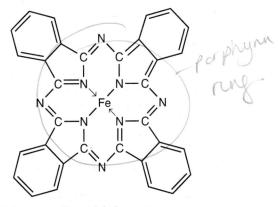

porphyrin ring

Figure 5 Structure of iron phthalocyanine

Don't be put off by the size of the molecule. You won't be expected to remember its structure, but you should be able to recognise some of its important features.

Four of the nitrogen atoms act as **ligands** to form a planar complex with the iron atom. If you have studied **The Steel Story**, you will remember that complexes of d-block metals are often highly coloured.

The 16-membered ring in iron phthalocyanine contains alternating single and double bonds. This type of arrangement is called a **conjugated system of bonds**. For each double bond, one pair of electrons is not confined to linking two particular carbon atoms like those in a single bond, but is spread out or **delocalised** over the whole conjugated system. The lone pairs of electrons on two of the nitrogen atoms are also involved, so the delocalisation extends over the whole 16-membered ring – and over the four benzene rings too. The result is a huge delocalised structure.

You met a conjugated bond system when you made a conducting polymer in **Activity PR4, The Polymer Revolution.**

The more that electrons are delocalised like this, the lower the energy of the molecule. So, iron phthalocyanine is a very stable pigment.

Molecules with extended conjugated systems also tend to be coloured. You will find out more about this later in the unit.

It's even better with copper

Molecules with similar structures have similar properties, so it is always worth making a series of related compounds in the hope that you come across one or two with even better properties than the ones you already have.

Once the structure of the blue iron compound was known, a team of chemists led by R. P. Linstead at Imperial College, London, set to work to investigate other phthalocyanines. They repeated and modified the original process, using other d-block metals instead of iron as the central atom for the molecule.

Within a few years of the original discovery, they had shown that a whole range of similar pigments could be made. Copper phthalocyanine was particularly promising. Writing about this in 1934, Linstead said:

'… it is even more stable than the other compounds of this series, and in this respect must be classed among the most remarkable of organic compounds. It resists the action of molten potash (potassium hydroxide) and of boiling hydrochloric acid. … It is exceptionally resistant to heat, and at about 580 °C it may be sublimed … in an atmosphere of nitrogen or carbon dioxide. … The vapour is deep pure blue and the crystals, which have the usual purple lustre, may be obtained up to 1 cm in length.'

By 1939, copper phthalocyanine was on the market as a pigment with the trade name **Monastral Blue** (Colour Index Pigment Blue 15: CI 74160).

The Colour Index

Most pigments and dyes are known by the name originally given to them by the manufacturer, rather than by a systematic name. So it's quite common for these compounds to have several names.

To avoid confusion, The Society of Dyers and Colourists in Bradford have drawn up a *Colour Index* in which coloured compounds are classified according to their chemical structures. Each compound is given a code number (CI number).

The commercial importance of Monastral Blue and other phthalocyanine pigments is due to a combination of factors:

- they have very beautiful bright blue to green shades and high colour strengths (which means that only a relatively small amount of pigment is needed to give a good colour)
- they are very stable pigments and have excellent fastness to light – they don't fade.

In **Activity CD2** you can make a sample of Monastral Blue. Your set can also join forces to produce a model of the pigment molecule.

CD3 *Chrome Yellow*

Artists are always on the look out for new and better pigments from which to make their paints. By the middle of the 18th century a variety of yellow pigments were being used. *Orpiment* (arsenic(III) sulphide) and *Yellow Ochre* (hydrated iron(III) oxide) had been known since earliest times. *Massicot* (lead(II) oxide) was introduced in the 16th century.

But there was still a need for a pigment capable of giving a bright lemon-yellow colour.

A new yellow pigment

Figure 6 Louis Vauquelin (1763–1829) discovered metallic chromium, Chrome Yellow and other artists' pigments

The French chemist, Louis Vauquelin, discovered chromium in 1797 whilst investigating a mineral called *Siberian red lead spar* from the Beresof gold mine in Siberia. The colours of samples of the mineral varied from orange-yellow to orange-red. We now know that the mineral was a form of lead chromate(VI) called *crocoite*, but at the time its composition was unknown.

Colourful compounds

A contemporary of Vauquelin described how the new metal got its name (*chroma* is the Greek word for colour):

'[The new element] … had the property of changing all its saline or earthy combinations to a red or orange colour. This property, and that of producing variegated and beautiful colours when combined with metals, induced him to give it the name of "chrome".'

By 1809, a new source of crocoite had been found in the Var region of France and the mineral became readily available in Europe. Within a few years, the enormous potential value of lead chromate(VI) as a yellow or orange pigment became clear. Painters particularly valued the dark lemon-yellow colour which lasted better than the pigments previously available.

In 1809, Vauquelin carried out a series of investigations to determine the best conditions for making the lead chromate(VI) pigment in the laboratory. He obtained it by **ionic precipitation**, using solutions of a lead salt and a chromate(VI), eg

lead nitrate(V)(aq) + sodium chromate(VI)(aq) →
sodium nitrate(V)(aq) + lead chromate(VI)(s)

Chemical Ideas 4.5 will help you to find out about ionic precipitation.

ASSIGNMENT 3

a For the reaction between lead nitrate(V) and sodium chromate(VI), write
  i a full balanced equation
  ii an ionic equation which shows only the ions involved in the precipitation reaction.
  Include state symbols in both your equations.
b Give equations for other possible ways of making lead chromate(VI) by precipitation.

Activity CD3.1 gives you an opportunity to repeat Vauquelin's work of 1809 and investigate factors which affect the colour of the Chrome Yellow produced.

Chrome Yellow was the first of a range of metal chromates containing lead, barium, strontium or zinc which can be used to produce pigments with different shades of yellow. Chrome Yellow is still widely used today in paints and printing inks.

What is a paint?

A paint is made up of two components:
• the colouring matter (the pigment)
• a liquid which carries the pigment and allows it to spread (the medium).

In watercolours, the finely ground pigment is suspended in water. The paint dries as the water evaporates and the pigment is absorbed into the paper.

In spray paints, the medium is a volatile organic solvent which quickly evaporates once the paint has been applied.

In oil paints, the drying process is slow. The oil does not evaporate. Instead, it slowly hardens as it reacts with air to produce a flexible film. The oil protects the pigment and helps to bind it to the surface being covered.

Figure 7 Yellow road markings contain Chrome Yellow pigment

Pigments can be poisonous

Many of the artists' pigments used in the past were hazardous in one way or another, and the artists were almost certainly unaware of the risks they were taking.

Some pigments, such as *Red* and *Yellow Ochre* (both forms of Fe_2O_3) are harmless – others like the green and yellow arsenic pigments can be deadly. We now know that lead, cadmium and mercury compounds are highly toxic, whereas chromates have been shown to be **carcinogenic** (they can induce cancers). So handle Chrome Yellow with care and follow the safety instructions!

Modern paints tend to be much less toxic. Lead compounds, for example, are no longer included in household paints. In many cases, inorganic pigments are being replaced by less toxic organic ones.

ASSIGNMENT 4

Modern cosmetics are carefully formulated to be beneficial to the skin – but this was not always the case. The pigments used in ancient Egyptian, Greek and Roman make-up read like a list from a poison cupboard!

- Face make-up (*White Lead*, $2PbCO_3.Pb(OH)_2$)
- Rouge (*Red Phosphorus*)
- Lipstick (*Cinnabar*, HgS)
- Eye-shadow (*Orpiment*, As_2S_3)
- Mascara (*Stibnite*, Sb_2S_3)

a What is the oxidation state of Pb in White Lead?

b Suggest two solutions which could be mixed to give a precipitate of $PbCO_3$.

c What are the modern names for Orpiment and Stibnite?

d Look up the hazard warning data for some of the substances above in a chemicals catalogue.

e Try to find out what pigments are used to colour modern lipsticks.

A famous wheatfield

During 1888, the Dutch artist van Gogh painted three pictures of *A Wheatfield, with Cypresses*. One of these (Figure 8) is in the National Gallery in London. If you are in Trafalgar Square, you can easily go in and see it.

During the 1980s this picture was cleaned and remounted. This gave scientists at the National Gallery a welcome opportunity to examine the materials and techniques which van Gogh used.

The pigments on the surface of paintings are coloured because they absorb some of the white light falling on them. **Activity CD3.2** will help you to understand this.

They photographed the picture in daylight and in both ultra-violet and infra-red light. These photographs give information about areas in the painting where particular pigments have been used. For example, *Zinc White* (zinc oxide, ZnO) fluoresces under ultra-violet light. *Emerald Green* (a pigment containing copper and arsenic) absorbs in the infra-red region, so areas painted with this pigment appear dark in infra-red light.

Figure 8 A Wheatfield, with Cypresses *by Vincent van Gogh*

Vincent Willem van Gogh (1853–1890)

Vincent van Gogh was the son of a Dutch clergyman. When he was 16, he started work in an art gallery, previously owned by his uncle. After a few years, he was sent to their London branch. While in London, he fell in love with his landlady's daughter, but the relationship was a one-sided and unhappy affair.

He abandoned the art business and eventually returned to Holland with the intention of entering the Church. But he did not complete his preparation for the ministry. Instead, he went to Belgium as a lay preacher, living there mostly as a tramp.

He was 28 and back in his parents' home town when he finally decided to become an artist. During the following 10 years he worked at his paintings with what one writer has described as 'a single-minded frenzy'. He produced no fewer than 800 paintings and as many drawings. Sadly, he ended his life in turmoil. In 1888 a piece of his ear was cut off during a quarrel with a fellow-artist, Gaugin. Shortly after that, he was admitted, at his own request, to a mental hospital. It was here that he painted *A Wheatfield, with Cypresses*. In July 1890 he shot himself.

Figure 9 Vincent van Gogh Self-Portrait 1888

The scientists took very small samples of different colours of paint from the edges of the painting and analysed them to find out which elements were present. One way they did this was to look at the lines in the **atomic emission spectrum** from each sample of paint. You will learn more about this technique later in the unit. They also used a scanning electron microscope to look at the tiny individual crystals in the paint (see Figure 10).

These investigations, combined with historical records, showed that van Gogh used Chrome Yellow, mixed with Zinc White and other pigments, to create the different shades of yellow in the wheatfield.

Table 1 shows an extract from the data obtained by the scientists at the National Gallery.

Paint sample	Pigment
darkest yellow of wheatfield	Chrome Yellow
mid-yellow of wheatfield	Chrome Yellow + Zinc White
lightest yellow of wheatfield	Zinc White + Chrome Yellow
dull yellow of wheatfield	Chrome Yellow + Zinc White + small amounts of Emerald Green
pale green bushes	Zinc White + Chrome Yellow + Viridian (a green pigment)

Table 1 Pigment mixtures used in A Wheatfield, with Cypresses *by Vincent van Gogh*

(a) Pure lead chromate(VI)

(b) Dark yellow wheatfield

(c) Light yellow wheatfield

Figure 10 Scanning electron microscope pictures of pure lead chromate(VI) and pigment samples from the wheatfield (the scale at the top of each picture shows 2 μm, ie 2×10^{-6} m)

a Explain how the electron microscope pictures in Figure 10 support the conclusions of the scientists shown in Table 1 concerning the pigments used in the dark yellow and light yellow areas of the wheatfield.

b Van Gogh used Cobalt Blue and Zinc White for the distant mountains. Both these pigments reflect infra-red light strongly. He used Emerald Green to produce the dark green of the cypresses. In infra-red light, the trees appear dark and the mountains cannot be distinguished from the sky. Explain why this happens.

CD4 *Chemistry in the art gallery*

The chemists involved in identifying the pigments used by van Gogh are *analytical chemists*. Their job is to find out which compounds are present in different substances. Some of the problems involved in restoring a painting can be very challenging. Solving them can involve a great deal of patience and ingenuity, a knowledge of chemistry and the application of some sophisticated techniques.

The Incredulity of S. Thomas

In 1504 an Italian artist, Cima da Conegliano, put the finishing touches to his altarpiece *The Incredulity of S. Thomas*. The painting now hangs in the National Gallery in London (see Figure 12). It is considered to be a masterpiece and is highly valued because of its rarity.

By the standards of the time, Cima used an exceptionally wide range of pigments in creating the altarpiece. Some of the substances he used will be familiar to you. For example, to produce certain shades of green, he used *Malachite* ($CuCO_3.Cu(OH)_2$, a basic copper carbonate). For reddish brown, he used *Haematite* (an ore containing Fe_2O_3, iron(III) oxide).

Many of the pigments, such as the blue *Natural Ultramarine* made from the semi-precious stone *lapis lazuli*, would have been quite expensive. In fact, there are several areas of blue paint on the altarpiece. These vary widely in colour from the rich turquoise blue of the ceiling to the pale blue drapery worn by the apostle to the left of Jesus Christ.

How do we know which blue pigments Cima used to achieve these colours nearly 500 years ago? One way to find out is to shine light on different areas of the painting and examine the wavelengths present in the reflected light. Different pigments absorb different wavelengths

from the incident light, so the resulting **reflectance spectrum** is characteristic of a particular pigment.

If you are ever fortunate enough to stand in front of Cima's painting in the National Gallery and look at its vast array of bright colours, you will find it difficult to believe how badly disfigured and fragile the painting was when restoration was started in 1969 (Figure 11). Layers of dirt and old varnish masked or dulled the colours. The paint was badly blistered and was flaking off in many places.

Figure 11 The Incredulity of S. Thomas *by Cima da Conegliano in 1969 before restoration*

Over the next 15 years a great deal of laborious restoration took place. Much of this was made possible by scientific analysis – not only of the pigments involved but also of the binding medium used to make the paint and of the foundation coating beneath the paint layer.

But first we will look at the story of how the painting got into such an awful state.

You can read about ultra-violet and visible spectroscopy in **Chemical Ideas 6.5**.

In **Activity CD4.1** you can find out how chemists can help in deciding which pigments Cima used to produce the different areas of blue in the altarpiece.

Figure 12 The painting in 1986 after cleaning and restoration

The history of the painting

The start of the trouble (1504–1870)

Cima's painting *The Incredulity of S. Thomas* was originally hung above an altar in a church in the Italian town of Portogruaro, about 50 miles northwest of Venice.

For some reason the paint began to flake and blister. In 1745, what may have been the first in a series of restorations was attempted. But the condition of the painting continued to deteriorate. Eventually it was sent to the Academy of Fine Arts in Venice where one of the foremost experts of the time, Professor Guiseppe Baldassini, restored it as best he could.

Between 1822 and 1830 the painting was stored in a ground-floor room of the academy while arguments were taking place over Professor Baldassini's bill. This led to the most disastrous episode in the troubled history of the painting: a sudden and unusually high tide flooded the room and the picture was submerged in salt-water for several hours.

More flaking and blistering occurred and there were several further attempts at restoration. Despite these problems, the painting caught the eye of Sir Charles Eastlake in 1861 while he was on a picture-buying expedition for the National Gallery. After some haggling over the price and a lengthy legal dispute about the ownership of the painting, it was bought for the National Gallery in April 1870 for £1800.

1870: to the National Gallery, London

At this point the gallery authorities made the emphatic recommendation that 'no restoration work should again be attempted'. But paint continued to flake off and there were repeated treatments over the next 80 years to reattach this flaking.

During the Second World War, the whole of the National Collection of art was housed in large artificial caves in a quarry near Bangor in North Wales. The conditions of stable humidity and temperature in the caves were far superior to those in the gallery, and the problems of warping wooden panels and blistering paint were much reduced.

It was when the collection was returned to London in 1945 that serious problems arose. The effect was particularly bad in the very cold winter of 1947, when the heat had to be turned up high to maintain a tolerable temperature for visitors to the gallery. The low humidity caused many paintings to dry out, resulting in cracking and flaking. Cima's poor altarpiece flaked more than almost any other painting.

When an oil painting is produced on a wooden panel, the wood is first coated with a stable inorganic substance bound together with an animal glue. In Cima's painting, *gypsum* (hydrated calcium sulphate, $CaSO_4.2H_2O$) was used for this purpose. This coating layer is called the *gesso* (the Italian word for gypsum).

In 1969, investigators found that the repeated flaking was due to the gesso layer becoming detached from the wooden support, and not to the paint coming away from the gesso. Worse still, it was found that the wooden panel had dry rot and woodworm!

Figure 13 The National Gallery, London

The challenge

In the light of all this, experts at the National Gallery decided to give the picture the most drastic form of treatment used in restoration. The delicate and priceless layers of paint and calcium sulphate were to be transferred from the wooden panel to a new support.

You might get some idea of the scale of the problem if you consider that the picture measures approximately 3 m × 2 m and that the thickness of the brittle paint and gesso together is only a fraction of a millimetre.

The first step was to cover the painting with layers of special tissue using an organic resin as an adhesive. It was then placed face-down on a temporary support and the original 5-cm-thick wooden panel was removed from the back. No high-tech here: it was a slow laborious process achieved by hand using small gouges, chisels and finally scalpels! What remained was a priceless film of paint and calcium sulphate.

Next, a heat-activated adhesive was used to secure the back of the painting to a new support. This consisted of a fibreglass plate secured to an aluminium honeycomb. Now the layers of tissue on the front of the painting could be carefully peeled away. After 500 years the painting was finally attached to something from which it was unlikely to come unstuck – at least not for a few more centuries.

Figure 14 The painting after cleaning and transfer to a new support – but before repairing the damaged paint layer

However, after all the years of hard work the painting was still unsuitable for exhibition (see Figure 14). The last stage was to repair the damaged paint layer.

So far, the scientific department at the National Gallery had played a relatively small role. In the final restoration, the *retouching* of the paint layer, the work of analytical chemists was crucial.

When retouching the painting, the restorers used modern pigments and modern *binding media* to make up the paints they used. They had to choose these carefully to make sure of two things:

- that any restorations could easily be removed without damaging the original work
- that the colours used in retouching were a good match to the original colours.

The first of these principles applies to the restoration of any work of art in any country. It ensures that a future generation can remove the work of the restorer if they decide that it is inappropriate or if scientific advances make better restorations possible.

Restorations can only be removed with ease if the modern binding medium dissolves in organic solvents more readily than the one used by Cima 500 years ago. So it is important to know exactly which binding medium Cima used.

The binding medium

The medium used to bind the particles of pigment together to form a paint must be viscous enough to prevent the paint from running as it is applied. But it must not be *too* sticky otherwise the artist's freedom would be restricted during painting.

Once the paint has been applied, the medium must then dry and become hard in order to produce a durable painted surface.

What medium did Cima use?

Throughout the history of painting, artists have experimented with different types of media. Egg yolk (known as *egg tempera* when used as a binding medium) was widely used in European paintings in the Middle Ages. Egg yolk is an emulsion of globules of fat and protein in water. It dries and hardens quickly as the water evaporates. You will be able to confirm this if you have ever had to wash up plates coated in dried egg.

Emulsions

An emulsion is a mixture of two liquids which do not dissolve in one another, such as oil and water.

For example, egg yolk is an oil-in-water emulsion. The oil droplets are so small that they do not settle out, and the mixture appears uniform and opaque.

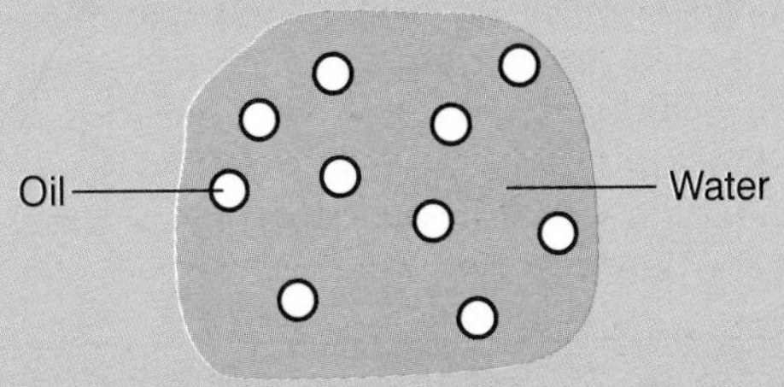

Oil ——————○   ———————— Water

Figure 15 An oil-in-water emulsion

By the time Cima was working on *The Incredulity of S. Thomas*, paints were more often prepared using oils as the medium. Oils dry more slowly than egg yolk and give artists more freedom. Natural oils, such as linseed or walnut oil, which dry and harden to develop a protective coating are suitable. They are called *drying oils*.

The drying oils which Cima might have used all contain significant amounts of **triesters** based on two carboxylic acids, *palmitic acid* and *stearic acid*. Different oils contain the palmitate and stearate esters in different ratios. So, if the palmitate and stearate ratio can be measured, we can tell with some confidence which oil Cima used to bind his pigments.

This ratio can be found using an analytical technique called **gas–liquid chromatography (g.l.c.)**. Figure 16 shows the gas–liquid chromatogram obtained from a small sample of paint from Cima's painting.

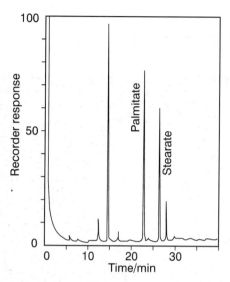

Figure 16 Gas–liquid chromatogram from a sample of paint from Cima's painting

The area under each peak in the chromatogram is proportional to the amount of each substance present. So you can work out the ratio of palmitate to stearate esters in the paint, and then compare this ratio with those obtained from known oils.

The paints used in the restoration were made using a synthetic polymer rather than oil as the medium. The polymer is soluble in hydrocarbon solvents. All the recent retouchings could be removed, if necessary, with a solvent-soaked swab in just a few hours, leaving behind only what remains of Cima's original work.

It will help to find out about the chemistry of oils and fats. You can do this by reading **Chemical Ideas 13.6**.

You met gas–liquid chromatography in **Developing Fuels**. You can find out more about it in **Chemical Ideas 7.6**.

In **Activity CD4.2** you can investigate what factors affect the drying potential of an oil.

You can work out which oil Cima used by doing **Activity CD4.3**.

What were the pigments?

You have already met some of the methods chemists can use to identify a pigment. One of the methods mentioned earlier is a form of atomic emission spectroscopy called **laser microspectral analysis (LMA)**. It proved particularly useful when analysing paint from Cima's altarpiece. It allows chemists to identify the *elements* present in a sample of paint. From this they can usually say which pigments are present. (If you have studied **The Steel Story**, you may remember that atomic emission spectroscopy is used to monitor the composition of steel during manufacture.)

You can remind yourself about atomic emission spectroscopy by reading **Chemical Ideas 6.1**.

Laser microspectral analysis

In this technique, a pulse of laser light is focused onto a small sample of paint. Laser light is a high-energy beam of light of a single wavelength. The energy of the pulse is high enough to vaporise the high boiling point metal compounds present in the pigments. A small plume of vapour rises from the paint sample into a region between two electrodes.

The atoms and ions in the vapour are then excited to higher electronic energy levels by an electrical discharge between the two electrodes. Each chemical element present gives rise to a characteristic **emission spectrum**.

The method is very sensitive and can be carried out on very small quantities of material. The sample of paint taken from a valuable picture is usually of the order of 10^{-5} g. Of this, a minor pigment component might comprise only 10^{-7} g -10^{-6} g.

Figure 17 shows the apparatus used at the National Gallery. The apparatus consists of four main parts:

A – a laser head to generate high-energy pulses of laser light (694 nm)

B – a microscope with a system of lenses to focus this light onto the sample

C – a pair of carbon electrodes and a power supply to generate a high-energy discharge

D – a u.v./visible spectrometer to separate the radiation emitted by the excited atoms and ions into its component frequencies and produce a record of the emission spectrum.

Figure 17 The apparatus used for laser microspectral analysis of pigments

ASSIGNMENT 6

The LMA emission spectrum obtained from a paint sample consists of a complex arrangement of lines corresponding to radiation of different frequencies.

a Explain why excited atoms only emit certain frequencies of radiation.

b Why are these frequencies different for atoms of different elements?

c How do you think chemists work out which elements are present in the paint sample from the lines in the LMA spectrum?

LMA is just one of the analytical techniques used to identify the elements present in a pigment. Scientific evidence is always used alongside information from other sources. Art historians, for example, can often provide additional information by studying contemporary manuscripts and by using what is known about other paintings from the same period.

Once the composition of the original pigment is known, a modern substitute can be chosen to give a good match for use in restoration.

In **Activity CD4.4** you can combine evidence from scientific and historical sources to identify the orange-yellow pigment Cima used for the robe of S. Peter.

Now you can try your hand at finding matches for two of the blue pigments in Cima's painting, in **Activity CD4.5**.

Activity CD4.6 allows you to review some of the work you have covered in Sections **CD1** to **CD4**.

CD5 *At the start of the rainbow*

During the 19th century, many new pigments became available as chemists investigated more and more compounds and learned to imitate the properties of natural substances.

The 19th century was also a time of great innovation in the production of dyes for cloth. Today, many of our more obviously high-tech industries are based on electronics; then, it was the colourist who enjoyed the regard we now have for software engineers and system analysts.

The story of the development of dyes is closely linked to the development of organic chemistry. Colourists learned both the methods of dyeing and the principles of chemistry as they moved about Europe selling their skills and knowledge.

To understand this section you will need to know about the special nature of benzene and the type of reactions benzene undergoes. You can do this by reading **Chemical Ideas 12.3** and **12.4**.

Three young entrepreneurs
Perkin

Figure 18 William Perkin (1838–1907)

William Perkin was only 18 years old when he invented a method of synthesising a dyestuff, later known as **Mauve**. He was a student at the Royal College of Chemistry in London and in those days the study of plant extracts dominated organic chemistry. August Hofmann, Director of the College, encouraged Perkin to try to make *quinine*, a natural product used to treat malaria. Perkin tried to do this during the Easter holiday of 1856 in his laboratory at home.

His starting material was a complex organic amino compound obtained from coal tar. Little was known of the structure of quinine, so Perkin's chance of success was minimal, and sure enough the experiment failed. But Perkin was not deterred. He repeated the process with a simpler starting material, **aniline (phenylamine)**, also obtained from coal tar. The reaction produced a purple solution – but again nothing related to quinine.

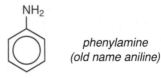

*phenylamine
(old name aniline)*

This type of reaction was already known to analytical chemists who often used reactions involving colour changes to test for compounds. Perkin realised that the purple substance might have other uses. Purple was a popular colour of fashion: the new colour was brilliant and held fast to a piece of cloth. Why not test it as a dyestuff?

The tests were promising and Perkin filed a patent for his discovery. It was the first *synthetic* dye. With the help of his father and brother, he built a factory to manufacture the dye. The difficulties were immense. For one thing, he had to devise a way of producing aniline on a large scale, but very little was known about the behaviour of reactions when scaled up. Figure 19 shows Perkin's reaction scheme and the type of equipment he used.

The venture was an overwhelming success. The colour was in great demand from the world of fashion and both Queen Victoria and the Empress Eugénie in France wore dresses dyed with the new dye. The dye was originally called *Aniline Purple*, but it was later named Mauve after the French for the mallow flower.

Perkin's discovery led to increased interest across Europe in aniline as a starting material. Other synthetic *aniline dyes* in a variety of colours soon followed.

You can investigate some typical reactions of arenes in **Activity CD5.1**.

In **Activities CD5.2** and **CD5.3** you can see the production of coal tar from coal and then follow Perkin's process through to the synthesis of Mauve.

Levinstein

Figure 20 Ivan Levinstein (1845–1916)

Perkin was not the only teenager to realise the potential of his college experiments. A German student, Ivan Levinstein, worked on the new aniline dyes at the Gewerbe Akademie in Berlin. In 1864, with the support of his family, he opened a factory there to make *Aniline Green*. The following year, aged 19, he moved to England and settled near Manchester.

Here he eventually started manufacturing *Aniline Red* in a row of cottages at Blackley and gradually built up the biggest British company in the field. In 1926, Levinstein's company was incorporated into ICI and the site of his factory became the headquarters of ICI Specialities (which later became ZENECA Specialities). Figure 21 shows an advert for dyes made by Ivan Levinstein's company in 1871.

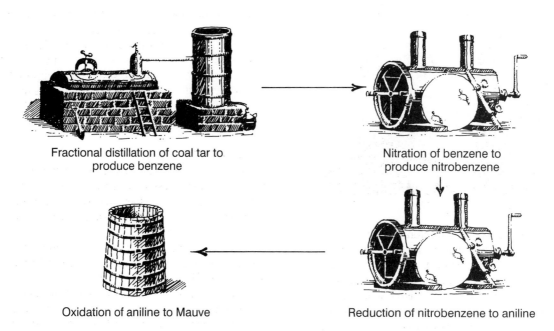

Fractional distillation of coal tar to produce benzene

Nitration of benzene to produce nitrobenzene

Oxidation of aniline to Mauve

Reduction of nitrobenzene to aniline

Figure 19 The manufacture of Mauve showing the type of equipment Perkin used

Figure 21 *An advert for dyes made by Ivan Levinstein's company in 1871. Manufacturers like Levinstein often started in their own homes using household appliances – to this day, the main building in any modern dyeworks is called the dyehouse*

Figure 23 *Empress Eugénie, wife of Napoleon III, wearing a dress dyed with 'Aldehyde Green' (a synthetic 'coal tar' dye) in the 1860s*

Caro

Figure 22 *Heinrich Caro (1834–1910)*

Another young German entrepreneur, Heinrich Caro, saw the economic potential of dye manufacture and made his way without family support. Caro was also a student at the Gewerbe Akademie before spending 7 years in Manchester as a colourist and plant manager in a dyeworks. He returned to Germany in 1866 and 2 years later joined the newly formed Badische Anilin und Soda Fabrik (BASF).

In Germany during the late 1860s, work centred on a systematic study of organic chemistry, as well as on possible commercial developments. Caro's skills in chemistry and chemical engineering enabled him to work out a key step in the synthesis of the colour of the natural madder dye (Figure 24 overleaf). Like Perkin and Levinstein, he was able to transform laboratory experiments into a successful commercial process.

But was it chemistry?

It is important to bear in mind the state of chemical theory at the time these young entrepreneurs were making their discoveries. Ideas that we now take for granted about atoms, atomic masses and periodicity were just beginning to emerge.

For example, the idea that carbon can form four bonds and is capable of forming long chains of carbon atoms emerged in 1858. Kekulé first reported his ideas about a ring structure for benzene in 1865. It was not until much later (in the 1880s) that chemists began to write the structural formulae of dyes in their scientific papers as a matter of routine.

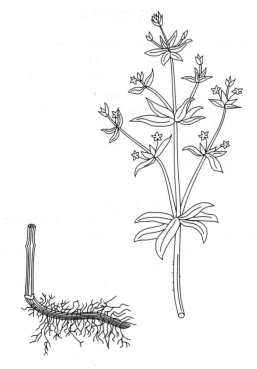

quinine

When Hofmann challenged Perkin to make quinine, it was thought that the empirical formula of quinine was $C_{20}H_{22}O_2N_2$ (although this was actually two hydrogens short). He therefore proposed the following synthesis, using sodium dichromate(VI) as the oxidising agent:

$$2C_{10}H_{13}N + 4O \rightarrow C_{20}H_{22}O_2N_2 + 2H_2O$$

This approach to tackling a synthetic problem now seems ridiculous, but at the time it seemed sound chemical theory! When the structure of Mauve was unravelled in the late 1880s, it turned out to be a mixture of compounds. The most important one, *Mauveine*, is a complex organic salt with the structure

Mauveine

So it was quite amazing that Perkin should stumble upon this molecule by chance – particularly as it was shown later that the formation of Mauve depended on the presence of impurities in the starting aniline. This also explained why Mauve was made up of more than one purple compound.

Alizarin

Until Perkin made his discovery, dyes had come mainly from plants, and vast areas around the world were given over to cultivation for the dyestuffs industry. The indigo plant was used to make blue dyes; red dyes came from the madder root. The colouring matter from the madder root is called **Alizarin**. We now know that it has the structure shown below:

Alizarin

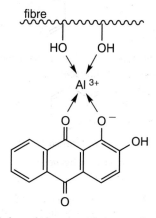

Figure 24 Madder plant and root

Alizarin only sticks fast to cloth which has been impregnated with a metal compound such as aluminium sulphate. The process is called **mordanting**. The colour of the dyed cloth depends on the metal chosen. When Alizarin is used with an aluminium mordant, the cloth is dyed red; when tin(II) is used the cloth is dyed pink; and iron(II) gives a brown colour.

The mordanting takes place under alkaline conditions so that the metal hydroxide is precipitated in the fibres. The metal ions firmly attach themselves to the cloth and then bind the dye molecules by forming chelate rings, as shown in Figure 25.

Figure 25 Chelate of Alizarin with the metal ion Al^{3+} (the two remaining ligand sites above and below the Al^{3+} ion could be taken up by OH^- ions)

ASSIGNMENT 7

a Write an *ionic equation* with state symbols for the precipitation of aluminium hydroxide by the reaction of an aluminium compound with alkali.

b What *type of reaction* takes place when mordanted cloth is dyed with Alizarin? What is the role of Alizarin in this reaction?

c Explain how the use of a mordant holds the dye in the fibres.

Alizarin had been used as a dye for thousands of years but no-one had any idea of its chemical nature until Carl Graebe and Carl Liebermann, two talented students of Adolf Bayer at the Gewerbe Akademie in Berlin, decided to find out. Bayer had recently developed a method for converting aryl compounds into their parent hydrocarbons by heating them with zinc dust. For example

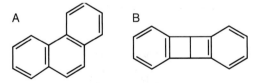

phenol

In January 1868, Graebe and Liebermann used this technique to show that Alizarin is derived from **anthracene**, a minor component of coal tar.

ASSIGNMENT 8

Graebe and Liebermann knew the molecular formula of anthracene. Its properties suggested that it was some kind of condensed aromatic system. Below are the two structures (A and B) that they suggested for anthracene in 1869:

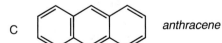

Compare structures A and B with the modern structural formula of anthracene C:

C   *anthracene*

a What is the molecular formula of anthracene?

b What is the relationship between the three structures A, B and C?

c Use your knowledge of bonding in organic compounds to explain why structure B is the least likely possibility.

Graebe and Liebermann then set out on a quest to find a method for synthesising Alizarin. They eventually devised the route shown in Figure 27 overleaf (Route I). Their method worked in the laboratory and they patented it in 1868, but the yield was very poor. Also, a route based on bromine was too expensive at that time for a larger scale process.

The last step of their route, in which the dibromo compound is heated with solid KOH, only added to the confusion of those later trying to work out the structure of Alizarin, because an isomerisation reaction takes place at the same time!

Once Graebe and Liebermann had announced their success, the race was on to find a cheaper commercial route to synthetic Alizarin – a route which was expected to bring rich returns to the first people to patent the process. Both Perkin and Caro joined in the competition.

The race turned out to be a tie. The competing chemists independently hit on the same solution in May 1869! It's the reaction scheme shown in Route II in Figure 27, but remember that the structures were not known at the time.

Perkin filed his patent in London on 26 June 1869. But an almost identical patent had been deposited at the Patent Office on the previous day on behalf of Caro, Graebe and Liebermann working for BASF. Chemists at the Hoechst company in Germany also solved the problem at the same time, but they didn't patent their process in London.

Figure 26 The 19th-century Turkey Red dyeing and printing process used Alizarin as the red dye: Turkey Red fabric was famous for its bright colour and distinctive patterns

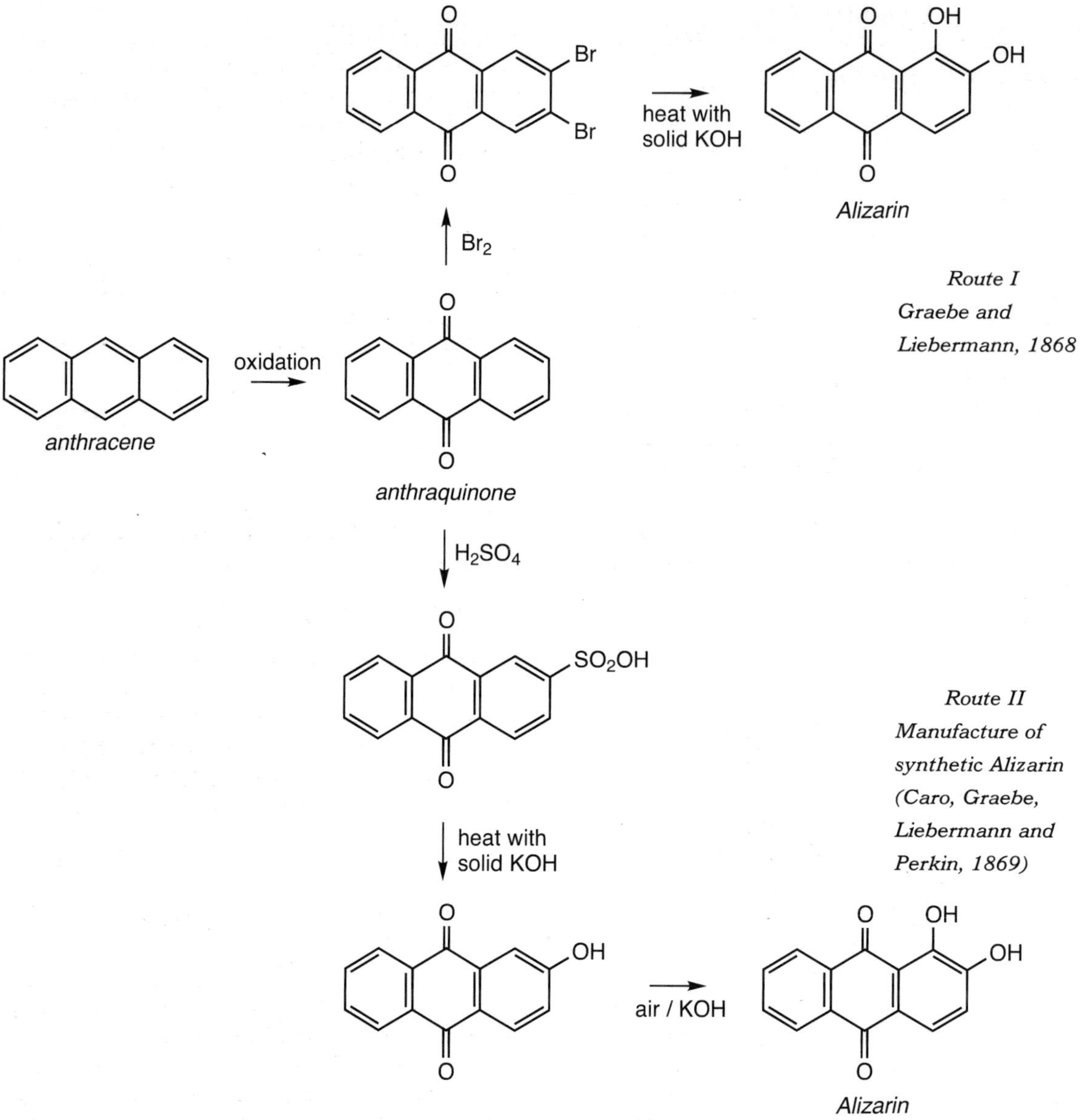

Figure 27 The conversion of anthracene to Alizarin

The situation was resolved amicably later in the year, when Perkin and BASF agreed to share the market in Alizarin. Perkin retained the UK trade while BASF was to dominate Europe and the USA.

The discovery of a route to synthetic Alizarin had a devastating effect on the madder industry. Hundreds of thousands of acres in Southern Europe and eastwards towards Asia were devoted to growing madder. In 1868 a crop of 70 000 tonnes of madder root was processed to produce around 750 tonnes of Alizarin. By 1873, just 5 years later, the madder fields had disappeared – Perkin's company alone produced 430 tonnes of Alizarin that year.

ASSIGNMENT 9

Compare the two reaction schemes (Routes I and II) for the synthesis of Alizarin in Figure 27.

a What is the essential difference between the two routes?

b Why was the second route a commercial success when the first was not? Would the same apply today?

c What *type of reaction* is involved in the reaction of anthraquinone in each route?

d Use a set of molecular models to build up the structure of anthracene. Now modify your model step by step through the stages shown in Figure 27 to arrive at the structure of Alizarin.

CD6 *Chemists design colours*

Figure 28 shows a cartoon of Kekulé's ideas about the structure of the benzene ring, in which monkeys appear instead of carbon atoms. This appeared in a hoax pamphlet put out by two of Kekulé's young disciples. One of them was Otto Witt a Swiss-trained chemist, who in 1875 was working for a dye-making company in Brentford near London.

Witt was working on a theory that related colour to structure. He wanted to know *why* certain structures led to coloured substances, and how small changes to the structure led to changes in colour.

To do this he was investigating the **diazo reaction**, known since 1858, which led to strongly coloured products which were insoluble in water.

To understand this section you will need to know about the structure and preparation of azo compounds. You can find out about these in **Chemical Ideas 13.8**.

Figure 28 Witt's cartoon lampooning Kekulé's ideas about the structure of the benzene ring: monkeys form single bonds by holding hands and double bonds by linking tails as well

The first azo dyes

The first azo dyes were made by coupling a **diazonium salt** obtained from phenylamine with one of a variety of **coupling agents**. Figure 29 shows one example of the reaction involved, in which the coupling agent is another molecule of phenylamine.

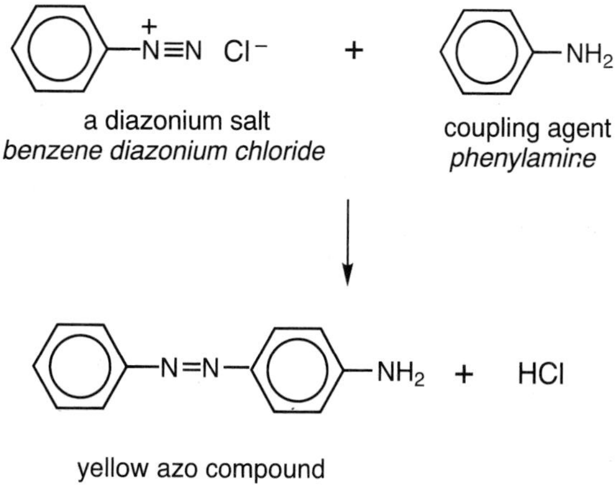

a diazonium salt
benzene diazonium chloride

coupling agent
phenylamine

yellow azo compound

Figure 29 Azo coupling reaction

Witt knew about this reaction. He also knew that the corresponding reaction using triaminobenzene as the coupling agent in place of phenylamine gave a brown azo compound.

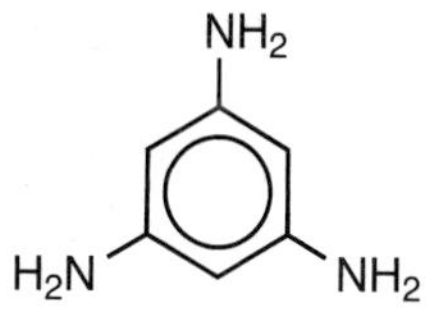

triaminobenzene

Witt thought that the colour of an azo compound was related to its structure. He predicted that the missing azo compound in the series, the one with *two* amine groups on the benzene ring, should be intermediate in colour. Sure enough, when he made this compound he found it was coloured orange, midway between yellow and brown. It proved to be a successful dye for cotton and was marketed as *Chrysoidine*. It was the first commercially useful azo dye.

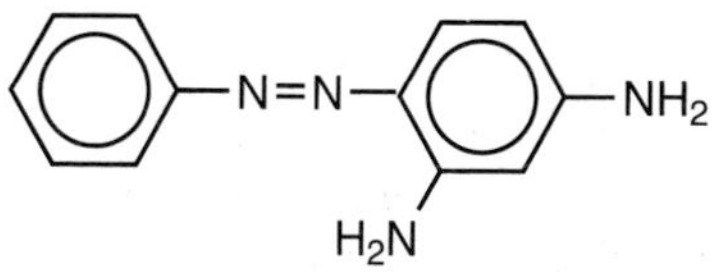

Chrysoidine

Ivan Levinstein manufactured a range of azo dyes at Blackley, but many other British manufacturers retired around this time. William Perkin sold his factory in 1874 having made his fortune. Meanwhile, the German companies Agfa, BASF, Bayer and Hoechst flourished. They set up research teams with links to the universities to invent new colours. By 1913, Germany was exporting around 135 000 tonnes of dyestuffs per year, while Britain was exporting only 5 000 tonnes.

ASSIGNMENT 10

a Write an equation for the azo coupling reaction Witt used to make Chrysoidine.

b In the early years, azo dyes could only be manufactured satisfactorily in winter. How do you account for this?

c Chrysoidine is a basic dye. Which group in the molecule is responsible for its basic properties?

How does structure affect colour?

Witt's work on azo dyes helped him to put forward a theory of colour in dye molecules which still influences our thinking today. A dye molecule is built up from a group of atoms called a **chromophore**, which is largely responsible for its colour.

We now know that chromophores contain unsaturated groups such as $C=O$ and $-N=N-$, which are often part of an extended delocalised electron system involving arene ring systems.

For Chrysoidine, the chromophore is the delocalised system shown in the box below:

chromophore $-\langle \bigcirc \rangle-N=N-\langle \bigcirc \rangle-NH_2$

H_2N functional group

Attached to the chromophore in Chrysoidine are two $-NH_2$ **functional groups** which interact with the chromophore to produce the orange colour.

Other functional groups may be added which can

- modify or enhance the colour of the dye
- make the dye more soluble in water
- attach the dye molecule to the fibres of the cloth.

All azo dyes contain the $X-N=N-Y$ arrangement. Chemists worked to make as many different XY combinations as possible to find new dyes with good colours, which were fast to fabrics and commercially viable. As they did this they began to understand the effect of chromophores and functional groups on the colour and properties of the dyes they produced.

A vast range of azo dyes is now available, produced by coupling one of 50 diazonium salts with one of 52 coupling agents to give a whole rainbow of colours – although these are mostly yellow, orange or red, with relatively few blues and greens.

In **Chemical Ideas 6.6** you can read more about chromophores and modern theories of colour.

In **Activity CD6** you can make a range of azo dyes using different diazonium salts and coupling agents.

CD7 *Colour for cotton*

The search for fast dyes

At the turn of the century, James Morton, a Carlisle weaver, made a trip to London. Standing outside Liberty's window in Regent Street, he examined a display of cotton tapestries he had designed. He was horrified by what he saw. The colours had faded after only 1 week in the shop window.

Immediately, Morton set out to find dyes that were fast to light and began manufacturing them. You can see an advert for some of his dyes in Figure 30.

Morton's success helped to re-establish the reputation of the dye industry in Britain. But cotton presented a problem in other ways. Dyes must be fast to washing and rubbing as well as to light. Many of the dyes which were fast to wool and silk did not bind at all well to cotton.

Figure 30 James Morton built up a range of unfadable dyes in the early 1900s called the Sundour range

How do dyes stick to fibres?

Protein-based fibres such as wool and silk have free
ionisable —COOH and —NH$_2$ groups on the protein
chains which can form electrostatic attractions to parts
of the dye molecule. For example, a sulphonate (—SO$_3^-$)
group on a dye molecule can interact with an —NH$_3^+$
group on a protein chain, as shown in Figure 31.

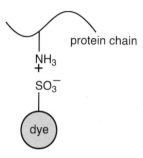

*Figure 31 Interaction between a dye molecule and a protein
chain*

Cotton, on the other hand, is a cellulose fibre
consisting of bundles of polymer chains with no readily
active parts. The polymer is a string of glucose units
joined as shown in Figure 32.

Dyes like Alizarin are bound to the fibres using a
mordant (look back to Figure 25 on p. 216). Indigo,
which is used to dye denim jeans, is a **vat dye**. Here
the cotton is soaked in a colourless solution of a
reduced form of the dye. This is then oxidised to the
blue form of Indigo which precipitates in the fibres.

Many azo dyes for cotton are trapped in the fibres
because they are insoluble. In contrast, **direct dyes**,
such as *Direct Blue 1* (see Figure 33) are applied to the
cotton in solution and are held to the fibres by
hydrogen bonding and instantaneous dipole-induced
dipole forces. Hydrogen bonds are weak compared
with covalent bonds and so these dyes are only fast if
the molecules are long and straight. They must be able
to line up with the cellulose fibres and form several
hydrogen bonds.

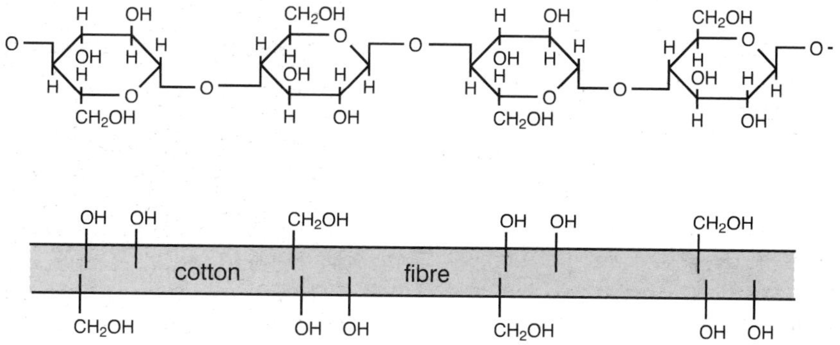

*Figure 32 Two ways of depicting a cellulose fibre: in the top diagram the molecule is shown to be a chain of glucose units; in the
lower diagram only the reactive —OH groups are shown*

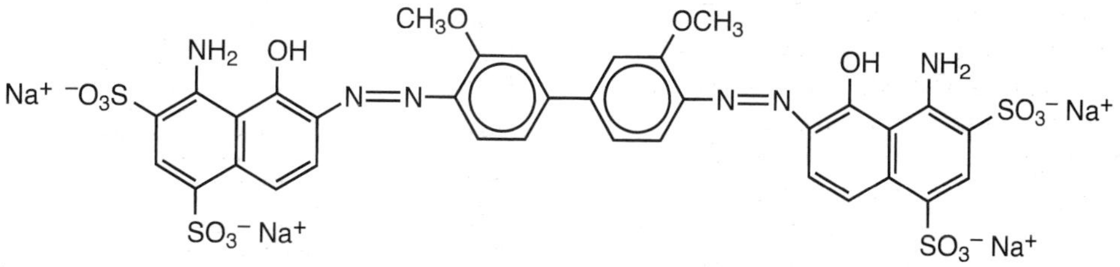

Figure 33 The structure of Direct Blue 1

ASSIGNMENT II

Look at the structure of Direct Blue 1 in Figure 33.

a Which groups of atoms do you think are
responsible for the fact that a compound with
such large molecules is soluble in water?

b Which groups of atoms would you expect to form
hydrogen bonds with cellulose fibres?

c Draw part of the molecule and part of a cellulose
fibre (in the style of the lower diagram in Figure 32)
to show how you picture these hydrogen bonds.

A dyemaker's dream

For many years chemists dreamed of developing dyes which would be held to fibres by strong covalent bonds instead of weak intermolecular forces. They knew that such dyes would be very fast to washing because they would react with the textile materials and become chemically part of the polymer molecules.

The story starts in the early 1950s with a group of chemists working at ICI's research laboratories in Blackley trying to find better dyes for wool.

William Stephen was part of the group. He started with azo dyes and modified the molecules by adding reactive groups, which he hoped might combine with the amino groups of proteins in wool. One idea was to modify an azo dye containing an amino group by reacting it with **trichlorotriazine** as shown in Figure 34.

Stephen took some samples of his modified dyes to Ian Rattee, the senior technician in the wool-dyeing section of the dyehouse. He hoped that the new dyes would react with wool as shown in Figure 35. However, the results were poor and Rattee was not impressed.

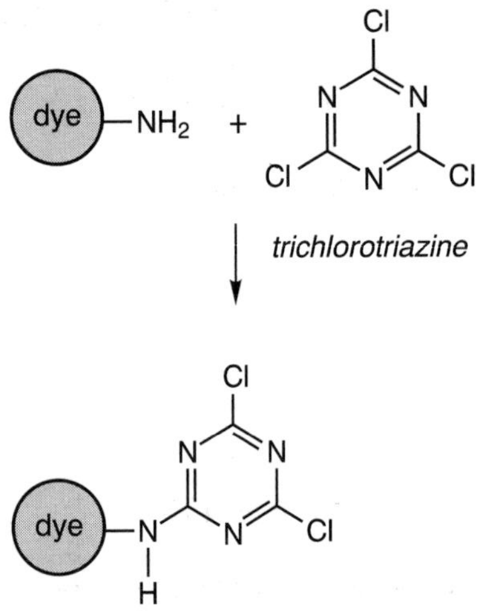

The dream come true

One morning in October 1953, Stephen and Rattee were discussing their experiments with reactive dyes. Stephen pointed out that the reaction of the new dye with the wool would be much more likely to happen under alkaline conditions. Unfortunately, the alkali would damage the wool at the same time.

ASSIGNMENT 12

Look at Figure 35 which shows the reaction Stephen was hoping to bring about between the modified dyes and wool.

a Why are there free —NH₂ groups in the protein molecules in wool?

b What is the second product of the proposed reaction?

c Why might this reaction be expected to go better in alkaline solution?

d Suggest an explanation for the fact that wool is damaged by alkali while cotton is not.

Stephen suggested that it might be worth trying the dyes with cotton, because cotton is not damaged by alkali in the way that wool is. The reaction they were hoping to use to bind the dye to the fibres can take place with hydroxyl groups on cotton as well as with amino groups.

Rattee saw the importance of this idea. Dyeing cotton was not part of his responsibility, but that afternoon he took samples of Stephen's dyes and showed that, as predicted, they would react with the hydroxyl groups on cotton when alkali was added.

Figure 34 Building a reactive dye to react with wool

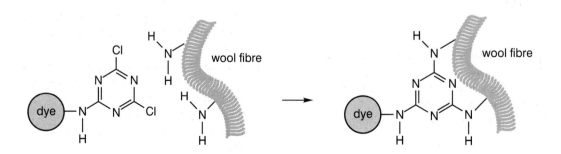

dye molecule becomes covalently bound to the wool fibre

Figure 35 The planned reaction of the new dye with amino groups in wool fibres

Figure 36 *The General Dyestuffs Research Laboratory at ICI, Blackley in the early 1950s*

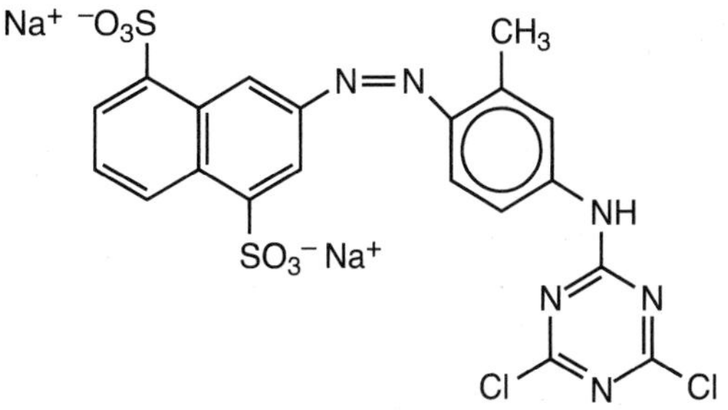

Na$^+$ $^-$O$_3$S ... CH$_3$ ... N=N ... NH ... Cl ... N ... N ... Cl

SO$_3^-$ Na$^+$

Procion Yellow RS

Na$^+$ $^-$O$_3$S ... SO$_3^-$ Na$^+$ ... N=N ... HO ... NH ... SO$_3^-$ Na$^+$ ... N ... N ... Cl ... N ... Cl

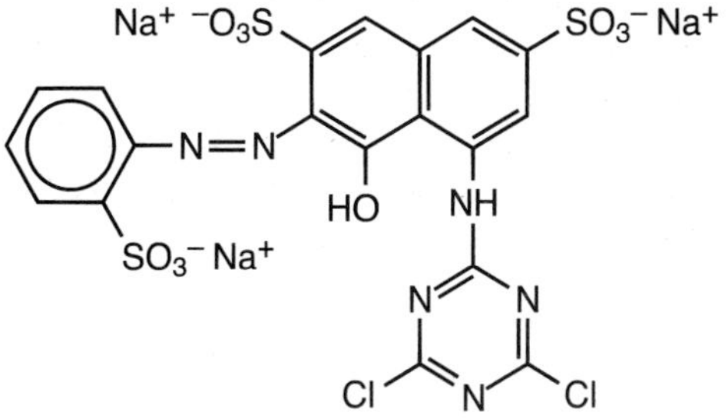

Procion Brilliant Red 2BS

Figure 37 *The first fibre reactive dyes*

The discovery had been made! The idea had at last become a reality – but it was far from certain that it could be made to work in textile mills. A great deal of work lay ahead to develop the innovation, demonstrate its potential and prove that it could be exploited successfully.

ASSIGNMENT 13

Draw a diagram in the style of Figure 35 to show what happens when a fibre reactive dye reacts with cotton in alkaline solution.

The first of the **fibre reactive dyes** are shown in Figure 37. Fibre reactive dyes are now so common that it is hard to recall the feverish excitement and energy released when it was realised that a search which had been going on for around 60 years might be coming to a climax.

In **Activity CD7.1** you can dye samples of cotton cloth with a fibre reactive dye and with a direct dye and compare the fastness to washing.

ASSIGNMENT 14

The two dyes in Figure 37 have the same chromophore.

a Copy the structure of one of the dyes and draw a ring round the chromophore.

b Which functional groups in the dye structure you have drawn help to make the dye soluble in water?

c Which part of the molecule you have drawn helps to attach the dye to the cloth? Explain how you decide on your answer.

d What are the differences in the structures of the two dyes which might account for the difference in colour?

You can investigate a mixture of different dyes using paper chromatography in **Activity CD7.2**.

Paradox and problem

The new dyes were fast because of the reaction with the hydroxyl groups in cotton, but this reactivity was itself a problem because there are hydroxyl groups in water too. The reactivity of the dyes was destroyed by hydrolysis.

This problem had to be overcome because commercial success with the textile industry depended on the possibility of using the dyes when dissolved in water. Stephen developed systems of **buffers** which kept the pH of the solution within strict limits and kept the hydrolysis reaction under control.

The action of buffers is explained in **The Oceans**.

The decision was finally taken to launch the new dyes in March 1956 – exactly 100 years after Perkin discovered his Mauve dye. There was an explosion of activity in all departments – research, patents, production planning, engineering, the dyehouse, costing, sales and publicity. The dream had finally become a reality.

ASSIGNMENT 15

Compare the structure of a fibre reactive dye with the structure of an acyl (acid) chloride such as ethanoyl chloride, CH_3COCl.

a What happens when ethanoyl chloride is added to water? Why is this reaction described as *hydrolysis*?

b Show what you would expect to happen when a fibre reactive dye is hydrolysed.

Figure 38 Colour co-ordination – the same colour can now be matched on different fabrics and materials

---

CD8 High-tech colour

The work of Stephen and Rattee heralded a new era of bright modern dyes which are fast to light and washing. Other types of reactive dyes soon followed, using different groups to bond the dye to the fibres. The 1980s saw the development of a range of extremely fast, brightly coloured dyes for polyester.

Colour chemists can now produce colours to order for a particular application. It is possible to have the exact shade of the season's fashion colour reproduced perfectly in a range of different fabrics – real colour by design.

One of the most exciting recent developments has been in the modification of dyes for high-tech uses, for example dyes used in high-speed ink jet printers and for electronic photography. In this last section, we shall look at these two applications in more detail.

A smudgy problem

Ink jet printers are a boon in many offices. The print-out is clear and sharp like that from a laser printer, but it is obtained at a fraction of the cost. The early machines had one big drawback though. The print was not permanent. A sweaty finger was enough to cause an embarrassing smudge and ruin an immaculate report.

How is an ink jet printer different?

In conventional printers, such as typewriters and dot matrix printers, the paper is struck by a key through an inked ribbon. In photocopiers and laser printers, charged ink toner particles are transferred electrostatically to the paper (see **The Polymer Revolution**).

The ink jet mechanism sprays drops of ink onto the paper from a nozzle in the print head. There are around 120 dots in each centimetre of print.

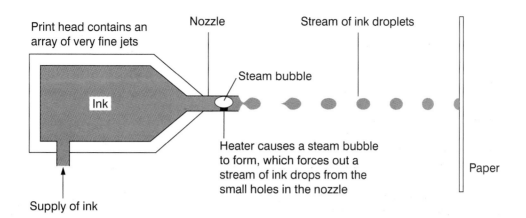

Ink
(pH 7.5–9.0, dye soluble in water)

Paper
(pH 4.5–6.5, dye insoluble in water)

Figure 39 An ink jet printer

The problem was this. For the method to work, the black dye used in the ink must be soluble in water in the print head, but once on paper it must be insoluble. You can see how one type of ink jet printer works in Figure 39.

Chemists at ICI Colours and Fine Chemicals at Blackley were called in to help sort out the problem. There are about 100 known black dyes to choose from, but none of them met the strict requirements necessary. The ICI chemists decided to concentrate on black food dyes like *Food Black 2,* which is used in fruit gums, since these dyes are cheap, non-toxic and light-fast. They then set about adapting the structure to give the required properties.

Their solution to the problem was beautifully simple. They made use of some elementary organic chemistry and the change of pH during the process: most modern papers are acidic whereas the ink solution is slightly alkaline, as shown in Figure 39.

They knew that arene carboxylic acids, like benzoic acid, are insoluble in neutral or acidic solutions, but dissolve in alkaline solution.

So why not replace some of the sulphonic acid ($-SO_2OH$) groups in the Food Black 2 molecule by carboxylic acid ($-COOH$) groups?

COOH insoluble in cold water ⇌ (OH^- / H^+) COO⁻ soluble in cold water

ASSIGNMENT 16

a Typewriters and photocopiers use a Carbon Black pigment. Why would this be unsuitable in an ink jet printer?

b Azo food dyes like Food Black 2 are fairly stable. If they break down, they tend to do so at the N=N linkage. It is important that any decomposition products are soluble in water. Explain how the dye is designed to achieve this.

c Why do you think only *some* of the $-SO_2OH$ groups in Food Black 2 were replaced by $-COOH$ groups in the new ink jet dye?

Food Black 2

When they did this, the new dye they obtained was a vast improvement, but still not quite perfect. The final refinement was to use the *ammonium salt* of the acid dye in the ink solution, rather than its sodium salt. You may have heated smelling salts, ammonium carbonate crystals, and seen them decompose into gaseous products:

$$(NH_4)_2CO_3(s) \xrightarrow{\text{heat}} 2NH_3(g) + CO_2(g) + H_2O(g)$$
smelling salts

The ammonium salt of the modified dye decomposes in a similar way on heating:

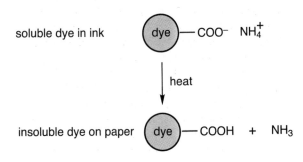

soluble dye in ink   (dye)—COO^- NH_4^+

heat

insoluble dye on paper   (dye)—$COOH$ + NH_3

The reaction, together with the change in pH, ensures that conversion to the insoluble carboxylic acid is virtually complete.

In **Activity CD8** you can investigate the effect of —SO_2OH and —$COOH$ groups on the solubility of arenes.

One in a million

The challenge here was to find three dyes with the right properties to print photographs taken by an electronic camera.

Electronic cameras are being developed to replace conventional silver halide photography. They contain no film. Instead, the photographs are recorded electronically on a magnetic disc and can be viewed on a television screen. You can then select the pictures you wish to print from the disc.

The printing process works like this. The colours come from just three dyes: a yellow dye, a magenta (or red) dye and a cyan (or blue) dye. These three dyes are dispersed, in sequence, in a thin polyester film which looks like a strip of multicoloured cling film. They then pass in turn beneath a row of thermal heads heated to about 400 °C. These raise the temperature and cause the dyes to diffuse from the ribbon to the white receiver sheet to give the final colour print. The amount of dye transferred depends on the temperature. Figure 40 shows how the printing process works. It's called the **dye diffusion thermal transfer process** (or the **D2T2 process** for short!).

The three dyes had to have some very special properties. Their colours had to blend precisely to cover the whole of the visible colour range – and they had to have a very high thermal stability up to 400 °C. Most organic dyes start to decompose long before this temperature is reached.

Figure 40 The D2T2 process for printing colour photographs from electronic signals: the temperature of each heating element in the thermal head is determined by an electronic signal linked to a point on the picture – the electronic signal triggers the diffusion of the right amount of each of the dyes

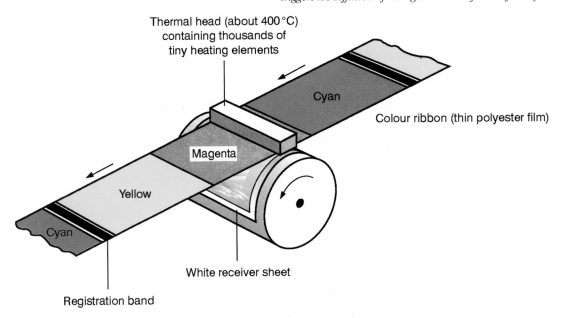

Thermal head (about 400 °C) containing thousands of tiny heating elements

Cyan

Colour ribbon (thin polyester film)

Magenta

Yellow

Cyan

White receiver sheet

Registration band

There are about 1 million known dyes in the world and none would do! Three completely new dyes had to be designed. The colour ribbon and the receiving sheet are both made of polyester, so a natural starting point was to look at existing polyester dyes and try to modify them. Computer models were a great help here: changes can be made to the structure of a dye on the computer screen, and the effect on the properties of the dye seen immediately.

The cyan dye was the most difficult to find. True cyan dyes are scarce. The best ones are the phthalocyanines but these were no good in this case because of their large molecules. The new dyes the researchers came up with are shown in Figure 41 and they all have relatively small molecules. Their structures are rather complex so don't try to remember them!

ASSIGNMENT 17

a Suggest why the large phthalocyanine dyes were unsuitable for the D2T2 process.

b Phthalocyanine dyes can be made by sulphonating Monastral Blue pigment with fuming sulphuric acid. Explain how this process converts the pigment into a dye.

CD9 *Summary*

Colour by Design is really two connected stories, one about pigments and paints and the other about the development of synthetic dyes. Both stories are a mixture of historical aspects and frontier applications of colour chemistry. They illustrate well the very diverse roles chemists play in society.

The chemists at the National Gallery use a variety of analytical techniques to investigate pigments and paint media. For example, ultra-violet and visible spectroscopy and atomic emission spectroscopy provide information about the chemical composition of pigments, while gas–liquid chromatography is used to determine the medium used to make the paint. Drying oils are unsaturated triesters of propane-1,2,3-triol (glycerol). The drying process involves reaction of the unsaturated chains with oxygen, followed by a polymerisation reaction in which cross-linking takes place between the chains.

The development of synthetic dyes over the last 150 years has been closely linked to the development of organic chemistry. Each contributed to the growth of the other. In this part of the unit you found out about the special structure of benzene and the types of reactions arenes undergo. An understanding of the relationship between the structure of a dye molecule and its function, and of the forces which bind dyes to fibres, is essential when designing new dyes.

Substances appear coloured because they absorb radiation in the visible region of the spectrum. The energy absorbed causes changes in electronic energy and electrons are promoted from the ground state to a higher energy level. Coloured organic compounds often contain unsaturated groups such as $C=O$ or $-N=N-$. These groups are usually part of an extended delocalised electron system called the chromophore. Functional groups, such as $-OH$ and $-NH_2$, are often attached to chromophores to enhance or modify the colour of the molecules. Many coloured inorganic compounds contain transition metals. Here, the radiation absorbed excites a d-electron to a higher energy level.

Activity CD9 will help you to review the important chemical ideas covered in this unit.

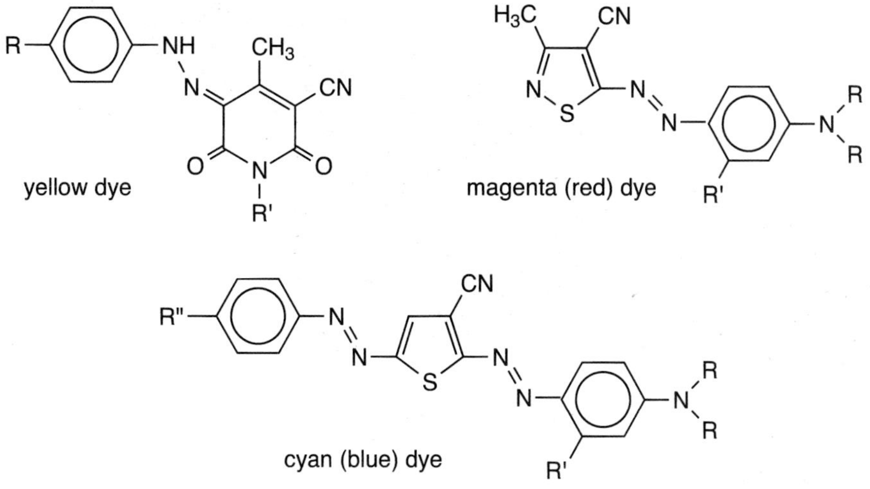

Figure 41 Dyes designed for the D2T2 printing process (R represents an alkyl group)

THE OCEANS

Why a unit on THE OCEANS?

To many people, the term 'ocean' probably conjures up an image of a seemingly endless expanse of water, of some biological interest but chemically inert.

Yet the oceans are far from being inert. They play an essential part in the cycling of many chemicals (sulphur and nitrogen compounds, for example) throughout the Earth. The oceans absorb and store carbon dioxide, and must be considered together with the atmosphere in any study of the greenhouse effect. The oceans play a further role in controlling our climate through their absorption of solar energy and the consequent production of water vapour and flows of warm water which help drive currents in the air and the seas.

The oceans help to make the Earth hospitable to life and have kept our planet habitable for over 3.5 billion years. Despite their importance, our understanding of ocean processes is far from complete, and they are one of the major sources of uncertainty in scientists' attempts to model future global conditions.

This unit attempts to raise awareness of the importance of the oceans to life on Earth, and to bring out some of the fundamental chemistry which lies behind some ocean processes. Major chemical ideas such as

- molecular-kinetic theory and energy distribution among molecules
- the role of entropy changes in determining the feasibility of chemical reactions
- applications of equilibrium to phase changes, solubility and the behaviour of weak acids

are developed, and linked (perhaps unexpectedly) to familiar objects such as shells and rocks, and to the behaviour of water itself.

Overview of chemical principles

In this unit you will learn more about ...

ideas introduced in earlier units in this course
- entropy (**Developing Fuels** and **From Minerals to Elements**)
- molecular motion (**The Atmosphere** and **Using Sunlight**)
- the ideal gas law (**Using Sunlight**)
- intermolecular forces (**The Polymer Revolution**)
- chemical equilibrium (**The Atmosphere**, **Engineering Proteins** and **Aspects of Agriculture**)
- Le Chatelier's principle (**Aspects of Agriculture**)
- dissolving and solubility (**From Minerals to Elements**)
- acids and bases (**From Minerals to Elements**)

... as well as learning new ideas about
- entropy and the distribution of energy quanta
- entropy changes in a system and its surroundings
- total entropy changes, spontaneity and equilibrium
- the structure and properties of water
- solubility products
- weak acids
- the pH scale
- buffer solutions.

0

THE OCEANS

01 *The edge of the land*

They that go down to the sea in ships …

In a French restaurant, a plate of shellfish is known as *fruits de mer*, or 'fruits of the sea'. For thousands of years mankind has farmed the sea for food, and the easiest creatures to catch must have been the shellfish. But the archaeological records of every seaside culture from Neolithic times onwards contain the remains of marine fish, and the hooks and harpoons used to catch them. Classical literature tells us that the Ancient Greeks devised complicated traps for catching fish and that the Phoenicians and Carthaginians founded many cities around the Mediterranean as fishing settlements – Sidon, for instance, a Phoenician city now in Lebanon, means 'the fishing place'.

Sea creatures provided these ancient cultures with more than just food. The name Phoenicia comes from the Greek word *phoenix* meaning 'purple'. One of the foundations of this country's vast commercial empire, from around 1500 BC to 800 BC, was trade in a brilliant purple dye, extracted from the shells of a species of marine snail. Tyrian Purple, as the dye was called, was used to colour the attire of kings and emperors, and was a symbol of great wealth and power. Tyrian Purple

Figure 1 Indonesian fishermen; fishing is one of the earliest skills and people have farmed the sea for food for thousands of years

is chemically similar to Indigo, the dye that the Ancient Britons extracted from the woad plant. What a coincidence that the two cultures should have used these two related dyes at about the same time – perhaps blues were in fashion!

Figure 2 The ancient dye, Tyrian Purple, was extracted from the shells of a species of sea snail. The Roman Empire decreed that only members of the ruling family (such as Julius Caesar, above) could wear robes dyed with Tyrian Purple

Indigo

Tyrian Purple

ASSIGNMENT I

Look at the structures of Indigo and Tyrian Purple. Both molecules are completely flat because electrons are delocalised around all four rings and across the double bond in the middle.

a What is meant by the term 'delocalised' in this context?

b From what you now know of the structure of Tyrian Purple, explain why the molecule does not exist as optical isomers.

c Tyrian Purple can be formed by substituting bromine atoms into Indigo. Describe a general method which is available to chemists for bringing about this kind of reaction.

Figure 3 (a) Traditionally, nori farmers cultivated the algae on brush bundles which they stuck into the mud of shallow estuaries. (b) Nowadays, the algae are encouraged to grow on netting stretched between bamboo poles

Less extensive use has been made of marine plants, but in Japan several species of marine algae (seaweed) are cultivated for food. The best known of these is the *Porphyra* plant, grown to make a seafood item called *nori*, which is rich in vitamins (Figure 3).

A similar seaweed is collected from the shores of North Wales where it is made into a dish called *laver bread*. There are other uses for seaweed: it can be spread on the ground as fertiliser and used as a source of chemicals. Seaweed ash has been a source of soda ash and potash (sodium carbonate and potassium carbonate) since the early 1700s; iodine was first extracted from it a century later.

So seaweed is rich in sodium, potassium and iodine, and the marine snail used to make Tyrian Purple is rich in bromine. Both the seaweed and the snail concentrate certain elements found in the sea-water they inhabit. Tyrian Purple, for example, contains 38% by mass of bromine, whereas the concentration of this element in sea-water is only 0.19%. Bromine is rare in the sea, but even rarer on land; that is why bromine is extracted commercially from the bromide ions in sea-water (see **Minerals to Elements** storyline, Section **M1**).

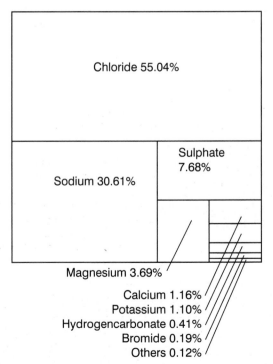

Figure 4 Percentages by mass of different ions in sea-water

Everyone knows that the sea is salty. Salts are ionic compounds and over 99% of all the dissolved substances in sea-water are ionic. Whilst they remain dissolved, of course, the ions are free in solution so – strictly speaking – the sea contains not salts, but a mixture of ions. Figure 4 shows the abundance of these ions. The proportion of one to another is remarkably constant whichever part of whichever sea you choose to sample.

The composition of sea-water has been known for over 100 years, but it is only recently that we have begun to understand in any detail how the sea became salty.

ASSIGNMENT 2

Use the information in Figure 4 to work out

a the amount in moles of positive charge present in 100 g of sea-water

b the amount in moles of negative charge present in 100 g of sea-water.

(Remember that 1 mole of doubly charged ions contains 2 moles of charge.)

Comment on the relative magnitudes of the answers you obtain in **a** and **b**.

You may find it useful at this point to refer back to the section on dissolving and energy changes in solution in **Chemical Ideas 4.5**, and the section on hydrogen bonding in **Chemical Ideas 5.3**.

Why do many ionic compounds dissolve so readily in water? **Activity 01.1** allows you to investigate the relationship between a solvent and the substances it dissolves. In **Activity 01.2** you can find out what changes occur when an ionic solid dissolves.

Salt of the Earth

There is an old Norse myth which tells of a magic salt mill grinding away at the bottom of the ocean, making the sea salt. Strangely enough, this notion is not so far from the truth.

It has been known for a long time that some of the salt comes from the land. Rainwater leaches salts from the soil and rivers wash them into the sea. But the sea contains in abundance some elements that are not found to any great extent in river water – chlorine, bromine and sulphur, for example. The source of these elements remained a mystery until we learned more about the structure of the ocean floors.

Underneath the sediments on the ocean floor are lavas, generated by long, thin, underwater volcanoes called *mid-ocean ridges*. The gases given off from these volcanoes are rich in chlorine, bromine and sulphur. Also, as molten lavas meet cold sea-water they solidify and shatter. Water streams down through cracks in the lava, scouring out soluble minerals. The superheated solutions which re-emerge through *hydrothermal vents* are much richer sources of elements like chlorine, bromine and sulphur than crustal rock. Figure 5 shows the sources of the dissolved ions in sea-water.

Scientists think that the water itself escaped from these deep-seated rocks and that sea-water was salty right from the beginning. The balance of ions is kept constant by a complicated geochemical cycle that scientists are only just beginning to understand.

Figure 5 The sources of dissolved ions in sea-water

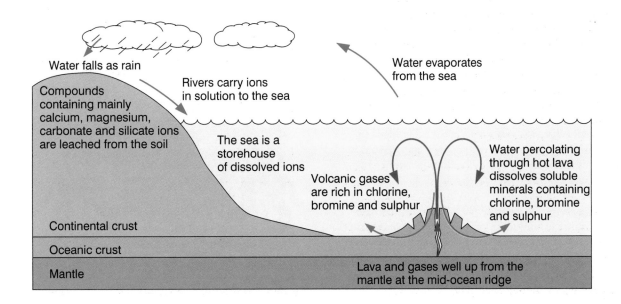

ASSIGNMENT 3

Bottled mineral water contains ions dissolved from the soil and rock through which the water has percolated. Most brands of bottled water give an analysis of the contents on their labels. Look at the labels of as many types of mineral water as you can find. Choose the still varieties as the fizzy ones have carbon dioxide added to them. Compare the contents with the analysis of sea-water shown in the table below.

Ion	Contents/mg dm^{-3}
Cl^-	19 300
Na^+	10 700
SO_4^{2-}	2700
Mg^{2+}	1300
Ca^{2+}	400
K^+	380
HCO_3^-	140
Br^-	65
Others	40

a What is the total mass of dissolved solids in 1 dm^3 (1 litre) of
  i sea-water
  ii the different sorts of mineral water?

b Comment on the difference between the total masses in **i** and **ii**. (Like the table above, the analysis of the mineral water will quote the concentrations in order, with the most abundant ion first.)

c Compare the analyses for the individual ions in the mineral waters with the figures given for sea-water. Comment on any differences. Which of the ions in sea-water cannot be accounted for by run-off of water from the land?

Salt sellers

Sea salt has almost the same composition wherever you get it from. However, the concentration of the salt in the water does vary from place to place. Where large volumes of fresh water enter the sea, the salinity (total salt content) is low. So those parts of the sea which are close to estuaries, abundant in icebergs or in areas of high rainfall are not very salty. On the other hand, in places where the rate of evaporation is high, the sea is saltier than normal. Water evaporates quickly in a hot, dry climate or where it is windy.

The two most abundant ions in sea-water are sodium (Na^+) and chloride (Cl^-). These ions are also present in the body fluids of all land creatures. An adult human contains about 300 g of dissolved sodium chloride (common salt). Some of this is excreted each day in urine and sweat, and must be replaced if the body is to function normally.

Our need for salt has been recognised for thousands of years and the substance has entered the language, superstition and history of all societies. The word *salary* means, literally, a payment in salt – as was the custom in the Roman legions. In medieval times, important guests sat 'above the salt' at a banquet – and the saying lives on. Spilling salt brings bad luck – a measure of its value hundreds of years ago. Not only was it important to eat enough salt; salt was also used to preserve food in the days before refrigerators and freezers had been invented.

The obvious place to get salt from was the sea. Along the east coast of Britain around 600 BC was a string of small salt-works. From the remains of their equipment it would seem that these early salters evaporated sea-water in shallow pottery dishes set on brick stands over fires.

When the Romans occupied Britain, they imported salt from France (Gaul) where it was possible to evaporate the water by the heat of the Sun. After the Romans left, the British salt industry thrived again. By AD 700, new ways of concentrating the salt had been devised. Sand was collected from the upper part of the shore, above the usual tide line, from the area only covered a few times per year by the spring tides. This sand has a high salt content, so it could be mixed with sea-water to make a more concentrated solution. Filtering through peat removed the sand, and the enriched solution was evaporated in lead pans over wood fires.

In medieval times, salt was big business. The Guild of Salters controlled the importation of foreign salt into Britain – mainly from the Bay of Biscay – and there were strict rules governing its handling. Salt could only be measured out by officials called 'salt meters' and carried by 'salt porters'. Large profits were made and the investments continue to produce income even today. The modern Salters' Company uses some of this income to support Chemistry teaching in schools.

Figure 6 The coat of arms of the Salters' Company: the motto means 'Salt savours all'

Although most of our salt now comes from underground deposits, one firm in Essex continues to extract salt from sea-water. Essex has a long coastline with numerous shallow inlets from which water evaporates, leaving sea-water with a high salinity. First the water is filtered, and heated by natural gas in large stainless steel pans. As the sea-water comes to the boil, some of the impurities rise to the surface as a froth and are skimmed off. Then the water is allowed to simmer. Calcium sulphate is one of the first salts to crystallise out and forms a hard scale deposit on the sides of the pans. As the solution becomes more concentrated, crystals of sodium chloride begin to form. This is partly because sodium and chloride ions are most abundant, and partly because the solubility of sodium chloride is relatively low.

After about 15 hours the pile of accumulated crystals reaches the surface of the liquid and heating is stopped. The crystals are raked to the sides of the pan and removed with shovels. It is important to do this before the bitter-tasting magnesium salts crystallise out and spoil the flavour. Luckily, they are present in smaller quantities and are more soluble than sodium chloride so they remain in solution for longer. The early salt makers must have learned by bitter experience not to evaporate sea-water to dryness.

Figure 7 Evaporating sea-water to make salt at the Maldon Crystal Salt Company in Essex

ASSIGNMENT 4

Human activities remove only a tiny percentage of salt from the sea. Suggest reasons why, when rivers, volcanic gases and hydrothermal vents continually supply the sea with dissolved ions, the composition of sea-water has remained constant for at least the last 200 million years.

... and occupy their business in great waters

The sea is a storehouse for fish and for minerals, and communities which have lived by the sea have always used it as such. Hannah Glasse wrote in 1747, 'Newcastle is a famous place for salted haddocks. They come in barrels and keep a great while'. Haddock were caught off the Northumbrian coast and sea-water, boiled over fires of sea coal, provided the salt for preserving. In the winter months, when it was too rough to put to sea, the salted fish provided the community with an assured supply of protein. These people used the coastal waters very much as others used the land. They exploited its resources, but their enterprises were small and inefficient enough to avoid over-fishing.

Nowadays, fishing is big business and many traditional fishing stocks have been depleted. Factory ships from Russia and other Eastern European countries travel as far as the waters outside Argentina, accompanied by fuel tankers, salvage tugs, repair boats and refrigerator ships that will hold 10 000 tonnes of fish. The pursuit of the whale, for food and for chemicals, has also led to the near extinction of some species.

Figure 8 Fishing on a large scale; catches must now be regulated to ensure adequate supplies for the future

Sea-water provides us with bromine, chlorine and magnesium. More recently, manganese-rich nodules have been collected from the ocean floors (see Figure 9 overleaf).

In future, scientists hope to use the sea as a source of more complex, organic compounds. Many sea creatures, especially those which have no shell to protect them, have evolved poisons which could perhaps be used as medicines. Some of these creatures have been known for thousands of years. For example, the tomb of the Egyptian Pharoah Ti, who lived nearly 5000 years ago, bears a picture of the pufferfish and a hieroglyphic description of its toxicity. In the 2nd century BC, similar information was published in the first Chinese pharmacopoeia, The Book of Herbs. In 1968, biochemists determined the nature of tetrodotoxin, the virulent poison produced by the pufferfish, and began to investigate its action.

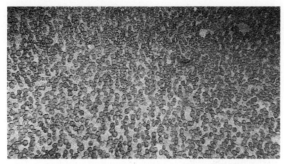

Figure 9 Manganese nodules on a deep ocean floor. The nodules (diameter about 5 cm) are mainly manganese and iron, but also contain traces of nickel, cobalt and copper. They could provide a valuable source of these metals in the future

The oceans, however, are not infinitely rich in food and chemicals, nor are they an ever-open bin into which we can throw our waste.

The North Sea, for example, is polluted by industrial effluent, sewage and excess of fertiliser that the major rivers of Northern Europe carry into it. Heavy metal ions poison fish stocks, and the increase in nitrate(V) concentration leads to rapid growth of algae.

You can read more about the search for new medicines from the sea in **Activity 01.3.**

02 *Wider still and deeper*

Surveying the seas

In December 1872 a small wooden warship, her guns replaced by scientific equipment, sailed out of Portsmouth. The ship was the HMS *Challenger*. She was fitted out by the Royal Society of London and her crew of 240 men was assigned to investigate 'everything about the sea'. Three and a half years later,

Figure 10 HMS Challenger. *Her voyage from 1872 to 1876 was the first systematic study of the oceans*

on 24 May 1876, the *Challenger* returned home. During a journey of over 100 000 km the expedition had collected information from most of the oceans, as well as samples of water, sediments and marine life. The voyage of the *Challenger* (see Figure 13) was the first systematic study of the oceans, and provided the scientific basis of modern oceanography.

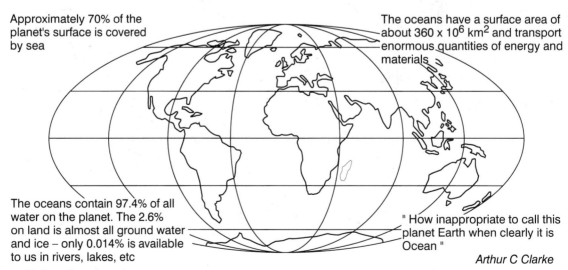

Approximately 70% of the planet's surface is covered by sea

The oceans have a surface area of about 360×10^6 km^2 and transport enormous quantities of energy and materials

The oceans contain 97.4% of all water on the planet. The 2.6% on land is almost all ground water and ice – only 0.014% is available to us in rivers, lakes, etc

" How inappropriate to call this planet Earth when clearly it is Ocean "

Arthur C Clarke

Figure 11 Some facts about the oceans

As we have learned more about the seas, we have realised that their role as a storehouse of food and chemicals is almost a sideline compared with the part they play in controlling our climate. Together with the atmosphere, the oceans are at the centre of the system which controls global conditions – the conditions in which we live and under which life has evolved for billions of years.

Perhaps we should have realised much sooner that the oceans have a regulatory role: they are so huge it would be hard to believe they did not influence what happens on Earth. But it is much harder to understand *how* the oceans work. Their vastness makes them difficult to study and it is only recently that our knowledge of them has really begun to grow.

The *Challenger* took samples and a range of measurements (such as water depth, the temperature at different depths, and the direction and speed of currents) at 360 sites in 3.5 years.

Even today an ocean survey ship, equipped with much more sensitive equipment, usually only makes measurements at one site per day, travelling 400 km between sites. But accurate information may be of little use if the system you are studying has changed significantly by the time you have finished collecting your data. Some of the events being studied are over in a matter of days or a few weeks. A satellite's greater speed is often a considerable advantage, even though the measurements it makes may sometimes be less accurate.

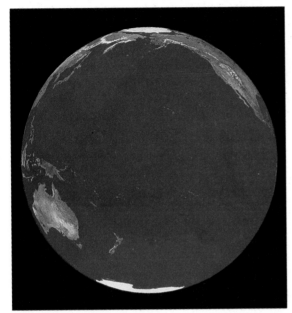

Figure 12 The watery planet: a view of the Earth showing the vast expanse of the Pacific Ocean

Figure 14 Area covered by a single satellite over a period of 10 days

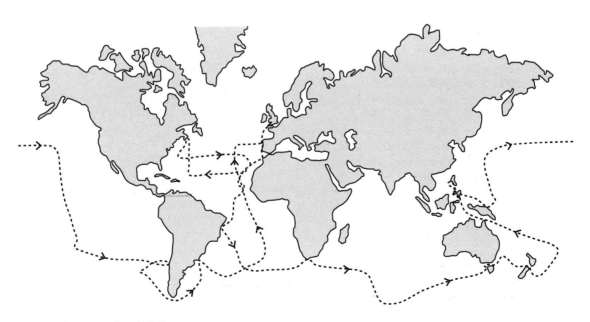

Figure 13 The voyage of HMS Challenger

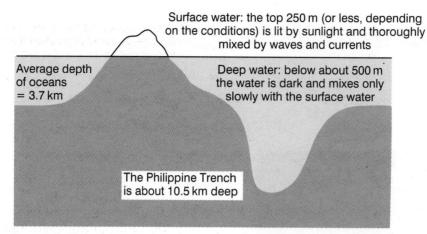

Surface water: the top 250 m (or less, depending on the conditions) is lit by sunlight and thoroughly mixed by waves and currents

Average depth of oceans = 3.7 km

Deep water: below about 500 m the water is dark and mixes only slowly with the surface water

The Philippine Trench is about 10.5 km deep

Figure 15 Underwater landscapes are more extreme than those we see above the water

Surveys have shown that the depth of the oceans is far from constant. In fact, underwater landscapes are more extreme than those we see above the water (see Figure 15). Mount Everest rises 8.85 km above sea level; there are several parts of the ocean which are deeper than 10 km.

ASSIGNMENT 5

Making accurate measurements on the oceans can be difficult, and errors can become significant when values are multiplied millions of times to scale them up to ocean-sized quantities. This assignment tells you about one example of such an error.

Fritz Haber was a brilliant German chemist, who developed a process for making ammonia (see **Aspects of Agriculture** storyline, Section **AA3**). Ammonia can be turned into explosives, and Haber's process was used to supply Germany's munitions factories during the First World War. When the war was over, Haber decided that his country's war debts could be paid off by another of his ideas – extracting gold from the sea.

Gold compounds are present in solution in sea-water. Their concentration is very low, but Haber calculated that vast quantities of the precious metal could be extracted by special devices fitted to ships. During the 1920s, German ships sailed around the world hoping to return laden with gold.

They didn't. Haber's figure for the gold concentration was hopelessly high, and our estimate has been falling ever since. For example, a survey carried out between 1988 and 1990 set a new maximum level at $1 \times 10^{-11}\,\text{g dm}^{-3}$; before 1988 it was thought to be $4 \times 10^{-9}\,\text{g dm}^{-3}$.

a Use the surface area and average depth of the oceans to estimate their volume in km^3 (see Figures 11 and 15).

b Convert your answer to **a** into dm^3 units. You should now be able to see the 'big number aspect' of calculations on the oceans.

c Estimate the maximum value for the total mass of gold thought to be in the oceans today.

d If all the gold could be extracted from the sea and shared equally among the Earth's population of 5×10^9 people, approximately what would be your share today?

e The price of gold varies from day to day, but it is currently about $6.71 \,£\,\text{g}^{-1}$.

  i How much would your share of the gold be worth?

  ii Explain why you would be unlikely to receive as much as this, and could even make a loss.

Unravelling a complex system

Here is an example of how our understanding of one global process has grown as we have learnt more about the interrelationship of life, the oceans and the atmosphere.

The problem of **acid rain** (or more correctly **acid deposition**) is serious in many parts of the world, and compounds containing oxidised sulphur are among the handful of chemicals involved. In the 1960s, scientists were trying to find out more about acid deposition by measuring the quantities of sulphur which circulated around the land, the oceans and the atmosphere. But their sums didn't add up ... there was a missing link in the sulphur cycle (see Figure 16).

It is now thought that dimethyl sulphide, $(CH_3)_2S$, produced by seaweeds and other marine algae, could be the missing compound in the cycle. Dimethyl sulphide is volatile and quickly finds its way into the atmosphere, where it is partly responsible for the smell of sea air. Once in the atmosphere, it can be oxidised to form acidic sulphur compounds.

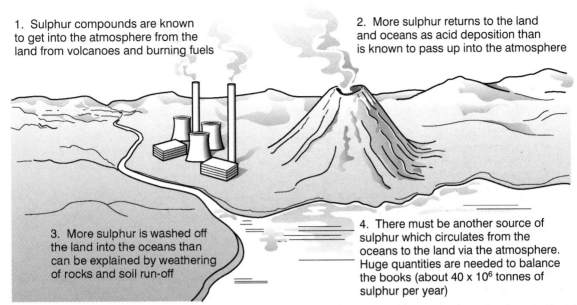

1. Sulphur compounds are known to get into the atmosphere from the land from volcanoes and burning fuels

2. More sulphur returns to the land and oceans as acid deposition than is known to pass up into the atmosphere

3. More sulphur is washed off the land into the oceans than can be explained by weathering of rocks and soil run-off

4. There must be another source of sulphur which circulates from the oceans to the land via the atmosphere. Huge quantities are needed to balance the books (about 40×10^6 tonnes of sulphur per year)

Figure 16 The missing link in the sulphur cycle

A recent North Sea survey showed how significant algal production of dimethyl sulphide can be. Maximum activity occurs in April and May along the coast from Germany to France and probably accounts for about 25% of all acidic pollution over Europe at that time. So when policy-makers are deciding what to do about acid rain, they need to be aware of the role of marine algae as well as the coal-fired power stations.

Later in this unit you will look at another element, carbon, and the role of the oceans in determining the amount of CO_2 in the atmosphere. But first you need to consider the part the oceans play in distributing energy around the Earth.

Figure 17 Microscopic marine algae: some types of marine algae produce dimethyl sulphide which is released into the atmosphere

ASSIGNMENT 6

a Draw a full structural formula for dimethyl sulphide. What shape would you expect the molecule to adopt?

b Sulphur is in Group 6 of the Periodic Table along with oxygen.
  i What do we call the series of compounds related to dimethyl sulphide in which the sulphur atom is replaced by an oxygen atom?
  ii Dimethyl sulphide, like its oxygen-containing relative, is volatile. Use your knowledge of intermolecular forces to explain why.

c $(CH_3)_2SO$ and SO_2 are two of the compounds produced in the atmosphere from dimethyl sulphide. Explain why formation of these products corresponds to oxidation of the sulphur.

03 *Oceans of energy*
The global central heating system

With the exception of *tidal power*, all our energy comes ultimately from nuclear sources. On Earth, we can mine radioactive compounds and produce from them fuel for *nuclear power stations*. Energy from the nuclear processes which go on in the core of the Earth can be tapped at suitable locations as *geothermal energy*.

But most of our energy comes from outside our planet – from a great nuclear furnace in the Sun. The Sun's rays heat the Earth directly, and through this drive the *winds* and *waves. Solar cells* convert sunlight into electricity. *Photosynthesis* uses sunlight to build up fuels: some are used almost immediately, and others have been changed over millions of years into *coal, oil* and *gas* (see **Using Sunlight** storyline).

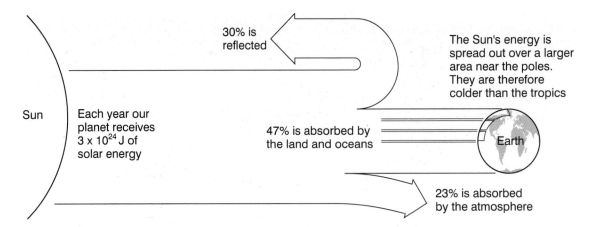

Figure 18 The fate of the Sun's energy reaching the Earth

When the Sun's rays reach the Earth they can be

- reflected
- absorbed by the atmosphere
- absorbed by the Earth's surface.

Roughly half the energy we receive from the Sun is absorbed by the land and the oceans, and this causes the Earth's surface to warm up. The Earth in turn radiates energy back into space (see **The Atmosphere** storyline, Section **A6**).

If the Earth was a dry lump of rock with no atmosphere, each part of its surface would soon settle down to a situation in which the energy being received from the Sun would, on average, be balanced by energy lost through radiation (see Figure 19). The tropics would be much warmer and the poles even colder than they are – and the Earth would be far less hospitable to life.

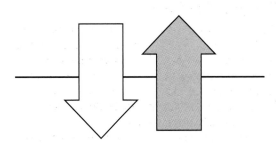

Incoming solar energy at any point is balanced by energy lost to outer space

Figure 19 A planet with neither atmosphere nor oceans

But the Earth is surrounded by water and gas – both fluids. Temperature differences set up currents in the oceans and atmosphere which spread out the heating effect of the Sun more evenly. Just like warm air from a radiator spreads around a room, currents in the sea and air take thermal energy from the tropics to the colder regions of the Earth.

In fact, the ocean/atmosphere system is even more effective at spreading out energy. Warm water can do more than circulate – it can *evaporate*. Energy is taken in when water evaporates, so the situation must be reversed, and energy must be released, when water condenses. The tropics are cooled by evaporation, and currents in the atmosphere carry the water vapour to colder, high latitude regions where condensation releases energy (Figure 20).

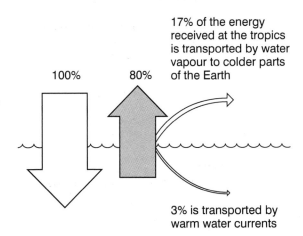

17% of the energy received at the tropics is transported by water vapour to colder parts of the Earth

3% is transported by warm water currents

Figure 20 At the tropics of a planet with an atmosphere and oceans, about 20% of the incoming solar energy is transported to colder regions

High latitude regions receive more energy than is provided by the Sun alone: they are wetter – but warmer. Figure 21 shows the balance of condensation and evaporation around the world.

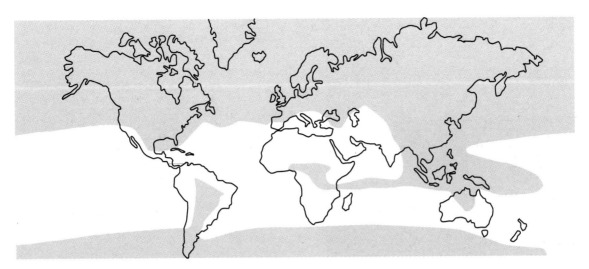

Figure 21 The condensation–evaporation balance of the Earth (shaded areas denote regions where condensation exceeds evaporation)

In the North Atlantic region, the winds and warm water currents flow from SW to NE. Northern Europe, including the UK, is warmed by energy which has been transported from the tropics and the Caribbean. In winter, as much as 25% of our thermal energy may come this way. Eastern North America does not receive this energy. So winters are much more pleasant in Lisbon, Portugal (latitude 38°N) than in Boston, USA (latitude 42°N) (see Figure 23).

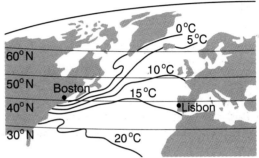

Figure 23 Average surface temperatures in the North Atlantic in February

ASSIGNMENT 7

The positions of three Canadian cities are marked on the map below. Explain the patterns in their winter and summer temperatures.

Figure 22

	Victoria	Winnipeg	St. John's
July maximum/°C	17	23	17
January maximum/°C	2	–19	–6

Chemical Ideas 4.4 reminds you of the behaviour of molecules in solids, liquids and gases, and explains it in terms of entropy.

Energy in the clouds

The molecules in liquid water and water vapour differ in one important aspect. In the liquid, there are attractive forces between the molecules – **intermolecular forces** – which hold the molecules onto one another and keep them quite close together. These forces are absent in water vapour where molecules are free to separate and take up far more volume.

When we evaporate water, changing it from liquid to vapour, the intermolecular attractions must be overcome – a process which takes in energy. The enthalpy change of vaporisation, ΔH_{vap}, is our measure of this energy. In the reverse process, condensation, molecules come together again, intermolecular attractions re-form and an equal quantity of energy is released. In other words, condensation is **exothermic** and the enthalpy change is $-\Delta H_{vap}$.

In **Activity O3.1** you can determine for yourself a value for the enthalpy change of vaporisation of water.

Figure 24 Energy is taken in from the surroundings when sea-water evaporates, and is released when the water vapour condenses in clouds

The UK may seem cold enough and wet enough most of the time, but imagine a world with propanone seas. The enthalpy changes of vaporisation of propanone, water and some other liquids are given in Table 1 (notice that kJ kg^{-1} units are used.)

Substance	Formula	ΔH_{vap}/kJ kg^{-1}
water	H_2O	+2260
ethanol	C_2H_5OH	+840
propanone	C_3H_6O	+520
hexane	C_6H_{14}	+330
mercury	Hg	+300

Table 1 Some enthalpy changes of vaporisation

If our present rain were replaced by the same mass of 'propanone-rain' it would release only about one-quarter of the energy. For enough 'propanone-rain' to fall to keep our temperature the same, there would have to be about four times more rain. Then there would be other problems – an increased fire risk, for example!

Perhaps it is a lucky chance, perhaps it is much more than that, but the properties of water make it an ideal liquid for spreading the Sun's energy around the world. Without it, the pattern of evolution and human development would probably have been very different.

Figure 25 illustrates the global water cycle. It summarises the major processes by which water circulates around the world.

Notice that more water evaporates from the oceans than is directly returned to them as precipitation (ie rain and snow). Each year, 36×10^{15} kg of water vapour produced from the sea falls as precipitation over the land. The process makes the land wetter and keeps the rivers flowing. It also makes the land warmer.

So evaporation and condensation of water affect the temperature of different parts of the Earth in two ways:

- by transferring energy from low latitudes to high latitudes
- by warming the land through condensation of water which comes from the oceans.

Figure 25 The global water cycle (figures represent fluxes in 10^{15} kg per year)

ASSIGNMENT 8

a Use the figures in Figure 25 and Table 1 to calculate the thermal energy released each year when water vapour carried from the oceans condenses out over the land.

b The output of a typical power station is about 2000 MW, in other words about 6×10^{16} J per year. Approximately how many power stations would be needed to produce the same energy as that transferred from oceans to land by evaporation and condensation?

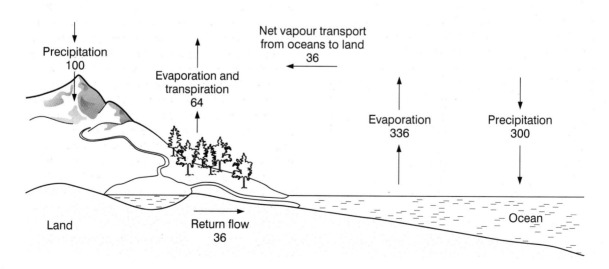

Precipitation 100

Net vapour transport from oceans to land 36

Evaporation and transpiration 64

Evaporation 336

Precipitation 300

Land

Return flow 36

Ocean

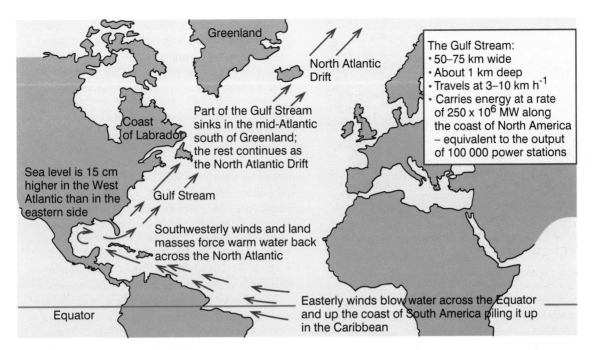

Figure 26 Ocean currents in the Atlantic

Warm water from the west

Western Europe is doubly fortunate with its climate. Winters are kept mild not only by the precipitation of rain but also by an 'ocean conveyor belt' bringing warm water from the tropics. The 'conveyor belt' is a surface current called the *North Atlantic Drift*. Surface currents are driven by prevailing winds and they alter course when they are deflected by large land masses.

We can find out how good a substance is at storing thermal energy by looking at its *specific heating capacity* (c_p). This is a measure of how much energy we have to put into 1 g of the substance to raise its temperature by 1 K. Looked at the other way, it tells us how much energy we can take out of a substance before it cools down by 1 K. Water has a large specific heating capacity: it will release quite a lot of energy without cooling down too much. Its specific heating capacity is given in Table 2 along with values for some other substances.

Substance	Specific heating capacity/J g^{-1} K^{-1}
water	4.17
ethanol	2.41
hexane	2.26
propanone	2.17
granite	0.82
copper	0.39
mercury	0.14

Table 2 Some specific heating capacities (c_p)

Water is one of the best liquids for transporting energy. A Gulf Stream in a 'propanone sea' would provide us with only half as much warmth.

Chemical Ideas 5.5 tells you more about water's unique properties and explains how they arise.

You can measure some specific heating capacities for yourself in **Activity O3.2**.

From Greenland's icy waters

On its way across the North Atlantic, the Gulf Stream meets two currents of cold water: one flows down the eastern side of Greenland, the other flows past the Labrador coast of Northeast Canada (see Figure 26). The currents are fed by melted ice and snow from the Greenland ice-sheet, so their salinity is low. The Gulf Stream has a relatively high salinity because it is a warm current: water evaporates from it leaving the salt behind.

The density of pure water varies with temperature in a complicated way, but as long as we don't go below 4 °C we can say that water is denser when it is colder. Salty water is also denser than pure water. When it meets the East Greenland and Labrador currents, the water in the Gulf Stream becomes much colder. The cold East Greenland and Labrador currents become saltier. The result of cooling the salty Gulf Stream and making the two cold currents saltier is a body of water which sinks because it is denser than the currents which feed it. The landmass of Greenland deflects the sinking water to the south, to produce a deep water cold current which follows the same route as the Gulf Stream but in the opposite direction (see Figure 27 overleaf).

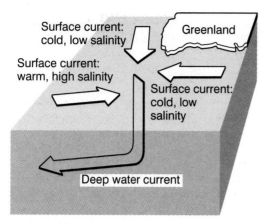

Figure 27 The deep water cold current in the Atlantic Ocean

Another deep water current is generated in the Antarctic. The temperature is much colder there than in Greenland so this current does not come from melted ice. Instead it results from sea-water freezing under the ice shelves. Salt is not taken up into the ice when this happens. It stays behind, so the residual water becomes saltier and sinks.

Activity 03.3 looks at the effect of freezing solutions of different concentrations.

The two deep water currents meet in the South Atlantic where the geography of the Earth and its rotation cause them to flow eastward. The water slowly rises back to the surface in the Indian and Pacific Oceans, and returns in surface currents to replenish the Atlantic, as shown in Figure 28.

The deep ocean currents transport huge volumes of water – 20 times more than all the world's rivers combined – and they move slowly. Water which sinks may take over 1000 years to resurface. Materials which are dissolved in the sinking water are also removed for a long time. We shall look at one of these materials – carbon dioxide – in the next section.

We are learning more about the ocean circulatory system and the oceans' role in controlling the Earth's heat energy balance. But we need to know much more before they can be included with confidence in global climate models – models which explain our present climate and predict how it may change in the future. We know that ocean currents are important but we cannot predict how they may change, and therefore how our climate may be affected, if the Earth warms up.

It seems possible that the deep ocean current was shut down during the last Ice Age, which was at its coldest about 18 000 years ago. The flow of warm surface water also stopped, making lands around the North Atlantic cooler by an extra 6°C–8°C. The currents were re-established at the end of the Ice Age as the Earth warmed up. But the warming caused the ice which covered much of North America to melt and flow out along the St. Lawrence river. The water in the North Atlantic became much less salty and it could not sink. The deep ocean current and therefore the warm Gulf Stream were switched off again. The ice took nearly 1000 years to melt and during that time Northern Europe stayed cold while the rest of the world warmed up.

The ice has gone from North America, but what might happen if global warming caused much more Greenland ice to melt? (In the early stages of global warming this is thought to be more likely than the melting of Antarctic ice.) Low salinity water might pour

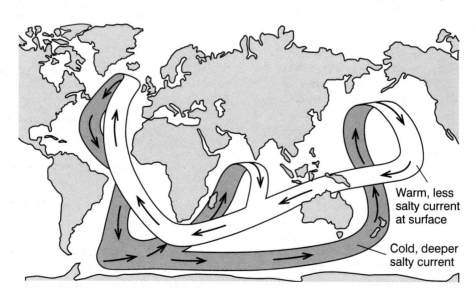

Figure 28 Deep ocean currents take cold salty water from the Atlantic to the Indian and Pacific Oceans on a giant 'conveyor belt'

into the North Atlantic once more, this time into the East Greenland and Labrador currents. The ocean circulatory system might shut down again and Northern Europe might become colder.

It is important to keep saying *might* because, until we have more knowledge, we cannot make accurate predictions. We are however sure that the consequences of global warming would be uneven. So Northern Europe could become colder while the rest of the world was getting hotter.

04 *A safe place to grow*
Storing carbon dioxide

Imagine you are planning a couple of hours on the beach in the middle of your summer holiday. You have a choice – to take cans of fizzy drink with you, or to leave them in the fridge to drink when you return. From experience you decide to leave the cans in the fridge. You know that more of the fizz stays in a fizzy drink if you keep it cool. If you leave a can standing in the Sun, the gas will come frothing out explosively when you open the top.

The carbon dioxide in the drink is like all gases: its solubility *decreases* as temperature increases. Table 3 shows this for carbon dioxide, oxygen and nitrogen.

Temperature/°C	Solubility/mg per 100 g water		
	CO_2	O_2	N_2
0	338	7.01	2.88
10	235	5.47	2.28
20	173	4.48	1.89
30	131	3.82	1.65
40	105	3.35	1.46
50	86	3.02	1.35

Table 3 Variation of the solubilities of some gases with temperature (at atmospheric pressure)

Carbon dioxide is put into fizzy drinks under considerable pressure – about 14 atmospheres in most cases. That's why there is such a 'pop' when you open the can. The high pressure makes more gas dissolve, as Figure 29 shows.

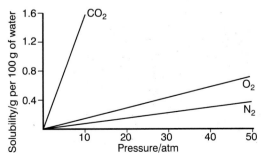

Figure 29 Variation of the solubilities of some gases with pressure, at 298 K

Eau so popular

Over 10^9 bottles of Perrier water are sold every year. Perrier is officially described as naturally carbonated, natural mineral water – which means that the fizz comes from carbon dioxide produced naturally underground rather than chemically manufactured gas added from a cylinder. Lots of people prefer the taste of bottled mineral water to their tap water, and many prefer the naturally carbonated drink to the other kind of fizzy water.

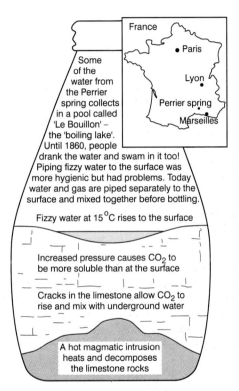

Figure 30

a Write an equation for the thermal decomposition of calcium carbonate.

b The pressure below the Perrier spring is 443 kPa (4.4 atm). How many times more soluble is carbon dioxide at this pressure than at atmospheric pressure? (Look at Figure 29 to find the way the solubility of carbon dioxide varies with pressure.)

c Why do you think the Perrier pool was called the 'boiling lake'?

d The Perrier company had problems when they tried piping the carbonated water out of the ground. Describe one difficulty they would have encountered and how it would be avoided by piping the gas and water separately.

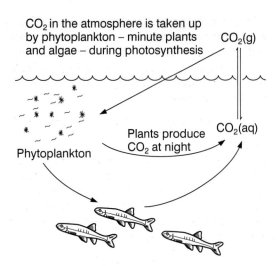

CO$_2$ in the atmosphere is taken up by phytoplankton – minute plants and algae – during photosynthesis   CO$_2$(g)

Phytoplankton

Plants produce CO$_2$ at night   CO$_2$(aq)

Phytoplankton is eaten and metabolised by animals which release CO$_2$ back into the water

Figure 31 Phytoplankton increase the rate at which carbon dioxide dissolves in the oceans

A high pressure of gas and a low temperature help to keep your drink fizzy. They also encourage carbon dioxide to dissolve in the oceans, which takes the gas out of the atmosphere and helps to maintain a stable environment on Earth.

You may find it useful here to refer to **The Atmosphere** storyline, Section **A8** and **Chemical Ideas 7.1**, which discuss the dissolving of carbon dioxide in the oceans.

The exchange of carbon dioxide between the atmosphere and oceans takes place quickly – more quickly than if you left some water in a beaker to come to equilibrium. Like so many environmental processes, we cannot explain it in terms of physical factors alone. Uptake of carbon dioxide by the oceans is speeded up by the action of marine life, as shown in Figure 31.

Table 3 and Figure 29 show that carbon dioxide is more soluble in water than oxygen or nitrogen. CO$_2$ molecules contain polar C=O bonds which can form hydrogen bonds with water molecules.

$$CO_2(g) \rightleftharpoons CO_2(aq) \qquad \text{(reaction 1)}$$

In addition, some of the carbon dioxide molecules react chemically with water and are removed from the equilibrium. More carbon dioxide therefore dissolves to maintain the equilibrium position:

$$CO_2(aq) + H_2O(l) \rightleftharpoons H^+(aq) + HCO_3^-(aq) \qquad \text{(reaction 2)}$$
$$HCO_3^-(aq) \rightleftharpoons H^+(aq) + CO_3^{2-}(aq) \qquad \text{(reaction 3)}$$

The reaction with water produces a mixture which contains mainly hydrogencarbonate ions (HCO$_3^-$) and H$^+$ ions together with some carbonate ions (CO$_3^{2-}$).

ASSIGNMENT 10

a Write an equilibrium constant expression, K_c, for the dissolving of carbon dioxide in water.

b Use the ideal gas law to work out the relationship between the concentration of a gas and its pressure.

c Explain the variation of gaseous solubility with pressure
  i by using your answers to **a** and **b**
  ii by reference to Le Chatelier's principle.

Much of the excess carbon dioxide we release into the atmosphere from the combustion of fuels is absorbed by the oceans. Estimates vary, but it seems likely that 35%–50% is removed this way. The oceans continue to soak up carbon dioxide because surface water, rich in CO$_2$, is constantly being removed and stored away for hundreds of years in the ocean deeps. The maximum amount of carbon dioxide is removed because this takes place in cold regions where CO$_2$ is most soluble. So currents, chemistry and marine life together make up a very efficient CO$_2$ removal system.

ASSIGNMENT 11

The oceans can keep on taking carbon dioxide out of the atmosphere because the dissolving of CO$_2$ takes place in what chemists call an *open system*. This means that material can enter or leave the system and so prevent equilibrium ever being established.

In this example, CO$_2$(aq) is removed to the deep oceans so more CO$_2$(g) dissolves to replace it. Drying washing on a clothes line and beer going flat in an open bottle are also examples of open systems which are never allowed to reach equilibrium.

Explain what happens in these two examples.

Sinking shells

Reactions 1, 2 and 3 are linked together – the product in reaction 1 is the reactant in 2, and so on. Let's simplify things by adding the three equations together to produce just one equation which shows how the reactants in 1 lead to the products of reaction 3:

$$CO_2(g) + H_2O(l) \rightleftharpoons 2H^+(aq) + CO_3^{2-}(aq) \qquad \text{(reaction 4)}$$

Remember, the reaction does not happen as simply as this, but the equation should make the next part of the story clearer.

Le Chatelier's principle tells us that any way of removing H$^+$ or CO$_3^{2-}$ ions from solution will cause more CO$_2$ to dissolve. Removing H$^+$ ions by adding a base is one way of doing this. You should already be familiar with this process: carbon dioxide is an acidic gas and it dissolves well in alkaline solution. That's why alkalis like sodium hydroxide are used to absorb CO_2.

Making the sea alkaline is not a very easy way of encouraging the oceans to take up carbon dioxide. But many marine organisms build protective shells composed of insoluble calcium carbonate using CO_3^{2-} ions in the sea-water. The shells are often very beautiful. They provide a way of mopping up carbon dioxide – perhaps from someone's factory chimney – and keeping the composition of our atmosphere constant.

At this point you may need to go back to **Chemical Ideas 8.1** to revise ideas about acids, bases and alkalis.

Figure 32 Mussels have protective shells made of calcium carbonate, made from carbon dioxide dissolved in the oceans

Billions of years ago, the Earth's atmosphere contained very much more carbon dioxide than it does now – probably about 35% carbon dioxide by volume. Once the process of photosynthesis had evolved, marine life had plenty of raw materials to work on in the form of carbon dioxide and water. Shell production flourished. Limestone and chalk rocks are the remains of shells of marine organisms which lived at that time and changed carbon dioxide from the atmosphere into solid calcium carbonate. When you go down into a cave you are quite literally making a journey into the past. When you walk on limestone hills or chalk downland, you are treading on Earth's prehistoric atmosphere.

Figure 33 The chalk cliffs of the Seven Sisters are the legacy of marine organisms which lived billions of years ago

Calcium carbonate is a good material for shellfish to use for protection at the surface of the oceans. It does not dissolve in sea-water. But it does dissolve, slightly, in pure water. It is an example of a **sparingly soluble solid**. The dissolving of sparingly soluble solids is controlled by equilibria like

$$CaCO_3(s) \rightleftharpoons Ca^{2+}(aq) + CO_3^{2-}(aq) \qquad \text{(reaction 5)}$$

in which the ions in the saturated solution are in dynamic equilibrium with the undissolved solid present.

The position of this equilibrium is determined in the normal way by an equilibrium constant which, because it describes the solubility of a compound, is called a **solubility product** (K_{sp}). The solubility product for reaction 5 is given by

$$K_{sp}(CaCO_3) = [Ca^{2+}(aq)] \, [CO_3^{2-}(aq)]$$

Its value is $5.0 \times 10^{-9} \, mol^2 \, dm^{-6}$ at 298 K.

Solubility products are discussed in more detail in **Chemical Ideas 7.7**.

One of two things can happen when Ca^{2+} ions and CO_3^{2-} ions are mixed together in a solution.

- Calcium carbonate may precipitate out of solution. This occurs whenever multiplying the dissolved calcium ion concentration by the dissolved carbonate ion concentration gives a value in excess of K_{sp}. (K_{sp} is the *maximum* value the product of the concentrations of $Ca^{2+}(aq)$ ions and $CO_3^{2-}(aq)$ ions can have in a solution at that temperature.)
- The ions may remain in solution. This will be the case whenever multiplying the concentrations of the two ions gives a number which is smaller than, or equal to, K_{sp}.

Calcium carbonate is a safe material from which to build sea shells because $[Ca^{2+}(aq)]$ and $[CO_3^{2-}(aq)]$ are already high enough at the surface of the sea for the calcium carbonate in the shells to be effectively insoluble. Remember, though, that the shells are in equilibrium with the ions in sea-water, and there will be a constant exchange of Ca^{2+} and CO_3^{2-} ions between the two.

ASSIGNMENT 12

a Use Hess's law and enthalpy changes of formation in the Data Sheets to calculate the standard enthalpy change for the process

$$CaCO_3(s) \rightarrow Ca^{2+}(aq) + CO_3^{2-}(aq)$$

b Explain in terms of equilibria how calcium carbonate production encourages more carbon dioxide to dissolve from the atmosphere.

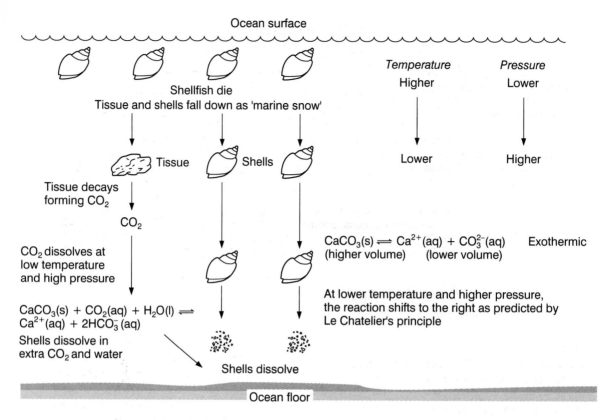

Figure 34 The dissolving of shells on the deep ocean floor

But things are different deeper in the ocean where the pressure is higher and the temperature is lower. The value of K_{sp} is greater under these conditions so calcium carbonate is more soluble. There is also a continuous downward drift of material from above. It's like a perpetual snowstorm. In fact the falling material is called *marine snow*. It contains the remains of dead organisms and the waste products from live creatures. Most of the organic material, such as tissue, is consumed or decomposed higher up, but some reaches the deeper water where bacteria break it down to produce carbon dioxide. The shells fall down intact, but then react with the extra carbon dioxide and dissolve. These processes are summarised in Figure 34.

In **Activity 04.1** you can investigate the dissolving of calcium carbonate.

There are no shells on the deep ocean floor: they've all dissolved. The creatures which live there cannot use calcium carbonate for a protective coating.

The calcium carbonate deposits which built up to form our limestone hills could not have formed in deep water. They must have been laid down when our landmass was in shallower seas. The abundance of life suggests also that it was warm, tropical water. Evidence like this helps scientists piece together the distant history of the Earth, and helps us explain how the continents have drifted and how the climate has changed throughout time.

ASSIGNMENT 13

Although the dissolving of calcium carbonate
$$CaCO_3(s) \rightarrow Ca^{2+}(aq) + CO_3^{2-}(aq)$$
is a slightly exothermic process, it is accompanied by a large decrease in entropy. We often assume that dissolving is accompanied by an increase in the entropy of the chemicals, but in this case ΔS_{sys} is large and negative. The entropy change which would occur if calcium carbonate dissolved is $-203\ J\ K^{-1}\ mol^{-1}$. Explain why you think dissolving might lead to such a large *entropy decrease* in this situation.

Now might be a good time to revise the properties of s-block elements such as calcium. You can read about these in **Chemical Ideas 11.2**.

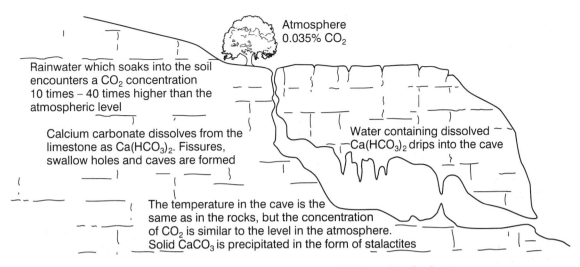

Atmosphere 0.035% CO_2

Rainwater which soaks into the soil encounters a CO_2 concentration 10 times – 40 times higher than the atmospheric level

Calcium carbonate dissolves from the limestone as $Ca(HCO_3)_2$. Fissures, swallow holes and caves are formed

Water containing dissolved $Ca(HCO_3)_2$ drips into the cave

The temperature in the cave is the same as in the rocks, but the concentration of CO_2 is similar to the level in the atmosphere. Solid $CaCO_3$ is precipitated in the form of stalactites

Figure 35 Formation of stalactites

ASSIGNMENT 14

Stalactites

Stalactites grow slowly. But they are worth waiting for. The growth rate depends on a number of factors, but the average rate is about 1 mm per year. The beautiful stalactite formations you can see in caves today have probably taken several thousands of years to form, and they have been created by the simple shifting back and forth of a chemical equilibrium.

The reaction involved is

$$CaCO_3(s) + CO_2(aq) + H_2O(l) \rightleftharpoons$$
$$Ca^{2+}(aq) + 2HCO_3^-(aq) \qquad \text{(reaction 6)}$$

It's the same reaction as the one responsible for dissolving shells deep under the oceans. Shells also dissolve in the formation of stalactites, but this time deep underground – the limestone rock which is the source of the calcium carbonate is itself composed of the shell-like remains of ancient marine organisms.

The same solution dissolves the calcium carbonate in the rocks and in the oceans. It is water with a higher than normal concentration of carbon dioxide which has been produced from decomposition of organic material. 'Marine snow' is broken down in the oceans; in the ground, the decomposer organisms work on the plant and animal remains which fall down into the soil.

So, in the oceans and on land, nature uses the same processes to dissolve and re-form structures using the simple compound, calcium carbonate.

a Use reaction 6 and Le Chatelier's principle to explain why a higher concentration of dissolved carbon dioxide in the ground water causes calcium carbonate to dissolve from limestone.

b Caves and their surrounding rocks are at the same temperature which stays close to 10 °C all year round. The carbon dioxide concentration inside a cave is close to the atmospheric level. Explain why calcium carbonate is precipitated when water drips through a cave.

c Give *two* reasons why stalactites would be unlikely to form on a planet without life.

Figure 36 Stalactites and stalagmites in the cave of the Black Spring, Wales

Million years ago		
4600	origin of Earth	first atmosphere lost from hot planet
3800	oldest sedimentary rocks organisms probably present	atmosphere consists of CO_2, NH_3, CH_4 and H_2S
3500	beginning of fossil record bacteria leave fossil remains	life probably uses energy released during fermentation, or from oxidation of organic molecules by sulphate ions and nitrate(V) ions
2800	first photosynthetic bacteria (blue-green bacteria or cyanobacteria)	oxygen produced for 1 million years it is used up in the oxidation of S^{2-} and Fe^{2+} ions no ozone is able to form in the atmosphere so life on the surface is impossible due to ultra-violet radiation bacteria live in the top 200 m of the ocean, screened from ultra-violet radiation by water
2000	first significant $CaCO_3$ deposits	removal of two greenhouse gases (CO_2 to form $CaCO_3$, and CH_4 by reaction with O_2) leads to major ice age
1800	oxygen begins to build up in the atmosphere	
1500	first green algae – plants with chlorophyll in their cells	
800	first sea animals	1% oxygen in atmosphere formation of ozone begins
400	first land plants	10% oxygen in atmosphere ozone layer protects plant cells from ultra-violet radiation
300	first land animals	20% oxygen in atmosphere

Table 4 The origins of life on Earth

Life on Earth

The Earth's early life forms evolved in the oceans – and that's where they stayed throughout most of the Earth's history. The planet was nearly 4 billion years old and life had existed for 3 billion years before life moved onto the land (Table 4).

Deep in the ocean, several kilometres down, there are cracks in the ocean floor called *hydrothermal vents* (see Section **O1**). They let out methane, hydrogen sulphide and clouds of black particles of sulphide minerals, which gives them their name – 'black smokers'. Colonies of tube worms up to 3 m long thrive around the vents. The energy the worms need for survival is provided by colonies of bacteria which live inside them. These bacteria must be very similar to the earliest life forms. They can live without light and oxygen because they gain their energy by using sulphate ions to oxidise the methane and hydrogen sulphide. This is life as it was 3500 million years ago.

Photosynthesis became possible with the evolution of cyanobacteria. They produced oxygen, but it was used up by reducing agents dissolved in the sea-water before it could build up in the atmosphere. This was just as well for the cyanobacteria because they cannot tolerate oxygen. Sulphate ions and nitrate(V) ions still had to be used as oxidising agents in respiration. It was only later that organisms could use free oxygen which was dissolved in the sea-water or which had built up in the atmosphere.

Figure 37 Colonies of huge tube worms thrive round hydrothermal vents in the ocean floor

The build-up of oxygen in the atmosphere is also discussed in **The Atmosphere** storyline, Section **A1**.

In terms of the Earth's history, the ozone layer is a very recent phenomenon. Most early life forms were resistant to ultra-violet radiation. Close relatives of cyanobacteria are alive today (there are plenty of places to hide away from the oxygen – in the mud of salt marshes or in a clump of dead seaweed, for example) · and they are still very tolerant of ultra-violet radiation.

The Earth's atmosphere has changed dramatically since the early days of life: reducing agents like methane and acidic gases like carbon dioxide have been largely replaced by a neutral, oxidising mixture of nitrogen and oxygen. If life had been forced to evolve on land in contact with the air, the primitive organisms would have become extinct. But they have been protected by their watery environment which has altered remarkably little over billions of years.

ASSIGNMENT 15

Molecules like 2-hydroxypropanoic acid and ethanol were probably present in small quantities in the early oceans. An example of an oxidation using sulphate ions, such as might have been carried out by a primitive bacterium, is shown below.

$$2CH_3CH(OH)COOH(aq) + SO_4^{2-}(aq) \rightarrow$$
$$2CH_3COOH(aq) + S^{2-}(aq) + 2CO_2(g) + 2H_2O(l)$$

a Explain why this equation represents a redox reaction.

b Calculate the enthalpy change produced by the oxidation of 2 moles of 2-hydroxypropanoic acid by sulphate ions. (Assume that the enthalpy changes of formation of the aqueous solutions of the acids are as follows: 2-hydroxypropanoic acid, $\Delta H_f = -694 \text{ kJ mol}^{-1}$; ethanoic acid, $\Delta H_f = -490 \text{ kJ mol}^{-1}$. Use the Data Sheets to find the other information you need.)

c i Write an equation for the complete oxidation of 2-hydroxypropanoic acid by oxygen to produce carbon dioxide and water.

ii Calculate the enthalpy change for the reaction in **c, i**.

d Use your calculations to explain which is more efficient: the aerobic respiration or anaerobic respiration of 2-hydroxypropanoic acid.

Absorbing the atmosphere

The ability of the oceans to withstand external changes has been essential for the unbroken evolution of life. For example, their pH has remained close to 8 for millions of years. Why were the oceans not very much more acidic when the atmosphere contained 35% CO_2 – 1000 times its present level?

One reason is that a solution of carbon dioxide in water is a **weak acid**. A weak acid reacts *incompletely* with water. If we represent the acid by the formula HA, we can show the reaction with water by the equation

$$HA + H_2O \rightleftharpoons H_3O^+ + A^- \qquad \text{(reaction 7)}$$

H_3O^+ ions (called **oxonium ions**) make the solution acidic. The position of equilibrium is well over to the left-hand side. Therefore, only a *fraction* of the acid added to the water reacts to produce oxonium ions. So the solution is not as acidic as it could be if all the acid had reacted.

The dissolving of carbon dioxide in water is also an equilibrium process. This means that the concentration of dissolved carbon dioxide will always be in proportion to the concentration of carbon dioxide in the atmosphere. Some of the dissolved carbon dioxide reacts with the water. The *proportion* which reacts is *greatest* when the carbon dioxide concentration is *low*; the equilibrium in reaction 7 then lies to the right-hand side because of the large excess of water in the dilute solution.

So the weak acid nature of carbon dioxide regulates the acidity of its solutions – only a small proportion reacts when carbon dioxide is abundant; most of it reacts when carbon dioxide is scarce.

Chemical Ideas 8.2 tells you more about solutions of weak acids.

You can compare some of the properties of strong and weak acids in **Activity O4.2**.

Keeping things steady

But the oceans are even more effective at controlling pH than this. They are an example of a **buffer solution** – a solution which remains within a narrow range of pH despite the addition of acid or alkali. This explains why the very much higher levels of carbon dioxide in the early years of the oceans did not lead to a significantly more acidic solution.

At this point it would help to read **Chemical Ideas 8.3** which will introduce you to the theory of buffer solutions. You may already have encountered buffer solutions in the **Colour by Design** storyline, Section **CD7** and in the **Aspects of Agriculture** storyline, Section **AA2** and in **Activity AA2.6**.

You can investigate some buffer solutions in **Activity O4.3**.

The commonest type of buffer solution is made up from a weak acid and one of its salts. The weak acid acts as a reservoir of H_3O^+ ions. These can react with any OH^- ions which are added and so prevent the solution becoming more alkaline. The anions from the salt act as bases. They can 'soak up' additions of H_3O^+ ions and keep the solution from becoming acidic.

If we represent the weak acid by HA and the anions in the salt by A^-, simple buffers rely on the shifting back and forth of the equilibrium

$$HA(aq) \rightleftharpoons H^+(aq) + A^-(aq)$$

(The role of water as a reactant has been omitted to keep the process clearer, and H_3O^+ ions have been replaced by the simpler formula, H^+.)

Buffering in the oceans looks at first sight to be much more complicated because four equilibria are involved. These are described by reactions 8, 9, 3 and 5 below. But if we focus on the dominant process – the production of hydrogencarbonate ions from dissolved carbon dioxide – the buffering action isn't very different from the one described already for a mixture of HA and A^- ions. To make things easier, we can regard dissolved carbon dioxide as equivalent to a weak acid with a formula H_2CO_3. It's as if the reaction

$$CO_2(aq) + H_2O(l) \rightarrow H_2CO_3(aq)$$

had occurred. Some people use the name 'carbonic acid' to describe a solution of carbon dioxide.

So, let's see how the process in reaction 8 can act to buffer the oceans

$$H_2CO_3(aq) \rightleftharpoons H^+(aq) + HCO_3^-(aq) \qquad \text{(reaction 8)}$$

Since H_2CO_3 is a weak acid, only a small fraction of it will react to form ions. There is therefore plenty of H_2CO_3 left to cancel out any effect which might otherwise make the oceans alkaline. What makes the oceans particularly effective is that a second reaction

$$CO_2(g) + H_2O(l) \rightleftharpoons H_2CO_3(aq) \qquad \text{(reaction 9)}$$

can be called upon to supply even more weak acid if it is needed. The carbon dioxide and water in the ocean/atmosphere system are therefore the ultimate sources of the weak acid which provides the ocean buffering.

What happens when changes occur which should make the oceans more acidic? Carbonic acid is a weak acid, so there are some HCO_3^- ions in solution to neutralise the influx of H^+ ions. There are also HCO_3^- ions which flow into the sea in the form of material dissolved in river water. But there are two other reactions which can provide an almost limitless supply of hydrogencarbonate ions. These are reactions 3 and 5 from pages 244 and 245:

$$HCO_3^-(aq) \rightleftharpoons H^+(aq) + CO_3^{2-}(aq) \qquad \text{(reaction 3)}$$
$$CaCO_3(s) \rightleftharpoons Ca^{2+}(aq) + CO_3^{2-}(aq) \qquad \text{(reaction 5)}$$

Figure 38 River waters provide a constant supply of HCO_3^- ions to the oceans from the weathering of limestone rocks

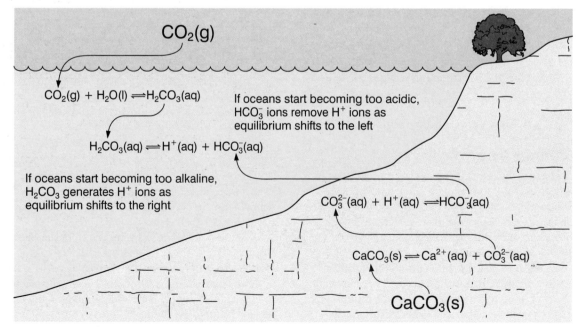

$$CO_2(g)$$

$$CO_2(g) + H_2O(l) \rightleftharpoons H_2CO_3(aq)$$

If oceans start becoming too acidic, HCO_3^- ions remove H^+ ions as equilibrium shifts to the left

$$H_2CO_3(aq) \rightleftharpoons H^+(aq) + HCO_3^-(aq)$$

If oceans start becoming too alkaline, H_2CO_3 generates H^+ ions as equilibrium shifts to the right

$$CO_3^{2-}(aq) + H^+(aq) \rightleftharpoons HCO_3^-(aq)$$

$$CaCO_3(s) \rightleftharpoons Ca^{2+}(aq) + CO_3^{2-}(aq)$$

$$CaCO_3(s)$$

Figure 39 The buffering action in the oceans

A rising concentration of H^+ ions will disturb the equilibrium in reaction 3. Carbonate ions will react with H^+ ions to restore the balance. Aqueous carbonate ions will then be replenished by dissolving of calcium carbonate in reaction 5. Reaction 3 is like a trigger – as soon as the concentration of H^+ rises, the reaction sets off the dissolving of calcium carbonate. The shells, chalk and limestone in the sea are therefore the reservoir of the anions needed for buffering.

It's a very neat situation. Instead of having the acid and anions permanently in solution (as happens in a simple buffer), the oceans keep them out of the way – in the atmosphere and rocks – until they are needed. The buffering action in the oceans is summarised in Figure 39.

What would happen if the carbon dioxide in the atmosphere rose to the high level of several billion years ago? Solid calcium carbonate would dissolve to produce the carbonate and hydrogencarbonate ions needed to remove the extra H^+ ions. The equilibrium constants are such that few CO_3^{2-} ions would remain. Most of the carbon would be in the form of HCO_3^- and dissolved CO_2. The sea would be like a mixture of Perrier water and bicarbonate of soda; the shells and white cliffs would disappear!

Limestone deposits could not form while the atmosphere contained 35% CO_2. The earliest sedimentary rocks are *silicaceous* (they consist predominantly of silicon dioxide). The first significant calcium carbonate deposits formed only about 2 billion years ago, over halfway through the Earth's lifetime. Much of the atmospheric carbon dioxide had been used up by then – so much so that its greenhouse effect had diminished and a major ice age had set in.

Figure 40 The three states of water: icebergs off the coast of Greenland

The carbon dioxide/calcium carbonate system is a fast acting buffer. In the longer term, ion exchange between H^+ ions in the water and Na^+ or K^+ ions in clay sediments provides another very powerful pH control mechanism.

This process can only take place at the bottom of the ocean where sea-water and sediment are in contact. Deep ocean water circulates slowly, perhaps taking 1000 years to complete one cycle. The ion-exchange buffer may be important over millions of years, but in the surface water and throughout the oceans on a shorter time scale it is the carbon dioxide/calcium carbonate system which keeps the pH of the ocean stable.

05 *Summary*

This unit has given you a glimpse of just a few of the processes going on in the oceans. The oceans provide a giant reservoir in the cycling of materials and energy around the Earth.

Some of these materials are useful and can be economically extracted. Others, like carbon dioxide, exert a profound influence on the Earth's climate. Life has evolved in the oceans, and these materials have become inextricably linked to the life-cycles of many creatures. Buffering in the oceans, and in the bloodstreams of marine animals, is largely controlled by chemical reactions involving carbon dioxide. But exactly the same systems are found in creatures on land, even humans.

The oceans play a major role in absorbing and redistributing the energy the Earth receives from the Sun. That they do this so effectively is due to the unique properties of water itself.

The oceans are very big. Finding out the details of processes like these can be difficult and slow, and accurate information is hard to obtain.

This unit dealt with the oceans; in a earlier unit you learned about the atmosphere. You may also be learning about plants and animals in other courses. One of the big challenges scientists face is to understand how human activities are likely to affect the global environment. What is becoming clear is that global conditions are determined by the way in which the oceans, the atmosphere, the land and life interact with one another. This is an enormous task involving all branches of science. As this unit has shown, chemistry has a major part to play.

Activity 05 will help you to summarise what you have learned in this unit.

MEDICINES BY DESIGN

Why a unit on MEDICINES BY DESIGN?

This unit describes some examples from an area of chemistry which has had a major influence on the quality of our lives. As we have increased our understanding of the way in which pharmacologically active compounds interact with the human body, so chemists have been able to design medicines which are more effective and have fewer undesirable side-effects than earlier remedies.

The unit begins with a look at ethanol, not a medicine but perhaps the most widely consumed pharmacologically active compound in Western society. It then moves on to look at how two widely different disorders – asthma and heart trouble – can be treated by medicines which selectively activate or deactivate one of the body's nervous pathways. The unit concludes with a study of two medicines which inhibit enzyme action: captopril inhibits the human angiotensin converting enzyme and penicillin inhibits a bacterial enzyme.

The chemical reactions which are used to synthesise and modify medicines are drawn almost exclusively from the field of organic chemistry, and this unit also serves as a good way of pulling together the organic reactions which you have encountered throughout the course.

Overview of chemical principles

In this unit you will learn more about …

ideas introduced in earlier units in this course

- pharmaceutical chemistry (**What's in a Medicine?**)
- the importance of molecular shape and molecular recognition in biological activity (**Engineering Proteins**)
- proteins and enzymes (**Engineering Proteins**)
- the interpretation of spectroscopic and g.l.c. data (**What's in a Medicine?** and **Colour by Design**)
- reactions of organic functional groups (several units)
- isomerism (**Developing Fuels**, **The Polymer Revolution**, **Engineering Proteins** and **Colour by Design**)

… as well as learning new ideas about

- the interaction of biologically active molecules with receptor sites
- alcohols
- aldehydes and ketones
- the synthesis of organic compounds.

MD
MEDICINES BY DESIGN

MD1 *Alcohol in the body*

Have you ever taken a *xenobiotic*? No? Well, if you hadn't you wouldn't be alive. Xenobiotics are substances which the body doesn't contain but which can affect it. They can be divided into three types:

- **foods** provide the molecules which give us energy and keep our bodies well maintained
- **drugs** alter the biochemical processes in our bodies, for example changing the way we feel and behave – drugs which lead to an improvement in health are called **medicines**
- **poisons** severely damage our biochemical processes and cause a deterioration in health or even death.

You must have eaten foods, and you would be very unusual if you had not taken at least one medicine. You would have been unwise if you had taken non-medicinal drugs or poisons.

But some substances can behave in more than one way. Their effect depends on the quantity you take and on your state of health. Ethanol, is an example; it is a source of energy, but it also affects behaviour, and, in excess, can cause liver damage and even death.

In this unit you will find out how chemists design medicines to perform specific tasks in the body. This involves making new compounds and modifying existing ones. To do this they need to have a 'tool-kit' of reactions which can be used to convert one compound into another. You can read about using organic reactions in this way in **Chemical Ideas 14.1** and **14.2**.

Alcohol as a food

Some people celebrate Christmas with a Christmas pudding ablaze with burning brandy. This is a reminder that energy is released when ethanol reacts with oxygen to produce carbon dioxide and water. Oxidation of ethanol in the body is more controlled and less complete, but it is still highly exothermic.

At the present time, alcoholic drinks contribute about 6% of the total dietary energy intake of people in the UK. In the 17th century they accounted for almost 25% – for children as well as adults. The common drink at that time was beer.

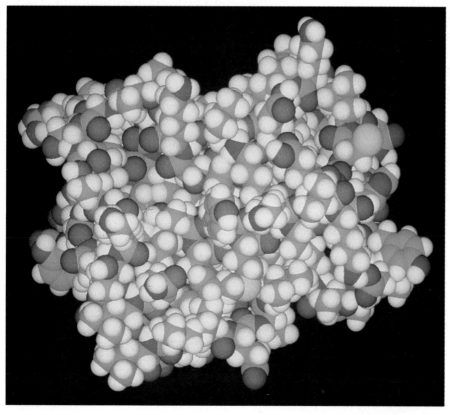

Figure 1 Molecular graphics systems are vital in the design of modern medicines. This shows a computer-generated graphic of interleukin-2, used in the treatment of some cancers

Alcoholic drinks also contain other nutrients, as shown in Table 1.

Year	Nutrient/mg per person per day				
	Iron	Calcium	Magnesium	Riboflavin	Nicotinic acid
1691	0.27	150	133	0.83	15.7
1741	0.20	110	97	0.61	11.5
1791	0.14	67	59	0.37	7.0
1841	0.09	47	41	0.26	4.9
1891	0.12	60	54	0.38	6.3
1941	0.05	27	24	0.15	2.8
1971	0.10	29	25	0.10	1.5
Recommended intake of nutrients for 18–35 year old	10.0	500	300	1.70	18.0

Table 1 The contribution of alcoholic drinks to English diets

Figure 2 It is very unwise to drink any alcohol at all before driving

ASSIGNMENT I

(You will need to refer to the Data Sheets to answer parts of this assignment.)

When ethanol burns, carbon dioxide and water are produced. Under more controlled conditions such as in bacterial metabolism, ethanol can be converted into ethanoic acid.

a Write a balanced equation for the complete combustion of ethanol. Look up the standard enthalpy change for this process.

b i Write a balanced equation for the oxidation of ethanol by oxygen to produce ethanoic acid and water.

  ii Using Hess's law and appropriate enthalpy changes of formation, calculate the standard enthalpy change for this reaction.

c Metabolism of ethanol in the human body releases about 770 kJ per mole of ethanol. Suggest what might be likely products of ethanol oxidation in human metabolism.

d Some ethanol is not metabolised. Suggest two ways in which ethanol can be lost from the human body.

Alcohol as a drug

Alcoholic drinks make many people feel better for a short time. They help them to relax or cope with stress. Alcohol can make them feel happier and relieve tension, anxiety or boredom. These effects are all outcomes of a single aspect of the behaviour of ethanol molecules in the body – they depress the activity of the central nervous system. This is explained in more detail in Section **MD2**.

This depression of nervous activity has important short-term effects. Drinking alcohol reduces vigilance, slows reaction times and impairs our judgement. It is largely because of these effects that so many laws have been introduced to control the use of alcohol. This is particularly important in relation to driving motor vehicles.

Blood alcohol concentration (BAC) is closely related to the extent of the effects of alcoholic drinks. It is usually defined as

BAC = mg of ethanol per 100 cm³ of blood

The quantity of alcohol needed to produce a particular BAC varies with age, sex, body weight, how quickly you drink and several other factors. The concentration of ethanol in the blood rises for some time after taking a drink, as the alcohol is absorbed. Then it slowly decreases as the ethanol is excreted or metabolised.

A 'unit' of alcohol is a convenient measure of how much ethanol is contained in a drink. It is an approximate measure, roughly equivalent to

- a half-pint of beer or lager
- a glass of wine
- a single measure of spirits.

Table 2 gives an idea of the quantities of alcohol needed to produce a BAC of 80 in a man of average weight. For women, the quantities would need to be reduced by about 30%.

Table 2 An estimate of the alcohol consumption needed to produce a BAC of 80 (the legal limit for driving) in a man of average weight

Number of units of alcohol	Time taken drinking/hours
4.0	1
5.0	2
6.0	3
6.5	4
7.5	5

ASSIGNMENT 2

The tables below show the results of a survey of the drinking habits of 933 men and 1063 women during 1 week. The figures are divided into age groups and show the percentage of the men or women in each age group who drank a particular number of units of alcohol during the week. The final column shows the percentages of the whole sample which fall into each alcohol band.

NB: These figures are not intended to give any indication of safe levels of drinking. Adverse symptoms are thought to arise at levels of about 18 units per week for men and 12 units per week for women.

a For each sex, which age range indulges in the heaviest drinking?

b What differences do you notice between the patterns of drinking of women and men?

To put the extent of our drinking into perspective, it has been estimated that an average of 18 units per week were drunk in 1984 by people over 16 years of age. This corresponds to an annual expenditure of £11.4 billion. This exceeds the money they spent on clothes and cars (each about £10 billion) over the same period.

Women

Units per week	Age range/years						%
	18–24	25–34	35–44	45–54	55–64	65+	
0	22	31	34	41	52	64	42
1–20	68	66	62	55	47	35	55
21–50	6	3	3	4	1	1	3
over 50	4	0	1	0	0	0	0

Men

Units per week	Age range/years						%
	18–24	25–34	35–44	45–54	55–64	65+	
0	7	12	17	23	32	46	24
1–20	44	54	52	52	49	43	49
21–50	36	26	24	20	15	10	21
over 50	13	8	7	5	4	1	6

"Excuse me Sir, …"

At present, 80 mg per 100 cm³ of blood is the legal limit for BAC for driving a motor vehicle. When a motorist who is suspected of drink-driving is stopped by the police, a roadside blood test is impractical. A quick BAC estimate is needed in order to decide whether or not to take things further.

Ethanol (the alcohol present in drinks) is almost the only commonly used drug which is sufficiently volatile to pass from the blood to the air in the lungs. This distribution

$$C_2H_5OH(blood) \rightleftharpoons C_2H_5OH(g)$$

is an example of chemical equilibrium, and it is governed by an equilibrium constant (K_c) which has a fixed value at a particular temperature.

In the human body, K_c for this process is 4.35×10^{-4}. A measurement of the ethanol concentration in the breath therefore gives an indication of the BAC.

The best known, and earliest successful, method of detection – the 'breathalyser' – is based on a familiar chemical reaction. Orange crystals of potassium dichromate(VI) turn green when they oxidise ethanol to ethanal and ethanoic acid. The extent to which the crystals in a tube change colour is a measure of the BAC.

Oxidation of ethanol is a redox reaction and involves electron transfer. An alternative way of finding the ethanol concentration is therefore to measure the voltage of a cell which incorporates the reaction. The 'Lion Alcolmeter' is a cell designed to do just this. Phosphoric acid is held in a porous plastic material between two electrodes. Oxygen is reduced to water at one electrode and ethanol is oxidised to ethanoic acid at the other. 'Breathalyser' tubes and 'Alcolmeters' are used by police forces in the UK and around the world.

The science behind the 'Alcolmeter' is fairly straightforward, but the technology needed to develop it is more challenging. For example, the instrument must be

- small enough for hand-held use beside the road
- rugged
- safe and easy to use
- reusable with a short turn-round time
- reliable – the consequences of the test can be serious for the person being tested.

Then it has to be marketed and sold.

Paul's story

Dr Paul Williams, who worked on the development of the 'Alcolmeter' and is now International Marketing Director for Lion Laboratories plc, Barry, South Glamorgan, describes his career since doing A-level Chemistry.

Figure 3 Paul Williams and the 'Lion Alcolmeter'

"After A-levels, and a degree in Applied Chemistry, I realised I was interested in forensic chemistry. Luckily for me, a research post was advertised on a project to develop an electrochemically based instrument for the breath alcohol testing of drink-driving suspects.

I got the job, gained an MSc and PhD while doing it, and at the end of 4 years had developed the 'Alcolmeter' instruments. During this time, I decided that the business life was for me – particularly marketing, where I could use my scientific training to talk to potential customers on their own level.

So, having developed the 'Alcolmeter', I went out and sold it! There is no better way to learn the trade than to hawk your wares from a company car for a year or so. That set me up to be made Marketing Director for Lion Laboratories.

Instead of selling, I was now formulating company marketing policy, and getting to talk to 'high fliers' in the alcohol field around the world. The Vauxhall gave way to a Boeing, and home became very often a room in the local Sheraton, Hilton or Intercon.

The opportunity to travel to South America, Africa and the Middle East annually, the USA at least three times a year and – of course – Europe, meeting police officers and forensic scientists, being able to talk with them and, in many cases, to educate and inform them, are features of the job which I enjoy and find intellectually satisfying.

Providing expert testimony in court is also a regular part of the job – daunting at first, but easier as it goes along.

I think my training did more to help me in my career than simply to provide the chemistry I needed. It improved my memory, and taught me to analyse and evaluate situations logically – which is very useful in the modern commercial world. If you are thinking of 'going commercial' it is probably best not to become too specialised. Keep a broad subject base and make sure your knowledge is practical – that way it is capable of being applied to the commercial job in hand."

ASSIGNMENT 3

a Write down the expression for K_c for the distribution of ethanol between the blood and the air in the lungs.

b The position of this equilibrium depends on temperature and pressure. These conditions will be the same in all drink-drive suspects. What values will they have?

c Under these conditions, in the human body, K_c for this process has a value of 4.35×10^{-4}. What will be the *breath alcohol concentration* (in mg of ethanol per 100 cm^3 of air) which corresponds to the 80 mg per 100 cm^3 legal limit for BAC?

ASSIGNMENT 4

a Write half-equations for the reactions at each electrode of an 'Alcolmeter'. (Remember to include water molecules and/or hydrogen ions where necessary to balance these equations.)

b State which electrode (positive or negative) each of your half-reactions will occur at.

You can read about alcohols and some of their reactions in **Chemical Ideas 13.2** and **13.4**. The reactions of alcohols are summarised in **Chemical Ideas 14.2**.

Activity MD1.1 investigates the oxidation of alcohols, and gives you a chance to check the reliability of some 'breathalyser' tubes.

Back at the station .....

The techniques used for roadside breath tests are not accurate enough or reliable enough to be used as evidence in court cases. If the roadside test indicates a high level of alcohol, the driver will be taken to a police station for a more accurate determination of BAC.

The method which has been in longest use involves collecting a blood or urine sample from the suspect and sending it away to a forensic science laboratory for analysis by **gas–liquid chromatography (g.l.c.)**.

A more recent method for accurate BAC measurement, which can be entirely performed at the police station, analyses the ethanol in the suspect's breath by absorption of infra-red radiation. This method does not require a doctor to take a blood sample, and provides the police and the suspect with an immediate result.

Gas-liquid chromatography is described in **Chemical Ideas 7.6.**

You can read about infra-red absorption spectroscopy in **Chemical Ideas 6.7.**

In **Activity MD1.2** you can find out more about the application of g.l.c. to blood alcohol analysis.

ASSIGNMENT 5

The infra-red absorption spectrum of ethanol is shown in Figure 4.

The ethanol concentration in the breath of a drink-drive suspect can be determined by measuring the intensity of one of the absorption bands in the ethanol spectrum. The absorption at about $3000\ cm^{-1}$ is used in the 'Lion Intoximeter 3000'.

The suspect's breath will also contain water vapour. This gives rise to strong infra-red absorptions centred at about $3800\ cm^{-1}$, $3600\ cm^{-1}$, $3200\ cm^{-1}$ and $1600\ cm^{-1}$.

a Compare the positions of the water absorptions in an infra-red spectrum with those of ethanol shown in Figure 4. Suggest why the $3000\ cm^{-1}$ band is chosen for ethanol detection.

b Explain why ethanol and water both give rise to infra-red bands in the same region of the spectrum.

c Look at the table of characteristic infra-red absorptions in the Data Sheets. What bond is responsible for the $3000\ cm^{-1}$ absorption in ethanol?

d People who suffer from diabetes often produce propanone vapour in their breath. Suggest why infra-red breath testing of a person with diabetes might appear to give a positive result even though the person had not been drinking alcohol.

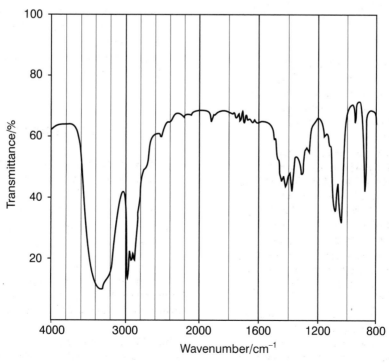

Figure 4 Infra-red absorption spectrum of ethanol

MD2 *The drug action of ethanol*

A touch of nerves

You need to know something about the human nervous system in order to understand how ethanol acts as a drug. The nervous system consists of two parts: the *central nervous system* (the brain and spinal cord) and the *peripheral nervous system* (all other nervous tissues which connect with the organs of the body). A simple overall picture of the nervous system is shown in Figure 5.

A more detailed look at the nervous system shows it to be immensely complex. It consists of thousands of millions of nerve cells or *neurons*. These are linked together at connections called *synapses*, as shown in Figure 6.

These interconnecting neurons provide an important system of communication in the body. This is what happens. An electrical signal called a **nerve impulse** travels along the axon until it reaches a nerve ending. There, the electrical signal causes release of small messenger molecules, called **neurotransmitters**, which carry the message across the synapse (see Figure 7). Neurotransmitters, released from nerve endings, cross the tiny gap to **receptors** on the dendrites of another neuron. Neurotransmitters can either excite or inhibit the electrical behaviour of the next nerve cell.

Central nervous system

Peripheral sensory nerves

Peripheral motor nerves

Detectors

Effectors

Stimulus

Response

Changes in the body's environment are detected and signals pass back to the central nervous system along sensory nerves

Effectors receive signals from the central nervous system via motor nerves and respond in the appropriate way

Figure 5 The essential parts of the nervous system

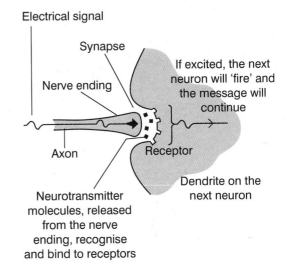

Figure 7 Signals pass from neuron to neuron by neurotransmitters released at the synapse

Figure 6 Connections between nerve cells

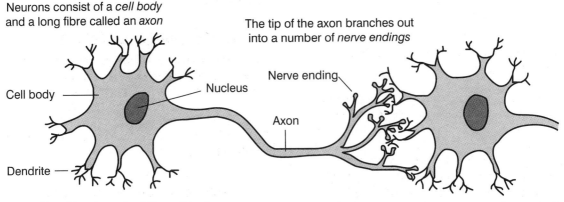

Neurons consist of a *cell body* and a long fibre called an *axon*

The tip of the axon branches out into a number of *nerve endings*

Nerve ending

Cell body

Nucleus

Axon

Dendrite

Dendrites branch off the cell body

Nerve endings on one neuron make contact with dendrites on another neuron at *synapses*

Some neuropharmacology

The brain has to process all the information coming in from the sensory nerves, and send out action signals to the appropriate motor nerves. There have to be lots of interconnections between neurons in the brain. At any instant some of these will need exciting (switching on so that they fire nerve impulses more rapidly) and some will need inhibiting (switching off so that they fire nerve impulses more slowly).

Switching on and switching off nerve cells is achieved by movements of ions in and out of the cells. Three ions are important: K^+, Na^+ and Cl^-. There are high concentrations of Na^+ and Cl^- *outside* the nerve cell, but the K^+ concentration is higher *inside*.

When the nerve is at rest, the nerve cell membrane is closed to Na^+ and Cl^- ions, so they can't get in. But K^+ ions can move freely in and out of the nerve through channels in the cell membrane.

Look at Figure 8. Some potassium ions will diffuse out of the cell to try to even out the K^+ concentration, but this leaves behind an excess of negatively charged groups which are attached to the inside of the cell. So the inside of the nerve cell becomes negatively charged. This makes it harder for the positively charged potassium ions to leave. An equilibrium is established in which the cell is at a negative potential of about 60 mV relative to the fluid outside. This is shown in Figure 9.

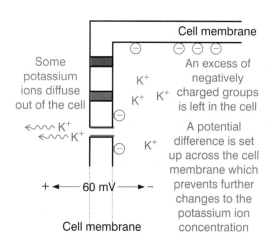

Figure 9 *The establishment of a potential difference across the cell membrane of a nerve cell which is at rest*

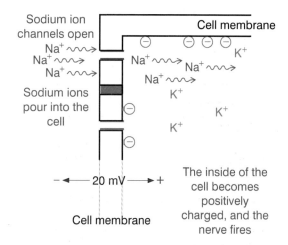

Figure 10 *A nerve cell 'fires' when sodium ions flood in through open sodium ion channels*

For nerve cells to 'fire' repeatedly, sodium ions are constantly being 'pumped out' of the cell and potassium ions replaced. This involves moving ions against their natural concentration gradients and uses a lot of energy.

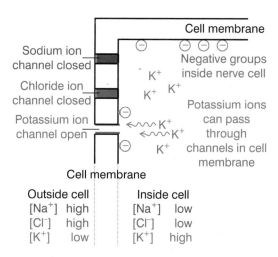

Figure 8 *The processes occurring at a dendrite of a nerve which is at rest*

This −60 mV is the cell's *resting potential*. The cell 'fires' when neurotransmitters, arriving from an adjacent neuron, cause the sodium ion channels to open. Large numbers of Na^+ ions then flood into the nerve cell. The inside of the cell becomes more positive, possibly to as much as +20 mV (Figure 10). This wave of positive charge is carried along the axon by further movements of Na^+ and K^+ ions, and constitutes the nerve impulse.

Nervous inhibition and GABA

The nerve cell is switched off – it is harder to fire – when its potential is made more negative. This is achieved by opening the chloride ion channels and allowing Cl^- ions to diffuse into the cell.

The compound *GABA* (gamma-aminobutanoic acid) is the neurotransmitter which switches off, or inhibits, nerve cell action in the brain.

$$H_2N-\overset{\gamma}{C}H_2-\overset{\beta}{C}H_2-\overset{\alpha}{C}H_2-COOH$$

γ–aminobutanoic acid (GABA)

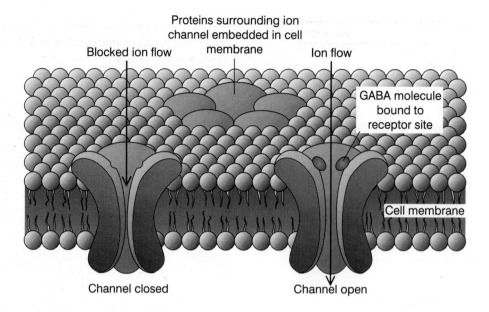

Figure 11 *Chloride ion channels in a cell membrane*

Each ion channel is surrounded by protein molecules embedded in the cell membrane (see Figure 11).

GABA molecules bind to receptor sites on these protein molecules, causing the protein to change shape and open the chloride ion channel. A simple illustration of how this could happen is shown in Figure 12.

Figure 13 illustrates what happens once GABA has bound to the nerve cell, causing the chloride ion channels to open.

Scientists think that one of the effects of drinking alcohol is that ethanol molecules bind to nerve cells near to the GABA receptors. This enhances the effect that GABA has.

Neurons are more inhibited if ethanol is present and the action of the nervous system is depressed. Other molecules have a similar effect and some are used medically to treat anxiety, eg benzodiazepines such as *Valium*.

It is very dangerous to drink alcohol if you are taking certain medicines. The benzodiazepines are an example. When ethanol and benzodiazepine molecules are bound to a nerve cell, the effect can be very much greater than when only one of them is present. The inhibition of the nervous system can be severe enough to be fatal.

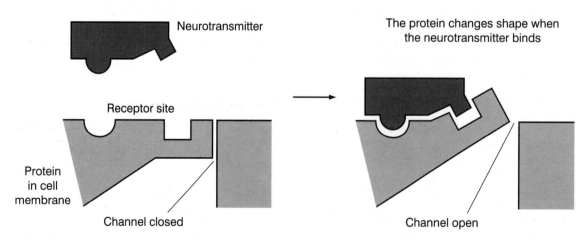

Figure 12 *An illustration of how binding to a receptor can open channels in a cell membrane*

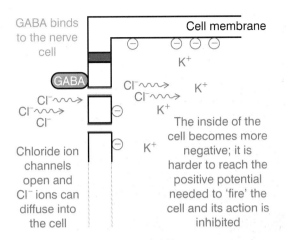

Figure 13 Nerve cell inhibition by GABA

ASSIGNMENT 6

Look carefully at the structure of the neurotransmitter GABA, γ-aminobutanoic acid. It is a γ-amino acid.

a In the body, GABA exists as a zwitterion. Draw out the structure of the zwitterion. (You may need to look back to **Chemical Ideas 13.7** to answer this question.)

b Unlike most α-amino acids, GABA does not exist in D and L isomeric forms. Explain why this is so.

MD3 *Medicines that send messages to nerves*

Discovering a new medicine

When they start out to design a new medicine, scientists focus their attention on two areas:

- developing a biological understanding of the disease or condition they want to cure
- finding a 'lead compound' (not a compound of the element lead, but a compound which provides a lead – shows some promise and gives some clues).

Sometimes, an idea for a lead compound comes from research into the chemical processes which go on in the body. As you have seen, scientists have some understanding of how the GABA neurotransmitter acts. In this section you will learn how our increased knowledge of another neurotransmitter, *noradrenaline*, has helped in the development of medicines to treat asthma and to combat heart disease.

Medicines have also been developed from lead compounds which are the active ingredients in traditional remedies. In **What's in a Medicine?** for

example, you learned how aspirin was developed from a natural remedy made from willow bark. In Section **MD4**, you can read about how studies of snake venom led to a medicine for treating high blood pressure.

Figure 14 Traditional medicines from plants can provide 'lead' compounds for new medicines

Some naturally occurring lead compounds have been discovered by accident. A classic example is the discovery of penicillin. You can learn more about this in Section **MD5**.

Finally, some medicines have been found from random screening – looking for activity in a very wide range of compounds, some of which might already be used medically to treat other things.

Despite the increasing success of medicine design based on scientific understanding of the chemical processes which go on in the body, only one in about 10 000 of the compounds which are synthesised survive today's rigorous testing procedures and become commercially available for medical use.

In **Activity MD3.1** you can use your knowledge of organic chemistry to build up a 'toolkit' of organic reactions.

You can then use these reactions in **Activity MD3.2** to plan the synthesis of some medicines.

Noradrenaline mimics

The noradrenaline molecule is the neurotransmitter in many of the synapses where nerves join organs in the body.

noradrenaline

Release of noradrenaline brings about a number of changes which give rise to the 'fight or fright syndrome' which you experience when you get scared. For example

- the heart rate is accelerated
- the bronchioles (airways in the lungs) become dilated (widened)
- sweating is increased.

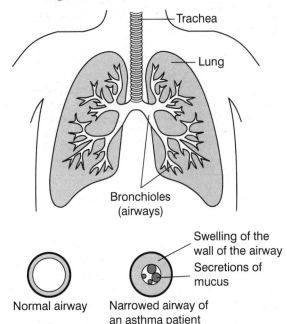

Figure 15 *Asthma patients become short of breath because of narrowing of the airways in the lungs*

About 5% of people suffer from *asthma*: a breathing difficulty which can be very disturbing and sometimes fatal. It is caused when the bronchioles narrow and become blocked with mucus (Figure 15). Noradrenaline brings about the opposite effect – *bronchodilation*. But it can't be used to treat asthma because of all its other effects – an extra dose of noradrenaline might cause a heart attack.

Noradrenaline has wide-ranging effects because it interacts with a number of receptors with very similar structures. Some of the receptors affect the airways and some the heart.

By making modifications to the noradrenaline structure, chemists have been able to design and synthesise molecules which interact more selectively with the receptors. The compound *isoprenaline* was used for many years. It relieves asthma without causing some of the other effects of noradrenaline. Unfortunately, it still affects the heart rate.

isoprenaline

In recent years, isoprenaline has been replaced by *salbutamol* which is even more selective and acts only by widening the bronchioles. It binds to receptors on the muscles of the airways, relaxing them and giving relief from breathing difficulties.

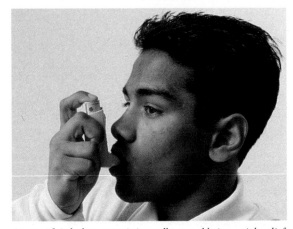

salbutamol

Neurotransmitters have to be reabsorbed by the nerve cells or changed into deactivated forms and detached from their receptors, otherwise their effect would go on forever. A medicine for treating asthma, however, needs to act for a long time. An advantage of salbutamol is that conversion of one of the phenol groups into a $—CH_2OH$ group slows down the rate at which it is metabolised, so its effects last longer than isoprenaline.

Figure 16 *Inhalers containing salbutamol bring quick relief in an asthma attack*

ASSIGNMENT 7

a Name three functional groups which are present in noradrenaline.

b In what way are
   i isoprenaline
   ii salbutamol

   different in structure from noradrenaline?

c How would you expect noradrenaline to react with the reagents listed below? Where possible, write structures for the reaction products.
   i $FeCl_3(aq)$
   ii $NaOH(aq)$
   iii $HCl(aq)$
   iv CH_3COCl.

d For each of the reagents in c, state whether or not you would expect salbutamol to react in a similar way to noradrenaline.

ASSIGNMENT 8

a The salbutamol molecule is chiral. Draw out the structure of the group of atoms which is responsible for the chirality.

b The enantiomers of salbutamol differ in their pharmacological activity. One isomer is 68 times more active than the other. Suggest a reason for the difference.

Activity MD3.3 looks in more detail at some of the chemistry and costs involved in producing salbutamol.

Agonists and antagonists

The structures of noradrenaline, isoprenaline and salbutamol have a common feature. Their activity depends on the presence of the structural fragment

This is the group of atoms which is involved in binding to the receptor. It's a case of **molecular recognition**. The structural fragment fits precisely into the shape of the receptor, and functional groups on both are correctly positioned to interact.

Molecular recognition is introduced in **Engineering Proteins**, where its importance with regard to DNA, RNA, protein synthesis and enzyme activity is discussed.

The structural fragment shown above is an example of a **pharmacophore** – a group of atoms which confers pharmacological activity on a molecule. The successful medicine, salbutamol, was made by modifying the pharmacophore with a phenolic OH group and a 2-methylpropyl substituent on the nitrogen atom to make it more selective as a bronchodilator.

Salbutamol is an example of an **agonist** – a molecule which behaves like the body's natural substance in the way it binds to a receptor and produces a response.

In some people the natural response may be a bad thing: for example, an increased heart rate can be dangerous for someone with a heart disorder. What these people need are molecules which compete with the natural, active compound for receptor sites but which have no effect when they are bound.

Molecules like this are called **antagonists**. An antagonist has a structure which is sufficiently like the pharmacophore to allow it to fit the receptor, but it produces no effect because it does not actually possess the pharmacophore. In the case of noradrenaline, if receptors are blocked by antagonists, the neurotransmitter cannot get to the receptor sites to stimulate an increase in heart rate (see Figure 17).

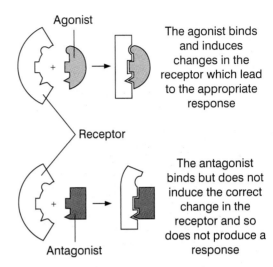

The agonist binds and induces changes in the receptor which lead to the appropriate response

The antagonist binds but does not induce the correct change in the receptor and so does not produce a response

Figure 17 An illustration of an agonist and an antagonist binding to receptors

Propranolol is a very successful noradrenaline antagonist. It binds to, and blocks, the type of noradrenaline receptors which control the heart muscles. These are called β_1-receptors, so drugs like propranolol are known as *β-blockers*. They are used by people with heart disorders to keep their hearts calm and avoid further trouble.

propranolol

(Since its development as a β-blocker, propranolol has found another use as a successful treatment for migraine. Its action here is not well understood, but it is not related to heart disorders.)

Figure 18 Inderal tablets contain the β-blocker, propranolol

ASSIGNMENT 9

a The structure of the propranolol molecule differs in two important ways from the noradrenaline agonists like salbutamol. These differences prevent propranolol triggering an electrical impulse when it binds to a receptor. What are the differences?

b The structures of three medicines are shown below. For each medicine state whether you would expect it to be a noradrenaline agonist, a noradrenaline antagonist, or show no effect related to noradrenaline. Briefly describe the reasons for your decisions.

i

ii

iii

angiotensin I. The enzyme which brings about the loss of the two amino acids in this conversion is called *angiotensin converting enzyme (ACE)*:

$$\text{angiotensin I} \xrightarrow{\text{ACE}} \text{angiotensin II} + \text{dipeptide}$$

An imbalance in the production of angiotensin II results in high blood pressure, so one method of treatment is to inhibit the enzyme which catalyses its formation. The medicine needs to be an *ACE inhibitor*. Captopril works in this way.

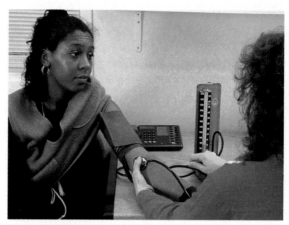

Figure 19 Measuring blood pressure helps to identify people who may be at risk of heart disease

Following the lead

The lead for the development of captopril was the discovery that the venom of the Brazilian Arrowhead Viper brought about its toxic effect by causing a fall in blood pressure. The venom is a complex mixture, but separation, analysis and further study of the components led to the identification of several small proteins which were powerful ACE inhibitors. Unfortunately, proteins are difficult to administer by mouth as medicines because they are readily broken down by digestive enzymes present in the stomach.

MD4 *Enzyme inhibitors as medicines*

Captopril – an ACE inhibitor

Receptors and enzymes are very similar. Both are proteins with precise structures designed to accommodate specific arrangements of atoms on another molecule such as a neurotransmitter or a substrate.

Just as antagonists are used to block receptors, so some medicines work by inhibiting the action of enzymes. A good example is *captopril* – which is widely used to treat high blood pressure (a condition called hypertension). Left untreated, this can lead to serious consequences such as a stroke or a heart attack.

A small protein built from eight amino acids is known to be a key factor in raising blood pressure. It is called *angiotensin II*. The body creates *angiotensin II* from an inactive 10-amino-acid protein called

Figure 20 The venom of the Brazilian Arrowhead Viper provided lead compounds for the development of medicines used to treat high blood pressure

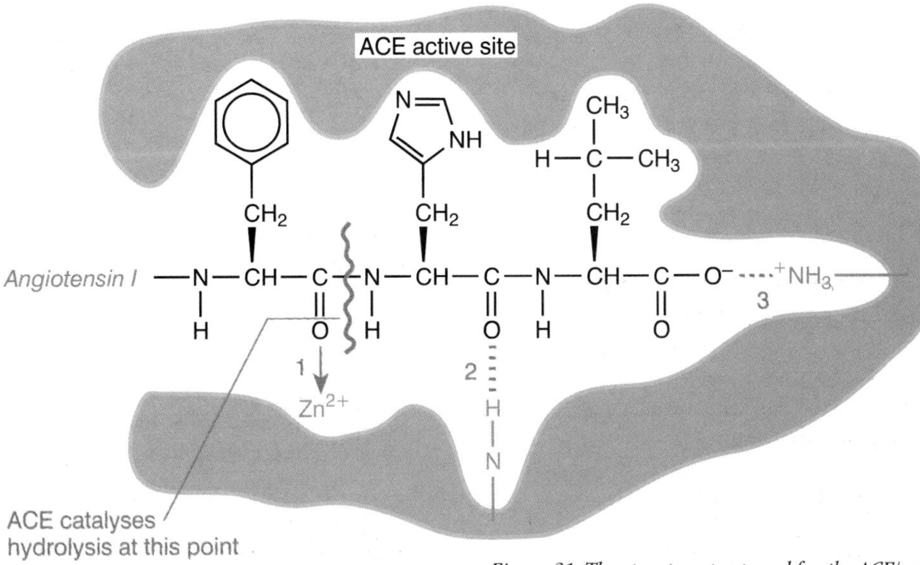

Figure 21 The structure proposed for the ACE/angiotensin I complex

The snake venom proteins could not therefore be used medically as ACE inhibitors, but their structures gave scientists clues about the enzyme's active site. They learned more by studying the way the enzyme changes angiotensin I into angiotensin II. From this they realised that ACE must be similar to another, better known, enzyme – *carboxypeptidase*.

Combination of these results led to a model in which the ACE enzyme binds to its substrate (angiotensin I) in three places by three different kinds of interaction:

1. a metal–ligand bond between a Zn^{2+} ion on the enzyme and an atom with a partial negative charge on the substrate
2. a hydrogen bond between an N–H group on the enzyme and a negatively charged atom on the substrate
3. an ionic interaction between a positively charged $-NH_3^+$ group on the enzyme and a negatively charged $-COO^-$ group at one end of the substrate.

These interactions (labelled 1, 2 and 3) between ACE and the three amino acid residues at the —COOH end of angiotensin I are illustrated in Figure 21. Notice too that the enzyme's active site has a precise shape which also fits other groups on the amino acid side chains.

It is essential for the action of ACE, and all enzymes, that the products are bound less strongly than the substrate. This ensures that the products will leave the enzyme and allow more substrate molecules to bind, thus continuing the reaction. In this case, angiotensin I (the substrate) is bound by three interactions, whereas angiotensin II (one of the products) is only bound by the metal–ligand bond (interaction 1 in Figure 21), and the dipeptide (the other product) is only held by the hydrogen bond and the ionic interaction (interactions 2 and 3 in Figure 21).

A successful ACE inhibitor needs to bind but not react, so it remains attached by all three interactions. The use of computer graphics to study the shape and charge density in the active site played a crucial role in the design of possible compounds.

In **Activity MD4** you can use a computer simulation to investigate the effect of different groups on the binding of substrate molecules to ACE. Although much simpler than the computer graphics used commercially in molecular design, the simulation clearly shows the power of this technique.

ASSIGNMENT 10

The primary structure of the angiotensin I substrate is:

Asp Arg Val Tyr Ile His Pro Phe His Leu

The part shown in Figure 21 is the Phe His Leu section at the —COOH end of the chain.

ACE catalyses hydrolysis at the position shown in Figure 21. Write down the primary structures of the two products of the hydrolysis.

Finding the best medicine

All the active proteins which were isolated from the snake venom had proline as the amino acid at the —COOH end of the chain. This was chosen as a good starting point for the development of an ACE inhibitor.

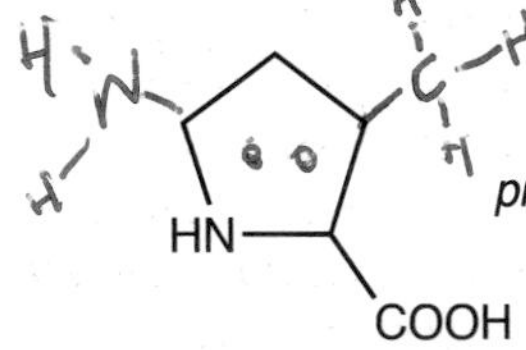

proline

Chemists set about synthesising hundreds of compounds with the general structure

R—C—N
||
O
COOH

each one with a different side chain. They were all capable of interacting at positions 2 and 3 with the ACE enzyme. The breakthrough came when it was discovered that derivatives which contained an —SH group in the right position to interact with the Zn^{2+} were particularly effective. Table 3 gives an indication of the effectiveness of three derivatives of this kind.

Derivative (Pro = proline residue)	Concentration needed to produce 50% inhibition of ACE activity/10^{-6} mol dm^{-3}
HS—CH$_2$—CH(CH$_3$)—CO—Pro	0.02
HS—CH$_2$—CH$_2$—CO—Pro	0.30
HS—CH$_2$—CH$_2$—CH$_2$—CO—Pro	9.70

Table 3 Effectiveness of various proline derivatives on ACE activity

Notice how the activity depends on the derivative's ability to fit precisely into the enzyme's active site. Small changes to the structure can lead to big changes in activity. In fact, very small changes may be significant. The orientation of the —CH$_3$ group in HS—CH$_2$—CH(CH$_3$)—CO—Pro is particularly important: the compound shown next, which is captopril, is much more active than the isomer with the —CH$_3$ group in the other configuration.

captopril

HS—CH$_2$—C—C—N
CH$_3$ (up)
H O
COOH

Figure 22 shows how captopril is thought to bind to ACE.

Captopril is not a protein and is not broken down by digestive enzymes when it is taken orally. The peptide link which is broken in angiotensin I is not present in captopril. At the corresponding position on the captopril–enzyme complex, there are S–C and C–C bonds which cannot be hydrolysed.

The development of captopril is an excellent example of the logical design of a molecule. The medicine passed the testing procedures and was launched in 1980. It is now in widespread use.

ASSIGNMENT II

Captopril is a much more active ACE inhibitor than its isomer with the methyl group in the other configuration.

a Discuss what you understand this statement to mean.

b Draw a structure for the other isomer of captopril.

c What other group in captopril is like the methyl group in being able to exist in another configuration in another isomer?

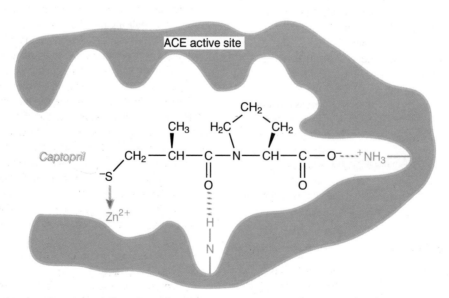

Figure 22 Captopril in the ACE active site (the —SH and —COOH groups on captopril are ionised in the form of the compound which interacts with the enzyme)

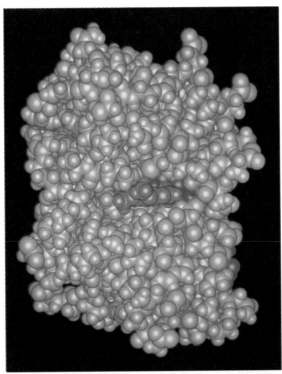

Figure 23 A computer-generated graphic of trimethoprim (in red), a medicine used to treat urinary infections, bound to the active site of an enzyme called dihydrofolate reductase (in green)

Types of bacteria

Bacteria are classified according to the shape of their cells and the way the cells organise themselves into colonies.

Staphylococcus

Streptococcus

Bacillus

MD5 *Targetting bacteria*

Some medicines inhibit the action of enzymes present in bacteria. As a result, the bacterial cells do not grow and divide, and infection is prevented. Of these medicines, *penicillin* is probably the most widely prescribed.

Penicillin first became available during the Second World War. Its use saved the lives of many injured people, who would otherwise have died from bacterial infections. It was hailed as a 'miracle cure'.

The discovery of penicillin occurred as a result of a chance observation. It proved to be an extremely valuable lead compound, and set the scene for the development of a vast range of **antibiotics**. These are compounds, obtained from micro-organisms, which selectively destroy disease-causing bacteria.

The production of penicillins on a large scale is an early example of the use of biotechnology.

The miracle cure

Natural materials have been used in many forms to treat infections in the past. The *Old Testament*, for example, describes the use of fungi and moulds to treat infected wounds.

In 1928, these remedies were shown to have a scientific basis, when Alexander Fleming noticed that a mould (*Penicillium notatum*) inhibited the growth of a *Staphylococcus* bacterium.

By some accounts, Fleming worked in a rather untidy manner. Accidentally, one of his experiments with bacteria became contaminated with a mould. Without realising this, he went away on holiday leaving the bacteria to grow. While Fleming was away, the summer temperatures were unusually low, causing the mould to grow faster than the bacteria. When he returned, Fleming noticed that bacterial growth was restricted in the areas where the mould had developed. He deduced that the mould had affected the bacteria by producing chemicals which he called **penicillins**.

The difficult task of isolating and purifying these substances was taken up by Howard Florey and Ernst Chain in Oxford, who, together with Alexander Fleming, shared a Nobel Prize for their work on penicillin.

In 1940, partially purified penicillin was shown to cure infected mice. A year later a girl was treated successfully. Luckily the traditional guinea-pigs had not been chosen for these tests. To them, penicillins are toxic substances.

During the 1940s, penicillin was extracted in bulk from mould cultures, both in the UK and the USA, and it became widely available.

Getting moulds to do the work

At first, scientists relied entirely on moulds to make penicillins.

The mould *Penicillium notatum* makes several antibiotic compounds as products of its natural metabolism. These were isolated and called, for example, penicillin F, G, K and X. Researchers found that the mould can be encouraged to produce just one penicillin, and that the type of penicillin produced can be altered by changing the nutrient on which the mould is grown.

For example, growing the mould with compound I as the nutrient gives just penicillin G. This was the first 'miracle cure'.

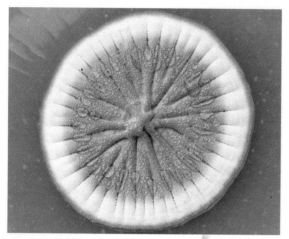

Figure 24 A penicillin mould

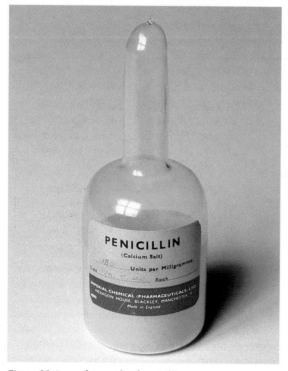

Figure 25 An early sample of penicillin

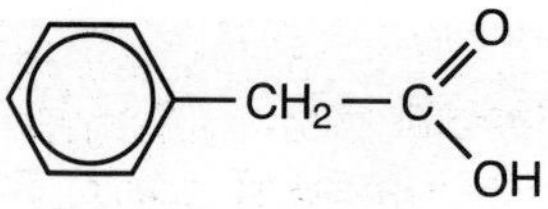

compound I

Unfortunately, penicillin G is only active against a limited variety of bacteria. Also, stomach acidity causes it to lose its activity, so it must be given by injection. Growing the mould with compound II gives the improved penicillin V, which is not so susceptible to attack by acids and can be taken orally.

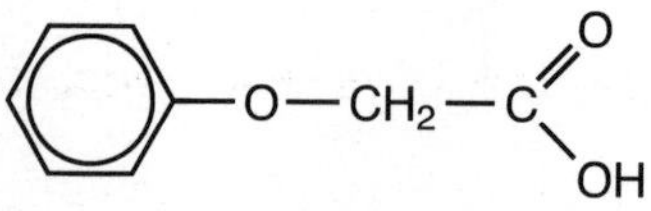

compound II

Improving on nature

When the National Health Service was set up in 1948, Beecham, known then as the 'pills and potions' company, decided to look more closely at the preparation of antibiotic compounds.

A major breakthrough came in the late 1950s. While trying to make a new penicillin, they found the penicillin 'nucleus', the central part of the penicillin molecule. They isolated this compound, called *6-aminopenicillanic acid (6-APA)*, and showed that it has the structure shown in Figure 26.

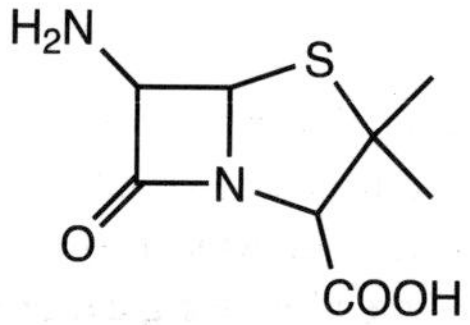

Figure 26 6-Aminopenicillanic acid (6-APA)

This was an important discovery because it helped to make sense of the different types of penicillins. It also enabled scientists to make new penicillins partially by chemical techniques, without relying completely on moulds to do the necessary reactions.

6-APA itself has little effect on bacterial growth, but if you add an extra 'side chain' to the amino ($—NH_2$) group you have a disease-curing penicillin. You can see the structure of a penicillin in Figure 27. The nutrient compounds I and II react with 6-APA to give different side chains.

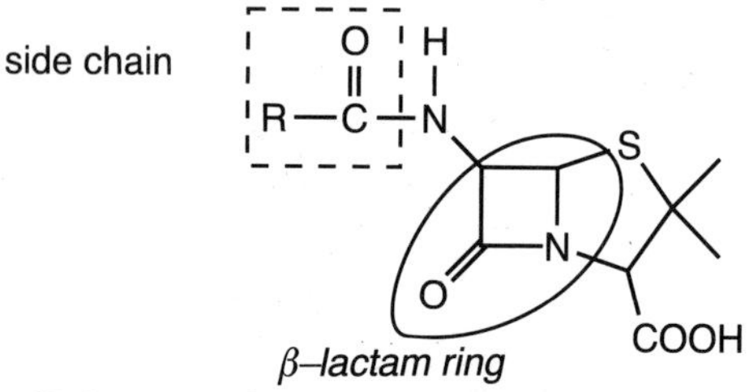

Figure 27 Structure of a penicillin – all penicillins have the same basic structure, only the R group varies

The β-lactam ring

Penicillin contains a fused-ring system containing a nitrogen atom and a sulphur atom. The four-membered ring contains a **cyclic amide** group and is called a β-**lactam ring**.

The simplest β-lactam ring is

$$H_2C - CH_2$$
$$| \quad\quad |$$
$$O{=}C - NH$$

You can think of it as arising from the β-amino acid

$$\overset{\beta}{H_2N} - CH_2 - \overset{\alpha}{CH_2} - COOH$$

by the —NH₂ group bending round and condensing with the —COOH group on the other end of the molecule.

β-Lactam rings are very sensitive to acids and alkalis. They react readily to give open-chain compounds. This is one of the reasons why it was so difficult to isolate and purify the first penicillins.

Research now focused on chemical reactions which would attach different side chains to 6-APA. An **acylation** reaction is used, as shown in Figure 29.

In **Activity MD5.1** you can make a semi-synthetic penicillin and test its antibacterial activity.

The different penicillins produced have different properties and ranges of antibacterial activity. A doctor decides which of the many penicillins available is the best one to use against the particular infection being treated.

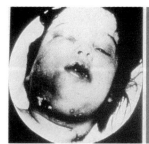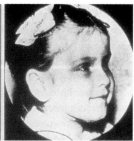

Figure 28 The first child to be treated with penicillin by Dr Wallace Herrell at the Mayo Clinic, USA. The photo on the right was taken 4 weeks after treatment

ASSIGNMENT 12

Use the 'tool-kit' of organic reactions you built up in **Activity MD3.1** to devise a synthesis for phenylpenicillin

from 6-APA and a benzyl alcohol (—CH₂OH) (3 steps).

For each step, give the essential conditions and write a balanced equation for the reaction. You will carry out the last step of the synthesis in **Activity MD5.1**.

Figure 29 Preparation of a semi-synthetic penicillin

---

acyl chloride
(inactive)

6-APA (from *penicillin G*)
(inactive)

+ HCl

penicillin
(active)

Making a so-called *semi-synthetic* penicillin involves making two biologically inactive molecules and clipping them together to make the active compound

One of the molecules is synthesised in the laboratory. This is the side chain in the form of an acyl chloride. The other is *6-APA*. This is obtained by treating naturally produced *penicillin G* with an enzyme to hydrolyse the amide linkage in the side chain

How penicillin works

Penicillin does not normally attack bacteria that are fully grown or in a resting state. Instead, it stops the growth of new bacteria by inhibiting the action of an enzyme responsible for constructing the cell wall.

A bacterium is protected by a rigid cell wall which is built up from a network of polysaccharide chains joined by polypeptide cross-links (see Figure 30). The shape of the penicillin molecule resembles that of the crucial amino acids used in the cross-linking process. The presence of penicillin confuses the enzyme which makes the cross-links.

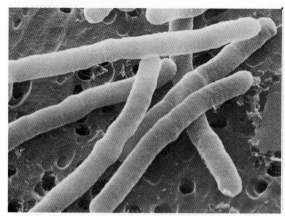

Figure 31 E. coli *cells 35 minutes after treatment with ampicillin; penicillin inhibits growth by inhibiting the action of an enzyme responsible for constructing the cell wall*

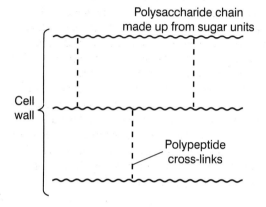

Figure 30 A simplified diagram of a bacterial cell wall

The enzyme never satisfactorily completes the wall, and eventually the contents of the cell burst out and the bacterium dies.

The structure of the cell wall in bacteria is unique and different from the cell walls in plants and cell membranes in animals. One of the amino acids used to make the polypeptide cross-links is D-alanine. Only its isomer, L-alanine, is found in humans. Penicillin is not toxic to humans and animals generally (although guinea-pigs are an exception). It selectively targets bacteria.

Nature fights back

Sometimes, penicillin-resistant bacteria cause serious outbreaks of infections in hospitals, especially in surgical wards. These bacteria produce an enzyme called *β-lactamase*, which attacks the four-membered β-lactam ring and makes the penicillin inactive.

Chemists have responded by developing new side chains that make the penicillin molecule less susceptible to attack by this enzyme.

ASSIGNMENT 13

New strains of bacteria appear as a result of *mutations*. These are spontaneous changes in the genetic material of the cell. They occur at random and are passed on when cells divide.

a Explain how penicillin-resistant strains of bacteria develop at the expense of susceptible ones.

b When you are prescribed a course of antibiotics, you should always finish the medicine, even if you feel better. Suggest a reason for this.

In **Activity MD5.2** you can make models of some penicillins and investigate how the structure of the side chain affects their antibacterial activity.

A group of scientists working at Beecham Research Laboratories tried a different approach. Instead of searching for penicillins with new side chains, they reasoned that a compound might be found that would inhibit the action of the β-lactamase enzyme, leaving the penicillin free to behave normally.

After investigating many possible compounds, they came up with a natural product called *clavulanic acid* (Figure 32). It has a structure similar to that of a penicillin molecule and is recognised by the β-lactamase enzyme.

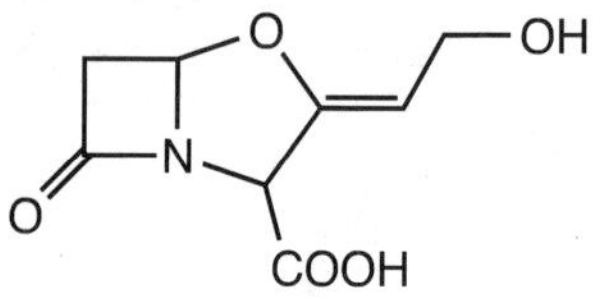

Figure 32 Clavulanic acid

Clavulanic acid alone has virtually no antibiotic activity, but, when mixed with previously ineffective penicillins, can be used against virulent bacteria with excellent results.

The story of penicillin doesn't finish here. Work continues to produce an ever-widening range of 'magic bullets' – compounds which are targeted at specific bacteria in particular areas of the body. Because bacteria are constantly changing, these compounds are in constant danger of becoming obsolete. Ways have to be found (like using the β-lactamase inhibitor, clavulanic acid) to prolong their usefulness.

ASSIGNMENT 14

Compare the structure of clavulanic acid (Figure 32) with that of the penicillin shown in Figure 27 on p. 268.

a What features, common to both molecules, might the active site of the β-lactamase enzyme recognise?

b Suggest how clavulanic acid might inhibit the action of the β-lactamase enzyme.

c The development of new penicillins, and compounds like clavulanic acid, involves a team of scientists working together. Find out what the role each of the following types of scientists might be and write a sentence to describe the work of each one:

- microbiologist
- pharmacologist
- chemist
- biochemist
- biotechnologist.

MD6 *Summary*

This unit has centred around the search for efficient medicines which are increasingly selective in the way they work. Once scientists understand the way in which a compound interacts with the human body, or with a bacterial cell, they can design new substances which fit selectively onto a receptor site and bring about a desired effect. This means that medicines can be more effective and have fewer side-effects.

Central to the storyline was the concept of molecular recognition. The shape and size of a biologically active molecule are crucial to its action. Its structure and precise shape must be known because certain groups may need to be in specific positions to bind the molecule to a receptor site. Computer-generated graphics help chemists to investigate the interactions involved and are the basis of modern drug design.

Synthetic organic chemists play an important role in preparing new compounds and modifying existing ones. So alongside the storyline, the chemical ideas introduced you to organic synthesis and allowed you to revise the various functional groups and organic reactions which you have encountered throughout the course. These were organised into a 'tool-kit' of reactions which you can use to write schemes for converting one organic compound into another.

Activity MD6 will help you to summarise what you have learned in this unit.

Figure 33 Industrial fermenters producing penicillin

VISITING THE CHEMICAL INDUSTRY

Why visit the chemical industry?

The chemical industry is a major contributor to our economy. All the principles of chemistry you learn in your chemistry course are applied in one way or another in the chemical industry. A study of the industry enables you to see the practical importance of chemical ideas.

This storyline is about some of the general principles of industrial chemistry.

Your visit to a particular chemical plant should enable you to learn some general principles about the way the chemical industry works.

Overview

The visit gives you an opportunity to

- have contact with local industry and the world of work
- improve your understanding of the relationship between industry and society
- see the industrial and social significance of the chemistry you are studying
- possibly collect ideas for your Individual Investigation.

You are going to visit a chemical plant in order to bring together your ideas on

- chemical manufacturing processes
- how chemical principles can be applied in order to:
  optimise efficiency
  ensure safety
  minimise environmental damage
  minimise economic cost.

VISITING THE CHEMICAL INDUSTRY

VCI1 *Introduction*

The UK chemical industry is a major contributor to both the quality of our life and our national economy. It is the only major sector of UK manufacturing industry which makes a positive contribution to the UK's balance of trade with the rest of the world.

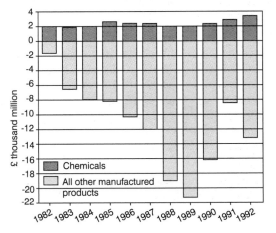

Figure 1 UK trade balance in chemicals and all other manufactured products, 1982–1992

All the principles of chemistry you learn in your chemistry course are applied in one way or another in the chemical industry. As well as chemists, chemical companies utilise people of most other disciplines to fulfil their activities, including accountants, lawyers, linguists, physicists, biologists, mathematicians, computer programmers and engineers of many kinds (chemical, mechanical, civil, electronic and so on).

The UK chemical industry is the nation's fourth largest manufacturing industry as measured by the value added, or money generated, in converting basic raw materials to more sophisticated, advanced chemicals and end products. The three largest sectors are: (i) food, drink and tobacco; (ii) mechanical engineering: (iii) paper, printing and publishing. It is the largest export earner among the manufacturing industries and, in global terms, is the fifth largest chemical industry behind the USA, Japan, Germany and France in terms of sales.

This study of the industry enables you to see the practical importance of some of the chemical ideas you have met.

An important part of this unit is your visit to a chemical plant. **Activity VCI1** will help you to get the most out of the visit.

Figure 2 ICI's new high-technology plant for making ammonia. It uses less energy and produces fewer emissions than more traditional plants

	Sales/10^9 US$	Location of Head Office
Hoechst	28.5	Germany
Bayer	25.6	Germany
BASF	24.1	Germany
Dupont	22.8	USA
Dow Chemical	18.8	USA
ICI*	15.7	UK
Rhône-Poulenc	14.5	France
Ciba-Geigy	14.2	Switzerland
Shell Chemical	11.2	UK/ The Netherlands
Enichem	10.9	Italy

*ICI demerged in 1993 to form two companies, ICI and ZENECA. The sales figure given here is for ICI alone

Table 1 *The ten biggest chemical companies in 1992 (not including oil companies)*

The chemical business

The chemical industry earns its money by carrying out chemical conversions and selling products either for further chemical modification or for formulation into final products. These final products perform a specific function, such as cleaners, paints, inks, medicines, dyestuffs, and soaps or toilet preparations.

The equipment needed to carry out the chemical conversions, the **chemical plant**, is specifically built or adapted to manufacture a required product. Plants are constructed according to the chemical process being operated and their size depends on the demand for the product. The process may be operated in continuous or batch sequences.

The important issues to address in deciding which product to make include

- what is the potential market size?
- will the product sell for a price which generates a profit for the company?
- how does the product 'fit in' with the company's other activities?
- does the company have sufficient expertise to develop the process and run the plant?
- what investment is required to manufacture the product?

Figure 3 *Sequence of unit operations in a chemical plant*

The plant is the major resource allocated to the manufacture of a product. The economic viability of the product will depend on the returns generated by the capital committed to the plant.

The marketing department will generate the necessary information to answer the above questions. The returns (selling price minus production costs) are derived from a number of factors which will be dealt with in turn in the following sections.

VCI2 *The operation of a chemical manufacturing process*

The chemical manufacturing process is the recipe, including specific instructions relating to the use of the equipment (plant), quantities and qualities of raw materials, mixing sequences, temperatures, pressures and so on, by which a product is made. Most chemical processes involve a sequence of events (called unit operations) which can be represented as in Figure 3.

ASSIGNMENT I

What are the main differences between the sequence in Figure 3 and a multi-step preparation you have done in your course (such as the preparation of a pure organic compound)?

For a particular process, this sequence may be organised in one of two ways: **batch** or **continuous.** A mixture of batch and continuous unit operations may be applied to achieve a given end product but each event is regarded as a unit operation.

In a **batch process**, the raw materials are put into a vessel and allowed to react together. The reaction is monitored and, when complete, the reaction phase is terminated. The product is separated from the reaction mixture. The process is then repeated in an identical manner, batch by batch, until the required amount of product is manufactured.

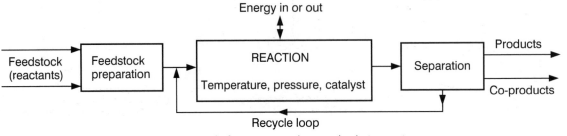

Figure 4 Making limestone using: (a) a batch process (an ancient lime kiln on Holy Island); (b) a continuous process (a modern rotary lime kiln)

In a **continuous process**, the raw materials are fed in at one end of the plant and product is withdrawn at the other end of the plant in a continuous flow. The process may proceed through various unit operations in specifically designed parts of the plant, each dedicated to a particular step in the sequence.

Plants capable of operating batch processes are generally more versatile than continuous plants. It is usually possible to carry out a variety of chemical reactions in batch operation using the same vessel with no, or only minor, modifications. Batch processes are most cost effective when relatively small volumes of products are required, although returns on sales of small tonnages would not usually be adequate to justify building a dedicated, single product plant. Batch processes are also more applicable to slow reactions where long residence time in the vessel would make adaptation to continuous operations difficult.

Batch and continuous: pros and cons

There are drawbacks to batch processes, relating to safety and contamination. In a batch reaction relatively large reacting masses might not easily be controllable in the event of an exothermic reaction. It may not be easy to cool the contents of the reaction vessel. Continuous processes tend to operate with relatively low volumes of reactants together at any time, allowing faster removal of energy and better control.

Contamination from batch to batch and product to product is also a potential problem in batch processing. Detailed clean-out procedures, which are time consuming and costly, must be followed to minimise cross-contamination.

Continuous processes are more suited to high-tonnage production of a single product. Once steady conditions have been established, the process can be run with minimal labour but relying heavily on instrumental and automatic control. To operate a continuous process, the plant is designed to produce product of consistent quality under optimum conditions, thereby minimising undesirable by-products and waste. Chlorine, ammonia and many other high-tonnage chemicals are made this way.

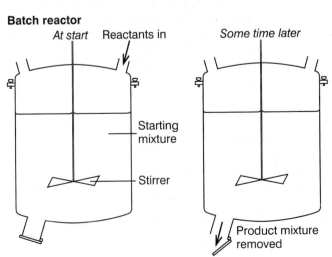

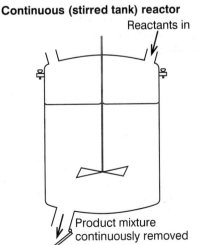

Figure 5 Comparison of batch and continuous tank reactors

Advantages	Disadvantages
Batch	
cost effective for small quantities; capital cost of plant much lower – possible to buy plant 'off the shelf'	charging and emptying the reactor is time consuming; no more product is being formed in this **shut-down** time
slow reactions can be catered for	larger workforce needed
a range of products can be made in the same vessel	contamination more likely
a greater percentage conversion is achieved compared with the same-sized continuous reactor for the same time	fast exothermic reactions can be more difficult to control
Continuous	
suited to high tonnage production	very much higher capital cost before any production can occur
greater throughput; shut-down may not occur for months or even years	not cost effective when run below full capacity
more easily automated and process is better controlled as fine adjustments are possible	
contamination risk is low when used for one product	contamination risk is higher when used for two or more products
consistent quality ensured	
requires minimal labour	
minimal waste and by-products	

Table 2 Advantages and disadvantages of batch and continuous processes

There are drawbacks to continuous processes, however. In particular, they require tailormade plant which is therefore less flexible. The economics of the process depend on the efficient usage of the plant, which may pose a problem if run at below full capacity. If the plant is used to make closely related products using the same chemical process but different feedstocks, the potential for contamination is even greater than for batch processes, since it takes time to flush previous products through the whole system.

Table 2 summarises the advantages and disadvantages of batch and continuous processes.

ASSIGNMENT 2

Explain which process, batch or continuous, you would employ to make

a a dyestuff?

b sulphuric acid?

c a pharmaceutical?

Figure 6 A glass-lined tank reactor

Plant construction materials

It is essential to choose construction materials which do not react with the feedstocks, catalysts, solvents and products involved in the process. The wrong choice can lead to lower efficiency, hazardous reactions, and product contamination – not to mention holes in the reaction vessels or pipes.

Glass-lined vessels, alloys or glass-reinforced plastics are widely used in place of steel components when there is a corrosion risk (Figure 6).

VCI3 *People*

The UK chemical industry employs around one-third of a million people from many disciplines with many different kinds of expertise and skills. It is necessary, because of the nature of chemical processes, that those directly responsible (chemists, chemical engineers, process operators) are highly qualified and extremely well trained. Such personnel work together as a team, with each individual contributing according to his or her different discipline.

The chemical industry is, by and large, capital rather than labour intensive and the relative size of the workforce reflects this. Indeed a large plant, such as one making concentrated sulphuric acid, may be operated by only four or five people. Computers and automation are used increasingly and new skills are needed from the fewer employees.

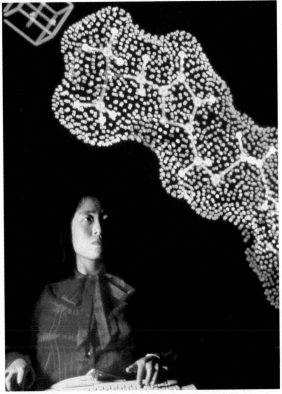

Figure 7 Computers play a major part in the chemical industry, for example in designing medicines

Comparisons of sales per employee between labour and capital intensive operations demonstrate this, as seen from comparing two of the largest companies in the world (see box).

Labour intensive versus capital intensive companies

General Motors (1991)
- Labour intensive
- Sales: US$123 × 10^9/756 000 employees
- Sales per employee: US$1.63 × 10^5

Shell Chemicals (1991)
- Capital intensive
- Sales: US$8.9 × 10^9/22 000 employees
- Sales per employee: US$4.1 × 10^5

The comparison shows that the capital intensive company sells over three times more per employee than the labour intensive company.

The list below shows some of the types of employee who might be required in a chemical plant.

Choose *four* from the list and suggest why they might be needed:

accountants
lawyers
linguists
physicists
biologists
computer programmers
engineers
– mechanical
– civil
– electrical
– production
– quantity
biochemists
analytical chemists
safety advisors
cleaners

caterers
transport workers
construction workers
fitters
clerical workers
laboratory technicians
market researchers
economists
librarians.

We'll now look at the various steps in the operation of a chemical plant.

VCI4 *Raw materials and feedstock preparation*

The reactants which go into a chemical process are called the **feedstock**. Feedstock is produced from the raw materials. Sometimes there may be more than one possible raw material to choose from. The choice will normally be decided by cost and suitability for the process.

There are five ways of manufacturing phenol (C_6H_5OH). Four of them start from benzene (C_6H_6) and one from methylbenzene ($C_6H_5CH_3$).

Methylbenzene is cheaper per tonne than benzene and this would seem to give an advantage over the route starting from methylbenzene.

a Calculate the mass of
  i benzene
  ii methylbenzene
  needed to manufacture 1 tonne of phenol.

b Explain how your answer to **a** shows that judging the most economical raw material is not always a straightforward matter of comparing price per tonne.

The raw materials usually have to be 'prepared' or treated to ensure that they are sufficiently pure and present in the correct proportion to use as feedstock. For example, by far the largest part of an ammonia plant is concerned with this 'feedstock preparation'. Methane, air and water are first purified by filtration and chemical treatment to remove potential catalyst poisons. Further chemical treatment is then carried out to produce the correct mixture of hydrogen and nitrogen for the main reaction.

An important part of feedstock preparation is getting the feedstock into a form in which it is easy to handle. Transferring gases and liquids is relatively easy because they can be transported by pipes. Even so, the cost of pumping may be high and so every effort is made to keep the number of pumps and length of piping down to a minimum. Solids are expensive to handle. Sometimes they are melted and maintained as hot liquids to reduce the transportation costs. For example, sulphur used in the manufacture of sulphuric acid is often delivered to, and used in, the plant as a liquid. Another way of handling solids is to mix them with a liquid to form a **slurry**; they can then be pumped for many kilometres along pipelines.

VC15 *The best conditions for the process*

Temperature and pressure

The efficiency of a chemical process depends on various physical factors such as temperature, pressure, rate of mixing, etc. When choosing the temperature and pressure for a particular reaction step it might seem appropriate to go for the highest possible, to maximise the rate at which the product is formed. However, it is not always as simple as this, and it is necessary to find the conditions that give the most economical conversion. For example, very high temperatures and pressures require very specialised, expensive plant to attain, and add to the difficulty in controlling the chemical reactions.

Even more important, the choice of conditions can have a significant impact on the *yield*. This is well illustrated by the main reaction step in the Haber process for ammonia synthesis (see **Aspects of Agriculture** storyline, Section **AA3**.)

In ammonia synthesis, too high a temperature reduces the yield. Too low a temperature reduces the rate of reaction. A compromise has to be made to allow a reasonable yield in a reasonable time.

ASSIGNMENT 5

Before you tackle this assignment, you will need to have studied **Chemical Ideas 10.2** on reaction rates and **Chemical Ideas 7.2** on equilibria.

ICI's new low pressure technology for the industrial production of methanol

The manufacture of methanol looks deceptively simple:

$$CO(g) + 2H_2(g) \rightarrow CH_3OH(g)$$

However, methanol production on an industrial scale is far from simple. Feedstock, catalysts, enthalpy changes, reaction rates, temperature and pressure all need to be considered. ICI's new low pressure technology, greatly simplified, involves three key stages:

- steam reforming of methane to produce synthesis gas (a mixture of CO, CO_2 and H_2)
- conversion of synthesis gas to methanol
- distillation of the methanol to give a high-purity product.

The conversion of synthesis gas to methanol involves several reactions. These include

$$CO(g) + 2H_2(g) \rightleftharpoons CH_3OH(g)$$
$$\Delta H = -90.7 \text{ kJ mol}^{-1}$$
$$CO_2(g) + 3H_2(g) \rightleftharpoons CH_3OH(g) + H_2O(g)$$
$$\Delta H = -49.3 \text{ kJ mol}^{-1}$$

The conversion is carried out over a catalyst at a temperature of 260 °C–270 °C and a pressure of 100 atm. Under these conditions, methanol is a gas. The methanol converter is designed to maintain this temperature. One way in which this is done is by using an internal heat exchanger.

a Use Le Chatelier's principle to decide what happens to the percentage of methanol in the mixture as
  i pressure increases
  ii temperature increases.

b Explain the reasons for the choice of reaction conditions in terms of achieving
  i a high yield
  ii a high rate.

Catalysts

A catalyst is a substance which alters the rate of a reaction by providing an alternative reaction route with a lower activation enthalpy. Many catalysts are made from precious metals; because they are not used up, it is economical to use them despite the high cost of the metal. Table 3 gives some examples of industrially important catalysts.

Most of the examples given in the table are *heterogeneous* catalysts. They are solids which bring about catalysis when their surfaces come into contact with the reactants in liquid or gas streams.

When the catalytic material is in the same phase as the reactants and can mix with them, it is called a *homogeneous* catalyst. Acids and alkalis are the most common homogeneous catalysts.

The performance of a catalyst is judged in terms of

- the effect it has on the reaction rate
- its life expectancy
- the percentage reclaimed when it is renewed.

The performance of catalysts deteriorates because of reactions with impurities in the feedstock (catalyst poisoning). Also, at high operating temperatures, a heterogeneous catalyst may melt and lose its high surface area. A catalyst may get covered in soot or other surface coating, and may need to be cleaned in a regenerator.

There is more about catalysts in **Chemical Ideas 10.4**.

ASSIGNMENT 6

Catalysts can be held in two main types of reactors. In **fixed bed** reactors, the reactants are passed over a bed of solid catalyst. The catalyst may be in a large vessel filled with porous pellets, or as a thin mesh of metal through which the reactants are blown.

Fluidised bed reactors have catalysts in the form of a fine power. Reactant gases are passed through the reactor at such a speed that the particles become suspended in the gas stream and behave like a fluid. In this type of reactor, the catalyst is regenerated by making the 'fluid' flow into a separate container for the regeneration process.

You can find an example of this type of reactor in the **Developing Fuels** storyline, Section **DF4**, under the description of catalytic cracking.

a Draw simple outline sketches to represent a fluidised bed reactor and a fixed bed reactor.

b Draw up a table to compare the likely effectiveness of the two types of reactor in terms of
i simplicity of design
ii ease of operation
iii ease of contact between catalyst and reactant
iv ease with which the catalyst can be regenerated
v heat transfer and temperature control.

c Explain the benefits of
i maximising contact between the catalyst and reactants
ii designing a reactor so that the catalyst can be easily regenerated.

Figure 8 An experimental fluidised bed burner for power generation from powdered coal

Reaction	Catalyst used
hydrogen and nitrogen to produce ammonia	iron
hydrogenation of edible oil for margarine	nickel
carbon monoxide and hydrogen to produce methanol	copper
oxidation of ammonia to give nitrogen(II) oxide for making nitric acid	platinum–rhodium alloy
oxidation of sulphur dioxide to sulphur trioxide for making sulphuric acid	vanadium(V) oxide
hydration of epoxyethane to give ethane-1,2-diol for antifreeze	0.5% sulphuric acid or sodium hydroxide solution

Table 3 Some important examples of industrial catalysis

Recycling

The reclamation and recycling of unreacted materials is an important aspect of process development for both economic and environmental reasons.

Recycling means separating unreacted feedstock from the reaction mixture, and this is not always easy. For example, it is important that impurities do not get recycled along with the unreacted feedstock. If an impurity is recycled but does not react, its concentration will build up in the reaction step and it will interfere with the reaction. For example, in the manufacture of ammonia, argon from the air is recycled along with the unreacted nitrogen and hydrogen. As argon is unreactive, it is difficult to remove it and so it is not possible to recycle continuously. The argon-enriched nitrogen and hydrogen mixture is bled off at intervals.

Energy matters

The efficient use of energy is significant in most chemical processes. During the past few years, often in response to high energy costs and environmental considerations, chemical companies have markedly reduced their energy consumption.

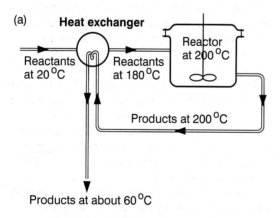

A stripped-down heat exchanger

Figure 9 Heat exchange

Many chemical reactions involve the release of thermal energy and this can be conserved by lagging pipes and by using heat exchangers. Energy from exothermic parts of the process can be used to supply energy to endothermic parts. The energy released in an exothermic reaction can be used to raise the temperature of the reactants.

Water or steam are the most usual agents for transferring energy in a chemical plant. Steam is a much safer alternative to oil, gas or electricity where flammable substances are involved.

In an integrated plant, energy (transferred in steam or hot liquid or gas streams) from one process can be used in a completely different part of the plant. This reduces the quantity of oil, gas and electricity that has to be purchased. By contrast, a small site would have to raise steam in a special boiler using purchased fuel oil, gas or electricity. The price of energy in the small plant would therefore be considerably greater than that in an integrated plant.

A few large-scale processes are sufficiently exothermic to enable electricity to be produced. Power stations which burn liquid sulphur to produce electricity have been built where sulphur is plentiful. The sulphur dioxide formed is converted to sulphuric acid for which there is a large market.

Co-products and by-products

When feedstock is passed through a reactor, a number of things might happen to it. The feedstock may

1. take part in the reaction to form only one product. For example

   nitrogen + hydrogen $\rightleftharpoons$ ammonia
   $N_2(g)$ + $3H_2(g)$ $\rightleftharpoons$ $2NH_3(g)$

2. take part in a reaction in which two products are formed. For example, propanone can be manufactured by passing propan-2-ol over a copper catalyst

   propan-2-ol $\rightleftharpoons$ propanone + hydrogen
   $CH_3CHOHCH_3$ $\rightleftharpoons$ CH_3COCH_3 + H_2

   The hydrogen formed in this reaction is an example of a *co-product*.

3. take part in a reaction other than the one that was intended. For example, epoxyethane, $(CH_2)_2O$, can be made in a one-step process in which ethene is mixed with oxygen and passed over a silver catalyst at 500 K and 15 atm. Not surprisingly, under these conditions there is also the possibility of the ethene being completely oxidised:

   ethene + oxygen $\rightleftharpoons$ carbon dioxide + water

   The carbon dioxide and water formed in this unwanted reaction are called *by-products*.

4. remain unreacted.

Chemical engineers calculate two values to show the extent to which these four possibilities have taken place in a particular reaction step. The **conversion** shows the proportion of the feedstock that reacts in one way or another:

$$\text{conversion} = \frac{\text{moles of reacting feedstock}}{\text{moles of feedstock in}} \times 100$$

The **selectivity** shows the proportion that gets turned into the product wanted:

$$\text{selectivity} = \frac{\text{moles of desired product}}{\text{moles of reacting feedstock}} \times 100$$

These two can be combined to give the **yield**

$$\text{yield} = \text{selectivity} \times \text{conversion}$$
$$= \frac{\text{moles of desired product}}{\text{moles of feedstock in}} \times 100$$

The higher the selectivity of a particular reaction step the better.

Low selectivity can produce a serious separation and disposal problem. Any hazardous by-products will have to be treated before disposal and this will add to the cost.

On the other hand, saleable co-products and by-products can sometimes make a significant contribution to the profitability of the process – it may even be the sale of the co-product that makes a particular route profitable. For example, one way of making phenol from benzene is

benzene + propene + oxygen ⇌ phenol + propanone

Six tonnes of propanone are produced for every 10 tonnes of phenol and the proceeds of its sale make a significant contribution to profits. The route would become uncompetitive if demand for propanone was to fall.

VC16 *Safety matters*

Safety is a major consideration in all operations in the chemical industry. All aspects of safety are affected by national and European Community legislation. In particular, the Health and Safety at Work Act places responsibility for health and safety with the employer.

ASSIGNMENT 7

a What other legislation do you know about which affects the safe handling of chemicals?

b Do they apply to the work which you do in your study of chemistry?

Figure 10 Protective clothing in the pharmaceutical industry

An analysis of all possible hazards and an examination of safety will be applied to any proposed project to build new or modified chemical plant. A Hazard and Operability Study (HAZOP) is a systematic procedure frequently used to carry out such an analysis. Every valve, pipe, vessel, pump, etc, is examined and the risk associated with failure is assessed and minimised by design.

Safety considerations play a crucial part in deciding the plant layout. Legislation requires specific design features to minimise risks of uncontrollable reactions and undesirable emissions. The designs of new plants have to demonstrate that the possible risks have been minimised and that emissions or leaks will be prevented.

On a site, there will be people who are responsible for considering specific aspects of safety and for ensuring that every person who works on the site or visits it constantly acts safely and is aware of all possible hazards. Training in the safe operation of the plant is therefore very important.

Personal safety is rated very highly and on a typical visit to a production site you may see eye-baths, showers, toxic gas refuges, breathing apparatus, emergency control rooms and, on larger sites, the company's fire brigade, ambulance service and a well-equipped medical centre with its own qualified doctors and nurses.

Figure 11 Safety training at ICI for a major accident

VCl7 *Environmental issues*

The environment is a major factor for chemical companies. It is not acceptable to allow harmful substances to escape into the environment. The resultant pollution which occurs if there is an accidental escape of materials from a plant or disposal of untreated waste products not only damages the environment but also jeopardises the future of the company itself.

There is an increasing quantity of legislation (local, national, European and international) which regulates the performance of chemical operations with respect to environmental issues. The worldwide voluntary 'Responsible Care' scheme has set new standards for chemical operations, leading to fundamental improvements in environmental matters.

Waste generation, treatment and disposal are major issues in process development. Minimising waste by getting the right conditions has already been discussed and the adoption of new clean technologies is helping in this area. However, chemical processes will always produce some waste which has to be dealt with.

Waste must be treated and can only be disposed of when in a state which is not harmful to the environment. Liquid waste from chemical works has to meet legal requirements on such things as pH and metal ion content before being released into natural waters or sewage systems. It must be treated appropriately, eg to neutralise any acid. Water containing organic waste cannot be discharged into rivers or canals if it would significantly reduce the oxygen content of the water, causing fish to die from lack of oxygen.

Gases which contain contaminants are purified by bubbling them through neutralising solutions to remove soluble contaminants; particles of dust can be removed by filtration or other methods.

Figure 13 It's not like this any more …

Figure 12 A treatment plant for recycling waste water

In the past, waste has been dumped into the nearest convenient place (the atmosphere, old quarry, river, lake, sea). Alternatively, it was contained in purpose-built ponds or tips which have caused problems with toxic materials leaching out into nearby streams and waterways. These methods are no longer acceptable and increasingly are becoming illegal.

VCl8 *Costs*

All of the factors considered so far contribute to the cost of the process. Major costs – such as research and development, plant design and construction, and initial production – are incurred before any product is sold into the market. Sales of the product have to generate enough return to offset these initial costs and generate a profit for the company.

The profit generated is the difference between the selling price and the costs of production. Production costs are made up of two elements: **fixed costs** and **variable costs.**

Fixed (or indirect) costs are those incurred by the company whether they produce 1 tonne or tens of thousands of tonnes of product. For example, as soon as it has been built, the production plant starts to lose value, or depreciate, regardless of how much product is made. Other fixed costs include labour costs, land purchase or rental, sales expenses, telephone bills, etc. Hence the fixed cost element in the production cost is calculated by spreading the total annual charges over the number of units produced per year. If only 1 tonne of product is produced per year then the fixed cost element of production cost will be significantly higher than if 100 tonnes are produced with the same fixed costs. As fixed costs are allocated against a product, it is best to divide the cost against the maximum output of product possible. This will only occur when the plant is operating at maximum capacity.

Variable (or direct) costs relate specifically to the unit of production. Raw materials are the most obvious variable cost, along with costs of effluent treatment and disposal, and the cost of distributing the product. If no production occurs then these variable costs will not be incurred whereas fixed costs will still have to be paid.

Capital costs relate to establishing chemical plant, buildings and infrastructures around which manufacture is based. These capital costs are recovered as part of the fixed cost element (depreciation). In general, for normal accountancy purposes, the life of a plant is assumed to be 10 years, after which it may be said to be 'written off'. This depreciation happens because chemical plants corrode, fall to pieces or are made obsolete by technological advances. In practice, many plants have a perfectly satisfactory life beyond 10 years. In estimating the profitability of a plant, it will be necessary to recoup the investment in capital costs (as well as covering the fixed and variable costs) before the plant is written off.

ASSIGNMENT 8

Explain why

a the capital cost of a 200 tonne day^{-1} chemical plant is less than twice that of a 100 tonne day^{-1} plant

b if you double the output of a chemical plant, you may double the variable costs, but you don't double the fixed costs.

ASSIGNMENT 9

Calculate the value of the sales per employee for the countries in Table 4.

a How does the UK compare with other countries in terms of value of sales per employee?

b Which country has the greatest value of sales per employee?

c Suggest what affects these figures.

	Sales/ 10^9 US\$	Number of employees
Germany	105.5	586 000
France	68.6	260 000
UK	52.8	305 000
Italy	52.0	208 000
Spain	39.9	216 000
Belgium	29.6	99 000
The Netherlands	24.6	87 000
Switzerland	17.1	71 000

Table 4 European chemical industry sales, 1992 (not including oil or man-made fibres)

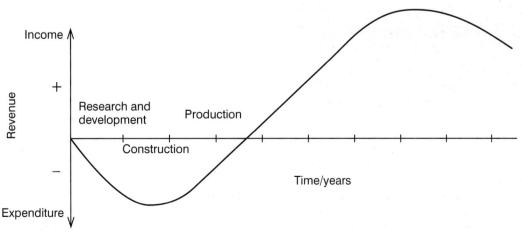

Figure 14 Expenditure and income for a chemical process against time

Figure 15 ICI Billingham by night has become a tourist attraction

VCI9 *Location*

The chemical industry in the UK grew up around either the source of its major raw materials or the customer industry which it served. With increasing specialisation in the UK and a much improved communication network, these factors are no longer the primary considerations in locating manufacturing sites.

New chemical plants are often built near to existing works. This may be because a district specialising in the manufacture of a particular product is more likely to be able to provide the skilled labour needed for new developments. That's why there are specialist steel producers in Sheffield, a traditional centre for steelmaking.

It may be that the feedstock for the new process is already being produced at the existing site. There may be less opposition to building a new plant at an existing works than to the development of a new site. In addition to these considerations, it may save money if facilities such as a canteen, medical centre and administration block are shared between existing and new plants.

However, many well-established locations are in built-up areas where the increasing concerns of the local population give rise to problems in extending plant or building new facilities. Increasingly, chemical companies are being forced to seek more remote locations for their operations.

The actual site chosen should be served by a good communications network, as building this from scratch would add significantly to the cost of opening the plant. Road, rail and water are all important means of transport, and deep sea access is useful for the import and export of bulk materials. Ideally the site would be level, free from danger of subsidence and have scope for further expansion. Waste treatment and disposal are always concerns to be borne in mind, but companies no longer choose locations on the basis of easy waste dumping.

ASSIGNMENT 10

Consider the company you have visited.

a Why is it on its present site?

b What are the constraints for further growth and employment in the existing area?

c What other locations in the UK or the rest of the world might be appropriate?

d What would the implications of a move be on
   i   the company?
   ii the local economy?
   iii the local environment?

Finally, try this longer assignment to check your knowledge and understanding of ideas about the chemical industry.

ASSIGNMENT II

Deeside Titanium

Titanium is an important strategic metal whose high strength-to-weight ratio makes it invaluable in the aerospace industry. In November 1982 a new £25 million titanium manufacturing plant was opened on Deeside, near Chester (see Figure 16). Why Deeside? The plant was originally planned for Hartlepool, but local residents objected and the Deeside location was chosen, attracted by government subsidies. The site was near to a steelworks which was in the process of closing down part of its plant. The site had a number of advantages, including access to a suitable means of waste disposal.

Making titanium

Titanium is manufactured from titanium(IV) chloride, $TiCl_4$, by reducing it with sodium. Deeside has two main suppliers for each of these two raw materials. These four suppliers are situated in France, Germany and the UK.

The raw materials are brought to the plant by road tanker or rail tanker. Both sodium and titanium(IV) chloride react violently with water, and sodium reacts with air.

The sodium metal is melted on delivery and is kept molten throughout the process. A precisely measured quantity of sodium is added slowly to liquid titanium(IV) chloride in a large pot filled with argon. A highly exothermic reaction occurs, and when it is complete the products, a mixture of titanium and sodium chloride, are allowed to solidify.

The contents of the pot are then broken into lumps by a small explosion so they can be removed. The lumps are washed with dilute hydrochloric acid which dissolves away the sodium chloride. The resulting solution is the main waste product of the process. It is neutralised and filtered before being discharged into the sea.

The Deeside plant can produce up to 5000 tonnes of titanium per year and guarantees a supply of high-quality titanium and titanium alloys to the British aerospace industry.

a List the factors which made Deeside a favourable location for the new plant.

b Suggest why Deeside Titanium has contracts with two suppliers for titanium(IV) chloride and two for sodium.

c Why is the sodium kept in a liquid state during the process?

d Why is the sodium added in a precisely measured quantity?

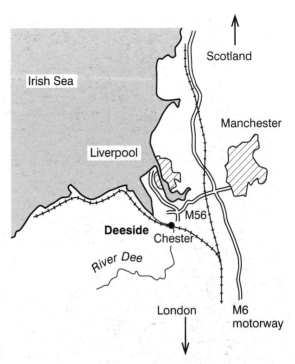

Figure 16 The location and transport connections of Deeside

e Write an equation, including state symbols, for the reaction in which titanium(IV) chloride is reduced to titanium.

f Why is the reaction vessel filled with argon?

g What would be an appropriate material for making the reaction vessel?

h Which type of process is this, batch or continuous? Why is this the more appropriate type for the process?

i i What is titanium's co-product in this process?
  ii What by-products would you expect the process to have?

j Name a chemical that could be used to neutralise the waste solution before pouring it into the sea. Give the reason for your choice.

k It is considered environmentally acceptable to discharge the waste from this process into the sea.
  i Explain why.
  ii Do you foresee environmental problems that may arise from this waste discharge, in spite of your previous answer?

l Identify
  i the major fixed costs
  ii the major variable costs
  in this process.

m What particular safety considerations would arise in the Deeside Titanium plant?

INDEX

Note: **CS** = Chemical Storylines; **CI** = Chemical Ideas;
    AA = Activities and Assessment

absolute temperature **CI** 47
absorbance **AA** SS1
absorption spectrum
   CS 198; stars 11–12; water 122
   CI 108–11; transition metals 218
   AA US3.1b
abstract writing **AA** A9
ACE inhibition **CS** 264–6
ACE modelling **AA** MD4
acid anhydrides **CI** 279–80
acid dissociation constant **CI** 151
acid rain
   CS 48, 236
   AA analysis M2.4
acid-base pairs **CI** 148
acid-base properties (period 3) **CI** 92
acidity constant **CI** 151
acids
   CS weak 249–50
   CI concentration/strength distinguished 148, 152;
     conjugate 148; defined 147; strong and weak 150–2
   AA strong/weak A8.2, O4.2
activation enthalpy
   CS and catalysis 155; and reaction rate 62
   CI 52, 173–4, 182–3, 186; and catalysis 189
acyl chlorides
   CS 141
   CI 278-9
   AA MD3.1
acylation
   CS for penicillin manufacture 269
   CI 240; agents 258–9, 278–9
   AA reactions MD3.1
addition polymerisation
   CI 230–1
   AA PR2.1
addition reaction **CI** alkenes 276; of ethene 228–30
adsorption **CS** 198
agonistic molecules **CS** 263
alcohol
   CS blood concentration 254–7; as drug 254, 258–61;
     effect on GABA 260–1; as food 253–4
   CI 246
alcohols
   CS energy in 19; as oxygenates 29
   CI 248–50, 276–8; condensation reaction 278;
     elimination reaction 277; –OH group 253;
     oxidation 254-5; polyhydric 249;
     reaction with HBr 277; substitution reaction 277
   AA DF4.5; ethanol DF1.1; A4.1; –OH group WM3;
     oxidation MD1.1; viscosity PR5.4
Alcolmeter **CS** 255–6
aldehydes
   CI 254–5, 277
   AA MD3.1
alizarin **CS** 216–18
alkali, defined **CI** 147

alkali metal halides **AA** M1.3
alkane series, physical property changes **AA** DF3.1
alkanes
   CS bromination 116; from cracking 27;
     isomerisation 26; in petrol 21, 22;
     for petrol blending 25-6
   CI 221–6; and alcohol synthesis 248;
     boiling points 74; branched 23; cracking 225-6;
     cycloalkanes 224; properties 225; reactions 225-6;
     shape 224–5; structure 223
   AA auto-ignition DF3.3; branched DF4.1;
     cracking DF4.4; naming DF4.1;
     octane numbers DF4.2; straight chain DF4.1;
     vapour, heat action DF4.4
alkenes
   CI 226, 227–31, 275–6; addition reactions 276;
     cycloalkenes 227; shape 228; *see also* ethene
   AA DF4.4; as hydrocarbon CD5.1;
     polymerisation PR2.1; test for DF4.4
alkoxy group **CI** 250
alkyl groups
   CI 223
   AA DF4.1
alkylation
   CI 240
   AA reactions MD3.1, MD3.2
alkynes **CS** 88, 90
alloys
   CS 159
   CI 208
alpha particles **CI** 15, 16
aluminium, in steelmaking
   CS 164
   AA SS2.4
aluminium atoms, zeolites **AA** DF4.3
amides
   CS 141
   CI 265, 266–7, 279
amines
   CS in nylon creation 92
   CI 263–5; coupling with diazo salts 271; reaction with
     acyl chlorides 279; substitution reactions 265
   AA EP2.1
amino acids
   CS 138–40; essential 140; formation 14–15
   CI 267–8
   AA EP2.1; α-amino acids EP2.4
amino groups
   CS 138
   AA MD3.1
aminopenicillanic acid (6-APA) **CS** 268–9
ammonia
   CS as refrigerant 66
   CI 200; as nucleophile 246; reaction with acyl
     chlorides 279; *see also* amines
ammonia leach, with roasted ores **AA** M2.3
ammonia manufacture kinetics **CI** 185–6
ammonia synthesis **CS** 191
ammonium ions
   CS and nitrification 188
   AA AA3.1

amphoteric
    CS tin 52, 174
    CI 92, 148
analgesic, *see* aspirin
aniline dye **CS** 213–15
angiotensin **CS** 264–5
angiotensin converting enzyme, *see* ACE
anions **CI** 27; *see also* zwitterions
antagonistic molecules **CS** 263
antibacterial activity **AA** MD5.1
antibiotics **CS** 267–71; resistance to 270–1
aramid **CS** 94
arenes
    CI 232–6, 281; reactions 237–41
    AA as hydrocarbon CD5.1; soluble in water CD8
aromatic hydrocarbons, *see* arenes
arseno-pyrites **AA** M2.6
art and chemistry, review **AA** CD4.6
asbestos **CS** 181
aspartame **AA** EP2.2
Aspects of Agriculture, summary activity **AA** AA5
aspirin
    CS marketing 107–8; safety 108; synthesis 106–7
    AA assay WM6.3; in medicines WM6.1, WM6.2;
       purity WM6.3; synthesis WM5, WM6.2
asthma **CS** 262
atmosphere
    CS changes in 248–9; structure 55–6
    AA carbon dioxide A8.3, A9; infra-red absorption A6;
       ultra-violet absorption ranges A2.3
Atmosphere, The, summary activity **AA** A10
atmospheric pollution **CS** 56
atmospheric pressure **CI** 9
atomic emission spectroscopy **CS** 162, 207
atomic mass, relative **CI** 1, 2
atomic number **CI** 14; and melting point 193;
    and periodic table 192
atomic orbitals **CI** 21–2
atoms
    CS number of, *see* mole
    CI models 14–15; size 32
    AA models EL4.1
auto-ignition **CS** 24
Avogadro's constant **CI** 2, 7
Avogadro's law **CI** 7
azo compounds **CI** 269–71
azo dyes
    CS 220
    AA CD6

bacteria, sulphate-utilising **CS** 248
bacterial leaching
    CS 49
    AA M2.6
baked beans can, detinning **AA** SS6.2
balloon molecules **AA** EP2.3
barium **AA** EL2.3
base **CI** amines as 264–5; ammonia as 200;
    conjugate 148; defined 147
base pairing **AA** EP2.7
base strength **CI** 148
batch process **CS** 274, 275–6
batteries **AA** US4.3
benzene
    CI 232–6; bromination 237–8;
       chlorination 239–40; nitration 238–9;
       stability 234–5; sulphonation 239
    AA MD3.2; Mauve CD5.3
benzenesulphonic acid **CI** 239

beta particles **CI** 15, 16
beta-blocker **CS** 263
beta-lactam ring **CS** 269
bifunctional compounds **CI** 267
bioconcentration factors, pesticides **AA** AA4.1
biodegradability **CS** 98
biodegradable plastic **CS** 148
biopolymers
    CS 97
    AA PR8.1
blast furnace
    CS 160–1
    AA impurities SS2.1
blood alcohol concentration
    CS 254–7
    AA MD1.2
blue pigments **AA** CD4.1 Information Sheets 1 and 5
body, elements in **CS** 3
Bohr's theory, and emission spectra **CI** 97–8
Bohr's theory of the atom **CI** 18
boiling point
    CI and hydrogen bonding 80;
       and intermolecular forces 74–7; of water 88
    AA DF3.1
bond breaking, and activation enthalpy **CI** 186
bond deformation, in infra-red spectroscopy **CI** 115
bond energy, *see* bond enthalpy
bond enthalpy
    CI 51; and bond length 51–2; measurement 52
    AA DF2.1, A3.1
bond fission **CI** 102–3
bond length, and bond enthalpy **CI** 51–2
bond polarity
    CI 30; and dipoles 77–8; and vibration 117
    AA PR5.3
bond type, and enthalpy change of combustion **CS** 18
bonding, *see* covalent bonding; hydrogen bonding; ionic
    bonding; polar bonds
bonding electron pairs **CI** 28
bonding and structure **CI** 91–2
bonds
    CI characteristic i.r. absorption 117; and enthalpy
       cycles 53–4
    AA conjugated PR4
bones, calcium in **CS** 6
BOS (basic oxygen steelmaking) process
    CS 161–4
    AA SS2.2, SS2.3
Boyle's law **CI** 9
breathalyser
    CS 255
    AA MD1.1
brine, electrolysis **AA** M1.2
bromine
    CS 41–2; alkanes 116; industrial use 42–3;
       production 40–2
    CI 202–4; reaction with benzene 237–8;
       reaction with ethene 228–9
    AA handling hazards M1.4; and hexane A3.2, A3.3;
       photodissociation A3.2; production M1.1;
       reactions CD5.1; recognition M1.3
bromine water **AA** DF4.4
1-bromobutane **AA** A4.2, A4.1, A4.2
Brønsted-Lowry theory **CI** 147
bubble gum **AA** PR7
buffers
    CS for reactive dyes 224; by ocean 249–50; in soil 185
    CI 154–5, 267–8
    AA soil AA2.6; solutions O4.3

butanedioic acid (succinic acid) **AA** EP6.2

butylamine **AA** EP2.1

by-products, industrial **CS** 280–1

cadmium telluride thin-film solar cells **AA** US5.2

caffeine, in medicine **AA** WM6.2

calcium
    CS deficiency 6
    AA EL2.3; in soil AA2.5

calcium carbonate
    CI solubility equilibrium 144–5
    AA solubility O4.1

calcium ions
    CS in neurotransmission 259
    CI and hard water 140

calibration errors **AA** II

calorimeter
    CI 47
    AA DF1.2

camera, electronic **CS** 226

cancer, skin **CS** 57, 69

Captopril **CS** 264–6

carbocation **CI** 229

carbohydrates, energy in **CS** 19, 20

carbon **CI** 197–9; allotropic 197;
    and organic chemistry 221

carbon cycle
    CS 79, 80
    AA A9

carbon dioxide
    CS absorption by sea 243–5; and greenhouse effect 73,
    75, 77–81; Kolbé synthesis 106; in oceans 244–5,
    249–51; in photosynthetic cycle 121;
    solubility 243–4; weak acid 249–50
    CI equilibrium with water 128–9
    AA concentrations A8.3; controls A9; weak acid A8.2

carbon oxides **CI** 198–9

carbonates, group 2
    CI 195, 196
    AA solubility EL2.3; thermal stability EL2.3

carbonic acid **CS** 249

carboxylic acids
    CS tests for 103
    CI 251–2, 277, 278–9; –OH group 253; strength 254
    AA –OH group WM3; solubility –COOH group CD8

carotene **AA** PR4

Carothers, Wallace **CS** 91–2, 93

cat cracking **CS** 28

catalase **AA** EP6.3

catalysis
    CS in cracking 28; enzymatic 154, 155–6;
    for reforming 29; by transition metals 166
    CI and electrode potential 169; and equilibrium
    position 139; mechanism of enzyme-mediated 182;
    and reaction kinetics 173, 182, 188–90;
    by transition metals 211
    AA rate of enzyme mediated EP6.5

catalysts
    CS industrial 279; organometallic compounds 87–8;
    Ziegler-Natta 89
    CI poisoning 190
    AA transition metal ions SS3.2; zeolites DF4.3

catalytic converter **CS** 33–4

catalytic cycle, Cl/ozone **CS** 61–2, 63

catenation **CI** 21

cation exchange
    CS 184
    CI 140

cations
    CS in silicates 181
    CI 27; *see also* zwitterions
    AA exchangeable in soil AA2.5

cells, electrochemical
    CI 161–6; calculation of potential 165–6
    AA US4.3, US4.5, SS4; voltage and concentration US4.4

cellulose **CS** 221

central nervous system **CS** 258

CFC
    CS greenhouse effect 73; as greenhouse gas 69;
    Rowland's predications 63–4; use 66–8
    AA A4.1, A4.4; international agreements A4.5

Chadwick, James **AA** EL4.1

chain reaction **CI** 104, 104–5

chair conformation **AA** DF4.1

chalcopyrite **CS** 45, 46, 47

charge density **CI** 32

Charles' law **CI** 9

chelate ring **CI** 215

chemical equilibrium
    CS of alkane isomerisation 26;
    carbon dioxide/water 244–5
    CI chemical 128–31; and entropy 63–4;
    solubilty 144–5; weak acid 150; *see also* partition
    equilibrium
    AA chemical A8.1, O4.1

chemical formulae **CI** 3–4

chemical industry, visiting **AA** VCI

chemical plant **CS** 274; costs 282–3; feedstock 277–8;
    labour 276–7; location 284–5; operation 274–6;
    pollution 282; processing conditions 278–81;
    safety 281

chemical properties, and electronic structure **CI** 25

chemical reaction, electrical energy from **AA** US4.2

chemical reaction enthalpy profile **CI** 52-3

chemical shift
    CI 120
    AA Data Sheets

chemical shifts for protons **AA** Data Sheets

chiral insulin monomers **CS** 151

chiral molecules **CI** 43

chlor-alkali **AA** industry M1.2; production M1.2

chloride formulae, periodicity **CI** 193

chloride ions, in neurotransmission **CS** 259

chloride structure (period 3) **CI** 92, 94

chloride-water reaction (period 3) **CI** 92, 94

chlorination of benzene **CI** 239–40

chlorine
    CS atmospheric 69
    CI 202–4
    AA manufacture M1.2; recognition M1.3

chlorine atom, and ozone removal **CS** 61; *see also* CFC

chlorine water, in bromine production **CS** 40–1

chlorofluorocarbons, *see* CFC

chlorophyll
    CI 170
    AA spectrum US3.1b

chloroplasts
    CS 118
    AA reduction reactions US3.1c

chromate(VI) ion **AA** A8.1

chromates, as pigments **CS** 205

chromatography
CS (gas-liquid) BAC 257; drying oil ratio 212; petrol 24–5; (thin layer) 103; hydrolysis permethrin 197
CI 141–3
AA (gas-liquid) drying oil ratio CD4.3; straight chain primary alcohols MD1.2; (thin layer) analysis of medicines WM6.2; hydrolysis aspartame EP2.2; willow bark extract WM2
Chrome Yellow
CS 204–7
AA CD3.1
chromium **CI** 206–7
chromophore
CS 220
CI 112
Cima da Conegliano **CS** 208
cis isomers **CI** 41
citrate ions, light affecting **AA** US2.3
clavulanic acid **CS** 270
clay
CS 181, 182
AA model making AA2.2; physical properties AA2.3
climate control, by sea **CS** 235, 238–43
co-products, industrial **CS** 280–1
coal **AA** as fuel DF1.1; products from CD5.2
coal tar
CS dyes from 202, 213, 217
AA CD5.2
codons **CS** 143, 144; alteration 152–3
collision theory of reaction **CI** 185–6
colorimeter
CI 109
AA SS1
colour
CS pigments, 115–16; of transition metals 167; *see also* dyes
CI 106–8; and absorbed radiation 111; chemistry of **CI** 112–13; and energy absorption 101; inorganic compounds 113; in transition metals 207, 216–18; organic compounds 112–3
AA compounds SS3.1; solution SS1
colour change
CI and ligands 113; in redox reactions 113
AA CD1; and molecular structure PR4
colour chemists **CS** 202
Colour by Design, summary activity **AA** CD9
Colour Index **CS** 204
colours, visibility **AA** CD3.2
combustion
CI analysis 222; enthalpy change 48
AA enthalpy changes DF2.1, DF2.2
complex formation
CS by transition metals 166–7
CI corrosion 171–2; effect on electrode potential 171–2; by transition metals 213–19
AA structure SS5.1
complex ions
CI nomenclature 214–15
AA A8.1; coloured SS3.3
complex organic molecules **AA** structure AA4.2; synthesising MD3.2
concentration
CI acids 152; effect on reaction kinetics 173, 174–84; and equilibrium position 134–5; solutions 11–12; symbol 129
AA changes, equilibrium mixtures A8.1

condensation reaction
CS in nylon creation 92; peptide formation 140
CI 257; –NH$_2$ group 268
AA polymerisation PR5.1
condensation-evaporation balance **CS** 238–9, 240
conductivity **AA** electrical M3; poly(pyrrole) PR4
conjugated bonds, iron phthalocyanine **CS** 204
conservation of energy **CS** 36
continuous process **CS** 275–6
conversion **CS** 281
–COOH groups **AA** CD8
coordination number **CI** 213–14
copolymerisation **CI** 86
copper
CS as catalyst 50; industrial production 44–9; origin 44–5; oxidation state 50; use 50
CI 206–7; as oxidising agent 160–1
AA production M2.3;
copper compounds
CS reduction 44, 45
AA from roasted ore M2.3; phthalocyanide CD2 sulphate M2.5;
copper ore **AA** M2.1
copper phthalocyanide **AA** CD2
copper(II) sulphate **AA** M2.5
copper-zinc half cells **CI** 162–3
copper-zinc redox reaction, direction of **CI** 167–8
CORN rule **CI** 44
corrosion
CS 167; *see also* rusting
CI and complexing 171–2
AA SS4.1, SS4.2
costs, chemical plant **CS** 282–3
coupling agents, dyes **AA** CD6
coupling reaction **CI** 269, 270–1
covalent bonding
CS in proteins 149
CI 28–9; dative 29–30; in group 4 197; halides 202
covalent molecule, shape **CI** 35
cracking
CS 27–8
CI 225–6
AA alkanes DF4.4
Crick, Francis
CS 145
AA EP2.8
cross-links, 'slime' **AA** PR2.2
crystalline polymers **CI** 85
crystallisation
CS 40–1
AA inorganic compound concentration O3.3
Culpeper, Nicholas (1616–54) **CS** 102
cyanide ions, with halogenoalkanes **AA** MD3.1
cycloalkanes
CI 224
AA DF4.1
cycloalkenes **CI** 227
cyclohexane
CI 234
AA DF4.1, CD5.1
cyclohexene **AA** CD5.1

d block (periodic table)
CI 205–19; *see also* transition metals
d sub-shell **CI** 20
database, isomer identification **AA** WM4.1, WM4.2
dative bond, *see* covalent bond
DDT **CS** 194
Dead Sea **CS** 39–40

decay, *see* radioactive decay
deep ocean circulation **CS** 251
deep water currents **CS** 241–2
degradation **AA** PR5.2
dehydration, alcohols **CI** 277
delocalised electrons
    CS iron phthalocyanine 204
    CI benzene 233; metals 208;
      phenols and carboxylicacids 254
    AA in polypyrrole PR4; in Monastral Blue CD2
density, water/ice **CI** 89–90
developer (photographic) **CS** 43
Developing Fuels, summary activity **AA** DF8
diabetes
    CS 135–8
    AA EP6.1
diaphragm cell **AA** M1.2
diazo coupling **AA** CD6
diazonium salt **CI** 269–70
diazotisation **CI** 270
dichromate(VI) ion **AA** A8.1
dienes **CI** 227
diffusion **CI** 54–5
dimethyl sulphide **CS** 236–7
dioxygen
    CS atmospheric 58
    CI 103–4
    AA A3.4
dipoles
    CS bonding in proteins 149
    CI 74–7; attractions 76; and bond polarity 77–8;
      dipole-dipole forces in water 88; dipole-dipole
      interactions 78–9; induced 78; intermolecular
      forces 75–6; permanent 74, 77
    AA moments PR5.3
direct dyes
    CS 221
    AA CD7.1
diseases, fatal **AA** WM1
dissolving
    CI and entropy 69
    AA M2.5; *see also* solutions
distillation
    CS vacuum 22
    AA A4.2; steam distillation AA3.1
DNA (deoxyribonucleic acid)
    CS 145–6
    AA modelling EP2.7
doping semiconductors **CS** 128
dose limit (radioactivity) **AA** SS6.1
dot-cross diagram **CI** 27, 35
double bond **CI** 28
double helix **AA** EP2.7
double salt **CI** 71
drug development
    CS costs 110–11
    AA WM7.1
drying oils
    CS 211
    AA CD4.2
dye diffusion thermal transfer (D2T2) **CS** 226–6
dyes
    CS 201–2; artificial 213–17; colour and structure 220;
      direct 221; fastness 220–4; fibre-reactive 222–3;
      for polyester 224; from snails 229–30
    AA azo CD6; direct and reactive CD7.1; fastness CD7.1;
      suitability for different fibres CD7.2; synthetic CD5.3
dynamic equilibrium **CI** 128–9

Earth
    CS energy balance 72; *see also* greenhouse gases
    AA infra-red radiation emissions A6
edta
    CI 216
    AA SS3.3, AA2.5
egg tempera **CS** 211
elastomers
    CS 85
    CI 82
electric arc furnace **CS** 165
electric vehicles **CS** 17
electrical conductivity **AA** M3
electrical energy, from chemical reaction **AA** US4.2
electrical units **CI** 162
electrochemical cells, *see* cells
electrochemical series **CI** 164–5
electrode potential
    CS for water decomposition 124
    CI charts 168; and direction of redox reaction 167–70;
      standard 164, 171–2; values 171
    AA US4.3, US4.4, US4.5, US4.7, SS3.1
electrolysis **AA** brine M1.2; water EL1
electrolytic refining **CS** 48, 49
electromagnetic spectrum **CI** 95
electron density maps **CI** 233
electron shell, *see* shell; sub-shell
electron transfer
    CS in photosynthesis 119–20;
      for water decomposition 123
    CI 113; *see also* redox
electronegativity **CI** 30–1, 78
electronic configuration **CI** 22; chemical properties 25;
    noble gas 27; and periodic table 19, 23–4; shells 18–19
electrons
    CS delocalised 204
    CI 14; in atomic orbital 21–2; delocalised 208, 233, 254;
      lone pair 28, 35; unpaired 103; *see also* β particles;
      radicals
    AA delocalised PR4, CD2
electrophilic addition **CI** 228–30
electrophilic substitution **CI** arenes 280–1; benzene 237–41
electrostatic attraction in ionic bonding **CI** 27
elements
    CS in body 3; discovery 6–9; formation 9–10;
      and periodic table 8–9
    CI determining percentage in compound 3
    AA effects on steel SS2.5; Group 2 EL2.3, EL3, EL6, M3;
      Group 4 M3; Group 7 M3; properties, and
      periodic table M3
Elements of Life, summary activity **AA** EL3, EL6
elimination reaction, alcohols **CI** 277
emission, evaporative **CS** 34
emission control (vehicle) **CS** 32–4
emission spectra
    CS stars 12
    CI 96; and Bohr's theory 97–8
    AA CD4.4, Information Sheet 4
empirical formula **CI** 4
employees, in chemical industry **CS** 276–7
emulsion **CS** 211
enantiomers, *see* optical isomerism
endothermic reaction **CI** 46, 47
energy
    CS in food 19; from fuel cell 132; hydrogen 131–2;
      industrial use 280; solar 113–15, 122–5, 126–30;
      see also combustion; photosynthesis
    CI and entropy 56, 57–63; levels 97–8;
      quantised 99–100; *see also* quanta

energy (enthalpy) level diagram **CI** 46
energy conservation **CS** 36
energy crop **CS** 121
energy density **CS** 20
energy levels **CI** 58–9, 97–8; *see also* quanta
energy transfer, by ocean **CS** 238–43
energy-matter interaction **CI** 99–101
engineering plastic **CS** 93
Engineering Proteins, summary activity **AA** EP7
enthalpy
 CI activation, *see* activation enthalpy; bond *see* bond
  enthalpy; and catalysis 189; defined 46;
  hydration 67; ionisation *see* ionisation enthalpy;
  lattice 64–6; solution 67–8; solvation 67
enthalpy change
 CS combustion 18; fuels 18
 CI 47, 47–8; and benzene structure 234;
  combustion 48; formation 48; reaction 48;
  vaporisation of water 89
 AA alcohol combustion DF1.3; calculation M2.5; fuel
  combustion DF1.2; oceans O3.3; solutions O1.2;
  spreadsheets DF2.1; vaporisation of water O3.1
enthalpy cycles **CI** 49–50, 52, 53–4, 68
enthalpy level diagram for solute **CI** 68
entropy
 CS 31
 CI 55–6; and dissolving 69; and energy 56, 57–63;
  and equilibrium 63–4; and freezing/melting 59–61;
  and laws of thermodynamics 58–63
enzyme binding of substrate **AA** EP6.2, EP6.3
enzyme catalysed reaction rates **AA** EP6.5
enzyme catalysis
 CI mechanism 182
 AA reaction rates EP6.3
enzyme inhibitor
 CS as medicine 264–6
 AA EP6.2
enzyme kinetics **AA** EP6.5
enzymes
 CS 154–7; industrial uses 156–7
 CI 188; *see also* catalysts; catalysis
 AA specificity EP6.1; and substrate concentration EP6.3
equations **CI** balanced 5; ionic 72–3;
 and rate equation 178; and reacting mass calculation 6
equilibrium
 CS of alkane isomerisation 26;
  carbon dioxide/water 244–5
 CI chemical 128–31; and entropy 63–4;
  solubility 144–5; weak acid 150; *see also* partition
  equilibrium
 AA chemical A8.1, O4.1
equilibrium constant **CI** 130, 131–5;
 effect of temperature 138; weak acid 151
equilibrium position **CI** 130; and catalysis 139;
 and concentration 134–5; and pressure 137–8;
 and temperature 138
errors **AA** II
ester
 CS aspirin as 107
 CI 257–9, 278, 279; fats as 260–1; hydrolysis 257, 259
esterification **CI** 278
ethanoic acid **AA** O4.2
ethanol, *see* alcohol
ethanoylation **CI** 258–9
ethene
 CS polymerised 85–7
 CI addition reactions 228–30; reaction with
  hydrogen 230; reactions 228–31

ethers
 CS as oxygenates 29
 CI 248, 250
evaporation **CS** 238, 239, 240
evaporation pans **CS** 40
exam revision **AA** AA3.3
excitation energy **CI** 111, 112
exhaust system, motor car **AA** SS4.2
exothermic reaction **CI** 46, 47
extraction techniques, willow bark **AA** WM2

f sub-shell **CI** 20
Farman, Dr J. **CS** 65–6
fats **CI** 262
fatty acids **CI** 262–3
feedstock **CS** 277–8; oil as 17
fertiliser **CS** inorganic 190–1; organic 188–90
fibre-reactive dyes **CS** 222–3
fibres
 CS artificial 85; nylon 94
 CI polymeric 83
fishing **CS** 233
fission **CI** bond 102–3; heterolytic, halogenoalkanes 244,
 245; homolytic, halogenoalkanes 243–4
flame colours **AA** EL4.2
flammability, hydrogen-air mixtures **AA** US6.1
flashbulb electrochemistry **AA** US4.2
flow diagrams **AA** bromine production M1.1;
 Mauve from benzene CD5.3; mineral extraction M2.3;
 steelmaking SS2.2; symbols DF5, Information Sheet;
 uses for DF5
fluorescence
 CS 116; of chlorophyll 117
 CI 107–8
 AA US2.1, US2.2
fluorine **CI** 202–4
food, from sea **CS** 229–30
food production **CS** 177
foods, reaction with tin can **CS** 172–3
formation, enthalpy change **CI** 48
formula determination, water **AA** EL1
formulae **CI** 3–4
fragmentation
 CI 124–5
 AA patterns WM4.1, WM4.3
Franklin, Rosalind **AA** EP2.8
freezing **CI** and entropy change 59–61; seawater 61–2
frequency **CI** 95
Friedel-Crafts reactions
 CI 240–1
 AA MD3.1, MD3.2
froth floatation **CS** 46–7
fuel cell
 CS 132
 AA US6.2
fuel combustion, enthalpy changes **AA** DF1.2
fuels
 CS and carbon dioxide increase 78;
  energy densities of 20; methanol as 35;
  oxygenated 18–19; from sunlight 114; *see also* petrol
 AA DF1.1, DF1.2; hydrogen US6.1; *see also* combustion
fullerenes **CI** 197
functional groups **CI** 39, 221
fungicides, *see* pesticides
fused ring systems **CI** 235
fusion, and element formation **CS** 9

GABA (gamma aminobutanoic acid) **CS** 259–61
galvanising **CS** 170
gamma rays **CI** 15, 16
gas laws **CI** 8–10
gas-liquid chromatograms **AA** CD4.3, CD4.3, Information Sheet 2
gas-liquid chromatography
    CS (gas-liquid) BAC 257;   drying oil ratio 212; petrol 24–5; (thin layer) 103; hydrolysis permethrin 197
    CI 141-3
    AA (gas-liquid) drying oil ratio CD4.3; straight chain primary alcohols MD1.2; (thin layer) analysis of medicines WM6.2; hydrolysis aspartame EP2.2; willow bark extract WM2
gaseous fuels, enthalpy changes **AA** DF1.2
gases **CI** 57;   entropy 59;   reacting volume 7–8
gasoline **CS** 21, 22; *see also* petrol
Geiger, Hans **AA** EL4.1
gene **CS** 146; alteration 152–3; transferred 147
generic names **CS** 107
genetic engineering **CS** 138, 147–8
geometric isomerism
    CS 90
    CI 40–2
    AA SS5.1
glassy substances
    CI 85
    AA PR7
global warming **CS** 74–6; and carbon dioxide 80–1; and greenhouse effect 72–4; and local cooling 242–3
glucose, in urine **AA** EP6.1
glucose level test **CS** 154
glycine **AA** EP2.1
gold **AA** M2.6
greenhouse effect **CS** 72–4; and carbon dioxide 77–81
greenhouse gases
    CS 72–3; CFC as 69
    AA A6, A9
grouping (periodic table) **CI** 192; group 1 properties 194–5; group 2 properties 194–6; group 4 197–9; group 5 199–201; group 7 202–4
group identification, mass spectrometry **CI** 124–5

Haber process **CS** 191
haemoglobin **CS** 4, 166–7
half-cells
    CI 161–5
    AA US4.5
half-equations
    CS copper reduction 48, 49
    CI 160, 161
half-life **CI** 17, 178–80
halide ions
    CI 202; reactions with halogens 204
    AA reaction with silver ions M1.3, A4.1
halogenoalkanes
    CI 243–7; comparative reactivity 244–5; properties 243; reactions 243–4; reactions with amines 265; substitution reactions 245–7; synthesis 246–7
    AA making A4.2; reactivities A4.1
halogenoalkenes **CI** 276
halogens
    CI 202–4; reaction with halide ions 204
    AA atoms A4.2; compounds M1.3; displacement reactions M1.3; elements M1.1, M1.2, M1.3, M1.4
hard water **CI** 140
heat balance **AA** SS2.3
heat exchanger **AA** DF5.1

heat transfer, by ocean **CS** 238–43
heating capacity, specific,
    CS 241
    AA 57, 89
hectare **CS** 186
helium nuclei *see* α particles
helium in Sun **CS** 12
herbalism
    CS 101–2
    AA WM1
herbicides
    CS 198–9; *see also* pesticides
    AA AA4.3
Hess's law **CI** 49
heterogenous catalysis **CI** 189, 211
heterolytic bond fission **CI** 102
heterolytic fission, halogenoalkanes **CI** 244, 245
hexane **AA** DF1.2; and bromine A3.2, A3.3; halogen solubility M1.3
hexanedioic acid **AA** PR5.2
HFC **AA** A4.5
high blood pressure **CS** 264, 264
homogenous catalysis **CI** 189, 190, 211
homolytic fission **CI** 102–3, 243–4
hormones **CS** 135, 136
Human Genome Project **CS** 146
humus **CS** 184
hydrated crystals **CI** 72
hydration **CI** 66–7, 72; and ion size 33
hydrobromic acid, reaction with alcohols **CI** 277
hydrocarbons
    CI 221; *see also* alkane; alkene; arenes; benzene
    AA comparing CD5.1; mixing DF4.7
hydrochloric acid **AA** O4.2
hydrogen
    CS in Sun 12; from water 122–5
    CI reaction with ethene 230
    AA as fuel US6.1 DF1.1; produced from water US5.3
hydrogen bonding
    CS dyes 221; in proteins 149
    CI 79–81; in alcohols 249; amines 264; and anomalous expansion of water 90; in water 88; *see also* water
hydrogen bromide
    CI reaction with ethene 229–30
    AA A3.3
hydrogen chloride, vibrational energy changes **CI** 99–100
hydrogen half-cell, standard **CI** 164
hydrogen peroxide
    CI decomposition 175–7; half-life 178–80
    AA EP6.3
hydrogen sulphide **AA** DF5.1
hydrogen-oxygen fuel cell **AA** US6.2
hydrogenation **CI** 230
hydrogencarbonate anions
    CS 78, 244, 250–1
    AA A8.2, O4.1
hydrolysis
    CI amides 266–7; of ester 257, 259; fats/oils 262; peptide group 267
    AA EP6.5; dyes CD7.1; halogenoalkanes A4.1; nylon PR5.2; peptide bonds EP2.2; precipitation of metal hydroxides SS3.3, SS4.1
hydroxide ions
    CS in rusting 168–9
    CI reaction with halogenoalkanes 245
hydroxides, group 2
    CI 195, 196
    AA solubility EL2.3

2-hydroxybenzoic acid
  CI 258, 259
  AA WM5
hydroxyl (–OH) group
  CI 253–6; acidic properties 253–4; oxidation 254–5
  AA WM3
hydroxyl radicals, and ozone removal **CS** 62–3
hyrogen emission spectrum **CI** 96

ibuprofen, from benzene **AA** MD3.2
ice, density **CI** 89–90
ideal gas law **CI** 9–10, 57
Incredulity of S. Thomas **CS** 208–11
indicators **CI** 113, 149
Individual Investigation **AA** II
induced dipole **CI** 75
information retrieval skills **AA** PR1
infra-red absorption of atmospheric gases
  CS infra-red radiation window 75
  AA A6
infra-red spectroscopy
  CS for carbon dioxide measurement 77; for ethanol 257;
    for salicylic acid 103–4
  CI 109, 114–18
  AA steroid hormones CD3.2; Data Sheets
inhibitor **CS** 264–6
initial rate method **AA** EP6.4
ink jet printer **CS** 224–6
insecticides
  CS 194–7, *see also* pesticides
  AA insecticidal activity AA4.2
instantaneous dipole **CI** 74–5
insulin **CS** 135–8; blood levels 137;
    genetic engineering 147, 151–3; monomers 151–2;
    structure 151
insulin hexamers **CS** 137, 149–50
insulin levels in blood **CS** 137, 152
interhalogen compounds **CI** 203
intermolecular forces
  CI 74–81
  AA PR5.4
interstellar medium **CS** 14
iodine
  CI 202–4
  AA partition between two solvents AA4.1;
    recognition M1.3
iodine clock technique **AA** EP6.4 AA2.1
iodine number, oils **AA** CD4.2
ion exchange
  CS in soil 183, 184
  CI 139–41; as partition equilibrium 137
  AA AA2.4; in soil AA2.5
ion exchange resins
  CI 33
  AA AA2.4
ion formation **CI** 32–3
ion shape **CI** 37
ion size **CI** 32–3; lattice enthalpy 65
ionic bonding
  CS in proteins 149; in soil 184
  CI 27–8
ionic equations **CI** 72–3
ionic lattice **CI** 71; modified 71–2
ionic precipitation
  CI 70
  AA Chrome Yellow CD3.1
ionic product of water **CI** 153

ionic solids
  CI 65, 66, 71; enthalpy cycle 68; solubility products 145
  AA dissolving O1.2
ionic substances, hydrated **CI** 72
ionisation enthalpy (energy)
  CS 98, 209
  AA Data Sheets
ionisation of water **CI** 152–3
ionising radiation **CI** 16, 101
ionosphere **CS** 55
ions
  CS in sea water 230, 231
  CI 91; hydrated, radius of 140; in mass
    spectrometry 123–4; metal, effect of ligands 171;
    molecular 124
iron
  CS in haemoglobin 4–5; rusting 167–70
  AA from blast furnace SS2.1; purity SS2.1;
    quantitative analysis EL2.1
iron alloys **CS** 159
iron deficiency **CS** 4–5
iron phthalocyanine **CS** 203–4
iron(III) chloride test **CI** 256
iron(III) ion **AA** A8.1; light affecting US2.3
isomerisation, and octane number **CS** 26
isomers and isomerism
  CS geometric 90; hydrocarbons 26;
    optical, in amino acids 141
  CI alcohols and ethers 248; alkanes 223;
    choice of isomers in synthesis 274; geometric 40–2;
    optical 42–4; structural 38–9;
    transition metal complexes 218
  AA alcohols DF4.5; complexes SS5.1;
    smell tests for optical isomers EP2.5; structural DF4.1;
    transition metal SS5
isotope peaks
  CI mass spectrometry 125
  AA WM4.1, WM4.2
isotopes, defined **CI** 15

kaolinite **CS** 182
K$_c$ (equilibrium constant) **CI** 131–5
Kekulé structure **CI** 233, 234
Kelvar
  CS 94–6
  CI 80
  AA PR6
kelvin **CI** 9
ketones
  CI 255, 277
  AA MD3.1
kinetic energy **CI** 57; and temperature 186–7
knocking **CS** 23–4
Kolbé synthesis **CS** 106

lactam ring **AA** MD5.1
laser microspectral analysis (LMA) **CS** 212
lattice enthalpy **CI** 64–6
Le Chatelier's principle
  CS and carbon dioxide removal 244–5
  CI 135, 137
leaching
  CS in soil 188
  AA bacterial M2.6
leaching ore **AA** M2.3
lead, in fuel, and catalytic converters **CS** 34
lead compound (medicine discovery) **CS** 261
lead compounds, anti-knock **CS** 25
ligand exchange reactions **AA** SS3.3

ligands
  CS in iron phthalocyanine 204
  CI 213, 215–16; amines as 265; ammonia as 200; and colour change 113; effect on electrode potential 171; polydentate 215–16; and transition metal colour 217, 218
  AA tetradentate CD2
light
  CS absorption and colour 115
  CI and colour 106; particle theory 96; wave theory 95
  AA decomposition of water US4.7; effect on chloroplasts US3.1c; effect on ions **AA** US2.3
light harvesting, photosynthesis **CS** 118, 119
light wavelength, photosynthesis **AA** US3.1a
lime requirement, soil
  CS 185
  AA AA2.6
limestone
  CS 245, 251
  CI 62
linear molecules **CI** 35–6
linseed oil **AA** CD4.2
liquids **CI** 57; entropy 59
LMA emission spectrum **AA** CD4.4
lock and key enzyme model **CS** 154–5
lode **CS** 45
lone pair electrons **CI** 28; in amines 264; in group 5 199; and hydrogen bonding 80; and shape 35
LPG (liquified petroleum gas) **AA** DF1.1

madder dye **CS** 215, 216–17
magnesium
  CS added in steelmaking 161; in chlorophyll 117, 118
  AA EL2.3; in soil **AA**2.5
magnesium ions, and hard water **CI** 140
manganese concentration, in steel **AA** SS1
manure **CS** 188–90
mass **CI** molar 2; reacting, calculation of 6; relative atomic 2; relative molecular 2, 3
mass to amount conversion **AA** EL1
mass of element in compound **CI** 3
mass number **CI** 14
mass spectrometry
  CI 123–5
  AA WM4.1, WM4.2
mass spectrum (salicylic acid) **CS** 104–5, 106
mass spectrum data **AA** WM4, Information Sheet
matter-energy interactions **CI** 99–101
Mauve
  CS 213–14
  AA CD5.3
Maxwell-Boltzmann energy distribution **CI** 186
medicine
  CS development costs 110–11; safety testing 109–11
  AA development WM7.1, WM7.2; discovery WM1; synthesis MD3.2
Medicines by Design, summary activity **AA** MD6
melting, and entropy change **CI** 59–61
melting point
  CI and hydrogen bonding 80; table 193
  AA DF3.1; organic solid PR5.2
melting temperature, polymer **CI** 85
membrane cell **AA** M1.2
Mendeleev, D. (1834–1907) **CS** 8
mercury cell **AA** M1.2
metal chlorides, spectroscopy **AA** EL4.2
metal hydrides **AA** US6.1
metal-ion/metal half cells **CI** 162–3

metal ions, effect of ligands **CI** 171
metallic bonding, transition metals **CI** 207–9
metallic properties **CI** and alloying 208–9; and periodic table 192
metals
  CI reaction with halogens 203; *see also* transition metals
  AA properties M3
methane
  CS formation 71; greenhouse effect 73; reaction with Cl 69
  AA as fuel DF1.1
methanol
  CS as fuel 35
  AA DF1.2, DF1.3; as fuel DF1.1
methyl benzoate, nitration **AA** CD5.1
methyl group **CI** 223
methylbenzene **AA** CD5.1
2-methylbutane **AA** DF3.3
mica
  CS 181
  AA AA2.3
microscope, rock samples **AA** M2.1
microwave cooker **CI** 100
migraine **CS** 263
mineral extraction, from sea **CS** 39–41
mineral spotting **AA** M2.1
mineralisation **CS** 184, 188
minerals
  CS in sea 233; in soil 179
  AA appearance M2.1
Minerals to Elements, summary activity **AA** M4
mixing of liquids **CI** 55
model making
  AA alcohols DF4.5; alkanes DF4.1; balloon molecules (shapes of molecules) EP2.3; DNA EP2.7; enzyme binding EP6.2; Monastral Blue CD2; penicillins MD5.2; silicates and clays AA2.2
molecular modelling
  AA ACE computer simulation MD4
molar atomic volume **CI** 192
molar entropy **CI** 56
molar mass **CI** 2
molar volume **CI** 7
mole (mol)
  CS 3
  CI 1-2, for concentration measure 11
molecular energy changes **CI** 101
molecular formula **CI** 4
molecular ion **CI** 124
molecular mass, relative **CI** 2, 3
molecular mixing **AA** DF4.7
molecular motion, and energy **CI** 58
molecular shape **CI** 34–6; and intermolecular forces 76
molecular sieves, zeolites
  CS 26, 27. 36
  AA DF4.3
molecular size
  CS and enthalpy change of combustion 18
  CI and dipole distance 79
molecular structure, and strength **CS** 95
molecules, shapes **AA** EP2.4
Monastral Blue
  CS 203–4
  AA CD2
monomers **CI** 82
Montreal Protocol
  CS Revised 70
  AA CFCs A4.5

mordant **CS** 216
Moseley, Henry **AA** EL4.1
MTBE **CS** 29–30

naphthalene **CI** 235
naptha **CS** 21
Natta, Giulio **CS** 88–9
nerve cell **CS** 258–61; inhibitors 196
neurotransmitter **CS** 258–61, 261–2
neutron **CI** 14
nickel **AA** SS3.3
nitrate(V) ions, determination in soil **AA** AA3.1
nitrates
    CS leaching 193; levels, soil/water 192–3
    CI 201
nitration
    CI of benzene 238–9
    AA methyl benzoate CD5.1
nitrile **AA** MD3.1
nitro-groups **AA** MD3.1
nitrogen
    CI 199–201
    AA in soil AA3.1
nitrogen balance, agriculture **AA** AA3.2
nitrogen cycle
    CS 187–9; fixation 187
    CI 200, 201
    AA AA3.2
nitrogen loss, from soil **CS** 188
nitrogen monoxide, and ozone removal **CS** 63
nitrogen oxides
    CS as pollutants 31–3
    CI 200
n.m.r (nuclear magnetic resonance)
    CS 104–5, 106
    CI 119–22; interpreting results 120–2
noble gas **CI** boiling points 74; electron configuration 27
nomenclature **CI** of complex ions 214–15;
    and oxidation state 159
noradrenaline **CS** 261–2, 263
North Atlantic Drift **CS** 241
N:P:K ratio in fertilisers **CS** 190
nuclear magnetic resonance, *see* n.m.r
nuclear power stations, scrap steel **AA** SS6.1
nucleic acids, structure **AA** EP2.8
nucleophiles **CI** 245–6; amines as 265
nucleophilic substitution **CI** 245–7, 265, 276, 277, 279
nucleus, and n.m.r spectroscopy **CI** 119
nutrient cycling **CS** 186–7
nutrient requirement, crop **CS** 186–7
nutrients, plant **CS** 177–8
nylon
    CS 85, 91–4; fibres 93–4
    CI 89, 268, as fibre 83
    AA PR6; making PR5.1; taking apart PR5.2

oceans
    CS as buffer 249–50; and carbon dioxide removal 78;
    currents 238–43
    AA density changes O3.3; management O1.3; pH O4.2
Oceans, The, summary activity **AA** O5
octahedral molecules **CI** 36
octane numbers
    CS 23
    AA DF4.6; alkanes DF4.2; booster (MTBE) DF4.6
octane rating **CS** blend for 25–9; and isomerisation 26;
    and reforming 28, 29

oil
    CS cracking 27–8; distillation products 21;
    as feedstock 17
    CI 260–2
    AA drying potential CD4.2; ester links CD4.3
oil refining **AA** DF5.1
optical brighteners
    CS 116
    AA US2.2
optical isomerism
    CS protein 141
    CI 42–4
    AA EP2.4, EP2.5, SS5.1
orbitals, *see* atomic orbitals
order of reaction
    CS 156
    CI 177–8; determination 180–1
ore samples, mineral extraction processes **AA** M2.3
organic chemistry **CI** 221; *see also* specific compound
organic molecules, interstellar **CS** 14, 15
organic reactions (summary of)
    CI 275–83
    AA MD3.1, MD3.2
organic solid, purification **AA** PR5.2
organic store (soil) **CS** 186
osteoporosis **CS** 6
oxidation
    CI 157–9, 160–1; alcohols 276–7; alkanes 225;
    of halides 204; *see also* redox
    AA alcohols MD1.1
oxidation catalyst system **CS** 33
oxidation states
    CS copper 50; transition metals 166
    CI group 4 197; halogens 203; number 157–9;
    of transition metals 207, 209–11
    AA vanadium SS3.1
oxides
    CI formulae periodicity 193; group 2 195;
    group 4 197, 198; nitrogen 200;
    structure (period 3) 92, 94
    AA group 2 reacting with water and acid EL2.3;
    from sulphide minerals M2.2
oxidising agent
    CS ozone as 58
    CI halogen as 203
oxonium ions
    CS in water 249–50
    CI 147
oxyanions **CI** 159
oxygen
    CS atmospheric 56, 248–9; enthalpy change of
    combustion 18–19; in polythene production 86,
    in silicates 180, 181
    CI dioxygen 103–4
    AA and ozone A3.1; in steel SS2.4
oxygen blow in steel making **CS** 162
oxygen production
    AA US3.1b; photosynthesis US3.1a
oxygen-oxygen bonds **AA** A3.1
oxygenates **CS** 29–30; and pollution control 34
ozone
    CS atmospheric removal 60–3; formation 58–9;
    motor pollution 58–9; as sunscreen 58; *see also* CFC
    AA concentrations A3.4; and oxygen A3.1
ozone depletion
    CS effects 69–70; 'hole' 65–6
    AA A4.4

p block (periodic table) **CI** group 4 197–9
group 5 199–201;   group 7 202–4
p sub-shell **CI** 20
paint
   CS 205;   binding medium 211
   AA analysis CD4.3;   cross-section CD4.4
paint identification, reflectance spectrum **CS**   208
paintings **CS** pigment analysis 206–7;   restoration 208–13
paracetamol **AA** from phenol MD3.2;   in medicine WM6.2
paraquat
   CS 198–9
   AA A4.3
particle theory of light **CI** 96
partition coefficient
   CS 196
   CI 134
   AA AA4.1
partition equilibrium
   CI 136–7
   AA AA4.1
pascal, defined **CI** 9
patents
   CS 107
   AA CD5.3
Pauling, Linus **AA** 220, EP2.8
PEEK **CS** 96
penicillins
   CS 267–71;   synthesis 268–9
   AA synthesis MD5.1;   modelling MD5.2;
      structure MD5.2
pentane **AA** DF3.3
peptide group
   CS 91–2, 140
   CI 266–8
   AA hydrolysis EP2.2
peptide link **CS** 91, 140
period 3 properties trends **CI** 92, 94
periodic table
   CS 8–9
   CI 191–2, and electron structure 19;   and electronic
      configuration 23–5;   and structure 92–4;   *see also*
      d block; *p* block; *s* block
periodicity **CI** 192–3
Perkin, William **CS** 213–14
Perkin's dye patent **AA** CD5.3
permanent dipole 74, 77
peroxide, polymerisation **AA** PR2.1
Perrier water **CI** 62–3
pest control, and genetic engineering **CS** 148
pesticides
   CS 193–7;   decay 197
   AA concentration in living organisms AA4.1
petrol
   CS blending 25–9, 30;   composition 21–2;
      and knocking 23–4;   octane number 23;
      pollution from 18;   seasonal blends 23–4;
      volatility 22–3;   *see also* octane number; octane rating
   AA auto-ignition DF3.3;   refinery processes DF4.8
petrol blend
   CS 25–9, 30;   and emission control 34;   seasonal 23–4
   AA DF4.6;   winter/summer DF3.2
petrol production, zeolites **AA** DF4.3
pH
   CS effect on soil 185;   and enzymatic catalysis 156;
      oceans 249
   CI 150;   and buffers 154
   AA control O4.2;   determination M2.4;
      measurements A8.2, A8.3;   oceans O4.2;   soil **AA**2.6
pH meter **AA** A8.3

pharmaceutical industry **AA** WM7.1;   origins WM1;
   statistics WM1
pharmaceuticals, from sea **AA** O1.3
pharmacy **CS** 101
PHB **AA** PR8.1
phenol group detection **CS** 103
phenols
   CS Kolbé synthesis 106
   CI 236, 249;   acidic strength 254;   coupling with diazo
      salts 270–1;   –OH group 253
   AA MD3.2;   –OH group WM3;
phenyl group **CI** 236
phenylamine **CI** 236
phenylethene **AA** PR2.1
photochemical reactions
   CS 113, 116
   CI chain 104
   AA redox US2.3
photochemical smog **CS** 31, 59
photoconductivity **CS** 84, 127
photocopier **CS** 83–4
photodegradability **CS** 97
photodissociation
   CS and ozone production 58–9
   CI 101
photography **CS** 42–3
photosynthesis
   CS 113, 114, 115, 117–21;   back reaction
      prevention 124–5
   CI 170;   as redox 161
   AA A9, US3.2, US3.1a
photosynthetic unit **CS** 118–19
photovoltaic cell **CS** 114–15
photovoltaic effect **CS** 126
photovoltaic power, marketing **CS** 130–1
physical state symbols **CI** 5
piezoelectricity **CS** 84
pigments
   CS 201;   toxicity 205
   AA art restoration CD4.5;   identification CD4.1, CD4.4
Planck constant **CI** 96
planets **CS** 13
plant breeding **CS** 148
plants, dyes from **CS** 202
plasticisers **CI** 86
plastics
   CS degradable 97–8;   dissolving 98–9;   engineering 93
   CI 82;   *see also* polymers
polar bonds **CI** 30, 74;   *see also* dipoles
polar molecule **CI** 91
polarisation **CI** bromine 238;   during addition reaction 228;
   molecular 74, 76;   water 88
polarity **CI** hydrogen-carbon bond 243;   and vibration 117
pollution **CS** 282;   in atmosphere 56;   motor vehicles 31–4;
   through nitrates 192–3;   through pesticides 194;
   petrol 18;   and recycling 99;   sea 234;   from smelting 48;
   from tailings 47;   and waste disposal 97–99
poly(ethene) **CS** 85–7, 90–1;   crystalline 88;
   high density 87–8
poly(ethenol) **AA** PR8.2
poly(hydroxybutyrate) (PHB) **AA** PR8.1
poly(phenylethene) **AA** PR2.1
poly(propene) **CS** 89
poly(pyrrole) **AA** PR4
poly(tetrafluoroethene) (ptfe) **AA** M1.2
poly(vinyl carbazole) **CS** 83
polyamides
   CS 92
   CI 268

polydentate ligands **CI** 215–16
polyester
   CS 93; dyes 224
   CI 258
Polymer Revolution, The, summary activity **AA** PR9
polymers
   CS characteristics 87; conducting 90; defined 85;
     disposal 97–9; doped 91; stereoregular 89
   CI 82–7; crystalline 85; effect of temperature 85–6;
     and hydrogen bonding 80; properties 83;
     strength 84–5
   AA PR1, conducting PR4; membrane cells M1.2;
     production PR1; structures and properties PR6
polythene *see* poly(ethene)
porphyrins
   CS 203–4
   AA CD2
potassium dichromate(VI) **MD**1.1
potassium halides **AA** M1.3
potassium ions, in neurotransmission **CS** 259
potassium manganate(VII) reaction with hydrocarbons
   AA CD5.1
potential calculation (cell) **CI** 165–6
potential differences **AA** US4.3
precipitation **CI** ionic 70; and solubility product 144–5
precision errors **AA** II
pressure **CI** atmospheric 9; defined 8–9
processing **CS** 274–6
protein
   CS 136, 138–44; bonding 149; catabolism 140;
     primary structure 140, 150; quarternary
     structure 150; secondary structure 149, 150;
     structure 148–51; synthesis 142–4;
     tertiary structure 149, 150
   AA peptide bonds EP2.2
protein engineering **CS** 138
proton **CI** 14
ptfe **AA** M1.2
purple, from snails **CS** 229–30
pyrethroids
   CS 194–7
   AA AA4.2
pyrites **AA** M2.6
pyrrole **AA** PR4

quanta **CI** 58–9, 99–100; emission spectra 97–8
quantifiable errors **AA** II
quantitative analysis **AA** EL2.1
quantity **CI** 1–4
quantum number **CI** 18
quartz
   CS 180
   AA AA2.3

radiation **AA** SS6.1; infra-red A6; ultra-violet A2.1, A2.3;
   visible A2.1, A2.3; *see also* infra-red;
   radioactive decay; ultra-violet
radical chain reaction **CI** 104–5
radicals
   CS atmospheric 58
   CI 103–5; in addition polymerisation 230–1;
     in halogenoalkanes 243–4
radioactive decay
   CS and element formation 13
   CI 15–17
   AA EL4.3
radioactivity, scrap steel **AA** SS6.1
radon **AA** EL4.3, SS6.1
rate constants, and temperature **CI** 187–8

rate determining step **CI** 181–2
rate equation **CI** 177; interpretation 181–2
rate of reaction *see* reaction kinetics; reaction rate
rate-determining step, and activation enthalpy **CI** 183
raw materials **CS** 277–8; costs 283
reacting mass calculation **CI** 6
reacting volume of gases **CI** 7–8
reacting volumes of solutions **CI** 12
reaction centre (photosynthesis) **CS** 118, 119
reaction conditions **AA** WM5
reaction enthalpy change **CI** 48
reaction kinetics **CI** 173–4; catalysis 173, 182, 188–90;
     concentration 173, 174–83; pressure 173;
     radiation intensity 173; surface area 173;
     temperature 173, 185–8
reaction rate
   CI defined 174–5; measurement 175
   AA and temperature AA2.1
reactions
   CS very fast 62
   CI collision theory 173–4, 185–6; order of 177–8, 180–1
   AA order of EP6.3, EP6.4
reactive dyes
   CS 222–3
   AA CD7.1
recombinant DNA technology **CS** 147–8
recycling steel **CS** 99, 173, 174, 280
redox
   CS chlorophyll initiated 119–20
   CI 157–9, 160–1; effect of complexing 171–2; and
     electrode potential 161–6; metal ion-metal 162–3;
     photosynthesis as 161; prediction direction of 167–70
   AA photochemical US2.3
redox colour change in transition metals **CI** 113
redox cycle, of corrosion **CS** 167
redox reactions
   CS and bromine production 41
   CI catalysis of 211
   AA US4.1, US4.6, SS3.1
reducing agents **AA** MD3.1
reduction **CI** 157, 158, 160–1; *see also* redox
references **AA** II
refining, copper **CS** 48, 48–9
reflectance spectra
   CS paint identification 208
   CI 110
   AA CD4.5 CD4.1
reflux **AA** A4.2, WM2
reforming **CS** 28, 29
refrigerant fluids and gases **AA** A4.1, A4.3
refrigerator **AA** A4.3
restoration, reversible **CS** 211
retention time **CI** (g.l.c) 143
reversible reaction **CI** 129; *see also* equilibrium
ribosome **CS** 143
risk assessment **AA** II
RNA (ribonucleic acid) **CS** 141–6; bases 142, 143;
   mRNA 141; rRNA 143; tRNA 141, 142
roasting, sulphide minerals **AA** M2.2
rock samples **AA** M2.1
Rothamsted Experimental Station **CS** 188, 189
Rowland, Prof. S. **CS** 63–4
rusting
   CS 167–70; prevention 169–70; and
     water conductivity 169
   AA steel SS4.1

s block (periodic table) **CI** 194–6
s sub-shell **CI** 20

sacrificial protection **CS** 170
safety
  CS industrial 281
  AA II
safety testing of medicines
  CS 109–11
  AA WM7.1
salbutamol
  CS 262
  AA costing MD3.3
salicylic acid
  CS 103–6; synthesis 106–7
  AA extraction WM2; mass spectrum WM4.1, WM4.2
salt
  CS source 231
  CI double 71
salt bridge **CI** 163
salt industry **CS** 232–3
sand **AA** AA2.3
saturation **CI** 221; *see also* unsaturation
sea
  CS carbon dioxide removal 78, 243–5; minerals in 230,
    233; pollution 234; surveys 234–6
  AA pharmaceuticals from O1.3
sea level rise **CS** 81
sea water
  CS ions in 230, 231
  CI energy changes during freezing 61–2
seaweed **CS** 230
semiconductors **CS** 126, 128; doped 128
separating funnel **AA** A4.2
sex hormones **AA** MD3.2
shape
  CS and enzyme inhibition 266
  CI and coordination number 213–14; and intermolecular
    forces 76; ionic **CI** 37; molecular 34–6
sheet structure **CS** clays 182; silicates 181
shells
  CS 245
  CI 18–19; closed 25; outer 19; sub-shells 20
side-chains, penicillins **AA** MD5.2
silicates
  CS 180–2; clay types 182–4; sheet 181
  AA chains AA2.2; physical properties AA2.3
silicon
  CS 127–9; as semiconductor 127–9
  CI 197–9; oxides 198–9
  AA solar cells US5.1
silver bromide **CS** 42–3
silver ions
  CI calculation of concentration 145;
    reaction with halides 204
  AA reaction with halides M1.3, A4.1
single bond **CI** 28
size **CI** atom/ion 32; molecular, and dipoles 79
skin cancer **CS** 57
slag, copper production **CS** 47
slime, making **AA** PR2.2
slip **CI** 208
smelting
  CS cooper production 47, 48
  AA sulphur dioxide M2.4
smog, photochemical **CS** 59
soap **CI** 262
sodalite cage **AA** DF4.3
sodium chloride lattice **CI** 71
sodium hydrogencarbonate **AA** A8.3
sodium hydroxide **AA** bromine handling M1.4;
  production M1.2; titration A3.3

soil
  CS clay 182–4; composition 178–9; effect of pH 185;
    fertility 186–93; ion exchange 183, 184;
    organic matter 184; silicates 180–2
  AA components AA2.5 CS2.6 CS3.1;
    ion-exchange AA2.5
solar cells
  CS 126–30; use 129–30
  AA hydrogen from water US5.3; silicon US5.1;
    thin-film US5.2
solids **CI** 57; dipole attractions 79; entropy 59
solubility
  CI group 2 196
  AA O1.1; calcium carbonate O4.1;
    halogen elements M1.3
solubility equilibria **CI** 144–5
solubility product
  CS calcium carbonate/water 245
  CI 144–5
solution **CI** energy changes 64–9; enthalpy 67–8;
  predicting reacting volumes 12; *see also* concentration
solvation **CI** 66–7
solvents
  CI and bond fission 244; non-polar 69
  AA O1.1
specific heating capacities **AA** O3.2
spectator ions **CI** 73
spectra, and energy changes **CI** 100–1
spectrometer **CI** 108, 109; infra-red 116–17;
  interpretation of results 110, 116–17; *see also* colorimeter
spectrometry, *see* mass spectrometry
spectroscope **AA** CD3.2
spectroscopy
  CS 11–12; absorption of stars 11–12;
    atomic emission 162; emission, of stars 12;
    i.r. for salicylic acid 103–4; n.m.r 104–5, 106
  CI 95, 108–11; infra-red 100, 114–18; *see also* n.m.r
  AA EL4.2
spin, electron **CI** 22
spreadsheets **AA** octane numbers DF4.6;
  steel BOS process SS2.2;
enthalpy changes of combustion DF2.1
S. Thomas, Incredulity of **CS** 208–11
stability constant
  CI 215
  AA SS3.3
stainless steel **CS** 170–1
standard conditions, and redox reaction direction **CI** 169
standard state **CI** 48
stars **CS** and element formation 9–10;
  spectroscopic analysis 11–12
state symbols **CI** 5
steady state, ozone production **CS** 60
steady state systems **CI** 130–1
steam distillation **AA** AA3.1
steel
  CS 159–60; recycling 163, 165, 173, 174; stainless 170–1
  AA affected by elements SS2.5; composition
    and use SS2.5; processing SS2.2, SS2.3;
    radioactive SS6.1; recycling SS6.1; rusting SS4.1;
    selection for use SS4.2
steel room **CS** 174
steel scrap **AA** SS6.1
Steel Story, The, summary activity **AA** SS7
steelmaking **CS** 160–5; addition process 164;
  electric arc furnace 165; monitoring 164;
  removing elements 161

stereoisomerism
CI 38–44; *see also* geometric isomerism; optical isomerism
AA inorganic compounds SS5.1
stereoregular polymers **CS** 89
steroids **AA** MD3.2
stoichiometric ratio **CS** 32
stratosphere
CS 55
AA A3.4
stratospheric gases *see* ozone
strength, and molecular structure **CS** 95
strong acids *see under* acids
strong adsorption capacity of soil **CS** 198, 199
strontium
CS in bones 6;
AA EL2.3
structural formula **CI** 222–3
structural isomerism **CI** 38–9
structure
CI and bonding 91–2; and periodic table 92–4
AA and properties AA2.3
study skills activities **AA** EL2.2, DF2.2, DF4.8, A5, US3.2, US4.6, EP2.6, SS3.4, AA3.3, CD4.6
sub-shells **CI** 20
substitution reactions **CI** (nucleophilic) acyl chlorides 279; alcohols 277; amines 265; halogenoalkanes 245–7, 276; (electrophilic) arenes 280–1; benzene 237–41
succinate dehydrogenase **AA** EP6.2
sulphides
CS metal production from 45
AA minerals, roasting M2.2
sulphonation of benzene **CI** 239
sulphur
CS steel manufacture 161
AA removal from oil DF5.1
sulphur cycle **CS** 236–7
sulphur dioxide
CS from copper smelting 48
AA environmental impact M2.4; from smelting M2.4
sulphur oxides, as pollutants **CS** 31–3
sulphuric acid, analysis by titration **AA** M2.4
summary activity **AA** Elements of Life EL3, EL6; Developing Fuels DF8; Minerals to Elements M4; Atmosphere A10; Polymer Revolution PR9; What's in a Medicine WM8; Using Sunlight US7; Engineering Proteins EP7; Steel Story SS7; Aspects of Agriculture AA5; Colour by Design CD9; Oceans O5; Medicines by Design MD6
Sun
CS 11; energy from 113–15, 237–8; radiation from 71–2; *see also* stars
AA radiation, atmospheric effects A2.3; spectrum A2.3
sunburn
CS 56–8; *see also* sunscreen
AA A2.1
sunlight
CS effect on skin 57
AA spectrum US2.2
sunscreens
CS 57–8
AA A2.1, A2.2
supernova **CS** 10
synthesis
CI 272–3; choice of isomer 274; yield 273–4
AA medicines MD3.2
systematic names *see* nomenclature

Tactel fibres **CS** 94
tailings **CS** 47
talc **AA** AA2.3
tapping temperature, steel **AA** SS2.3
technological and economic appraisal, pharmaceuticals **AA** WM7.2
temperature
CI absolute 9, 47; and rate constants 187–8; and reaction kinetics 173, 185–8
AA and reaction rate AA2.1
temperature control **AA** SS2.3
temporary dipole **CI** 74–5
tensile strength, of polymers **CI** 84–5
tetradentate ligand **AA** CD2
tetrahedral molecules **CI** 34, 35
thermochemical (Hess) cycle **CI** 49
thermochemical measurements **AA** M2.5
thermodynamics **CI** first law 59; second law 61
thermoplastics **CI** 83; effect of heat 85–6
thermosets **CI** 83–4
thin layer chromatography (t.l.c.)
CS (gas-liquid) BAC 257; drying oil ratio 212; petrol 24–5; (thin layer) 103; hydrolysis permethrin 197
CI 141-3
AA (gas-liquid) drying oil ratio CD4.3; straight chain primary alcohols MD1.2; (thin layer) analysis of medicines WM6.2; hydrolysis aspartame EP2.2; willow bark extract WM2
thiocyanate ion **AA** A8.1
Thomson, Joseph J. **AA** EL4.1
tin **CS** amphoteric oxide 174; mining 50–2; reaction with alkali 174; recycling 52; use 52
tin cans
CS 171–3; recycling 174
AA recycling SS6.2
titanium, as polymer catalyst **CS** 88
titration
CI titration calculations 12–13
AA estimation of iron EL2.1; acid base M2.4; bromine-hexane reaction A3.3; ion exchange capacity of a resin AA2.4; ion exchange capacity of a soil AA2.5; nitrogen content of soils AA3.1
TMS (tetramethylsilane) **CI** 120
toxicity **AA** WM7.2
toxological testing **AA** A4.5
trace elements **CS** 4; calcium 6; iron 4–5
trade balance **CS** 273
trans isomers **CI** 41
transition metals
CS 165–7; as catalysts 166; colour 167; complex formation 166; oxidation states, variable 166
CI catalytic activity 211; characteristics 205–11; chemical properties 209; colour 207, 216–19; colour changes in redox reactions 113; complex formation 212–19; electronic configuration 205–6; ligands 215–16; metallic bonding 207–9; oxidation states 207, 209–11;
AA as catalysts SS3.2; complexes SS3.3; properties SS3.1
triester (triglyceride) **CI** 261
triple bond **CI** 29
triplet base code, for amino acids **CS** 143
troposphere **CS** 55; composition 56
tropospheric gas, *see* greenhouse effect; methane

ultra-trace elements **CS** 4
ultra-violet radiation
  CS effect of increase 69–70;   ozone production 58–9;
    sunscreen against 57–8
  CI absorption 101;   and fluorescence 107–8
  AA absorption A2.1, A2.3;   effect on compounds US2.1,
    US2.2
ultra-violet spectroscopy, *see* spectroscopy
underwater landscape **CS** 236
units, electrical **CI** 162
unsaturation **CI** 230
urease **AA** EP6.5
Using Sunlight, summary activity US7

vaccines, through genetic engineering **CS** 148
vacuum distillation **CS** 22
vacuum filtration **AA** M2.3
value engineering **AA** SS4.2
van Gogh, Vincent (1853–90) **CS** 207
vanadium **AA** oxidation states SS3.1;   reduction SS3.1
vaporisation enthalpy change **CI** 89
vapour lock **CS** 23
volatility, of alkanes **CS** 25
voltage, cells, and concentration **AA** US4.4
volume **CI** molar 7;   reacting 7–8
volume measurement **CI** 7

washing powder
  CS 157
  AA ultra-violet light US2.1, US2.2
washing-up liquid, ultra-violet light **AA** US2.1, US2.1
waste, industrial **CS** 282
waste disposal of polymers **CS** 97–9
waste treatment, enzymes in **CS** 157
water
  CS absorption spectrum 122;   as greenhouse gas 73, 75,
    76;   as hydrogen source 122–5
  CI dipoles 77;   in equilibrium 128;   hydrogen bonding
    in 88–90;   ionisation 152–3;   as nucleophile 246;
    reaction with group 2 elements 195;   *see also*
    freezing; hydrogen bonding; melting; oxonium ion;
    seawater
  AA decomposition US4.7;   determining formula EL1;
    specific heating capacities O3.2

water of crystallisation **CI** 72
water cycle **CS** 240
water molecule dipoles **CI** 77
Watson, James D. **AA** EP2.8
wave theory of light **CI** 95
wavelength **CI** 95
wavenumber **CI** 109, 115, 117
weak acid, *see* acids
weathering **CS** 179–80
weed control, and genetic engineering **CS** 148
What's in a Medicine, summary activity **AA** WM8
white light spectrum **AA** EL4.2, CD3.2
Wilkins, Maurice **AA** EP2.8
William, Dr P. **CS** 256
willow bark,
  CS 102;   identifying active principle 103–5
  AA extraction techniques WM2
'window' for radiation emission **CS** 75

X-ray diffraction studies, and protein structure **CS** 152

yellow pigments **AA** CD3.1; CD4.4, CD4.4,
  Information Sheet 3
yield
  CS industrial 278
  CI of synthesis 273–4

zeolites
  CS as molecular sieves 26, 27, 36
  CI 139–40;   as catalysts 189;   *see also* ion exchange
  AA DF4.3;   card models DF4.3;   Type A DF4.3;
    Type Y DF4.3
Ziegler catalysts **CS** 87–8
Ziegler-Natta catalysts **CS** 89
zinc
  CS sacrificial 170
  CI as reducing agent 160–1
zinc dust, copper production **AA** M2.3
zinc-copper half cells **CI** 162–3
zinc-copper redox reaction, direction of **CI** 167–8
zwitterions **CI** 267